RECASTING EUROPEAN WELFARE STATES

BOOKS OF RELATED INTEREST

The Changing French Political System
edited by Robert Elgie

Compounded Representation in West European Federations
edited by Joanne B. Brzinski, Thomas D. Lancaster and Christian Tuschhoff

Politics and Policy in Democratic Spain: No Longer Different?
edited by Paul Heywood

Britain in the Nineties: The Politics of Paradox
edited by Hugh Berrington

Crisis and Transition in Italian Politics
edited by Martin Bull and Martin Rhodes

Southern European Welfare States: Between Crisis and Reform
edited by Martin Rhodes

The Euro-Mediterranean Partnership: Political and Economic Perspectives
edited by Richard Gillespie

The State in Western Europe: Retreat or Redefinition?
edited by Wolfgang C. Müller and Vincent Wright

The Regions and the European Community
edited by Robert Leonardi

The Regional Dimension of the European Union
edited by Charlie Jeffery

National Parliaments and the European Union
edited by Philip Norton (new in paperback)

The Crisis of Representation in Europe
edited by Jack Hayward

The Politics of Immigration in Western Europe
edited by Martin Baldwin-Edwards and Martin A. Schain

Recasting European Welfare States

Editors

MAURIZIO FERRERA
MARTIN RHODES

FRANK CASS
LONDON • PORTLAND, OR

First Published in 2000 in Great Britain by
FRANK CASS PUBLISHERS
Crown House, 47 Chase Side,
Southgate, London N14 5BP

and in the United States of America by
FRANK CASS PUBLISHERS
c/o ISBS, 5824 N.E. Hassalo Street
Portland, Oregon, 97213-3644

Website: www.frankcass.com

British Library Cataloguing in Publication Data

Recasting European welfare states
   1. Welfare state 2. Public welfare – Europe 3. Europe –
Social policy
I. Ferrera, Maurizio II. Rhodes, Martin, 1956 Feb. 23–
361.6'5'094

ISBN 07146 5103 6 (hb)
ISBN 07146 8143 1 (pb)

Library of Congress Cataloging-in-Publication Data

Recasting European welfare states / Maurizio Ferrera, Martin Rhodes.
     p. cm.
Includes index.
ISBN 0-7146-5103-6 – ISBN 0-7146-8143-1 (pbk.)
   1. Europe – Social policy. 2. Welfare state.
   I. Ferrera, Maurizio. II. Rhodes, Martin.

HN373.5 .R43 2000
361.6'5'094 – dc21   00-029044

This group of studies first appeared in a Special Issue of *West European Politics*
(ISSN 0140-2382) Vol.23, No.2 [Recasting European Welfare States]

Printed in Great Britain by Antony Rowe Ltd, Eastbourne

Contents

Recasting European Welfare States:
An Introduction

MAURIZIO FERRERA AND
MARTIN RHODES

Since the establishment of compulsory social insurance in Wilhelmine Germany back in 1883, the welfare state has made a fundamental contribution to the modernisation of European society: its programmes have greatly contributed to consolidating democratic institutions and to harmonising economic growth with changing social needs. Yet, despite its unquestionable historical success, the welfare state is entering in its second century of life in conditions of strain and uncertainty. A child of the nation state and industrial society, it stands somewhat disoriented amidst the new socio-economic and political context, characterised by the rapid transition to post-industrialism, increasing globalisation, sweeping changes in demography and social relations, trends towards supranational integration and a new, 'post-cold war' politics. No institution can survive without adapting: thus the European welfare state is now faced with a difficult challenge of internal restructuring, involving a 'recasting' of many of its traditional instruments and objectives.

But what exactly is the nature of this challenge? What specific features of social protection 'European style' are most in need of adaptation? How advanced is the restructuring process in the various countries, in terms of actual reforms? And what social and political factors can facilitate this process? These are the main questions addressed by the chapters contained in this volume.[1] By way of introduction, we will briefly articulate these broad questions and present some of the specific themes discussed by the various authors.

In public debates on both sides of the Atlantic, the European 'model' of the welfare state – based on universal coverage and generous levels of protection – is frequently accused of being 'unsustainable', not only with respect to fiscal imperatives, but also because it allegedly constitutes a burden for Europe's economy and thus puts it at a disadvantage in the new context of global competition. In this perspective, the roots of the crisis would appear as primarily exogenous. As shown by recent research, however, there are many good reasons for believing that the overall impact of globalisation has been exaggerated, as have its potentially adverse consequences for employment and social standards in Europe. Unemployment problems and the need for the modernisation of social protection systems should, on the whole, be attributed mainly to other developments (such as the 'post-industrialisation' of advanced economies) to which external pressures (many of which are not so new) may make some contribution but cannot on their own explain.

While serious if critical attention should be paid to arguments that financial market globalisation limits government policy autonomy and that open borders unleash tax competition, in the first instance – as a number of contributions to this volume note – it is European integration and economic and monetary union that really count among the most heavily felt recent exogenous pressures. These have been resisted by some but welcomed by others as timely support for reform in their respective battles with the forces of inertia and conservatism (see especially the contribution on Italy by Maurizio Ferrera and Elisabetta Gualmini). All European welfare states must become 'competitive' to the extent that simultaneously meeting their fiscal, solidarity and employment creation objectives requires a creative new mix of policies in an era of open borders and increasingly competitive product markets. This is the single market's most important contribution to the current new world in which the welfare state finds itself, exerting a much more significant set of constraints than international trade, which accounts for only around some ten per cent of total EC exports and imports. That said, and as we argue in our concluding chapter in this volume, various types of institutional setting and forms of social, social security and labour market policy may be equally compatible with competitiveness both in Europe and with the outside world. There is little evidence of convergence on neo-liberal solutions, or in terms of policy making and implementation, for a trend towards unilateral, Thatcher-style reformism.

Nor is there much evidence of welfare becoming a battleground between capital and labour in which the stakes are raised to the point in which there can only be a zero-sum outcome. Even in the German case, discussed here by Philip Manow and Eric Seils, employers are not using the social-insurance linked employment crisis to engineer a substantial shift of power in their favour, as did their British counterparts so effectively in the early 1980s. Indeed, in many countries, the 'new politics' of welfare actually involve a much closer and consensual relationship between the social partners than in the past, sometimes consolidated in social pacts with varying degrees of formality and institutionalisation.[2]

Far from the issue of 'globalisation' being at the centre of policy concerns, the real challenge for each national system is that of clearly identifying those specific programmes and regulations that have become 'incentive incompatible' and 'employment unfriendly' and of devising new solutions, at both the macro and the micro level. As also discussed in our concluding chapter, for different national systems a careful sequencing of negotiated reform in employment, social security and health care policies seems essential, and a process on which most countries have already embarked. For the European Union as a whole, the challenge is in turn that of appropriately addressing at the supranational level those strains generated by the process of market-making and 'negative' integration. In neither the domestic or supranational arenas is the pessimism often expressed with regard to the future of national welfare systems or the European 'social model' justified. To generalise the title of Stein Kuhnle's article on Scandinavia to the rest of the region, Europe's welfare states are challenged yet remain viable. News of their demise has been much exaggerated.

As we also stress, although we acknowledge the constraining nature of external developments, the principal sources of this challenge are internal. The most important and demanding are socio-economic, stemming from a number of well known developments: demographic change (causing a shift in the ratio of active citizens to passive welfare recipients); the rising cost of health care (due to ageing, higher disposable incomes and greater insurance coverage, but also to technological improvements and rising real prices); low economic growth and high unemployment; the changing nature of the labour market; and new household patterns and family/gender relationships. These transformations have generated mounting pressures on institutional arrangements that were not only designed under very different 'environmental' circumstances, but which also have become increasingly rigid over time. To quote Paul Pierson, 'irresistible forces' are meeting 'immovable' objects, provoking clashes and conflict, but also – of necessity – generating a search for new and sustainable solutions.[3]

The scope and intensity of such pressures are obviously filtered (or obstructed) by the 'objects' – that is, national institutions and traditions and the web of vested interests that welfare programmes tend to produce. As the case studies in this volume clearly show, in each country the reform agenda responds to specific problems with differentiated solutions – necessarily given particular national circumstances, both facilitating and constraining, and different types of problem constellation. However, as the broad priorities are very similar, a number of common trends and key orientations can be observed across systems.

The first of these trends is constituted by structural adjustments in response to socio-demographic developments. In the field of pensions, the 1990s have witnessed a substantial wave of reforms that in some cases (for example, Sweden or Italy) have altered the fundamental architecture of the system – a 'third order' change, to use the terminology of Peter Hall employed by Bruno Palier in his contribution to characterise certain recent reforms of the French social security system. Most countries, though, have kept within the boundaries of 'first' and 'second order' changes in that they modify existing instruments or remain within the logic of the existing system, taking steps in one or more of the following directions: increasing the age of retirement, tightening qualifying conditions, restricting indexation rules and strengthening the link between contributions and benefits. In the field of health care – which is also greatly affected by population ageing – reforms have been introduced with a view to enhancing efficacy and efficiency in the allocation of resources and in the provision of services through better incentives at both the micro and the macro level. In the social services, new relationships have emerged between central and local authorities. In both cases policy reform has had important consequences for traditional institutional arrangements.

As illustrated by Richard Freeman and Michael Moran, a basic trend of these endeavours in health systems has been the adoption of a 'public contract' approach – which in some cases may also change the basic architecture of the system – in the relationships between purchasers and providers with a view to fostering forms of 'managed competition'. Fiona Ross also refers to new public sector management as one of the techniques whereby otherwise constrained politicians can assert their power to deal with 'immovable objects' in the policy system. One fascinating outcome, as Freeman and Moran discover, has been that, as a result of its interventions to foster markets, the state inevitably takes on a new and more central role. As they conclude, state intervention becomes ever more essential as the regulator of external pressure and internal demand: 'In health care we encounter the wider paradox of public policies that try to strengthen market forces: markets need states, and strengthening markets demands assertive states.' Various efforts have also been made to consolidate the net of social services, as presented in the chapter by Valeria Fargion. As her account of recent developments across Europe shows, trends towards greater fiscal austerity coupled with an expected increase in social needs render more expansive provision unlikely. But coping with what she calls 'confining conditions' produces different results in different countries, depending on the timing of innovation in the provision of social care and distribution of responsibilities between central and local government. While in some countries local governments become more purposive actors as a result of decentralisation, in others their activities become more constrained by arrangements for funding.

A second general trend is a move from a passive to an active approach in the management of schemes for work incapacity (for example, sickness and invalidity) and especially for unemployment. The new emphasis is clearly on rehabilitation, training and insertion, with a view to preventing long-term dependency on income support. In the course of the 1990s the 'job first' principle has gradually made its way throughout European (un)employment protection systems. This type of policy orientation, which also includes 'in work' benefits or work subsidies, is sometimes seen as 'neo-liberal' and coercive, but actually has a long and honourable history as part of Swedish social democratic active labour market policy. As argued by Jochen Clasen, this policy shift has been especially pronounced recently in the UK and in Denmark, particularly as regards the young unemployed. As he also points out, in other systems – specifically the German case – such reform is harder to introduce to the same degree, since, in this case, activation policies would have to be implemented and funded at local level, and therefore face powerful obstacles from regional governments. In that country, successful policy innovation truly would have the character of 'third order' change given the degree of institutionalised opposition to it. Nevertheless, the 'activation' of benefits is now a widespread phenomenon in Europe, meeting political demands for an end to 'something for nothing' welfare in certain countries while also – if successful – giving hope to the long-term unemployed and ending the cycle of short-term jobs punctuated by periods out of work for those on the margins of the labour market.

A third trend is a greater 'targeting' of resources towards those most in need. Targeting has become an important ingredient of the policy recommendations formulated by international organisations such as the OECD or the World Bank, and its virtues praised by the international and supranational exponents of community welfare policy. Even for those countries that do not use this conception of the term, there has been a new emphasis on *selectivity*. But different strategies – often with different purposes – have been experimented with in this direction, also depending on institutional constraints and opportunities.

As described by Rhodes in his analysis of the British case, targeting in the UK has been concentrated at the bottom of the social security system, with a greater use of means-testing and the introduction of stricter eligibility rules for accessing most cash benefits. By contrast, as shown by Kuhnle, in

Scandinavia – the historical cradle of full universalism – the 1990s have witnessed the inauguration of relatively novel forms of targeting 'from the top', by using an income test in order to trim the social entitlements of higher income groups. In the insurance systems of continental Europe, the only kind of selectivity that is practicable is *exclusive* and not *inclusive*: since everyone is already covered by generous programmes, the very rich can only be excluded from certain services. Thus, a more general process of 're-calibration' of social protection has been launched, whereby the generous formulas protecting the 'old' risks have been reduced (for example, pensions) while at the same time strengthening the so-called 'safety net'. The establishment of minimum income schemes and of new programmes to fight social exclusion (discussed in the contributions on France and Italy) represent clear efforts on this latter front. In Italy, as in the rest of southern Europe, the institutional configuration of this area makes grafting selectivity easier in principle, but in fact even more difficult and risky than in continental Europe. Nevertheless, both the 'over-protection' enjoyed by certain categories within the social security system, and considerable gaps in the income support net legitimise policies that prune back benefits, and smooth the way for selectivity, despite the insurance legacy in the system.[4]

A fourth common trend finally involves the financial side of social protection. Here two main trends can be observed, especially in continental Europe. The first is the attempt at reducing charges on business and labour, particularly in the form of non-wage costs. This trend is primarily motivated by 'competitiveness' preoccupations, but also by the wish to neutralise the vicious circles that are generated by 'contribution-heavy' social insurance systems: the institutional pathologies of such systems are emblematically reconstructed by Manow and Seils for the German case. In a strong counter-claim to the argument that the German unemployment crisis can be attributed mainly to macroeconomic austerity and the costs of the unification years, Manow and Seils attribute strong responsibility to the way in which the broader economy interacts with the social insurance system to create a particular unemployment pathology. Thus, non-wage labour costs, in particular continuously rising social insurance contributions, have adverse effects on job growth in the low wage (service) sector and on the competitiveness of German industry in world markets. All insurance-based systems confront this problem to one degree or another, and while not making it as central to his analysis as Manow and Seils, Palier shows that similar concerns have driven recent social security reforms in France. This produces a second trend, which is the search for a more rational, transparent and equitable 'division of labour' between social security contributions and taxes in the overall financing of the welfare state. As underlined by Palier, the issue of separating the social security from the 'national solidarity' sectors – for economic, but also for political reasons – has been especially contentious in France during the last decade: but reforms in a similar direction have also been undertaken in Italy, Spain, Belgium and Germany.

While it is clear that in all European welfare states a process of internal restructuring is well under way, the actual effectiveness (as well as extent) of the reforms introduced so far varies significantly across countries and 'regimes'. At one extreme, as Stein Kuhnle concludes, we find the Scandinavian countries: their systems of social protection have basically 'stood the test' posed by the long crisis initiated in the 1970s and culminated in the turbulent first half of the 1990s. The Nordic welfare states have been adjusted, but have basically remained 'universal, comprehensive, redistributive and employment-oriented' – and so they are likely to remain in the foreseeable future. At the other extreme, we find the big continental countries. While it cannot be denied that the French, Italian and German welfare states have shown some important signs of 'defrosting' – to use Bruno Palier's phrase – they still appear short of having reached a new 'virtuous' equilibrium. In these cases, the 'frozen landscape' metaphor of Esping-Andersen remains appropriate.[5] But given that 'frozen' in this case implies sclerosis rather than a stable and sustainable situation, recasting will become more and more irresistible as problems of financing, equity and the pathology of dysfunctional outcomes become overwhelming. In the German case, the old institutional pathologies have only been marginally tackled so far and greater political investments are required from policy makers in order to bring about the necessary changes. In the Italian case, although, as shown by Ferrera and Gualmini, important innovations have occurred, there is still a need for further reform in, for example, pensions and health, to make these sub-systems of welfare affordable and equitable (in the first case) and efficient and responsive to needs (in the second).

This leads us to the last set of general questions raised above, that is, those addressing the political factors that shape welfare reforms. Recasting the welfare state generates a 'new politics' highly conditioned by 'entrenched interests and sticky institutions'. As the experiences of the 1990s have shown, there are in fact powerful vested interests devoted to defending transfer-heavy welfare states and their traditional redistributive outcomes. But policy innovation has indeed taken place – in some instances

quite incisively. What accounts for more or less change? As Ross underlines
in her analysis, political agency remains important in triggering institutional
change. Although, as she clearly demonstrates, the 'sandwiching' of
political leadership between structural necessities and institutional and
political constraints serves to circumvent the critical role political agency
can play in welfare reform, there is still room for political leadership and
manoeuvre. Indeed, pointing to one aspect of our first trend, introduced
above – the New Public Management – Ross notes that some leaders have
dramatically reorganised their public services in accordance with market
principles – reforms that have had significant consequences for their welfare
agenda. In the UK, as discussed by Rhodes, this has definitely also been a
means of disempowering entrenched interests and marginalising potential
sources of opposition within a strong-state, unilateral process of radical
reform of the public sector in general. As shown by Freeman and Moran,
competition as such, as a principal of organisation in health care, may well
prove transient; competition has turned relatively quickly into collaboration
between larger units with more clearly defined functions of planning and
providing care. More than anything, reinforcing Ross's point, it served its
purpose as a destabilising strategy, breaking up old rigidities and
expectations in systems resistant to reform.

However, in other areas, especially where employment, social insurance
and tax systems intersect, and where the accommodation of powerful
interests is inevitable, a quite different approach to initiating reform can be
just as successful, if considerably less dramatic. In most European
countries, without the benefit of the loosely organised and centralised
institutional structure of the UK, politicians truly are 'sandwiched' between
other, non-governmental powers and the interpenetration of policy domains
and constituencies in insurance-based systems makes reform a much more
complex business. Electoral incentives, 'institutional stickiness' and the
veto points created by powerful vested interests devoted to defending
transfer-heavy welfare states and their redistributive outcomes make
anything other than incremental reform very difficult. As Pierson puts it, the
'new' politics of the welfare state in these countries – and, one might add,
the exercise of political agency – 'involves a complex two-level game,
incorporating both an electoral arena and a corporatist arena'.[6] Indeed, the
interest-group arena has if anything become more important in gaining
support for reform in many countries in recent years than the parliamentary
domain.

For while there has been a gradual convergence of political opinion on
the inevitability and direction of reform in many of those countries facing

the most difficult problems, either of financial restructuring or benefit recalibration, the social partners, welfare professionals and citizen groups with stronger opinions, and sometimes more direct stakes as welfare clienteles, have moved to centre-stage. Reforms to pensions systems and labour market regulation all require a careful process of adjustment if social cohesion as a governing principle of these systems is not to be sacrificed and if core constituencies and their representatives are not to erect insuperable impediments to change. In our conclusion we elaborate further on the forms of productive interaction that 'new' corporatist paths to reform can provide. As shown by the contributions of Ferrera and Gualmini for the Italian experience and by Hemerijck and Visser for the Dutch (compared with the Belgian) case, potential blockages in the process of reform can be avoided by the creation of new coalitions behind the reform agenda, most notably through new types of concertation and negotiation.

In sum, the process of welfare state 'recasting' involves a number of dimensions of change in response to a set of pressures which are largely domestically generated. Globalisation is compatible with several different institutional and normative projects, including those projects that aim at reconciling the imperatives of economic growth with the quest for more cohesion, solidarity and 'real' freedom. Recasting implies resetting old instruments, introducing new instruments and changing in some crucial respects the very objectives of the welfare state. Given the rapidly changing nature of advanced economies, in terms of demographics (ageing), patterns of employment and social risks, as well as the apparent permanence of 'austerity', recasting is also likely to be an ongoing process. If European societies wish to reset themselves on a course of *just growth*, they will not only have to re-adapt their welfare institutions to the new context, but must also increase their *adaptability*, enhancing their social and policy learning capabilities and inaugurating novel institutional combinations to avoid zero-sum trade-offs between competitiveness and solidarity, and flexibility and security.

NOTES

1. Most of the articles in this volume originate in the Research Forum on 'Recasting the Welfare State' directed by the editors at the European Institute, Florence, Italy in 1998–99. The remainder stem from a project on 'Work and Welfare in Open Economies' at the Max Planck Institute in Cologne in which the editors were also involved.
2. See, e.g., M. Rhodes, 'The Political Economy of Social Pacts: "Competitive Corporatism" and European Welfare Reform', in P. Pierson (ed.), *The New Politics of the Welfare State* (Oxford: Oxford University Press 2000).
3. P. Pierson, 'Irresistible Forces, Immovable Objects: Post-Industrial Welfare States Confront Permanent Austerity', *Journal of European Public Policy* 5/4 (1998), pp.539–60.

4. For a more complete comparison, see M. Ferrera, 'The Four Social Europes: Between Universalism And Selectivity', in M. Rhodes and Y. Mény (eds.), *The Future of European Welfare: A New Social Contract?* (London: Macmillan 1998), pp.81–96.
5. G. Esping-Andersen, 'After the Golden Age? Welfare State Dilemmas in a Global Economy', in G. Esping-Andersen (ed.), *Welfare States in Transition: National Adaptations in Global Economies* (London: Sage Publications 1996), pp.1–31.
6. Pierson, 'Irresistible Forces', p.556.

Interests and Choice in the 'Not Quite so New' Politics of Welfare

FIONA ROSS

The 'new politics of the welfare state' is a term coined by Paul Pierson to differentiate between the popular politics of welfare expansion and the unpopular politics of retrenchment.[1] In contrast to the distributive and legitimising politics of welfare state enlargement, in the current era of austerity political leaders are sandwiched between economic and demographic pressures threatening the foundations of their post-industrial welfare states and broad public support for social programmes, entrenched interests and sticky, path-dependent institutions.[2] Forced to govern under conditions of continuous constraint, leaders are impelled to reformulate their costly and inefficient welfare states while minimising the risks of electoral defeat. The new politics, therefore, is primarily one of blame-avoidance.[3] This is a particularly arduous challenge in that electorates punish losses more readily than they reward gains.[4] They are both more attuned and more reactive to the costs of cuts. Focusing on the power of entrenched interests, Pierson draws on the 'logic of collective action' to explain the inherent dangers of withdrawing resources: losers incur clear, high, concentrated costs, while winners receive unclear, small, thinly spread benefits.[5]

Without question, the new politics literature has advanced the analysis of retrenchment politics and, to a lesser extent, welfare reformulation in important and innovative ways. We are now much more aware, for example, of how the timing and sequencing of welfare commitments condition the entrenchment of interests, the extent of policy lock-in and the degree of risk leaders must embrace in pursuing a reform agenda.[6] Such variables can claim considerable success in explaining cross-national variations in sectoral reforms such as pensions. Likewise, programmatic structure and the availability of blame-avoidance strategies (for example, 'obfuscation, division and compensation') have shed much light on cross-national departures in retrenchment politics.[7] Theories of path dependence and institutional stickiness have contributed greatly to our understanding of continuities in social policy across time and particularly the welfare state's resilience in the face of mounting pressures.[8] Pierson's path-breaking work has redefined many of the core issues for welfare studies. Indeed, it is the justified success, not shortcomings, of his insightful conceptualisation of welfare state politics that informs the thesis of this article: that the role of political leadership, interests and choice deserve much greater attention in our analyses of welfare state restructuring.

Despite bringing politics much further into the centre of social policy analysis, especially in comparison to power-resource theories of welfare expansion, this article argues that much of the new politics debate remains heavily de-politicised. Its neglect of political leadership, opportunity and choice has serious implications for how it conceives of new welfare challenges and the availability of political responses. Indeed, all policy transitions need to be understood in terms of a relationship between structural possibilities and political agency.[9] While making a compelling case for the importance of policy institutionalisation and the consequent resilience of deeply entrenched welfare programmes to retrenchment initiatives, the new politics has presented an overly institutionalised portrait of the welfare state and underestimated the role political leadership can play in the restructuring process.

Indeed, among the forces of social policy stability the only elements of political choice are entrenched interests and public preferences. De-politicising the new politics further, Francis Castles rejects the notion that even entrenched interests play a role in the restructuring process: 'in our account pressure group resistance to programme cuts plays no discernible part. Thus, rather than identifying the characteristic mode of contemporary public sector decision making as a "new politics" of blame-avoidance, our preferred focus is on the emergence of a "new political economy" of economic and institutional constraint.'[10] Increasing returns arguments do incorporate an element of choice at the margins: institutionalised policy paths are not simply accepted due to inertia or the technicalities of policy lock-in such as high start-up costs.[11] Rather, previous policy investments actually make the *status quo* or only incremental adjustment more *appealing* to policy-makers.[12]

Yet nowhere in this constellation of new politics variables do we find a defining role for political leadership, for elite choice, for elite influence over policies, institutions or public opinion. We have little understanding, for example, of how symbolic politics, the strategic deployment of political discourse, elite diffusion of political ideas and policy framing can serve as elite strategies of agenda control. The mechanisms by which leaders can shape public opinion, aggregate interests and expand leadership options under conditions of constraint require much greater attention. Moreover, we should bear in mind that political leaders can and have fundamentally reformed their governing institutions. Nowhere has this been more clear than in the extensive public sector reforms sweeping across and beyond post-industrial societies. Often portrayed as one of the major constraints placed upon elected officials due to some inconsistent combination of bureaucratic inertia and artful, power-hungry bureaucrats,[13] leaders have dramatically reorganised their public services in accordance with market principles – reforms that have had significant consequences for their welfare agenda. Crafted to cut costs, impose losses, disempower entrenched interests and marginalise potential sources of opposition, the New Public Management reforms appear to be a particularly astute method of liberating elected officials from both bureaucratic routines and purposeful opposition.

One of the principal reasons why more malleable political variables, such as leadership, have been marginalised in the new politics is due to its emphasis on explaining the lack of welfare retrenchment. Indeed, the puzzle for the new politics has been to explain why *despite* the political will of rightist governments to impose losses and restructure their welfare states and *despite* exogenous and endogenous pressures bearing heavily upon social programmes, surprisingly little reform has occurred. The welfare state debate, therefore, has very much focused on the sources of resistance to change, drawing heavily on institutionalist arguments of constraint. As welfare states have exhibited greater movement since the early to mid 1990s the new politics has paid greater attention to globalisation, demography and programmatic imperatives as possible explanations for these adjustments. To its credit, the new politics has resisted over-exogenising welfare state transition and has recognised the importance of endogenous pressures. These endogenous sources of change, however, are also de-politicised: demographics, programme maturation and slow growth urge leaders to restructure costly and inefficient social programmes.[14] With welfare reformulation often occurring under the leadership of leftist governments, de-politicising the forces of change has an obvious logic.

Yet politics also needs to be brought back into our analyses as an independent variable. With policy driving politics in the new politics, the answer to the question 'what drives policy?' has been reduced to objective events not politics in any ideological, partisan or leadership sense. To the extent that partisan leadership has entered the new politics, it has been implicit at best: it is assumed that parties of the right will embrace welfare reform to the greatest extent that electoral risk will allow, and that parties of the left will seek to defend welfare institutions to the greatest extent that economic and demographic transformations will permit. Castles has recently examined aggregate expenditures across OECD democracies only to conclude that parties *do not matter under conditions of constraint*.[15] Such de-politicisation has not gone unchallenged. Both Jonah Levy and I have argued, albeit for different reasons, that leftist parties can play a critical leadership role in the welfare reform process.[16] Whereas blame-avoidance is a mode of leadership defined by hidden-hand manipulations, welfare restructuring can offer electoral opportunities for the left.

Much greater attention should therefore be paid to the role of political leadership, opportunity and choice in the new politics of welfare. In no sense does this approach imply that the objective forces impinging upon welfare states are irrelevant. On the contrary. Leadership is situated within an institutional context and within an international context. Moreover, the concept of leadership is most useful *precisely* when political actors are constrained. What is suggested here is that political choice matters, that it needs to be explained and that even if leadership appears to be a rather small part of the governing equation under conditions of constraint we should be mindful of a point well made by path dependence theories: seemingly small events or choices can have far-reaching consequences.

De-problematising issues of choice does injustice to the proactive elements of the restructuring process and leaves too many questions unanswered. How, for example, can we explain why Britain's Tony Blair has chosen to abandon social democracy to a far greater extent than demanded by either globalisation or post-industrial transformations?[17] How can we explain why parties of the left in many places have chosen to reform their welfare states more dramatically than their conservative counterparts?[18] Public opinion may well constrain political leaders in their restructuring endeavours, yet this is proving not to be a constant across partisan actors or time. Indeed, we have reasons to believe that leftist leaders can actually shift public opinion on the welfare state rather than simply being constrained by it.

These arguments for bringing politics, especially leadership politics, further into the centre of our analyses are illustrated in the next section by a comparison of the old and new politics of welfare and in the following one through a review of structural and choice-based explanations for welfare state change. We conclude by considering the implications of these arguments for social policy convergence/divergence across welfare states.

THE OLD AND NEW POLITICS OF WELFARE

The new politics starts from the premise that, in contrast to the legitimising politics of welfare state expansion, retrenchment is inherently unpopular. Consequently, it cannot be explained in terms of dominant theories of welfare state growth, such as power resources, economic development, a 'logic of industrialism' or state strength.[19] This point of comparison, however, may not be the most appropriate one and may well have led us prematurely to fashion a *new* politics of welfare in overly stylised blame-avoidance terms. Accounts of welfare state expansion based on working class mobilisation, economic growth and state strength were more or less effectively deployed to explain parsimoniously sweeping historical differences in expenditure and/or outcomes across clusters of regimes that had been configured over the best part of a century. Indeed, it would be surprising if theories of historical departure did explain comparatively small differences in welfare reformulation across affluent societies.

Moreover, the search for grand theories of welfare contraction is premature at this juncture, especially given the lack of clarity concerning the dependent variable and the declining consensus regarding just how much change has occurred across welfare states and the precise nature of this change.[20] Approached less from the stance of grand theory and more from a general policy leadership perspective we find that leaders find it difficult to do many things, not simply retrench. This is not to deny the pertinence of Pierson's observation that the new *goals* and *context* of social policy have affected the politics of the welfare state in critical ways.[21] Goals have changed from welfare expansion to slow-downs and retrenchments. The context of the welfare state has been changed by its own growth. The elaborate array of interest groups now attached to social programmes and the sheer number of people now tied to the administration and receipt of welfare services have surely affected the salience of welfare politics. This, of course, explains why reform can pose a formidable challenge even where labour movements and social democratic politics are weak.[22] Most importantly, in Pierson's words, 'The welfare state now represents the status quo, with all the political advantages that this status confers. Non-decisions generally favour the welfare state'.[23]

The political salience and institutionalisation of welfare programmes undoubtedly intensifies the leadership dilemma. Yet are these constraints of such qualitatively different proportions from other contentious policy problems that they merit both a new conceptualisation and a specifically tailored set of explanations? Understood in less 'bottom-up' and institutionalised terms, we might find them to be exaggerations of standard policy leadership challenges rather than distinctively different. The dominance of power-resource models of welfare growth has overshadowed the fact that the founding of welfare states was far from a credit-claiming and legitimising process for social democratic governments responding to class needs.[24] On the contrary, just as we now find leftist parties playing a critical role in retrenching and reformulating welfare policy, bourgeois parties often assumed a pivotal position in laying the foundations of the welfare state. Indeed, both processes have involved counterintuitive modes of partisan leadership.

Likewise, it was noted above that a particular focus of the new politics has been to explain why welfare retrenchment has been so incremental.[25] If we adopt a general policy leadership perspective it becomes clear that the vast majority of policy change, not simply welfare reform, is incremental. This slow and adaptive pattern of change cannot be attributed to the institutionalisation of welfare programmes or the unpopularity of restructuring initiatives. Welfare state expansion was incremental – even during the so-called Golden Age when the political and economic conditions for non-incrementalism were ripe. Welfare states were not built over a decade or two, so why would we expect them to be dismantled over a decade or two? Pierson is undoubtedly convincing when he argues that welfare expansion and contraction are far from 'mirror image' processes.[26] However, it is not so clear that the changed goals and context of social policy should lead analysts to discard many of the established lessons of public policy leadership in approaching the welfare restructuring process.

It is becoming increasingly clear, for example, that the neo-corporatist tools of Golden Age welfare governance are playing an integral role in the reformulation of welfare states. Neo-corporatist mechanisms are resurrecting themselves in various guises, especially around the European peripheries.[27] According to Martin Rhodes, these modes of concertation are even *more* important in certain countries now than during the Golden Age, providing leaders with vital mechanisms for exercising political control under conditions of constraint. Moreover, mounting evidence indicates that negotiated settlements are among the most effective strategies for reform.[28] In a word, traditional mechanisms for effective welfare leadership are highly relevant to the restructuring process – even in the Bismarkian welfare states that, squeezed so severely between structural pressures and entrenched institutions and interests, should be heading for disaster.

A similar point could be made with respect to how the new politics has conceived of institutions more generally. The unpopularity of welfare retrenchment initially implied that power-sharing structures would help leaders retrench by diffusing responsibility for unpopular initiatives. Centralised institutions reduce the power of opponents but they simultaneously leave leaders politically exposed – a particularly important factor when leaders want to hide.[29] More recently, Pierson has argued that 'on balance' the ability of majoritarian institutions to reduce opposition is a greater leadership asset than the capacity for blame-avoidance.[30] This may well reflect the fact that welfare restructuring is not as unilaterally unpopular as originally envisaged or simply that the magnitude of popularity has less effect on leadership choices than has been assumed. Whether broadly popular or unpopular initiatives are on the agenda, majoritarian structures facilitate change.

Not only are many of the standard tools and rules of policy leadership highly relevant for understanding welfare restructuring, but the new politics' failure to bring a wider policy leadership perspective to the restructuring debate is distorting its analysis of critical actors and institutions. For example, the importance of bureaucratic politics has been eclipsed by the new politics' heavy emphasis on public opinion. The new politics tends to envision policy as formulated by electorally driven politicians with the ballot box at the forefront of their minds. Yet unelected civil servants have played a critical role in retrenchment politics.[31] The assumption that civil servants simply administer the decisions of their political masters leads Pierson to comment:

> ... there is little reason to expect that bureaucratic capacities will be particularly important in an age of retrenchment. Can we administer it? may be an important question in a discussion of new or greatly expanded public initiatives, but for advocates of retrenchment the primary goal is to dismantle existing programs. Closing offices, curtailing services, and cutting benefits do not require formidable administrative capacity.[32]

This assumption is problematic for at least four reasons. First, career civil servants are a notable source of policy obstruction, especially where austerity limits the research and analysis needed to demonstrate the sagacity of a new course of action.[33] As Patricia Ingraham and Charles Barrilleaux contend, 'Career executives are, in a very real sense, the change agents who bless reform and/or retrenchment with their cooperation and direction, or doom it by their disapproval and failure to cooperate'.[34] The authors cite one government manager as saying: '... for many [managers] loyalty is at the program level. People come to identify in a very close personal way with a program they have worked on for years, and they may identify very closely with those served by the program. ... Real pain comes from seeing programs that you really put yourself into, and that you thought were really important, go down the tubes.'[35]

Second, the new politics of welfare is not simply about cutbacks. On the contrary, restructuring initiatives have been largely about regulating behaviour and changing the relationship between citizens and the state, especially in the English-speaking world. Third, the role of bureaucratic politics should be especially relevant to the new politics because administrative actors, who have a heavy hand in policy formulation and not simply implementation, are *un*elected. Indeed, civil servants are exempt from the public pressures that Pierson sees as fundamentally constraining elected officials in their retrenchment endeavours. Fourth, it is unclear how a group-based analysis of welfare state retrenchment, emphasising the power of pluralistic interests attached to diverse social programmes, can survive without an analysis of the public bureaucracy.

Given the heavy emphasis placed upon the exceptional unpopularity of welfare restructuring in the new politics and how this pivotal assumption, along with institutional stickiness, has defined the distinctiveness of welfare reform as an electorally driven politics of blame-avoidance, it is worthwhile taking a moment to consider its robustness. The third section argues that recent developments in Britain suggest that the popularity assumption is neither as robust nor as relevant as has been assumed.

The Popularity Assumption

Evaluating the 'crisis' of the welfare state almost two decades ago, Hugh Heclo cautioned that 'glancing over one's shoulder ... may help temper some of the assumptions about the uniqueness of our own times'.[36] The notion that the welfare state enjoys a depth and breadth of public support that is truly exceptional at face value best captures the historically transitory Golden Age – an atypical episode in welfare state expansion during the 1950s and 1960s when welfare growth seemed possible without economic trade-offs or competing policy costs. What marked this peculiar era of welfare development was the seeming absence of tension between sound economic policy and just social policy, resulting in a marked de-politicisation of welfare spending and the so-called 'end of ideology'.[37] Heclo warns against such naivety, however, when he opens his article with the following quote from Asa Briggs written during the height of the Golden Age;

> ... recent writings from all sides make it abundantly clear that the ideals which inspired the achievement of a "welfare state" are now no longer universally shared. Comprehensive notions of a "welfare state"

based on complete "equality of citizenship" no longer receive universal assent (or lip service). Against a background of recurring fiscal crises, "paying for services" has replaced "fair shares for all" as a current political slogan.[38]

The new politics argument that welfare states are broadly popular can hardly be denied. Opinion polls across affluent societies continue to reveal broad support for both social programmes and the values that underlie welfare institutions.[39] Moreover, as Pierson has pointed out, the intensity of welfare state support encourages political mobilisation in its defence and, representing the *status quo*, its champions enjoy a distinct institutional advantage.[40] Consequently, median voters and/or pivotal voters are strategically positioned to protect their popular social programmes.[41]

Yet this support has sat uncomfortably alongside the election of right-wing governments and the refusal of voters to entertain further tax increases to support their welfare states. Electorates are also increasingly willing to choose private alternatives, especially in health and pensions. Moreover, inconsistencies between public attitudes and behaviours are often apparent. For example, while Elim Papadakis and Clive Bean detect quite high levels of support for government spending in the United States (albeit lower than in other countries), the unusually punitive 1996 Personal Responsibility and Work Opportunity Reconciliation Act, 'ending welfare as we know it', proved to be a highly popular initiative for the Clinton administration and Republican-controlled Congress.[42] Indeed, less the 'Middle-East of domestic politics' than it was 20 years ago, welfare reform has increasingly been subject to bi-partisan consensus-building efforts and enjoyed broad public support.[43] While the United States stands out among the English-speaking countries as a retarded and residual welfare state, where the principle of workfare has deep roots in the work houses of the last century, the work relief programmes of the New Deal and the Work Incentives Program of the late 1960s, more recently workfare has come to approximate an ideology.[44]

The depth of support for welfare institutions may also have shifted since the 1970s. As Heclo comments, just as the depression of the 1930s 'undercut faith in any party program that relied entirely on the private sector to solve problems', so the turmoil of the mid to late 1970s discredited the state's ability to provide the answers to all manner of social and economic difficulties.[45] Continuing, Heclo writes, despite enduring public support for the welfare state, 'political disaffection, electoral volatility and distrust in traditional appeals' were notable political reactions to economic stress.[46] Indeed, the resilience of public support for the welfare state remains unclear.

Through generational turnover and natural cohort effects, public opinion would be expected to shift over time.[47] As Kees van Kersbergen has argued, cohorts born in the mid-1970s are apt to view the welfare state as a troubled institution that offers little safeguard against hard times.[48]

While this does not necessarily imply a permanent erosion of public support for the welfare state,[49] it does suggest that social programmes will be less resistant to political attack in the short to medium term. Indeed, while most elements of the welfare state continue to enjoy impressive levels of support, voters across western Europe show a significantly deeper attachment to policies that aim to improve security compared with those targeted towards equality – especially equality of result.[50] As Edeltrand Roller comments:

> It is the provision of a guaranteed income – a policy aiming at establishing national minima – which gets the weakest support among West European publics. The essence of this policy is that it entitles people to financial benefits without doing anything for them. However, the related policy of providing jobs gets more support. But in this case people are not provided with financial goods, only the wherewithal to earn financial rewards. Guaranteeing a minimal level of income, it seems, offends more against the widely accepted achievement principle than guaranteeing people a job. According to this argument, support for moderate socio-economic equality policies reaches its boundaries when national minima policies leave no space for the achievement principle to operate.[51]

Regime theory, of course, would lead us to expect substantial variation in levels of support for welfare programmes across countries. Support for the welfare state is certainly thought to be less resilient in the English-speaking countries due to their liberal, residualist welfare culture where the principle and habit of means-testing are well established and leftist politics and labour movements are comparatively weak. By extension, there should be a natural division between the bulk of the tax-paying public and welfare recipients. Indeed, Pierson acknowledges that the more 'right-leaning' pivotal voter in these countries does tend to be less attached to the welfare state than their counterparts elsewhere.[52] Papadakis and Bean, however, find little evidence for a systematic relationship between regime type and welfare state support.[53] Stefan Svallfors detects a loose one yet also finds strong similarities in group-based (class and gender) attitudes across countries.[54] Indeed, while regime-type may well reveal baseline differences in public attitudes towards welfare, it gives little indication of how these attitudes are changing.[55] Moreover, the commonalities in group-based attitudes suggest that support for the welfare state may be more influenced by socio-economic interests and less deeply entrenched on a normative and cognitive level than assumed by regime theory.

In a word, the popularity of welfare states should not be taken as frozen. Investigating trends in voter ideology across a sample of democracies, Hee Min Kim reports that, despite the ideological gap continuing to divide the English-speaking countries and other Western societies, both groups have shifted rightwards since the 1970s.[56]

Consequently, political leaders enjoy some latitude for shaping public attitudes towards the welfare state. We would expect publics to shift their opinions to some degree in accordance with elite positioning on social policy. Through active framing, leaders can help mould public opinion, especially as voters with first-hand recollection of the collective traumas of depression and war die out. Statistical evidence indicates that electorates do shift their opinion in the direction of the incumbent government,[57] although the importance of political framing is perhaps most starkly illustrated by the host of 'spin doctors' and media personnel employed in the political arena.[58]

Arguing that elites can shift and shape public opinion, of course, does not tell us whether they seek to do so. While the new politics may over-emphasise public opinion as a source of constraint, elites may also be supportive of the *status quo*. Rhodes captures differences in mass and elite perspectives well, however, when he argues that, while 'public opinion polls continue to indicate widespread support for the welfare state, among politicians of all parties there is a profound loss of confidence in "collective", public sector solutions in favour of either privatised or "marketised" social services'.[59] We should also be mindful of the fact that national leaders are also subject to supra-national leadership efforts on welfare-related matters, especially from bodies such as the IMF and WTO that heavily promote free-market ideology. Moreover, as far as the English-speaking countries are concerned, the contraction of the welfare agenda across parties of both the left and right, coupled with the erosion of the trade unions as a pro-welfare lobby, has produced a high degree of elite consensus regarding the superiority of market solutions. This narrowing of political discourse should, over time, be reflected among the public.

In sum, while welfare programmes, especially security-related ones, remain popular, it is not so clear that the unpopularity of retrenchment (together with institutional stickiness) should lead us to relinquish much of the 'conventional wisdom' on effective policy leadership. Leaders employ tried and tested policy strategies in their restructuring endeavours and the politics of welfare state contraction is perhaps less distinctive than might appear from a comparison with grand theories of welfare state growth. Policy leadership *per se* is difficult. It has undoubtedly become more difficult. But it has not become so uniquely and distinctively difficult that it can be reduced to little more than an exercise in blame-avoidance. The new politics' failure to appreciate these similarities not only derives from the point of departure it takes for evaluating welfare reform (macro-explanations of sweeping historical difference) but also from its exaggeration of the constraints public opinion places upon leadership choices. Given that the popularity assumption may not be as robust or as pivotal as portrayed in the new politics, we must consider how political leaders are choosing to reform their welfare states.

STRUCTURE AND CHOICE IN WELFARE POLITICS

Pierson captures what seems to be the critical conundrum for the future of the welfare state: 'what happens when the irresistible forces of post-industrialism meet the immovable objects of the welfare state?'[60] Without doubt, this is an enticing and eloquently posed puzzle. Yet conceiving of the new welfare dilemma in these terms all but precludes a role for political choice in driving the restructuring process.

This section presents a brief overview of the two main factors impelling leaders to restructure their welfare states: exogenous global pressures and endogenous post-industrial stresses. While both tensions are highly relevant to welfare state restructuring, we also need to be able to explain why leaders have sought to impose reforms where exogenous and endogenous pressures are comparatively weak. That is, we need to conceive of welfare restructuring as driven by a combination of structural pressures and political choices. Structural forces alone cannot explain why reform has occurred.[61] The most they can do is provide a potential set of explanations for why political leaders have felt compelled to pursue particular initiatives. In the following section, the role of political choice is illustrated by a short discussion of welfare restructuring under Britain's New Labour. This case is particularly interesting because despite comparatively weak structural pressures, the party has chosen to implement a number of retrenchments. These initiatives offered modest budgetary savings and seemed designed as a matter of principle above all else. According to the logic of the new politics, not only is this unexpected from a leftist party but these types of retrenchments should also demand a blame-avoidance style of political leadership. Yet far from hiding, welfare reform for New Labour has come closer to a credit-claiming exercise.

Globalisation and Post-Industrial Pressures for Change

Despite heavy criticism of the globalisation thesis, there can be little doubt that exogenous pressures now place constraints upon national leaders that were not present two decades ago. Nation states are bound by a growing number of international requirements that reach further and further into national policy domain. Leaders can no longer make policy and spending choices in isolation of their implications for international competition and regulation and deficit politics are now a luxury of the past.[62]

The fact remains, however, that none of these pressures is having as strong a bearing on national welfare states as originally envisaged.[63] While 'workfare' schemes are becoming increasingly visible across Europe, providing capital with an ever more flexible labour force, global competition and financial integration have yet to force the erosion of most labour market protections. In their quest to attract increasingly mobile capital (and repel mobile claimants), nation states have yet to engage in a 'race to the bottom' and, as yet, there is little evidence of 'social dumping' across Europe. Indeed, Rhodes contends that globalisation is interacting with domestic institutions in ways that may be encouraging greater social and economic justice.[64] While market pressures are increasing, so are incentives for the accommodation of social and economic interests. Rather than being crushed by globalisation, the social partners are showing signs of being reinvigorated (except in cases where their demise had already occurred). Globalisation and the welfare state, in other words, are neither in direct competition nor in a mutually hostile relationship.

This is not to imply that welfare states are stress-free. Pierson highlights the importance of endogenous tensions gnawing at the peripheries of post-industrial welfare states.[65] Arguing that the relationship between globalisation and social policy constraint reflects a coincidence of timing and is largely spurious, Pierson contends that welfare states would still be under fundamental pressure to restructure *irrespective* of global trends.[66] The most pressing tensions have come from within societies themselves as they have become 'post-industrial' – a transition founded upon three dominant 'irresistible' developments: (a) lower productivity and slower growth following the replacement of manufacturing with a service-based labour market;[67] (b) programmatic maturation and the weak capacity of entrenched programmes to meet emerging social needs; and (c) demographic developments, specifically an ageing population and the stress this places upon health and pension sectors. Pierson argues that the first development displays only a modest, indirect connection to globalisation while the latter two trends bear no obvious relationship to economic or financial openness. Moreover, there is little reason to expect globalisation to exhibit any relationship to the politics of health or pensions. If anything, only social security compensation should be affected by economic competition.

By offering an endogenous set of explanations for the climate of austerity confronting the welfare state, Pierson draws our attention to variations in pressures for reform across countries. What we find is that welfare states exhibit an inverse relationship between the severity of their post-industrial pressures and the reach of their reform agenda. Post-industrial pressures for reform are weakest among the English-speaking nations, yet these cases have reformed their welfare states in the most significant ways. Conversely, the most severe tensions afflict the conservative regimes of continental Europe where a combination of onerous payroll taxes, a heavy, skewed pension burden, high unemployment, low birth rates, and the exclusion of women from the labour market place immense stresses upon social programmes, yet these regimes are proving to be the most resistant to change.[68]

This inverse relationship is accounted for by the other half of Pierson's new politics equation: the strength or weakness of the welfare state's defences. While the post-industrial pressures bearing down upon welfare states are least severe in the English-speaking nations, so are the welfare state's buffers (public support and sticky institutions). With post-industrial pressures and forces of resistance broadly proportional in each regime, this chain of reasoning is better at explaining stability than change.

To account for change more effectively, therefore, the new politics needs to be infused with a source of political agency. We cannot simply explain restructuring as the net effect of the 'irresistible forces of post-industrialism' colliding with the 'immovable objects of the welfare state'.[69] To obtain political significance, objective trends must be defined as both salient and pressing. Their importance and urgency rarely speak for themselves.

Political Choice

Two alternative, mutually consistent forces driving welfare restructuring are ideas and interests. The former are beginning to attract more attention as the weakness of structural explanations grows more apparent. Ideas, in interaction with existing state capacities, have played an important role in explaining why a logic of no alternative and market liberal orthodoxy has become so prominent in the English-speaking countries since the 1980s and not elsewhere. Historical institutionalists, such as Peter Hall, have argued that in order to be compelling ideas must resonate with the underlying norms and values of a society.[70] The lack of resonance between market liberal principles and the norms and values of conservative and social democratic welfare regimes helps explain their resistance to New Right ideas even under crisis conditions.

Agenda change, of course, requires individuals to grab new ideas and promote them. As Bryan Jones contends, 'ideas are not self-sustaining without advocates'.[71] They typically must be promoted by influential material interests that enjoy institutional access.[72] In New Zealand, the classical New Right ideas driving change from the mid-1980s onwards were embraced by a small clique of strategically situated actors, notably the Cabinet, the Treasury, the Reserve Bank and the Business Round Table.[73] The majoritarianism of New Zealand's institutions allowed a narrow group of elites to capture the agenda and bring about radical restructuring between 1984 and 1993 *irrespective* of widespread public opposition.[74] Indeed, the interaction of ideas and institutions helps explain why, under non-crisis conditions, political leaders on the left in many of the English-speaking countries have continued to restructure their welfare states when the objective pressures (and according to the new politics, electoral interests) for doing so are comparatively low. Britain's New Labour, for example, has embraced structural dependency theses with a vengeance, portraying itself as heavily beholden to global capital and international financial markets.[75]

Interests, however, have been all but excluded from the analysis of social policy restructuring due to the new politics' pivotal assumption that retrenchment and restructuring are unpopular, risky initiatives that require elected officials to avoid blame. It is assumed that rightist preferences for change will, for the most part, be subordinated to these overwhelming electoral interests, thereby discouraging welfare reform – an assumption that appeared to be borne out by the behaviour of conservative governments across Europe during the 1980s and early 1990s.[76] The political left is generally assumed to have neither the desire nor an interest in welfare restructuring.[77] This has not been the case, however, with Britain's New Labour.

Electoral Interests: The Case of New Labour

It was against the background of four successive electoral losses and a rising tide of public anxiety over the future of the public sector that Labour returned to power. The 1997 election was widely perceived to be a verdict on the Conservative government's handling of social policy, in tandem with the associated baggage of crime, corruption, injustice and neglect. Of some surprise, therefore, may be the substance of the agenda that Labour offered in order to gain credibility with British voters – an agenda that confined the party to (artificially austere) Tory spending plans for at least its first two years in office, an unambiguous refusal to increase direct taxes, inclemency on crime and intolerance towards those 'unwilling' to work.

Labour's agenda involved 'thinking the unthinkable', in its leader's words, on a range of issues in comparison to which Tory initiatives paled. Within less than six months of returning to office, New Labour had confirmed cuts in single parents' benefit, leaked plans to chop disability benefit and sick pay, was busy devising its welfare-to-work scheme, and university tuition fees had been placed squarely on the agenda. In addition, 'stake-holder' pensions were under review. Surprisingly, the party maintained a steady 20–30 per cent lead in the polls – even with the revelation that hospital waiting lists had expanded (twice) since taking office. Indeed, the most strident opposition to the government arose from within the parliamentary party (47 MPs voted against the government and 14 abstained on the cuts in single parents' benefit).

Why, despite the supposed popularity of the British welfare state and the lack of structural pressures urging reform, did New Labour introduce these initiatives? One answer is found in the dynamics of electoral competition and prolonged periods spent in opposition: New Labour, in other words, had compelling electoral interests in introducing seemingly contentious welfare cuts. New Labour's agenda developed during the party's lengthy confinement to the opposition benches and four successive electoral defeats. In the early 1980s, Labour was perceived to be splintered and extreme, with the infamous 'loony left' exerting a significant impact on party policy. By the 1983 election, the party (led by Michael Foot), offered a far left agenda that appeared anachronistic and was subject to considerable ridicule. Unsurprisingly, Labour polled appallingly (gaining only 27.6 per cent of the vote). In October of that year, Neil Kinnock replaced Foot as party leader.

While Kinnock did much to prepare the way for the emergence of New Labour in terms of disabling the hard left and shedding the party of a string of uncompetitive policies, Labour only managed to attract 30.8 per cent of the vote in 1987. Increasingly reflective and reformatory, Kinnock initiated a significant review of party policy between 1987 and 1989. Still, the vestiges of socialism remained, albeit symbolically more than substantively. At the 1992 election, Labour increased its share of the vote to just 35.2 per cent (as against 42.8 per cent polled by the Tories). Following two electoral defeats under Kinnock, John Smith assumed the party leadership in 1992 until his death in 1994. By this time, Labour had been professionalised in organisation and modernised in policy. The central role of the market, for example, was rarely questioned among Labour's upper echelons. Indeed, most senior figures appeared satisfied with the extent of Labour's transformation.[78]

Under the tutelage of Kinnock, Labour was transformed from an organisation for the excluded and working class to one that could 'articulate the "aspirations of the majority"'.[79] Still, core electoral constituencies (notably the skilled manual and lower white-collar workers Labour targeted after 1992) doubted the sincerity of Labour's conversion, specifically its pledge not to increase the middle class tax burden. The final phase of Labour's conversion emerged with Tony Blair's succession to the leadership following Smith's death. As Patrick Seyd recalls, 'Just 15 months after his election as leader, Blair was engaged in initiating changes in his party more fundamental than any since Labour adopted a new constitution and program in 1918. By the time the Labour party was elected in May 1997 it had a new constitution, new policies, new internal structures and a new image.'[80]

After gaining the confidence of voters, Labour was anxious to demonstrate its resolve by confronting its own back-benchers over the controversial cut in single-parents' (91.5 per cent of whom are mothers) benefit. The Treasury amassed such minuscule savings from the measure that it seemed designed to send a message to the public that New Labour could make tough choices and could govern as *New* Labour. For sure, the government blatantly illustrated its resolve on one of the most politically vulnerable groups. Moreover, the savings gained from assailing single parents would be diverted towards middle class services, for example, education and health – universal provisions for the more 'deserving'. Indeed, while New Labour flaunted the issue of hard choices and maintaining Tory budgetary estimates, economics was plainly just one consideration. *The Economist* estimated that the measure would cut £60 million per year from a welfare budget of £97 billion.[81] Single mothers and the unemployed account for a tiny section of total welfare spending in Britain (whereas the elderly account for 42 per cent).

While the cut in single parents' benefit was not popular with the British people, Blair was commended for withstanding leftist pressure. Moreover, it served the purpose of showing middle Britain that New Labour was a genuinely transformed organisation. The political capital the government exhausted among its own backbenchers, however, was considerable. Prior to the revolt over the sharp cut in single parents' benefit, for example, the British treasury decided against a planned cut in unemployment benefit due to a threatened back-bench revolt. New Labour's decision to make the unemployed wait a full week (rather than three days) before qualifying for

Job-Seekers' allowance was also shelved largely due to internal party opposition.

All parties are institutionally constrained by both their allies and competitors. Alliances can render agenda change both laborious and impractical. In many respects, the Tories prepared the way for Labour's shift rightwards. Thatcher massively increased Labour's policy flexibility by crippling the unions, clearing the way for structural changes in New Labour's policy-making apparatus (vital to its subsequent policy reversals). For example, thanks in part to Thatcher, New Labour was able to strip the enfeebled union movement of considerable policy authority by first reducing its voting power at the party conference and, second, by reducing the role of the party conference in the policy-making process.[82]

That is not to suggest that electoral interests and organisational changes can fully account for the individual-level transformations necessary for Labour (or any collective body for that matter), to reverse positions on many of its defining policies. The electoral competition argument, for instance, assumes that significant numbers of Labour's policy-making community were willing to suspend their policy preferences for the sake of electoral victory (irrespective of whether they themselves were subject to electoral pressures). Similarly, the structural argument speaks to leaders' ability to orchestrate policy swings once they have been agreed upon.

As intimated earlier, ideas often interact with interests in important ways. With a radical swing rightwards in the governing paradigm since the late 1970s and early 1980s, policy shifts have seemed imperative for the left. The old social democratic alternatives consistent with an era of redistribution and interventionism no longer seem appropriate for an age of market liberalism *irrespective* of their feasibility in structural terms. Frames for policy evaluation have switched from social redistribution to individual responsibility. While leaders' core preferences may not have changed, their choices are restricted by what they see as a new 'logic of appropriateness'.[83] Jones explains that 'changes in choice are caused not so much by changes in preferences as by sensitivity to contextual cues. Humans are sensitive to context because they are not just preference maximisers, they are also problem solvers and problem solving is related to changes in ones task environment'. Changes in the governing context since the late 1970s, in other words, have brought forth a fundamental shift in political ideas, in turn affecting leaders' perception of viable and unattainable policy alternatives.

Preferences, of course, should not be discounted. The transformation of the British Labour Party owes much to the selection of a leadership cadre that is, by taste, more liberal than socialist, thereby providing a commitment to a centrist agenda that seems unlikely to emerge from sensitivity to contextual cues alone. Genuine non-leftist preferences on the part of Blair and many members of his central entourage (combined with the iron grip the leadership exerts upon leftist back-benchers), are important to understanding why New Labour has shifted its agenda so far rightwards. Leaders' basic policy preferences condition *how much* they are willing to move for contextual reasons. Recall, for example, that John Smith had no designs on pushing Labour nearly so far to the right as Tony Blair, irrespective of an equivalent set of contextual cues.

In sum, domestic politics, including interests and ideas, do not simply serve as constraints in the welfare restructuring process, buttressing the *status quo* and locking in popular welfare institutions. They also drive the reform process. Of course, this is far from a complete account of New Labour governance and the party's agenda for the welfare state has not been uni-directional. What this overview illustrates, however, is that, far from being wedged between structural pressures and popular institutions, there are instances when elected leaders, especially those on the political left, have compelling electoral interests in initiating retrenchments and restructuring their welfare states.

This leaves us with the question of whether there really is a new politics of welfare? Without question, the changed goals and context of the welfare state have affected the politics of social policy in critical respects.[84] Both exogenous and endogenous pressures bearing down upon welfare states have constrained the range of policy choices and policy instruments available to decision-makers. Policy and expenditure choices involve more costly trade-offs and bear a greater electoral risk. It is not so clear, however, that we can reduce these complex and dynamic political shifts to a collision between structural imperatives and popular institutions, with political leaders 'sandwiched' in between. Indeed, the new politics is not simply one of passivity or blame-avoidance. The changing politics of the welfare state is more conditioned by interests, choices and ideas than has been allowed for. By implication, many of the standard tools and techniques for effective policy leadership deployed during previous era of welfare state governance are highly pertinent for understanding the politics of welfare reform. While the popularity/unpopularity of policy initiatives is far from irrelevant to both political choices and how those choices are pursued, it is not so clear that this is a principal pillar (along with policy institutionalisation) upon which a new politics of welfare can be distinguished from an old politics of welfare.

CONCLUSION: THE MULTIPLE POLITICS OF WELFARE

Predictions for the future of the welfare state fall into two broad groups. Globalisation and structural dependence theories predict increasing convergence across regimes as global competition forces governments to residualise their welfare states in a means-tested direction. Conversely, explanations for divergence tend to be path-dependent accounts of institutional difference.[85] Not only are deeply entrenched institutions extremely difficult to change but the changes that do occur are unlikely to be uniform. Differences in the timing and sequencing of policy commitments affect the degree of policy lock-in and how deeply consolidated programmes are by the time they come under stress.[86] The depth of entrenchment of all welfare states suggests that historical differences are unlikely to be unravelled.[87] These institutionalist accounts of divergence have been especially critical of convergence theses on the grounds of economic determinism and their tendency to deploy a functionalist or rationalist logic: not only are global trends determinative of social policy options, but there is only one rational or functional response to these pressures.

How does bringing politics into the centre of our analysis bear upon these predictions for the future of the welfare state? It has been argued here that political leaders are not simply wedged between structural imperatives driving them towards restructuring and sticky institutions, entrenched interests and public support urging them to practice modesty. Just as politics, in the sense of partisan leadership, ideas, interests and choice, has been integral to the construction and expansion of the welfare state, so it is crucial to the reformulation of the welfare state. By extension, in order to formulate hypotheses about the welfare state's future we need to understand the politics of choice in relation to the structural constraints placed upon political choice.

The structural pressures bearing down upon welfare states are far from constant across affluent societies. For the most part, these stresses are far more severe in continental Europe than in the English-speaking world. The forces of resistance, Pierson's 'immovable objects of the welfare state', also differ significantly across and within welfare regimes. So do political choices. There are also significant differences in both stresses and responses *within* clusters of nations.[88]

Bringing politics into the centre of our analyses, of course, reminds us that convergence can occur for reasons of choice, such as policy transfer. Indeed, it is not inconceivable that international success stories (or perceptions thereof), such as the Netherlands, will encourage a greater sharing of policy solutions. Certainly, as the mechanisms for political integration grow more important we might expect further policy convergence for reasons of learning and choice at the sectoral level. Yet in calling for greater attention to the role of political choice in the new politics of welfare, it should not be implied that structural and institutional forces are of secondary importance. Any degree of convergence based on political choice is also likely to be very partial. Indeed, convergence across welfare states is heavily contingent upon converging structural pressures, converging choices and the erosion of prevailing institutional differences.

NOTES

Many of the ideas presented in this article developed over the course of a year I spent with the European Forum 1998–99: Recasting the European Welfare State: Options, Constraints, Actors. I am very grateful to the many forum participants who offered valuable feedback. I am especially indebted in this regard to Ann Shola Orloff, although she is in no sense liable for any of the arguments presented. Funding for this project has been kindly provided by the Training and Mobility of Researchers Program of the European Commission's Marie Curie Foundation. I should also acknowledge that several of the arguments critiqued in the previous pages are ones that I have contributed to in my own work.

1. P. Pierson, 'The New Politics of the Welfare State', *World Politics* 48 (1996), pp.143–79.
2. Ibid.; P. Pierson, 'Coping with Permanent Austerity: Welfare State Restructuring in Affluent Democracies', in P. Pierson (ed.) *The New Politics of the Welfare State* (Oxford: Oxford University Press 1999).
3. K.R. Weaver, 'The Politics of Blame-Avoidance', *Journal of Public Policy* 6 (1986), pp.371–98; P. Pierson, *Dismantling the Welfare State: Reagan, Thatcher and the Politics of Retrenchment* (Cambridge, MA: Cambridge University Press 1994).
4. R. Lau, 'Two Explanations for Negativity Effects in Political Behavior', *American Journal of Political Science* 29 (1985), pp.119–38; Pierson, *Dismantling the Welfare State*.
5. Pierson, *Dismantling the Welfare State*; M. Olsen, *The Logic of Collective Action: Public Goods and the Theory of Groups* (Cambridge: Harvard University Press 1965).
6. P. Pierson, 'Not Just What, But When: Issues of Timing and Sequences in Comparative Politics', article presented at the *American Political Science Association* Boston, MA (2-6 September 1998); J. Myles and P. Pierson, 'The Comparative Political Economy of Welfare Reform', article presented at the *RSC*, European University Institute (24 Feb. 1999).
7. Pierson, *Dismantling the Welfare State*.
8. P. Pierson, 'Increasing Returns, Path Dependence and the Study of Politics', *EUI Working Article*, EUF No. 44/97; D. Wilsford, 'Path Dependency, or Why History Makes it Difficult but Not Impossible to Reform Health Care in a Big Way', *Journal of Public Policy* 10 (1997), pp.251–83.
9. J. Campbell, 'Institutional Analysis and the Role of Ideas in Political Economy', *Theory and Society* 4 (1998), pp.376–403.
10. F. Castles, 'When Politics Matters: Public Expenditures Development in an Era of Economic and Institutional Constraints', article presented at the *RSC*, European University Institute (26 Nov. 1998), p.33.
11. See B. Arthur, *Increasing Returns and Path Dependence in the Economy* (Ann Arbor, MI: University of Michigan Press 1994).
12. See Pierson, 'Increasing Returns', for an excellent discussion.
13. B.G. Peters, *The Politics of Bureaucracy*, 4th edn. (New York: Longman 1995).
14. Pierson, 'The New Politics of the Welfare State'; P. Pierson, 'Irresistible Forces, Immovable

Objects: Post-Industrial Welfare States Confront Permanent Austerity', *Journal of European Social Policy* 5 (1998), pp.539–60.

15. Castles, 'When Politics Matters'.
16. J. Levy, 'Vice into Virtue? Progressive Politics and Welfare Reform in Continental Europe', *Politics and Society* 27 (1999), pp.239–73; F. Ross, '"Beyond Left and Right": The New Partisan Politics of Welfare', *EUI Working Article* EUF No. 99/4.
17. M. Wickham-Jones, 'The Constraints Upon Social Democracy: History, Expertise and Reformism', article presented at the American Political Science Association, Atlanta GA (2–6 Sept. 1999).
18. C. Green-Pedersen, 'The Danish Welfare State Under Bourgeois Reign: The Dilemma of Popular Entrenchment and Economic Constraints', *Scandinavian Political Studies* 22 (1999), pp.243–60; F. Ross, 'A Framework for Studying Unpopular Policies: Partisan Possibilities and Institutional Liabilities', article presented at the International Political Studies Association, Seoul, Korea (1–6 Aug. 1997).
19. H. Heclo, 'Toward a New Welfare State?' in Peter Flora and Arnold J. Heidenheimer (eds.), *The Development of Welfare States in Europe and America* (London: Transaction Books 1981); Pierson, 'The New Politics of the Welfare State'.
20. Pierson, 'Irresistible Forces, Immovable Objects'; Pierson 'Coping with Permanent Austerity'; R. Clayton and J. Pontusson, 'Welfare State Retrenchment Revisited: Entitlement Cuts, Public Sector Restructuring and Inegalitarian Trends in Advanced Capitalist Societies', *World Politics* 51 (1998), pp.67–98.
21. Pierson, 'The New Politics of the Welfare State'.
22. Ibid., p.175.
23. Ibid., p.174.
24. Heclo, 'Toward a New Welfare State?'; K. van Kersbergen, *Social Capitalism: A Study of Christian Democracy and the Welfare State* (London: Routledge 1995).
25. But see Clayton and Pontusson, 'Welfare State Retrenchment Revisited'.
26. Pierson, *Dismantling the Welfare State*.
27. M. Rhodes, 'Globalisation and West European Welfare States: A Critical Review of Recent Debates', *Journal of European Social Policy* 6 (1996), pp.305–27; M. Rhodes, 'Globalisation and the Welfare State: The Emergence of Competitive Corporatism', *Swiss Political Science Review* 4 (1998), pp.99–107.
28. G. Esping-Andersen (ed.), *Welfare States in Transition* (London: Sage 1996).
29. K.A. Weaver and B.A. Rockman (eds.), *Do Institutions Matter? Governing Capabilities in the US and Abroad* (Washington, DC: Brookings Institution 1993); Pierson, *Dismantling the Welfare State*; Ross, '"Beyond Left and Right"'.
30. Pierson, 'Coping with Permanent Austerity'.
31. S. Goldfinch, 'Remaking New Zealand's Economic Policy: Institutional Elites as Radical Innovators 1984–1993', *Governance* 11 (1998), pp.177–207; J. Kelsey, *The New Zealand Experiment: A World Model for Structural Adjustment?* (Auckland: Bridget Williams Books 1995).
32. Pierson, 'The New Politics of the Welfare State', p.153.
33. C. Levine, 'Organizational Decline and Cutback Management', *Public Administration Review* 38 (1978), pp.315–25.
34. P.W. Ingraham and C. Barrilleaux, 'Motivating Government Managers for Retrenchment: Some Possible Lessons from the Senior Executive Service', *Public Administration Review* 43 (1983), p.393.
35. Ibid.
36. Heclo, 'Toward a New Welfare State?' p.383.
37. Ibid.
38. A. Briggs, 'The Welfare State in Historical Perspective', *Europäisches Archiv für soziologie* 2 (1961), pp.221–58; cited in Heclo, 'Toward a New Welfare State?', p.383.
39. J. Stephens, E. Huber and L. Ray, 'A Welfare State in Hard Times', in H. Kitschelt *et al.* (eds.), *Change and Continuity in Contemporary Capitalism* (Cambridge: Cambridge University Press 1998); E. Papadakis and C. Bean, 'Popular Support for the Welfare State: A Comparison between Institutional Regimes', *Journal of Public Policy* 13 (1993),

pp.227–54; P.A. Pettersen, 'The Welfare State: The Security Dimension', in O. Borre and E. Scarbrough (eds.), *The Scope of Government* (Oxford: Oxford University Press 1995); E. Roller, 'The Welfare State: The Equality Dimension', in O. Borre and E. Scarbrough (eds.), *The Scope of Government* (Oxford: Oxford University Press 1995); Pierson, 'Coping with Permanent Austerity'.

40. Pierson, 'Coping with Permanent Austerity'.
41. See Pierson, ibid., for a discussion of this distinction.
42. Papdakis and Bean, 'Popular Support for the Welfare State'.
43. J. Califano, cited in L. Mead, 'Welfare Policy: The Administrative Frontier', *Journal of Policy Analysis and Management* 15 (1996), p.589
44. T. Skocpol, *Protecting Soldiers and Mothers: The Political Origins of Social Policy in the United States* (Cambridge, MA: Harvard University Press 1992); idem, *Welfare Reform Network News* (Cambridge, MA: Harvard University Press 1997).
45. Heclo, 'Toward a New Welfare State?' p.391.
46. Ibid., p.387.
47. H. Wilensky, *The Welfare State and Equality: Structural and Ideological Roots of Public Expenditures* (Berkeley, CA: University of California Press 1975); R. Inglehart, *The Silent Revolution* (Princeton, NJ: Princeton University Press 1977); R. Inglehart, *Culture Shift in Advanced Industrial Society* (Princeton, NJ: Princeton University Press 1990).
48. K. van Kersbergen, 'The Declining Resistance of Welfare States to Change', in S. Kuhnle (ed.), *The Survival of the Welfare State* (London: Routledge 1999).
49. See G. Garrett, *Partisan Politics in the Global Economy* (Cambridge: Cambridge University Press 1998).
50. Roller, 'The Welfare State', p.168; Pettersen, 'The Welfare State'.
51. Roller, 'The Welfare State', p.195.
52. Pierson, 'Coping with Permanent Austerity'.
53. Papdakis and Bean, 'Popular Support for the Welfare State'.
54. S. Svallfors, 'Worlds of Welfare and Attitudes to Redistribution: A Comparison of Eight Western Nations', *American Sociological Review* 13 (1997), pp.283–304.
55. Ibid.
56. H. Kim, 'Explaining Ideological Swing in Western Democracies: A Comparative Analysis, 1952–1989', article presented at the International Political Science Association, Seoul, Korea (1–6 Aug. 1997).
57. Ibid.
58. Campbell, 'Institutional Analysis'.
59. Rhodes, 'Globalisation and West European Welfare States', p.308.
60. Pierson, 'Coping with Permanent Austerity'.
61. See E. Overbye, 'Convergence in Policy Outcomes: Social Security Systems in Perspective', *Journal of Public Policy* 14 (1994), p.149.
62. 1See F. Scharpf, 'Globalisation: The Limitations on State Capacity', *Swiss Political Science Review* 4 (1998), pp.92–8.
63. Ibid.; Rhodes, 'Globalisation and the Welfare State'; Garrett, *Partisan Politics in the Global Economy.*
64. Rhodes, 'Globalisation and the Welfare State'.
65. Pierson, 'Coping with Permanent Austerity'; Pierson, 'Irresistible Forces, Immovable Objects'.
66. Pierson, 'Irresistible Forces, Immovable Objects'.
67. T. Iversen and A. Wren, 'Equality, Employment and Budgetary Restraint: The Trilemma of the Service Economy', *World Politics* 50 (1998), pp.507–46.
68. Esping-Andersen, *Welfare States in Transition.*
69. Pierson, 'Irresistible Forces, Immovable Objects'.
70. P. Hall (ed.), *The Political Power of Economic Ideas: Keynesianism Across Nations* (Princeton, NJ: Princeton University Press 1989). See Campell, 'Institutional Analysis', for an excellent discussion.
71. B.D. Jones, *Reconceiving Decision-Making in Democratic Politics: Attention, Choice, and Public Policy* (Chicago: University of Chicago Press 1995), p.24.

72. Campbell, 'Institutional Analysis'.
73. Goldfinch, 'Remaking New Zealand's Economic Policy'.
74. Ibid.; Kelsey, *The New Zealand Experiment*.
75. Wickham-Jones, 'The Constraints Upon Social Democracy'; C. Hay and M. Watson, 'Rendering the Contingent Necessary: New Labour's Neo-Liberal Conversion and the Discourse of Globalisation', article presented at the *American Political Science Association*, Boston (3-6 Sept. 1998).
76. QBut see Clayton and Pontusson, 'Welfare State Retrenchment Revisited'.
77. See Levy, 'Vice into Virtue?', for an exception to this rule.
78. P. Seyd, 'Tony Blair and New Labour', in A. King (ed.), *New Labour Triumphs: Britain at the Polls* (Chatham, NJ: Chatham House 1997), p.50.
79. S. Fielding, 'Labour's Path to Power', in A. Geddes and J. Tonge (eds.), *Labour's Landslide* (Manchester: Manchester University Press 1997), p.23.
80. Seyd, 'Tony Blair and New Labour', p.49.
81. *The Economist*, 20 Dec. 1997, p.79.
82. D. Denver, 'The Government That Could Do No Right', in A. King (ed.), *New Labour Triumphs: Britain at the Polls* (Chatham, NJ: Chatham House), p.39.
83. J. March and J. Olsen, *Rediscovering Institutions: The Organizational Basis of Politics* (New York: Free Press 1989).
84. See Pierson, 'The New Politics of the Welfare State'.
85. Pierson, 'Increasing Returns'; Myles and Pierson, 'The Comparative Political Economy of Welfare Reform'.
86. Myles and Pierson, 'The Comparative Political Economy of Welfare Reform'.
87. Pierson, 'Not Just What, But When'.
88. F. Castles and C. Pierson, 'A New Convergence? Recent Policy Developments in the United Kingdom, Australia and New Zealand', *Policy and Politics* 24 (1996), pp.233–45; H. Schwartz and M. Rhodes, 'Internationalisation and the Liberal Welfare States: The UK, Australia and New Zealand', article presented at the *RSC*, European University Institute (19–20 Oct. 1998).

Reforming Health Care in Europe

RICHARD FREEMAN AND
MICHAEL MORAN

Health care policy has been a crucible of welfare reform in Europe for a quarter of a century and for good reason: there is a tremendous amount at stake. We argue that the 'epidemic' of reform – to use Rudolf Klein's word[1] – has been driven by three linked forces. The first arises from what might be called the welfare dimension of health care. Health care matters. Not often, but sometimes, it is a matter of life and death. More usually, it represents a powerful means of alleviating the anxiety, discomfort and incapacity that come from sickness and ill health. Being able to go to the doctor is one of the hallmarks of citizenship in most advanced industrial countries. Not least because of this, health care programmes are – alongside education – generally the largest in European welfare states, and efforts to restructure the wider welfare state inevitably involve efforts to reshape the 'health care state'.[2] In particular, health care has been deeply implicated in the fiscal pressures on modern welfare states.

The second dimension of health care might be summarised as the power dimension. Because health care matters, it is the object of conflict – between those who use health services, those who provide them, those who pay for them and those who make the rules. Health care policy arenas are populated by dense networks of institutions, all representing complex constellations of actors. Reform of the substance of health care policy almost always has major implications for the power and authority of these institutions and their associated interests. Reform constitutes a thoroughgoing re-examination and reconstruction of public authority in the health sector: it amounts to a continuing process of organisational stocktaking. In this continuing process, there is one particularly serious point of friction. Across western Europe, fiscal imperatives have inexorably drawn states deeper into the health care arena in the search for reform. But that arena has been populated – indeed dominated – by a variety of non-state actors, of whom medical professions are the most important. Attempts to solve fiscal problems have often clashed with the economic interests of doctors; but they more often still involve friction about the historically established authority of the medical profession. That friction is given an extra sharpness by the particular historical trajectory of health care systems. The health care systems examined in these pages are all embedded in systems of pluralist democracy. But the emergence of doctors as a well-organised interest in health in most cases preceded the development of democratic politics. In some cases – of which Germany is the most important instance – doctors achieved a dominant position in the whole health policy process not only before the advent of democratic politics, but through the agency of non-democratic politics.[3] Part of the issue of power, therefore, involves an extra friction between democratic states and interests empowered under pre-democratic political arrangements.

These conflicts are necessarily national ones. But there is a third aspect to health policy which connects national politics to international economic conditions. This arises from what might be called the industrial dimension of health care. Although we instinctively think of health services as being about the delivery of a personal service to individual patients, that delivery involves a considerable industrial infrastructure. One indicator of that infrastructure is the presence of health institutions in modern economies: health care employment, for instance, has been one of the most rapidly growing sectors of most west European economies for a generation. A second indicator is provided by the way health care is linked to the prosperity of other, crucial sectors of modern industrial economies. This is most obviously revealed in the role of medical technology. Health care is a personal service, but it is a personal service characteristically delivered using a range of technological artefacts, some of great scale and technical complexity. These artefacts are supplied by industries which are not only major contributors in their own right to economic prosperity – consider the significance of the pharmaceutical industry – but are also important to key sectors not obviously linked to health care: for instance, manufacturers of the largest, most sophisticated and most expensive medical devices are major customers of the electronics industries. This industrial dimension to health care immediately introduces tremendous tensions into any reform process for a very obvious reason: fiscal pressures push policy makers in the direction of cost containment; industrial imperatives push them in the direction of expanding the demand for health care goods and services. And the decisions now facing health policy makers can only be taken with reference to international economic considerations.

The discussion that follows is shaped by the complex dimensions of health care reform. We begin with the fiscal imperatives, and trace responses to them. We describe associated changes to the organisation and management of health systems, assessing the extent to which (and reasons why) many of them have become more alike. Through an account of reform processes in different countries, we discuss the strengthening position of the state in the regulation of health care. We then explore the implications of the internationalisation of the health care industry. The significance of the state, we conclude, is in managing the increasingly difficult relationship between internal and external pressures on the finance and delivery of health care.[4]

We concentrate on five cases: Britain, Sweden, France, Germany and Italy. The choice is dictated by an eclectic set of reasons. Some have to do with the wider theme of this issue, the changing welfare state in Europe: the range includes some of the most discussed welfare state 'models' and explains, in particular, the inclusion of the Swedish case. Some have to do with health care itself. Our range includes the biggest health care systems in western Europe. It also includes the most important representatives of the main 'types' of health care system in western Europe: 'national health service' systems, funded mostly from taxation (Britain, Sweden); 'late developing' national health service systems of the Mediterranean (Italy); and systems financed through schemes of compulsory insurance, of which the prototypical case is Germany.

THE FISCAL IMPERATIVE

Health care spending in Europe has followed the trajectory of spending in the wider welfare state. The 'long boom' in the advanced capitalist economies funded the 'golden age' of the welfare state in the 30 glorious years up to the mid-1970s, and in the process funded a great extension in health care entitlements and a great rise in health care spending. By 1975, in France, Germany and Sweden, public spending on health absorbed more than twice the proportion of GDP it had in 1960: in Italy, health spending had grown by more than two-thirds and in the UK by more than half. Because the labour costs and tax rates needed to finance high levels of welfare spending make countries unattractive for economic investment, this continued rise in health spending constituted a 'fiscal imperative' for reform throughout the 1980s.[5] In the 1990s, it was exacerbated by further recession and the pressure placed on public budgets by governments keen to meet the Maastricht criteria for European monetary integration.

It was in this context that governments set out to control the volume of resources consumed by the health sector. Their strategies for doing so included setting limits to whole budgets or to some of their component parts, and reducing employment and capital investment. In 1977, for example, the German government introduced the principle of an income-oriented expenditure policy for the health insurance system, reinforcing it in 1989. In the UK, government had always been able to control the total amount of NHS spending by fixing its annual budget in advance; in 1980, cash limits were made legally binding on health authorities. Between 1990 and 1993, central government in Sweden imposed a freeze on local taxation, the bulk of which is used to fund health care. In Italy, as a result of a raft of changes made in 1992–93, health spending not met by central allocations was to be financed by regional governments. In 1998, insurance-based funding was replaced by a regional tax paid by firms and the self-employed. France moved to set a social security budget in 1996.

Prospective budgets for ambulatory care were introduced in Germany in 1977 and in Sweden in 1985. In Germany, physician fees were tied to the development of sickness fund revenues between 1991 and 1995. Prospective budgeting was introduced in the hospital sector in France in 1984 and in Germany in 1986. In France and Germany likewise, governments have sought to negotiate global drug spending with the pharmaceutical industry. Reference pricing was introduced in Germany in 1989 and a total pharmaceutical budget fixed prospectively in 1993. Ambulatory care doctors have been given indicative drug budgets, both in Germany and in the UK.

Personnel cuts were imposed on regional and district Health Authorities in the UK in 1983, while the Italian government blocked further recruitment to the Servizio Sanitario Nationale (SSN) in the same year. In both countries, too, new restrictions were placed on the additional earnings of doctors working in the public sector. Germany restricted the registration of new doctors in 1986 and introduced doctor-to-patient ratios in 1993. In France, physician access to sector 2 (which allows doctors to impose supplementary bills on patients) was frozen temporarily in 1990. Meanwhile, the growth of capital spending on major items of medical equipment was checked by introducing regional planning arrangements in Italy in 1984. Existing arrangements in France were extended to cover the use as well as acquisition of such technology in 1991. The UK closed hospital beds in the mid to late 1980s, and there were similar closures in France and Sweden in the early to mid 1990s.

These changes were about limiting – governments have almost never been able to reduce – the volume of financial flows into health care.

Attempts to raise more revenue for health care or to reduce the scope of entitlements have been the exception not the rule, even though the reason health systems had become more expensive was because more people had come to use more services more often: most of the growth in health spending was to be explained by rising rates of health care utilisation.[6] Access to publicly funded health care had become effectively universal, while advances in medicine meant that a greater range of treatments was possible. Chronic illness, which is less easily or readily treated than acute illness, was more prevalent than before. A more informed public had learned to express greater demand for services, coupled with higher expectations of quality and privacy. At the same time, services themselves had become more expensive because they involved more sophisticated equipment and more specialised staff.[7]

If systems had grown to limits reform had limits, too. Remember that the health systems of western Europe are embedded in specific social, political and economic systems. The health care state has three faces: it is not simply a 'welfare state', but also a 'capitalist industrial state' and a 'pluralist democratic state'.[8] 'Health care systems help shape capitalist economies and are shaped by those economies; they help shape democratic politics, and are shaped by democracy'.[9] The economic orthodoxy of the 1980s was that economic performance was being inhibited by the ever-increasing 'social wage' – that proportion of earnings absorbed by taxes and contributions to finance welfare. To spend more on health care would progressively reduce the capacity of the economy to fund it at all. Meanwhile, the increased use of health services, while the principal explanation of rising costs, testified to the increasing importance of access to health care in people's lives. Retrenchment of any kind was likely to be highly contested, and governments would risk much by embarking on it. In this way, the pluralist democratic face of the health care state militated against the significant curtailment of benefits, and its capitalist industrial face against much additional revenue raising,

The partial exception to this is co-payments or user charges, which have been raised and extended in most countries, often more than once. They have been most used in Italy, where there has also been ultimately muted discussion of allowing individual and group opt-outs from public provision.[10] Co-payments were increased in conjunction with other legislation in Germany in 1981–82, 1983–84, 1989 and 1993, while a small additional health insurance contribution was levied for hospital maintenance between 1997 and 1999. In France, charges were raised in 1986 and 1993, and in the UK most notably in 1989, when they were introduced for eye tests and dental checks (though NHS prescription charges have been raised at other times, too). The expansion of sector 2 provision in France by definition brings with it extra billing. However, co-payments tend to be applied only to what might be termed medical peripherals, such as food and accommodation costs in hospitals, prescription drugs, dentistry and ophthalmics, and they are invariably paralleled by elaborate exemption arrangements. No country moved to reduce basic entitlements in this period, and core funding arrangements in tax-based and social insurance systems have remained unchanged.[11] Health care is still very much a public affair.

ORGANISATIONAL CHANGE: MANAGEMENT, QUALITY AND COMPETITION

For key contextual reasons, therefore, the fiscal imperative has come to be focused on the providers and administrators of health care rather than those who use and/or pay for it. In general terms, too, macro-level cost containment measures have been effective. Global budget growth is no longer a serious problem in European health care systems. However, a significant indirect effect of limiting resources without reducing output may be to drive down quality. It is because of this that cost containment has everywhere been accompanied by administrative changes designed to affect individual and organisational decision making about the allocation and use of resources.[12] Direct control of spending has been complemented by increasing the managerial functions of both payers and providers, by making quality norms and standards more explicit, and by introducing elements of competition. Most countries have also sought to direct activity away from hospitals.

General management was introduced into the NHS in the mid-1980s, and is now a feature of Italian districts (ASLs) and hospitals as well as the public hospital sector in France. In the UK, hospital doctors were allocated budgetary responsibility for clinical directorates in 1986. In 1989, German sickness funds were given a new freedom to terminate contracts with inefficient hospital providers. In 1990–91, the Dagmar 50 project in Sweden studied ways of improving productivity and performance in hospitals. The introduction of the internal market into the NHS from 1991 enhanced the managerial responsibilities of health authorities, and effectively invented those of GP fundholders and hospital Trusts (though fundholding was abolished by the Labour government elected in 1997).

Governments have also used changes in patterns of funding to manipulate patterns of health care provision. Fee-for-service payment of doctors in ambulatory care was replaced by a capitation system in Sweden in 1985. Similar changes were made in Germany in 1993, where, at the same time, hospitals began to be paid by diagnosis rather than for each day a bed was filled. More specifically, physicians' prescribing practice can be constrained by listing drugs not covered by respective public schemes (a negative list) or, alternatively and more effectively, drawing up a limited list comprising only those drugs which are (a positive list). A negative list was introduced in France in 1983, and a limited list announced in the UK in 1984. In Germany, similar schemes have been proposed but not so far implemented. Meanwhile, medical audit was strengthened in Germany in 1977 and again in 1989, and introduced in the UK after 1990. Clinical guidelines were introduced in France in 1993, and hospital accreditation procedures tightened in 1996. Performance indicators were established for UK health authorities in 1983, and waiting list initiatives set up there in 1989 and in Sweden in 1991.

Competition is a key feature of new health policy environments. It features much more strongly in health policy debate and change in national health services than insurance systems – perhaps necessarily, since the separation of purchase from provision is characteristic of social insurance systems almost by definition.[13] Hospital ancillary services were made subject to compulsory competitive tendering in the UK in 1983. With the introduction of the internal market, providers of medical care such as the new hospital Trusts also came to compete for Health Authority contracts. This pattern is echoed in some Swedish counties. In Italy, competition among providers for patients is much less regularised. In Germany, it was made possible for individuals to move between different kinds of sickness fund in search of lower premiums and improved benefits. The strategy underlying these changes is better described as 'public competition' than marketisation. These bounded markets – in so far as they are markets at all – are very different from those which the introduction of highly integrated national health services was intended to replace. In the wake of reform, competition takes place among public providers for contracts held by public bodies and financed by public money. The managerial functions associated with contracting (information-gathering, planning, professional regulation) are starkly counterposed to naive conceptions of the market.

Medical care is expensive, and hospital care its most expensive component. The financial and organisational reform of health care in Europe has been accompanied by strategies of dehospitalisation and demedicalisation, both explicit and implicit. In different countries, various incentives work to reduce the length of in-patient hospital stays, and to encourage the relocation of patients (and budgets) to social care facilities. German hospitals, for example, have been allowed to provide outpatient care, while minor surgical procedures are now also provided by doctors in local practice, both in Germany and in the UK. Meanwhile, responsibilities for social care have been separated from health care more clearly than before, and accorded to local authorities in the UK in 1991 and to Swedish municipalities in 1992. Germany introduced a social care insurance scheme in 1995. At the same time, most countries made attempts to strengthen the profile of prevention in health policy.

CONVERGENCE

As this summary suggests, there is a remarkable similarity of tone and purpose to health reform in different countries, even if different institutional arrangements have meant that different instruments have been employed in realising it. In broad terms, Italy, Sweden and the UK have all sought to improve the micro-economic efficiency of their health systems by increasing elements of management and competition, albeit to different degrees and in different ways. France and Germany have sought to increase macro-economic control over costs with more assertive central regulation, while also enhancing the element of selectivity in agreements formed between purchasers and providers.[14] What emerges from this is some convergence between systems, from different directions, on what the OECD has identified as the 'public contract' model of health provision.[15] In essence, this means that health care is financed from public sources, either through taxation or through compulsory insurance contributions; that health finance is administered by public agencies who are not also health care providers, and that providers, if not independent or even private bodies, are invested with the organisational and managerial autonomy to compete for contracts with purchasers. What is important about the model is that it seems suited to both macro-economic and micro-economic efficiency.

In many respects, reform appears to have had a common functional or technical rationality. In part, this reflects the commonality of problems faced by policy makers in different countries – notably the achievement of both micro- and macro-efficiency in the context of resource constraint. But it also points to wider and deeper social processes of convergence and diffusion. At the most general level, the health care state in Europe had emerged in the course of the nineteenth and twentieth centuries as a correlate of industrial capitalism and liberal democracy. Its concomitants were theirs: urbanisation, party politics, free professions and economic boom. A generalised pattern of reform indicated a turning point – one of the many definitions of 'crisis' – in that development and also that it was common to all. The reform processes of the 1980s were prompted by changes to the increasingly international economic environment in which governments worked. Meanwhile, the international diffusion of technologies meant that medicine and its management shared common characteristics and concerns. The diffusion of new medical technologies,[16] led often by multinational firms, was matched by that of what might be called new managerial technologies, such as Diagnosis-Related Groups (DRGs).[17] If much of this was driven by commercial interests, cheap air travel and telecommunications meant that professional and research networks also functioned on an increasingly international scale.

These multi-layered economic and social processes of convergence and diffusion help to explain why different systems began to change at more or less the same time. But they do not fully explain why they should do so in such strikingly similar ways. For that, a stronger concept of policy transfer is required. By the 1980s, common or at least comparable solutions to health policy problems began to be drawn from a general, international currency of reform ideas. These were propagated by quickly developing, sometimes sector-specific organisations and networks, such as the European Healthcare Management Association (EHMA). The OECD has been influential in defining policy problems, disseminating comparative data on the performance and reform of health care systems with increasing frequency since 1977.[18] Most notably, the American health economist Alain Enthoven's idea of managed competition became incorporated into a general discourse of health policy and planning.[19] Policy reform in the UK in 1989–91 drew heavily on his treatment of the NHS,[20] and then, in turn, informed policy discussion and debate in the Italian SSN.[21] Sweden's HSU 2000 Committee, similarly, referred its report to an international panel of health policy advisers for consideration.[22]

POWER, POLITICS AND THE HEALTH CARE STATE

Evidence of convergence, diffusion and transfer raise key questions about the autonomy of states.[23] Here, in the health sector, they imply that government action is at best reactive, at worst a *fait accompli*. In almost every instance, however, the paradoxical effect of cross-national pressures has been to extend the power of national governments to regulate and reorder highly complex systems of health provision. For cost containment, management, competition and quality control are all predicated on public (state) intervention in what was once thought of as a realm of 'private government'. If, formerly, the role of the health care state was simply to finance and administer health services provided by medical professions, these changes imply that, far from being in retreat, the state has made a significant advance. This applies to the substantive content of reform, that is, to the nature of health policy, as well as to health politics, that is, to the political process by which it was realised.

Some of the more general cost-containment measures excepted, most of the instruments of health policy reform are local. They operate at the level of the firm – the practice or hospital – and the district, and sometimes the region. Everywhere, however, they are predicated on the centralisation of regulatory authority. The introduction of managed competition, for example, more characteristic of national health services than social insurance systems, has been dependent on the kind of central government authority only the most integrated systems could generate: 'it is precisely the firmness of their external constraints which has permitted them to adopt the freedoms of the market within their publicly funded systems'.[24] The very purpose of management was to enable the 'corporate rationalisers' to make rational decisions, for purchasers to be more discriminating in their relations with providers and for providers to be more efficient in production terms.[25] Even in Germany, where users have become entitled to move between different kinds of sickness fund, a centralised system of redistribution of resources between funds has been required for competition among them to become effective. There, it is a cumulative process of reform which has served to strengthen the hand of government; this now seems likely to be deployed in the increased regulation of purchaser–provider contracts.[26]

The corollary of the enhanced presence of the state is the exclusion of medicine from health policy decision making. As Paul Godt established:

> In devising strategies to deal with overriding macro-economic concerns in an era of intense international competition, the French, British and West German states have come to view the medical profession as simply one interest group among many. There are still important aspects of health policy ... in which physicians' technical expertise prevails ... But in those areas which are crucial to broader public purposes, professional power has had to yield.[27]

One of the clearest examples of this is in the UK, where the Working for Patients document which formed the basis of reform discussion in the UK between 1989 and 1991 was drafted by a small group of ministers chaired by the Prime Minister. It published no evidence and undertook little consultation. 'In formulating, publishing and implementing its plans for change, the Thatcher administration ignored the medical profession and defied its campaign of opposition'.[28] In Sweden, too, aggressive medical opposition testified to the exclusion of professional interests. The government's proposed Family Doctor Scheme provoked a series of strikes by doctors in early 1994.[29] This was towards the end of a period of reinvigorated party conflict prompted by the change of government in 1991,[30] and the liberal–conservative proposal was eventually blocked by the Social Democrats in parliament. In Germany, structural reform in 1993 deserved the name only by virtue of having excluded established provider interests. Here too, the health political arena was briefly reoccupied by parties.[31]

Until recently, however, policy change in the health sector has been unusual, big change even more so. For all the conflict of the last decade or so, it is worth remembering that the universalisation of the health care state in the post-war period had been broadly consensual. Access to health care satisfied patients, doctors and employers, that is, both users and providers as well as those who ultimately paid for it. It also established organisational interests such as sickness funds and health authorities, on whom the administration of existing policy and the implementation of reform depended. Particular policies create particular institutional environments; they sustain particular sets of interests which in turn tend to sustain them. Ordinarily, institutional interests may be described as 'locked-in' to the systems of which they form a part.[32] Change, where it takes place, tends to be incremental. Decision-making is shaped by institutions and interests, which have themselves been shaped by previous decisions: later decisions are constrained by earlier ones. In this sense, normal patterns of policy making may be described as 'path dependent'.[33]

So what accounts for deviations from established paths of policy making? Why do they occur in some systems rather than others; at some times rather than others? What are the conditions which make reform possible? Change is a product of the interaction between the institutional and procedural routine characteristic of any given health system, and the pressures on that system from its environment. The different systems of health care finance and administration developed in west European countries in the post-war period afforded greater or lesser opportunities for regulatory steering (even if, ordinarily, governments had intervened relatively little). Sources of growing pressures on those systems were of two kinds, political and economic, and they were naturally interrelated. What mattered for the reform of health care was the combination of relative pressure on government, and its relative capacity to do something about it.

Change has to do with the relationship between structure and conjuncture: 'structures are the institutions and processes that form the infrastructural framework for policy [decisions] within which dynamic events unfold over time. This may be thought of as an endogenous universe, which then may be subject to exogenous shocks, that is, conjunctures'.[34] Among social insurance systems, the reform process has been more far-reaching in Germany than in France; among national health services, more radical in the UK than Italy or Sweden.

At the end of the 1980s, with even the experienced and ambitious Labour Minister Norbert Blüm outmanoeuvred by the lobbying of health political interests, it was difficult not to see the post-1975 period in Germany as one of reform blockade.[35] Both doctors and the pharmaceutical industry had links to the liberal FDP, the Christian Democrats' partner in government, and used them well, while the hospitals were protected by the Länder. Yet 1992 brought change of a more substantial kind. Horst Seehofer, a new Health Minister who had formerly been deputy to Blüm, had been appointed early in the year. He was able to use his position – the coalition had had a powerful majority since the first post-unification election in 1990 – to negotiate cross-party agreement on structural reform, working as much with the opposition Social Democrats as with the Liberals. The background economic pressure imposed by a combination of world recession, high German wage costs and the deepening effects of unification strengthened Seehofer's hand,[36] and meant, too, that the reform arena belonged to political parties, not the sectional interests of Concerted Action.[37] And the 1993 reform was genuinely structural: it affected physician fee levels and methods of payment, hospital funding and pharmaceutical pricing and effectively ended the segmentation of the insurance system into different kinds of fund. On the strength of those changes, further reform followed in 1997.

Reform in France, meanwhile, has tended to focus on public hospitals – that part of the system for which the government has exclusive and unambiguous responsibility. The key change came as early as 1984, with the shift in hospital funding from per diem payment to prospective budgeting. Here, too, contextual political and economic factors were crucial to its being realised. A Socialist government had been elected in 1981 and tried unsuccessfully to spend its way out of recession, reverting to a policy of economic austerity in 1983; in the Health Ministry, the tenacious Jean de Kervasdoué was appointed Director of Hospitals at the same time.[38] An increased economic need for reform matched an increased political ability to carry to it through. The government's established institutional strength allowed it to reform mechanisms of hospital planning and management again in 1991.

As long as hospital budgets brought some success in containing costs, there was little to be gained by intervening in ambulatory care. But social security deficits continued to mount through the late 1980s and into the 1990s: the government's calculation came to be that there was more to be lost, in respect of broader economic policy, in allowing contributions to grow than in restricting spending. Then 1995 brought a new President (Jacques Chirac) and a new Prime Minister (Alain Juppé) who were, moreover (in contrast to the period of 'cohabitation' between François Mitterand and Eduard Balladur which had gone before), close political allies. The Plan Juppé constituted an extensive project of welfare reform. The proposed reduction of public sector pensions it contained was blocked by public protest, but health reform measures were passed in 1996.[39] They included setting a prospective budget for the social security system as a whole, and by parliament rather than by the funds themselves, and also began to rewrite the rules governing the provision of ambulatory care. Overspending will now make practitioners liable to financial penalties, while patients consulting GPs first rather than going directly to specialists of their choice are entitled to enhanced reimbursement. The implicit assault is on physician freedom of practice and patient freedom of consultation in turn. The underlying government project, meanwhile, appears to be to universalise the statutory insurance system, increasing the proportion of its finance derived from taxation and legitimating greater central control.[40]

The 1989–91 period in the UK is described as 'Big Bang' reform.[41] This cannot be explained by immediate economic circumstance: Britain was doing at least as well as, if not better than, most of its European competitors, while spending much less on health care in doing so (although, of course, it was the severity of the UK's economic decline in the 1970s and early 1980s which had precipitated the extended neo-liberal project of successive Conservative administrations). This government entered its third term in 1987 with a large majority in parliament and a dominant Prime Minister personally committed to a specific set of market-oriented policy goals. Earlier health policy decisions, such as the introduction of management in 1984–86, had created new organisational interests (managers themselves) who in many cases supported reform of the health sector. In the event, reform was prompted by political crisis in 1987–88, engendered by the failing performance, expressed in ward closures and lengthening waiting lists, of a cash-starved NHS. Because, in the UK, central government is responsible for the funding and organisation of the health care, their problems were laid at its door. But, for the same reason, the government had greater capacity to respond to them than had its counterparts in France and Germany, Italy and Sweden. 'The lesson of the British case ... is that strong, centralised state structures in a policy domain can sometimes lead, paradoxically, to greater departures from the established policy path. That is, wholly new trajectories are made more easily possible by strong structures.'[42]

In Italy, a long period of legislative stasis since 1978 was punctuated by reorganisation in 1992–93. The USLs (the local administrative bodies in the health system) had been running deficits throughout the 1980s. In 1988 and 1989, health ministry reform initiatives had been blocked by the parties in parliament and under pressure from health sector lobbies.[43] But the party system was to collapse in the early 1990s, leading to the formation of two so-called 'technical' governments, the first in mid-1992. While Italian public debt continued to worsen, the new government was charged with managing public finances so as to meet the Maastricht criteria for European monetary integration. Legislation was passed allowing the government wide discretion to design and implement reform in key sectors, including health care.

The Swedish economy experienced a sharp and unexpected downturn at the end of the 1980s. In 1991, the Social Democrat government was replaced by a multi-party coalition led by Bildt and committed to economic deregulation, tax reform and the reduction of public spending. The HSU 2000 committee was convoked to consider wholesale alternatives to existing arrangements for the finance and organisation of health care, though its proposals were buried among the claims of different parties in the non-Socialist coalition. Its work had petered out even before the election of 1994.[44] The economic position had steadily and significantly worsened, despite the new government's austerity measures, and the Social Democrats were returned to power. The economic incentive to reform was undoubtedly significant, but the authority of the centre was insufficient to change the rules of the institutional game. Major reform would have implied renegotiating the position of county councils in relation to central government, a constitutional reordering clearly beyond the power of a fragile and short-lived administration. Instead, less systematic change has taken place at sub-central level, taken up by the counties themselves.

The experience of the health sector in the 1980s and 1990s is that political and economic conjunctures in different countries have shaped reform as decisively as the performance of respective systems. That said, structural features of those systems – essentially the regulatory power they afford to government – filter conjunctural pressures in different ways. What matters in each case is the relative effect of structure and conjuncture. In

Germany, the limited institutional authority of the centre was compensated by both political and economic factors, creating an opening for government which it continues to exploit. In France, until very recently, structural limitations have restricted change by and large to hospital care. A new conjunctural moment seemed to arrive in 1995, though whether it established sufficient authority for government to pursue a more extended project of reform remains an open question. In both cases, the real significance of environmental pressures lies in the extent to which they facilitated (or even forced) changes in institutional arrangements: conjuncture changes structure. In the UK, the endogenous power of the centre, already higher than elsewhere, was made greater by external political factors. There, structure worked with, rather than against, conjuncture. In Italy and Sweden, reforming governments were offered brief windows of opportunity: severe economic constraint was common to both, but while the conjunctural weakness of parties in Italy worked in favour of systemic change there, the structural decentralisation of policy competence worked against it in Sweden.

The picture of an increasingly state-centred politics is complemented by what might be described as a decentring of health systems. Health care states were invariably built on the sub-central government of finance and administration, and recent reform has consolidated the regional structure of health governance. Reform has instigated processes of scaling up from the district or locality as well as down from the centre, aggregating local administrations and interests as well as disaggregating national ones, often as an indirect effect of other changes. In many cases, financial and managerial responsibilities have been devolved more clearly than before to sub-central bureaux, and the number of those bureaux has been reduced. But regionalisation is the reverse of disintegration. As the NHS reform in the UK took effect, some neighbouring Health Authorities (then known as District Health Authorities as distinct from Regions) began to merge, as some DHAs did with Family Health Service Authorities, the separate bodies which had formerly administered GP contracts. In 1995, Regional Health Authorities were replaced by half the number of Regional Offices of the NHS Executive. Some fundholding general practices made group purchasing arrangements – which are now to be replaced by Primary Care Groups comprising all practitioners in a local area – with hospital providers (Trusts). In Italy, the number of local administrative bodies (formerly USLs, now ASLs) was also reduced, while the financial accountability of regional government was more clearly defined. In France, regional systems for planning hospital care and the use of expensive medical technology were introduced in 1991, as they were in Italy in 1984. In France, too, new regional organisations are being established to co-ordinate social insurance administration at regional level.[45] The reform of health insurance in Germany opened the way for the amalgamation of district funds. Earlier, exclusive responsibility for hospital building had been allocated to the regional states in 1985, and new arrangements made for authorising registrations of new physicians on the basis of regionally defined need. In Sweden, the counties were made responsible for all aspects of health service planning in 1983. They have become increasingly self-confident *vis-à-vis* the National Board of Health and Welfare, while some are being merged to form 'super-counties'.[46] Questions of access and entitlement continue to be regulated by the centre, though regional autonomy in respect of reform has left the counties operating what are in administrative terms a number of different health care systems.

Across countries, there were economies of scale to be made by doing things on a regional basis which had formerly been done locally, if at all. But more than that, by increasing their relative size, regionalisation has strengthened the hand of the planners and purchasers against that of the providers. In determining the allocation of health care resources, public bodies – health authorities, sickness funds and local and regional governments – have been made increasingly ready and able to punch their weight. Third party payers had always met access and insurance functions – guaranteeing citizens' access to health care and covering its costs – though their agency function had been relatively underdeveloped.[47] Now, as buyers, they were to become more discriminating. In turn, this has tended to increase the local and regional diversity of the health care state, as different administrative agencies have taken up, often with central encouragement, a new freedom to experiment. Coupled with macro-level convergence, this may make for a pattern of increasing regional variety within increasing national similarity among west European health care states.

INDUSTRY, ECONOMY AND EUROPE

Convergence has made for regionalisation. How far it is making for, or could in the near future make for, internationalisation is a matter of some uncertainty. It is possible to tell two very different stories – one stressing the limits of internationalisation, the other stressing its great potential.

The first story – about the limits to internationalisation – begins by noting that convergence is the result of systems with similar functions (the finance and provision of health care) being subjected to similar cross-national pressures. It does not erode their distinct identities, nor imply that the health care state is about to be supplanted by authorities which operate across national boundaries. Though the reform of health care in Europe has been paralleled by a process of international integration, institutionalised in the widening and deepening of the European Union, it is remarkable how little one has had to do with the other. For the moment, the development of European integration appears perfectly compatible with continued cross-national diversity in the health sector.[48] In principle, EU intervention in national policy making is legitimate only where it is required to facilitate or protect the mobility of goods, services, capital and labour between member states. In practice, as far as health issues are concerned, this has meant some standardisation of health and safety regulations in the workplace, and the issuing of reciprocal guarantees of the validity of worker entitlements and professional qualifications across countries. The Commission has no explicit competence in health policy as such, though it is beginning to stake such a claim in respect of public health. Title X (Article 129) of the Maastricht Treaty on European Union declared that 'The Community shall contribute towards ensuring a high level of human health protection by encouraging co-operation between the Member States and, if necessary, lending support to their action'. Specific programmes (Europe against AIDS, Europe against Cancer) have been funded, though it is notable that while they address areas of high legitimacy they require limited substantial intervention. Both here and in respect of health care, EU regulation complements, but does not replace, national provisions. It is concerned primarily and specifically with cross-border issues and claims as raised, for example, by the increased mobility of workers, pensioners and tourists. These markets remain closely regulated by states. There is some movement of skilled medical labour as individuals move away from areas of high physician density (and unemployment) such as Germany. Historically, however, greater numbers of doctors have come to Britain from former colonial countries. Medical migration then and now is shaped by national authorities. Some patients travel to other countries for treatment although, here again, this is neither new nor yet substantial enough to be significant. In the eighteenth and nineteenth centuries, the wealthy might travel to visit spas and sanatoria; now they might travel to specialist private clinics. Other, more routine movement across borders seems to be determined by geographical proximity, as takes place between the Benelux countries or from health authorities in southeast England to providers in northern France.

So much for the story of the persistence of national power. The way to tell a different story, stressing both internationalisation and Europeanisation, is to focus on the industrial face of health care. If much of health care is a personal service produced and delivered locally, there is also a large part which is locked into a wider global economy of production and marketing. That large part is closely identified with the medical technology industries, notably with drugs and devices. Across Europe these industries have a twofold significance: as part of the foundations of modern curative medicine and as part of the foundations of modern industrial economies. In both the United Kingdom and the Federal Republic of Germany, for instance, the pharmaceutical industry is estimated to provide over 100,000 jobs; in Denmark, a considerable industrial economy has been built on the success of Danish medical technology in exporting.[49] In turn, the medical technology industries are locked into wider structures of the industrial economy: two obvious examples are the connections between the pharmaceuticals and chemicals industries and the way the most sophisticated 'big ticket' medical technologies incorporate advances in computing hardware and software. These industrial structures cannot be understood in isolation from a wider picture still: the existence of world markets in medical technologies in which European producers operate in competitive markets alongside powerful producers from across the globe, notably the United States and Japan. These facts have some obvious consequences for the international dimension of health care. Most obviously, they mean that the industrial face of health care is part and parcel of the wider diplomacy of international trade. The most significant way this has had an impact on Europe is in the trend to the creation, at the level of the EU, of institutions and networks concerned with the management of interests at the level of the whole Union. Easily the most significant impact is observable in the pharmaceutical industry, where the Union (and especially the Commission) has assumed a three-fold importance.

First, in the drive to create a single market, and to manage the interests of that market in competition with other major capitalist blocs (notably North America and East Asia), the Commission has emerged as a key negotiator. Thus, one purpose of EU participation (with the United States and Japan) in the International Conference on Harmonisation of Technical Requirements for Registration of Pharmaceuticals for Human Use is to help harmonise the technical requirements for registering new medicines.[50] This initiative must be seen against the background of the use of safety requirements and licensing procedures as non-price barriers to trade: Japan, for instance, has consistently argued that the unique racial make-up of its population means that only products passing Japanese standards can safely be marketed domestically.[51]

The second area of impact concerns the EU-wide harmonisation of product licensing. EU directives go back as far as 1965, while the European Court of Justice has built up an extensive case law on the industry.[52] This process, which resulted in the incremental creation of a European regulatory system over a period of over two decades, was given a sharp impetus by the passage of the Single European Act and, from 1992, the project to accelerate the creation of a Single European Market. The process of incremental change has already produced agreements on directives on advertising, good manufacturing practice, and on provisions relating to labelling, package inserts, and the licensing of wholesalers. In 1995 the EU established a central regulatory agency, the European Medicines Evaluation Agency (EMEA), in London. The establishment of the Agency introduced three sets of registration procedures for pharmaceuticals across the Union: a centralised procedure, administered by the new agency, for innovative products, leading to a single Union-wide authorisation valid in all member states; a decentralised procedure, expected to apply to a substantial majority of products, based upon the principle of mutual recognition between member states; and a national procedure, for applications of local interest concerning a single member state.[53]

The growth of the EU as a regulatory actor helps explain its third area of impact, on interest representation. There now exists a well-organised system of EU-level interest representation, notably for the pharmaceutical industry, using peak associations centred on Brussels.[54] The process by which the European Medicines Evaluation Agency (EMEA) came to be established in London shows how the governing system is evolving to create a complex series of relationships between industrial interests and state agencies at EU level. The siting of the EMEA in London (in the redeveloped Docklands complex at Canary Wharf, perhaps the most important symbol of the British state's effort to use private and public sector partnerships to regenerate decaying urban industrial areas) was the result of a combined campaign by the Department of Health and the Association of the British Pharmaceutical Industry (ABPI). Two calculations were at work; they both emphasise the significance of the 'industrial' face of health care. The first has to do with wider competition within the Union to influence the location of Union institutions because of the benefits to regional and city economies: agencies like EMEA bring jobs and demand for other goods, like property. The second calculation resembles that at work in the contest to determine the location of the other European regulatory agencies, like the European central bank: that the location of a regulatory agency will have long term effects on where product development takes place. The calculation is particularly important in the case of pharmaceuticals, for the industry is an especially heavy investor in R&D: it usually ranks among the four or five top industries in international comparisons, alongside those like electronics, aerospace and computers. The explicit theory behind the campaign to locate the EMEA in London is hence that it will encourage a concentration of R&D activities in the vicinity of the Agency – and thus will reinforce British strength in the world pharmaceutical industry. What we are witnessing here is a particular model of internationalisation, of a kind identified by Mohan: one where the inward investment strategies of the state are used to try to strengthen the position of particularly favoured metropolitan locations.[55]

THE CHANGING GOVERNANCE OF THE HEALTH CARE STATE

We began with the notion that health care policy had three dimensions: a welfare dimension, a power dimension, and an industrial one. The governance of health care is changing in complex – and often apparently contradictory – ways because radical change is taking place along all three dimensions.

The 'end to growth' was only one aspect (if, for welfare states, the defining one) of a more general restructuring of capitalist economies.[56] Among its key characteristics were: the emergence of a specialised service sector, rooted in technology-based expansion and entailing the formation of a new managerial class; the de-skilling and sometimes re-skilling of the traditional workforce; and the emergence of a group of newly differentiated and demanding consumers. At the same time, the capacity of states to meet productive and redistributive functions was called into question, as a resurgent liberalism turned to market mechanisms for allocating goods and services. In industrial and commercial firms as well as government, meanwhile, administrative hierarchies were being broken down into networks of semi-autonomous units. Hierarchies of knowledge were challenged, making the privileging of scientific rationality no longer certain or self-evident. The corollary of this was that the political consensus about the pre-eminence of the state and the medical profession in health policy and provision had eroded. The working assumption of the post-war era had been that the role of the state was simply to guarantee the financial and administrative framework within which medical care was to be delivered, according to professional judgement, to increasing proportions of European populations – and it no longer held.

Of the principal reform instruments described here, the purpose of macro-level cost-containment measures has been to ensure the continued viability of public health care. In almost every part of the health system, it has necessitated the development of enhanced management capacities. The function of management (as distinct from administration) is to recognise the constraints under which organisations operate, to define and redefine organisational goals and to promote the organisational change required to meet them. Among its guiding principles are the pursuit of quality and efficiency. Competition, meanwhile, perhaps the signal term in the international discourse of reform, may well turn out to have been one of the more transient. In the UK, where it was promoted most vigorously, and in Sweden, competition has turned relatively quickly into collaboration between larger units with more clearly defined functions of planning and providing care. More than anything, it served its purpose as a destabilising strategy, breaking up old rigidities and expectations.[57]

Regionalisation, for its part, may have been among the least recognised elements of reform. In context, it is the continuing expression of an historic tension in health politics between core and periphery, between central and local authority. In an increasingly tense distributional environment, it served partly as a means of blame diffusion, representing 'states' efforts to distance themselves from hard choices'.[58] There may have been other ways of doing this, but depoliticisation by decentralisation was both more subtle and more legitimate than by marketisation. As described here, the process of 'decentring' is properly the coalescing of systems (whether fragmented or integrated) into multiple centres. It deserves the name only in so far as the (re)construction of the management responsibilities of regions and localities is predicated on the accretion and assertion of central government authority. This assertion of government authority reveals the paradox of reform in health care: an era when reform was pictured in the imagery of liberal economics was in truth one where state control was actually strengthened. Economic and political change threatened to undo many of the assumptions on which the public provision of health care was based. This made reform of some kind likely, if not inevitable. Market liberalism in health policy was not only imagery; there were real changes in the exposure of health systems to market forces. The question remains, however, why state regulation of health care not only persists, but in many ways has been strengthened through reform. And this despite the end to growth and the declining influence of organised labour, both of which had been so important in the universalisation of the health care state in the period following the Second World War. In part, new policies have created a new politics, in which the health care state has become, in a sense, self-sustaining. In economic terms, public health care represents a key market, a prime source of employment and a highly prized benefit. In turn, these are sources of political demand that it be maintained. But what is significant here is that, in order that it be maintained, it must reach some accommodation with other, external sources of economic and political pressure. As these multiply, state intervention becomes ever more essential as the regulator of external pressure and internal demand. In health care we encounter the wider paradox of public policies that try to strengthen market forces: markets need states, and strong markets need strong states.

NOTES

This paper draws on material in our two separately authored books: R. Freeman, *The Politics of Health in Europe* (Manchester: Manchester University Press 2000), and M. Moran, *Governing the Health Care State: A Comparative Study of the United Kingdom, the United States and Germany* (Manchester: Manchester University Press 1999). Michael Moran gratefully acknowledges the financial support of grants from the Nuffield Foundation and the UK Economic and Social Research Council. The paper was drafted while we were both Jean Monnet Fellows at the European University Institute, Florence in 1999, as part of the European Forum on 'Recasting the European Welfare State: Options, Constraints, Actors'. We are grateful to other Forum Fellows for many stimulating discussions, and in particular to the co-directors, Maurizio Ferrera and Martin Rhodes, for advice, comments and encouragement.

1. R. Klein, 'Health Care Reform: The Global Search for Utopia', *British Medical Journal* 307/6907 (1993), p.752.
2. M. Moran, 'Three Faces of the Health Care State', *Journal of Health Politics, Policy and Law* 20/3 (1995), pp.767–81.
3. M. Moran, *Governing the Health Care State: A Comparative Study of the United States, United Kingdom and Germany* (Manchester: Manchester University Press 1999).
4. The issues treated here are well represented in what is now an extensive literature – OECD, *Reform of Health Care: A Comparative Analysis of Seven OECD Countries* (Paris: OECD 1992), and OECD, *The Reform of Health Systems. A Review of Seventeen OECD Countries* (Paris: OECD 1994) – are wide ranging, though now dated. More recent coverage is provided by C. Altenstetter and J.W. Björkman (eds.), *Health Policy Reform, National Variations and Globalization* (Basingstoke: Macmillan 1997); M.W. Raffell (ed.), *Health Care and Reform in Industrialized Countries* (University Park, PA: Pennsylvania State UP 1997); R. Saltman and J. Figueras, *European Health Reform: Analysis of Current Strategies* (Copenhagen: World Health Organization 1997); and R. Saltman and J. Figueras, 'Analyzing the Evidence on European Health Care Reforms', *Health Affairs* 17/2 (1998), pp.85–108. A Special Issue of the Journal *Health Affairs* (18/3, 1999) is devoted to the theme of international health reform, and includes papers on Britain and Germany, as well as the United States, Australia, Canada and Japan. L. Brown, 'Exceptionalism As the Rule: U.S. Health Policy Innovation and Cross-National Learning', *Journal of Health Policy, Politics and Law* 23/1 (1998), pp.35–51 sets some European experience against that of the biggest health care system in the world, the American. Many of the general arguments in this paper are elaborated in R. Freeman, *The Politics of Health in Europe* (Manchester: Manchester University Press 2000), and in M. Moran, *Governing the Health Care State: A Comparative Study of the United Kingdom, the United States and Germany* (Manchester: Manchester University Press 1999).
5. D. Wilsford, 'States Facing Interests: Struggles over Health Policy in Advanced Industrial Democracies', *Journal of Health Politics, Policy and Law* 20/3 (1995), pp.571–613.
6. A.J. Culyer, 'Cost Containment in Europe', in OECD (ed.), *Health Care Systems in Transition. the Search for Efficiency* (Paris: OECD 1990); M. Pfaff, 'Differences in Health Care Spending Across Countries: Statistical Evidence', *Journal of Health Politics, Policy*

and Law 15/1 (1990), pp.1–67; G.J. Schieber and J.-P. Poullier, 'Overview of International Comparisons of Health Expenditures', in OECD (ed.), *Health Care Systems in Transition.*

7. A. Gray, 'International Patterns of Health Care, 1960 to the 1990s', in C. Webster (ed.), *Caring for Health: History and Diversity* (Buckingham: Open University Press 1993).

8. Moran, 'Three Faces of the Health Care State'.

9. M. Moran, 'Explaining the Rise of the Market in Health Care', in W. Ranade (ed.), *Markets and Health Care. A Comparative Analysis* (Harlow: Longman 1998), p.21.

10. For detail, see M. Ferrera, 'The Rise and Fall of Democratic Universalism. Health Reform in Italy, 1978–1994', *Journal of Health Politics, Policy and Law* 20/2 (1995), pp.275–302.

11. W. Ranade, 'Conclusions', in Ranade (ed.), *Markets and Health Care*; Saltman and Figueras, 'Analyzing the Evidence on European Health Care Reforms'.

12. OECD, *Reform of Health Care.*

13. M. Moran, 'Health Care Policy', in J. Clasen and R. Freeman (eds.), *Social Policy in Germany* (Hemel Hempstead: Harvester Wheatsheaf 1994).

14. R. Freeman, 'Competition in Context: the Politics of Health Care Reform in Europe', *International Journal for Quality in Health Care* 10/5 (1998), pp.395–401; W. Ranade, 'Conclusions'.

15. OECD, *Reform of Health Care.*

16. S. Kirchberger, *The Diffusion of Two Technologies for Renal Stone Treatment Across Europe* (London: King's Fund Centre 1991); B. Stocking, *Factors Affecting the Diffusion of Three Kinds of Innovative Medical Technology in European Community Countries and Sweden* (London: King's Fund Centre 1991); M. McClellan and D. Kessler, 'A Global Analysis of Technological Change in Health Care: The Case of Heart Attacks', *Health Affairs* 18/3 (1999), pp.250–55.

17. J.R. Kimberley, and G. De Pouvourville, *The Migration of Managerial Innovation. Diagnosis-Related Groups and Health Care Administration in Western Europe* (San Francisco: Jossey-Bass 1993).

18. OECD, *Public Expenditure on Health* (Paris: OECD 1977).

19. A.C. Enthoven, 'The History and Principles of Managed Competition', *Health Affairs* Supplement (1993), pp.24–48.

20. A.C. Enthoven, *Reflections on the Management of the National Health Service* (London: Nuffield Provincial Hospitals Trust 1985).

21. G. Bevan, G. France and F. Taroni, 'Dolce Vita. Inside Italy's NHS', *Health Service Journal* (27 Feb. 1992), pp.20–23.

22. P. Garpenby, 'Health Care Reform in Sweden in the 1990s: Local Pluralism Versus National Coordination', *Journal of Health Politics, Policy and Law* 20/3 (1995), pp.695–717.

23. C.J. Bennett, 'Review Article: What is Policy Convergence and What Causes It?', *British Journal of Political Science* 21/2 (1991), pp.215–33.

24. OECD, *Reform of Health Care*, p.142.

25. Freeman, 'Competition in Context'.

26. K. Kamke, 'The German Health Care System and Health Care Reform', *Health Policy* 43 (1998), pp.171–94.

27. P. Godt, 'Confrontation, Consent and Corporatism: State Strategies and the Medical Profession in France, Great Britain and West Germany', *Journal of Health Politics, Policy and Law* 12/3 (1987), p.478.

28. R. Klein, 'Big Bang Health Care Reform – Does it Work? The Case of Britain's 1991 National Health Service Reforms', *Milbank Quarterly* 73/3 (1995), p.302; J. Mohan, *A National Health Service? The Restructuring of Health Care in Britain Since 1979* (Basingstoke: Macmillan 1995).

29. E. Brunsdon and M. May, 'Swedish Health Care in Transition?', in E. Brunsdon and M. May (eds.), *Swedish Welfare: Policy and Provision* (London: Social Policy Association 1995).

30. Garpenby, 'Health Care Reform in Sweden in the 1990s'.

31. N. Bandelow, 'Ist Politik Wieder Autonom? Das Beispiel Gesundheitsreform', *Gegenwartskunde* 4 (1994), pp.445–56.

32. P. Pierson, *Dismantling the Welfare State? Reagan, Thatcher and the Politics of Retrenchment* (Cambridge: Cambridge UP 1994), pp.39–50.

33. D. Wilsford, 'Path Dependency, or Why History Makes it Difficult but not Impossible to Reform Health Care Systems in a Big Way', *Journal of Public Policy* 14/3 (1994), pp.285–309.
34. Ibid., pp.257–8.
35. D. Webber, 'Krankheit, Geld und Politik: Zur Geschichte der Gesundheitsreformen in Deutschland', *Leviathan* 16/2 (1988), pp.156–203; D. Webber, 'Zur Geschichte der Gesundheitsreformen in Deutschland – Ii Norbert Blüms Gesundheitsreformen und die Lobby', *Leviathan* 17/2 (1989), pp.262–300; B. Rosewitz and D. Webber, *Reformversuche und Reformblockaden im Deutschen Gesundheitswesen* (Frankfurt: Campus 1990); C. Altenstetter, 'Health Policy-Making in Germany: Stability and Dynamics', in Altenstetter and Björkman (eds.), *Health Policy Reform*.
36. Wilsford, 'Path Dependency'.
37. Bandelow, 'Ist Politik Wieder Autonom?'.
38. Wilsford, 'Path Dependency'.
39. D. Wilsford, 'Caught Between History and Economics: Reforming French Health Care Policy in the 1990s', in M. Schein and J. Keeler (eds.), *Policymaking in France in the 1990s* (New York: St Martins Press 1996).
40. B. Palier, 'A "Liberal" Dynamic in the Transformation of the French Social Welfare System', in J. Clasen (ed.), *Social Insurance in Europe* (Bristol: Policy Press 1997).
41. Klein, 'Big Bang Health Care Reform'.
42. Wilsford, 'Path Dependency', p.265.
43. G. France, 'Constrained Governance and the Evolution of the Italian National Health Service Since 1980', Paper Presented to Workshop 'Beyond the Health Care State. New Dimensions in Health Politics in Europe', 24th ECPR Joint Sessions of Workshops, Oslo, 29 March to 3 April 1995.
44. Garpenby, 'Health Care Reform in Sweden in the 1990s'.
45. Palier, 'A "Liberal" Dynamic.
46. R. Saltman, 'Health Reform in Sweden: the Road Beyond Cost Containment', in Ranade (ed.), *Markets and Health Care*.
47. Ranade (ed.), *Markets and Health Care*.
48. C. Altenstetter, 'Health Policy Regimes and the Single European Market', *Journal of Health Politics, Policy and Law* 17/4 (1992), pp.813–46.
49. P. Lotz, 'Demand As A Driving Force in Medical Innovation', *International Journal of Technology Assessment in Health Care* (1993), pp.174–88.
50. J. Abrahams and M. Charlton, 'Controlling Medicines in Europe: the Harmonisation of Technology Assessed', *Science and Public Policy* 22/6 (1995), pp.354–62.
51. S. Foote, *Managing the Medical Arms Race: Public Policy and Medical Device Innovation* (London: University of California Press, 1992), p.186.
52. M. Burstall, 'Europe after 1992: Implications for Pharmaceuticals', *Health Affairs* 10/3 (1991), pp.157–71.
53. H. Treece, 'An Evaluation of Medicines Regulation', *Medical Law International* 2/4 (1997), pp.315–36.
54. J. Greenwood, 'The Pharmaceutical Industry: A European Business Alliance that Works', in J. Greenwood (ed.), *European Business Alliances* (Hemel Hempstead: Prentice Hall 1995).
55. J. Mohan, 'The Internationalisation and Commercialisation of Health Care in Britain', *Environment and Planning A* 23 (1991), pp.853–67.
56. Mohan, *A National Health Service?*
57. Freeman, 'Competition in Context'.
58. J. White, 'Market Choices', *Health Service Journal*, 8 April 1993, p.25.

Timing and the Development of Social Care Services in Europe

VALERIA FARGION

Over the last decade a growing body of literature started addressing a variety of questions related to the development of the personal social services. What is driving the new interest in social care is the increasing awareness that new social needs are emerging in all European societies: notably frail elderly care, child care and care of the disabled, the mentally ill, and the chronically sick.

If we consider the nature of the demands stemming from such needs – especially in terms of services – it is quite clear that local governments have recently been facing increasing pressure. But have they been in a position to respond positively to such challenges? This study attempts to shed some light on the background conditions underlying local policy action; particularly the financial constraints that local authorities have had to cope with over the last decade and in the 1990s. Future prospects for the development of this policy area will be discussed on the basis of current unfavourable 'confining conditions'.

CHANGING SOCIAL NEEDS

In order to grasp fully the extent to which changes in the content of social needs actually challenge existing arrangements of social protection it is useful to review some quantitative indicators. Ageing of the population is by far the highest on the list. Indeed, over the past 30 years the proportion of people over 60 years of age has constantly grown in the European Union, going from 15.3 per cent of the total population in 1960 to the current 20.7 per cent. Such an outcome reflects among other things the success of the social protection programmes enacted by European welfare states, yet it clearly also creates new policy problems. Benefits and services designed for the elderly over the post-war period were certainly not meant for such large numbers. Moreover, if we disaggregate the figures by age group, we can see that the largest increase refers to the age bracket above 80 years, namely to those elderly who are least self-sufficient and require more health and social care services. Although absolute values still remain low, we are nonetheless talking of 3.9 per cent of the population in the European Union as against 1.8 per cent only 30 years ago.

These demographic changes are coupled with even deeper changes in traditional family structures which evoke a whole variety of new family arrangements. The spreading of such new arrangements follows a north–south gradient and is basically characterised by more flexible and definitely less stable solutions than traditional marriage. The transformation of the Western family goes well beyond the scope of this account, but, again, a few data are in order.[1] We can start by mentioning the steady growth in the number of births out of wedlock. In 1994 children born out of wedlock in the European Union represented as much as 21.7 per cent of the total. In France and the UK the figure was over 30 per cent while in Denmark and Sweden it reached a high of 46 and 50 per cent, respectively. If we consider divorce rates, whereas according to Eurostat only 14 per cent of marriages embarked upon during the 1960s ended or will end in a divorce, the corresponding figures for marriages begun in the 1970s and 1980s are 22 and 27 per cent. Turning to single parent families, in 1994 such families accounted for 5.8 per cent of the total (EU 12) and for as much as nine per cent in Ireland and the UK.

Needless to say, for families without the stable presence of both parents, childcare becomes a very demanding task and the care of other dependent members – be they elderly, disabled or sick – becomes even more burdensome. And future prospects do not seem any brighter considering the rise in cohabitation, which is definitely a more precarious relationship compared with marriage. Although the numbers are still rather small, the scenario could change quite rapidly given that as many as 28 per cent of couples under 30 years of age are now cohabiting.

Yet, as we very well know, it is not just a matter of the increasing precariousness of family arrangements; referring exclusively to families risks overshadowing the crucial role played by women in providing care to dependent family members. But again this is being deeply affected by structural and cultural changes. If we consider activity rates for women between 20 and 59 years of age, in the early 1990s we are confronted with an average of 62 per cent for the European Union ranging from a minimum of 46 per cent in Spain and Greece to a maximum of 84 per cent in Denmark. Even the Netherlands (where female employment has traditionally been extremely low) have witnessed a strong upward trend during the 1980s, reaching substantially similar levels to nearby France and Germany. Employment is usually higher among single rather than married women,[2] but on average the difference is only about seven percentage points.[3] Therefore, we can safely maintain that housewives in a position to take care of dependent family members on a full-time basis now represent a minority and their numbers are likely to decrease even further.

Thirty years ago the picture in Europe was quite different: high levels of female employment were confined to the Nordic countries. But household arrangements already complicated the care of the elderly within the primary network. Except for southern Europe, three-generation households were no longer the rule and had been largely replaced by the nuclear family and the subsequent separation of dwellings between the elderly and their adult children. Available statistical data show that by the 1970s the elderly living with their children represented at most 20 to 25 per cent, not only in the northern countries but also in continental Europe. Even in a country such as the Netherlands, with a strong Catholic sub-culture, most elderly people were already living on their own. The decline in the extended family accelerated over the 1980s and – except for Spain,[4] Italy and Ireland – this type of family is about to disappear. Under these circumstances it is no surprise that in the EU statistics households including the elderly and their adult children are labelled as *ménage atypique* (untypical household).

The changes we have been discussing inevitably reduce throughout Europe the practical possibilities for inter-generational co-operation, thereby increasing the difficulties in the performance of caring functions within the primary network. Indeed, the problems arising from the interaction of these demographic, labour market and family changes are most likely to continue increasing in the near future. Demographic projections by Eurostat illustrate the extent to which population ageing will affect European societies over the next ten to 15 years.[5] Whereas in the mid-1990s people over 65 years of age represented more than 20 per cent of the population only in a few areas – notably in central Italy – by 2015 this is likely to be the rule for a large part of Europe.

THE EARLY DEVELOPMENT OF PUBLIC SOCIAL CARE SERVICES: THE SCANDINAVIAN EXPERIENCE

The societal changes we focused on in the previous section exert the greatest pressure on local authorities. This is hardly surprising given that potential demands stemming from such changes call for the provision of personal social services, which have an inherently local dimension. Notably in the Nordic countries local government moved very early in this direction. As the literature documents, over the 1960s and 1970s local authorities developed a widespread network of public social services; to the point that, referring to Scandinavia, Jorma Sipilä wonders: 'should we speak of welfare municipalities instead of welfare states?'[6] As is well known, what is specifically Scandinavian about this model is the extensive coverage of social care services and their universal accessibility to everyone who needs them.

It is my contention that examining the peculiarities of the Scandinavian experience can provide useful insights into the analysis of the different paths taken by other European countries. With this in mind, despite the recent prevailing interest in differences among the Nordic welfare states, we shall concentrate on their common traits. More specifically, to grasp the course of action taken by policy actors in Scandinavia, we consider a number of factors ranging from the timing in the emergence of the aforementioned needs to the specific cultural mediation legitimating such needs, as well as the institutional arrangements backing the policy process.

We have already mentioned that in the Scandinavian countries demographic and, to a greater extent, occupational and family changes occurred at an earlier stage compared to the rest of Europe. In the early 1970s, as many as 67 per cent of women between 15 and 64 years of age were working in Sweden and in Denmark, while in Finland the corresponding figure was 64 per cent. But this is just the first part of the story. Structural variables need first of all to be complemented by a careful consideration of the cultural lenses which mediate how social needs are perceived. We might usefully recall how, with an analysis confined strictly to structural variables, Anneli Antonnen and Sipilä are unable to explain why France and Germany – despite similar levels in female employment – display such different levels in childcare services.[7]

Cultural Factors

While having implications for a wide range of values, the social changes we are concerned with affect most dramatically how the family and women's roles within the family are conceptualised. Depending on the extent to which the traditional vision of women's responsibilities is entrenched, we might expect social care issues to enter the policy agenda sooner or later. In short, the cultural heritage of any given country can either enhance or hinder legitimating the externalisation of caring functions traditionally confined to the family domain. Elsewhere I have suggested labelling this process as the 'defamilisation' of caring functions.[8] Other authors have also referred to this concept, although using a slightly different wording. But I would argue that, with respect to the current usage, we can turn this concept into a more powerful analytical tool. In detail, we can view 'defamilisation' along a continuum where subsequent steps – corresponding to the externalisation of different caring functions – are progressively more disruptive with respect to the traditional ideology of family responsibility. From this angle, the starting point would be the discharge of caring functions related to elderly family members, while the end point is represented by the legitimisation of child care outside the family. Indeed, it appears much more difficult to question caring functions that are connected to the very foundations of the family institution, namely to child rearing. In Western industrialised countries such functions have always been intimately associated with women, giving rise to the social construct of mothering.[9]

Given these premises, Sweden, Denmark, Finland and (albeit to a lesser extent) Norway appear as the European countries most inclined and better equipped to push 'defamilisation' to its limits. Broadly speaking, this process entails 'rejecting the long-standing image of wives as institutionally supplying altruism in a gender-asymmetric setting', and emphasising instead the value of individual autonomy. It is hard to dispute that deeply rooted ideas stressing such a value thrived in the Nordic countries, leading to the early individualisation of social rights.

As to this point, Lars Tragardh's interpretation of the *ethos* underlying the Nordic model of social protection is particularly illuminating and innovative:

> Despite the common perception of the collectivist nature of the Nordic welfare state, what is even more surprising is the extent to which behind the Gemeinschaft of the so called people's home one can find a Gesellshaft of autonomous and atomised individuals ... the Nordic welfare state and in particular the Swedish one can be seen as a gigantic pact through which individuals are collectively enfranchised from personal, individual responsibilities, disguised as solidarity run by the state.[10]

According to this line of thought, the origins of the family policies developed especially from 1970 onwards are historically grounded in the northern populations' intolerance of and antipathy for any bond which might develop into some form of dependence.

Whether one agrees with this interpretation or whether one prefers the more comfortable image of a women-friendly society, what remains is that the cultural lenses filtering emerging social care demands did not represent a barrier to 'defamilisation'. Quite the contrary, they helped to propel public intervention as a means for alleviating women's caring burden, and promote equality of opportunity in the labour market and in society at large. Clear evidence of the early cultural shift from the family to the individual as the subject of social rights can also be found in civil code provisions. In Sweden, children were exempted from the responsibility of supporting their parents way back in 1956; in 1964 the same occurred in Norway, and in 1970 in Finland, whereas in Denmark this responsibility was never written into the law.

The Strength of Local Government

So far we have highlighted the early emergence of social care issues in the Nordic countries and the pro-active role played by the cultural heritage. Yet, to understand why and how the Scandinavian countries were able to set up such an extensive system of public social care services we need to consider that they could count on a particularly strong system of local government. During the 1950s, local authorities had accumulated substantial and multifaceted experience in public service management: they were responsible for a wide range of functions in the fields of education, housing, health and hospital care. Hence, for local government the acquisition of new responsibilities in the social sphere did not represent something totally new, and could largely be viewed as broadening previous commitments in favour of citizens' well-being.

Moreover, as a result of the 1950s and 1960s reforms, and especially of the amalgamation process,[11] local authorities acquired the structural and organisational capacity to handle new responsibilities effectively. By reducing the number of municipalities, local government reforms were clearly meant to provide territorial dimensions which allowed for an effective and efficient delivery of services, thereby overcoming the practical and financial difficulties that confronted the smaller units.

However, what appears even more important is the considerable fiscal autonomy which Scandinavian local authorities enjoyed. The power to levy taxes at the local level was already well established in the early 1960s and is still unparalleled in Europe. However, considering the driving force behind the expansion in social services was represented by national legislation, this argument might appear controversial. Scandinavian municipalities are often viewed as 'efficient implementation machines of nationally decided policies' or along the same lines as 'non-autonomous service delivery agents'.[12] Yet the establishment of such a diffused network of public social care services can hardly be understood without the consistent support offered both in terms of legitimisation and financial support by local institutions. Indeed, taxing power goes hand in hand with the people's perception of local government as the primary channel for democratic participation, which in turn is instrumental in meeting citizens' needs. Not surprisingly, the right of municipalities to levy their own local taxes is considered a cornerstone of local autonomy and democracy. That is not to suggest we disregard the regulatory power and, in particular, the crucial standard-setting role played by the central level of government in the establishment of statutory social care services. It is not a matter of setting the local against the central level, especially considering that both levels of government shared long-standing Social Democratic rule. Actually, for a long time this was perhaps the strongest co-ordinating device at work in Scandinavian centre–periphery relations. The point is simply that with respect to the existing literature greater emphasis should be placed on the fiscal autonomy of local government as a critical factor in the development of the Scandinavian social care model.

The data in Table 1 highlight the extent to which the financial conditions of Scandinavian local governments differed from the rest of Europe during the original expansion of social care services. The information is drawn from a 1975 study by the Council of Europe,[13] and the figures are averages for the period 1960–64, which largely corresponds to the 'take-off' of the Scandinavian social care system. The evidence presented documents how Swedish, Danish and Norwegian local government definitely had a more prominent role compared with all other European countries, in terms of spending and taxing capacity.

TABLE 1

LOCAL EXPENDITURE AS A PERCENTAGE OF GNP AND OF TOTAL PUBLIC EXPENDITURE, AND LOCAL DIRECT TAXES AS A PERCENTAGE OF GNP IN SELECTED EUROPEAN COUNTRIES (AVERAGES FOR 1960–1964)

	Local expenditure as % of GNP	Local expenditure as % total public expenditure	Local taxes as as % of GNP
Sweden	13.7	35.9	5.3
Norway	12.9	36.8	8.4
Denmark	8.4	30.1	5.4
Netherlands	13.2	28.2	0.3
United Kingdom	10.3	25.4	3.1
Ireland	9.9	25.6	3.0
Germany	7.8	23.4	3.1
France	6.9	23.6	2.8
Italy	7.9	26.1	2.6

Source: Council of Europe, *The Financial Structures of Local and Regional Authorities in Europe*, 1975

TABLE 2
TYPOLOGY OF EUROPEAN LOCAL GOVERNMENTS (EARLY 1960s)

| | | Local Spending | | |
		High	Medium	Low
Local Taxation	High	Sweden Norway	Denmark	
	Medium		Great Britain Ireland	Germany
	Low	Netherlands		France Italy

However, in order to appreciate fully the differences among the countries under consideration, the results are cross-tabulated in the first and third column, which take GNP as a common reference point. Thus, we can easily identify different combinations of local expenditure and taxation (Table 2). Whereas in northern Europe local institutions combined a tradition of high spending with considerable taxing power, quite the opposite holds true in the case of France and Italy, where the low level of resources spent locally goes along with a very limited fiscal autonomy. Great Britain and Ireland fall in between these two poles, while Germany displays a similar tax-raising power but a substantially lower level of local spending. The greatest imbalance between taxing and spending capacity occurs in the Netherlands. In sum, nowhere in Europe was local government better equipped than in Scandinavia to address emerging social care demands and to respond positively to them.

Timing

In the previous section we have – albeit loosely – referred to the favourable combination of social demands, cultural filters and institutional arrangements pertaining to the local government system in Scandinavia. However, in order to take full advantage of the evidence presented so far we need to go a step further. What appears to be crucial is exactly *when* the three processes under scrutiny intersect. As Paul Pierson reminds us, '*when* a particular issue or conflict emerges in a society may be critical for two reasons. On the one hand, the repertoire of possible responses is historically determined. On the other hand, once a response is adopted, it may generate self-reinforcing dynamics that put politics on a distinctive long-term path'.[14]

Both points are particularly relevant in our case. Starting with the first, what appears of paramount importance are the economic possibilities available at the particular time we are considering. How can we depict these possibilities in the case of Scandinavian countries? In the introduction to what is perhaps the most comprehensive study of the development of social care services in Scandinavia, Sipilä provides us with the following straightforward answer:

> since it had been decided that social care services were to be made available to all mothers and daughters who needed them, service production had to be started on an unprecedented scale. This was indeed what happened in all Scandinavian countries from the 1960s onwards, *in a situation where the economy was posing no restrictions on the growth of the welfare state.*[15]

Indeed, the process we are considering was set in motion during the golden age of the economy and could clearly benefit from the financial opportunities offered by a context of economic growth, as well as from the social and political expansionary climate surrounding it. As the pie was growing, policy makers did not have to struggle with fiscal constraints, and could pick from a wider range of policy alternatives compared with the context of fiscal retrenchment and austerity, typical of the next two decades.

By following this line of argument, we are in a better position to approach the comparative analysis of social care services in Europe. In sum, to shed light on cross-national differences in the development of this policy domain, we need to emphasise that the Scandinavian social care model was set in place before the international downturn of the economy and the spread of fiscal imbalances across the Western countries. Consequently, we might expect quite different country trajectories depending on the economic opportunities available at the particular historical juncture when the social care issue arises.

Yet it is not just a matter of the configuration of economic variables at the point in time when the trajectories relevant to the social care issue interconnect opening a policy window for decision makers. Once more the Scandinavian countries can provide interesting hints. If we extend the time span of our analysis, we are confronted with a sort of ratchet mechanism whereby the service expansion process that Scandinavian policy makers set in motion during the 1960s and 1970s continued well beyond the end of the golden age. To put it differently, by adopting a long-term perspective, we can clearly notice that subsequent policy steps in all four Nordic countries display a substantially self-reinforcing dynamic.

As the large body of theory on path dependency suggests, the critical mechanism is some form of positive feedback loop where initial moves in a particular direction encourage further movement along the same path.

Although this is by no means an inevitable outcome, social policies have repeatedly been depicted as a privileged area for path-dependent processes. And in our case we can easily list a number of factors favouring lock-in effects. In particular, we can hardly avoid considering that potential backlashes had to meet not only with the opposition of very large numbers of beneficiaries but also with the entrenched interests of a considerable share of the workforce directly engaged in the provision of the services themselves.

Further, a high degree of fiscal autonomy offered local authorities a crucial lever in bargaining with the central level of government, as the economic scenario progressively got worse. This point requires further elaboration and we shall return to it in the final section. For the moment, what should be stressed is that, as a result of self-reinforcing mechanisms and of unintended consequences stemming from earlier policy steps, the gap between Scandinavian countries and the rest of Europe widened (if possible) even further as the former proceeded along the policy track they originally set out on during the 1960s.

THE TIME LAG IN CONTINENTAL AND MEDITERRANEAN EUROPE

If we now turn to the other European countries, throughout the 1960s and 1970s societal pressure for a reduction in the household's social care responsibilities still appeared very limited compared with Scandinavia. On the whole, women's employment was considerably lower compared with Nordic levels. However, in a number of countries – namely in France, Germany and the UK – female labour force participation was significant. Moreover, in continental Europe the shift from the extended to the nuclear family was already a widespread phenomenon, which meant that social care services for the elderly could not be considered a remote issue. In short, the types of demographic, family and occupational changes that triggered the 'defamilisation' process in Scandinavia were already taking place in many other European countries but had yet not reached a critical threshold.

Further, the cultural background in most continental – let alone Mediterranean – countries represented a formidable obstacle to any far-reaching attempt to shift the care burden from the family to the public sector. Germany is certainly a case in point. In this country, the establishment of statutory care services was most clearly hindered by a cultural orientation deeply resistant to upsetting traditional family roles; an orientation largely reinforced by institutional mechanisms and normative devices. According to the German constitution, marriage was formally granted privileged state protection. Not surprisingly, the only type of social care service that received some public attention and funding in this country was targeted at the elderly, reflecting just the initial and less controversial steps of the 'defamilisation' process.

Yet, over the decade of the 1980s and into the 1990s the whole bundle of issues related to care giving and care services gradually came to the forefront, and crept into the policy agenda even in countries with the most unfavourable cultural background – namely Germany and the Netherlands. As the societal changes discussed in the first section of the article spread along the north–south axis and were filtered by progressively more secularised national cultures, social care acquired increasing political salience across continental and Mediterranean countries.

However, the time lag with respect to the Nordic countries set the rest of Europe on quite different grounds with respect to its forerunners. Most notably from the 1980s onward the context was no longer characterised by an expansionary climate; rather it was dominated by retrenchment and austerity efforts within the broader framework of international recession and world-wide competition. It is against this scenario that we need to consider domestic policies more directly affecting the field of interest.

To appreciate fully the implications of this new scenario, we need to focus once more on the relative strength of local government in individual countries.[16] As the multifaceted demands emerging from the impact of the 'defamilisation' process first and foremost on local authorities, it is crucial to shed light on the set of constraints and opportunities that framed their action at this particular point in time.

Across Europe, this period witnessed a renewed interest in decentralisation. At first glance this might appear as a positive opportunity. But as soon as we take a closer look, this impression changes. Compared with the earlier devolution of powers from the central to the local level of government, the principles underpinning this second decentralising wave appear of a quite distinct nature. In the previous decades, relevant policy measures were spurred on by functional requirements.[17] In the 1980s and 1990s the discourse on decentralisation has reflected primarily the market reorientation stemming from predominant neo-liberal values. Quite interestingly, both left- and right-wing interpretations of neo-liberalism supported decentralising policies. While the left emphasised devolution in order to improve responsiveness to citizen's needs, the right argued for decentralisation in terms of cost-containment, freedom of choice, individual responsibility, fiscal competition and subsidiarity.

Yet how does this exactly relate to social care policies and their future prospects? According to Bennett, altogether ongoing changes 'leading to a reorientation towards more consumer-based approaches using market structures' are bringing about a 'post-welfare model' of local government, with different implications depending on the starting point in each system. Southern countries, for instance, 'may bypass much direct provision by moving directly towards para-state, quasi-state and market approaches to service delivery'.[18]

A lot of field research is still needed in order to pinpoint what exactly is going on. Yet investigating broad trends at work in centre–local relations across Europe can provide crucial information to put into prospective policy developments not only in the field under scrutiny but also in other increasingly important areas, notably public assistance and active labour policies. Although institutional arrangements differ across countries, sub-national levels of government have increasingly been involved in sharing the financial burden of public assistance programmes (France, Belgium Germany) – not to mention the cases of Spain and Italy,[19] where up until now the responsibility exclusively rested on regional and local governments. Similar considerations can be expressed with respect to the growing set of measures aimed at bringing the unemployed back into the workforce. Irrespective of the different national tendencies towards the British model of workfare or the French ideal of '*insertion*', policies fighting unemployment and social exclusion are increasingly falling under the jurisdiction of local government and requiring local financial support.

How can sub-national levels of government meet these new challenges in a context where overall increases in fiscal pressure are essentially ruled out? Under these circumstances, the issue at stake is clearly how public resources are actually allocated among different levels of government.

LOCAL GOVERNMENT SPENDING IN THE CONTEXT OF RETRENCHMENT

The thrust of the argument here is that, given the different timing in the emergence of the social care issue, continental and Mediterranean countries were in no position to follow the Scandinavian path, that is, to establish a locally based public system of social care services. As a result, in addressing social care issues policy makers in these countries had almost no alternative than to take an approach which would first of all allow them to turn to a variety of non-public bodies, thereby widening the range of funding sources and service providers. Within this broad context, national outcomes clearly differed depending on what policy makers could 'pick' from: the powerful network of competing religious institutions traditionally operating in

Germany could hardly be compared to the French non-profit associations or the *mutuelles*.

A good starting point to articulate this line of argument is the overall trend in spending levels by local government in the time period under consideration. Is there some common trend underpinning individual countries' trajectories? In detail, can we detect some upward or downward movement in local expenditure largely shared by these countries? Or on the contrary, are we confronted with essentially divergent and country-specific trends? OECD statistics provide an excellent data source for this purpose, though their figures are not directly comparable with the Council of Europe figures presented in Table 1. Figure 1 furnishes data for six European countries: the UK, Germany, France, Italy, the Netherlands and Belgium. The figure provides a first answer to the question, illustrating cumulative annual changes in local spending and the relevant contribution by individual countries.[20] In detail, the figure focuses on percentage point changes from the previous year providing a visual depiction of overall change for the six countries, the direction of such change and the national components thereof.

The figure shows that as we move from the mid-1980s to the mid-1990s the total amount of variation substantially diminishes, and a downward

FIGURE 1
CUMULATIVE ANNUAL CHANGE IN LOCAL EXPENDITURE (1990 CONSTANT VALUES) FOR SELECTED EUROPEAN COUNTRIES 1985–96

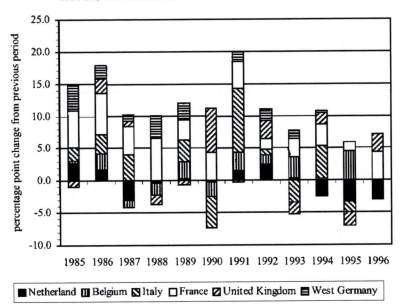

trend is progressively more visible. Whereas in the mid-1980s there was still room for some – albeit limited – expansion of local intervention, the picture for the 1990s shows a substantial stabilisation of local expenditure levels with minimal upward or downward adjustments. It is against this backdrop that we can attempt a closer examination of individual national cases. Due to space limitations, the discussion is concentrated on the Netherlands, Italy and France. Spain, which also experienced a significant restructuring of the balance of centre–local government power and administration, is also added to the analysis.

PASSING THE 'HOT POTATO' IN HYPER-CENTRALISED SYSTEMS: THE CASES OF ITALY AND THE NETHERLANDS

It appears most instructive to start by considering what happened to local government in the countries originally located at the opposite end of the spectrum from Scandinavia. By going back to the evidence presented in Table 1, the Netherlands and Italy (closely followed by France) were clearly the countries with the highest degree of political-administrative centralisation and the lowest fiscal autonomy. Turning to the 1980s and 1990s, what is striking is how the development of centre–periphery relations in the two countries is similar, and how the implications for the local government system are largely the same.

As Figure 2 illustrates, in the mid-1980s the Dutch and the Italian sub-national levels of government accounted for roughly one-third of total current expenditure by the public sector.[21] However, by the mid-1990s in both countries the share of local government spending was reduced to just over one-quarter of the total. The common drop actually reflects two distinct trajectories. In the Dutch case, the level of local spending (in constant terms) was persistently either blocked or shrinking over the ten-year period (see Figure 1). Apparently, turning the Dutch disease into the Dutch miracle was not without consequences for local authorities. On the other hand, Italy still experienced a period of rising sub-national expenditures over the 1980s which can largely be attributed to increased spending in the health care system. This upward trend only came to a halt over the following decade.

It is perhaps even more interesting to notice what occurred meanwhile with respect to local government financing. As Figures 3 and 4 document, over the period 1984–96 in Italy as well as in the Netherlands local taxing power was progressively upgraded to an unprecedented level – a move clearly aimed at compensating the concurrent drop in central government transfers.

FIGURE 2
LOCAL GOVERNMENT CURRENT DISBURSEMENTS AS A PERCENTAGE OF
GENERAL GOVERNMENT CURRENT DISBURSEMENTS IN ITALY AND THE
NETHERLANDS (1984–96)

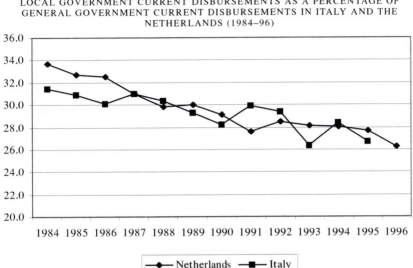

FIGURE 3
LOCAL DIRECT TAXES AND GOVERNMENT TRANSFERS AS A PERCENTAGE OF
LOCAL CURRENT DISBURSEMENTS IN THE NETHERLANDS (1984–96)

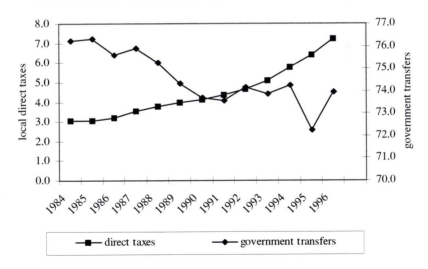

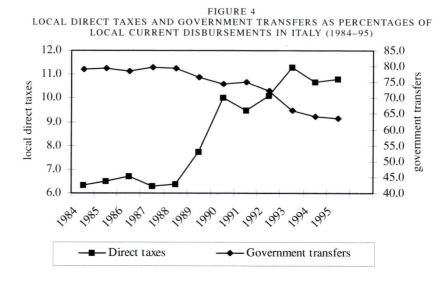

FIGURE 4
LOCAL DIRECT TAXES AND GOVERNMENT TRANSFERS AS PERCENTAGES OF
LOCAL CURRENT DISBURSEMENTS IN ITALY (1984–95)

The Netherlands

In the Dutch case, the share of current disbursements covered by local direct taxes never exceeded throughout the post-war period the negligible figure of three per cent. All of a sudden this revenue source doubled. If we combine this piece of information with the evidence presented in the previous figures on the shrinking size of local spending, the prospects for the policy areas we are interested in appear quite bleak. An increase in local fiscal autonomy exactly when harsh restructuring was taking place was hardly welcomed by local authorities who were not used to considering their citizens as taxpayers. This was even more true given that pushing the public revenue ceiling was politically unrealistic.

These comments seem most appropriate considering the new types of pressure that the Netherlands were facing with respect to caring responsibilities, especially from the 1980s onwards. Up until the 1970s, Dutch female employment was the lowest in continental Europe. This situation radically changed over the 1980s to the point that in just a few years the country reached European levels. Although most employed women were working on a part-time basis, this new scenario certainly contributed to the erosion of the traditional cultural vision of women's role, especially with respect to childcare. Jet Bussemaker offers an insightful account of how political discourses and ideological assumptions preventing any consistent public involvement in childcare were finally superseded in the 1980s by a rationale calling for active policy measures.[22]

It is within this context that for the first time the Dutch government passed legislation aimed at expanding childcare services. But at this time the Scandinavian solution was clearly not on the agenda. In fact, in 1996 the responsibility for childcare shifted from the national level to the municipalities. However, in the light of the evidence presented above, we can expect local government involvement to have largely divergent implications and effects compared to the similar strategy pursued by Nordic countries 25 years earlier. Local authorities found themselves 'squeezed' between growing demands and the economic and political difficulty of exacerbating fiscal pressure.

This uncomfortable position was certainly not confined to childcare. Notably, Dutch sub-cultural pillarisation produced a model of solidarity based on clearly distinct political-religious beliefs. In turn, this resulted in a proliferation of charitable bodies, with over-arching umbrella organisations, usually referred to as the 'fifth power'.[23] The literature documents how these non-profit organisations traditionally 'short-circuited' local authorities, and turned directly to the centre for financial support, obtaining almost a monopoly in social services. The situation hardly changed as a consequence of the decentralising policies pursued by the central level of government in recent years. As in the case of childcare, the national level – to alleviate pressure – tried to pass the 'hot potato' on to local authorities. However, in the context of the 1990s, local governments were constrained essentially to serve as a filter for the third sector or – depending on the case – for employers, citizens' associations and private service providers.

Italy

Turning to the case of Italy, although the national ingredients are obviously different, the structural dynamics at work appear largely similar, and are in fact even more marked. All three main trends discussed for the Netherlands can be detected in the case of Italy. First, Italian national legislation increased the range of regional and local competence; second, the share of total public spending accounted for by sub-national levels decreased; and, third, local fiscal autonomy substantially increased, especially over the 1990s. However, in order to provide an accurate account of recent policy developments in this country, one also needs to consider the historical role played by charitable bodies and the impact of the north–south cleavage.

The power of the church and the strong Catholic tradition of the country meant that there were a far greater number of these institutions than in other European countries. Throughout this century, charities carried out their functions with maximum independence, operating in effect as private bodies despite their public legal status. Along with religious bodies directly linked to holy orders, charities always represented the main providers of institutional care for the elderly as well as for children and the disabled. The establishment of the regions in 1970 opened new opportunities for modernising the system, but the results across the country turned out to be highly uneven.

Italy is in fact two countries in one. If we consider factors such as the ageing of the population, female labour force participation and changes in family structure, the centre-north of Italy looks very much like the rest of continental and northern Europe. In contrast, demographic indicators in southern Italy more closely resemble those of Greece, Portugal and certain southern regions of Spain, where the basic problem is a high dependency ratio and insufficient wage income for a substantial number of families. Hence, the two parts of the country differ both in their respective structures of social needs and the cultural perception of those needs. Importantly, the policies pursued by regional governments further increased the gap between these two parts of the country.

The constitution entrusted the regions with legislative power in the field of public assistance and social services. But the national parliament never passed the required guidelines, letting regional governments differentiate their policies to a greater extent than institutionally envisaged. As a result, while southern regions largely maintained an archaic system of public assistance, from the start northern and central regions committed their course of action to innovation.[24] They stimulated the expansion of a wide range of community services. Particularly, the regions run by leftist majorities aimed at establishing a comprehensive network of public social care services directly managed by local authorities.

However, the regions could only provide extremely limited funding for the new services, and essentially left the financial burden with local authorities. The latter were in no better position to meet the new legislative requirements. Municipalities almost exclusively relied on state transfers, and, especially, especially from the 1980s, were limited by the central government's actions to curtail local funding and impose a hiring freeze for local-level personnel. In short, local authorities in central and northern Italy were still engaged in the initial phase of implementing regional social care legislation when they had to confront a variety of restrictions imposed by the centre. Indeed, this approach to sub-national authorities contrasted with the easy spending predominant in practically all other fields. But, as a result, Italian local authorities were in no way sheltered from the retrenchment climate prevailing across Europe. Especially urban municipalities were increasingly 'squeezed' between mounting social care demands (fully legitimated by regional legislation) and the growing inability to provide the services directly – particularly given the freeze on hiring.

Under these circumstances, one can better understand how and why local authorities increasingly turned to non-statutory service providers.[25] The latter allowed an albeit limited policy response while short-circuiting the freeze on hiring. Considering that traditional charities were ill-equipped to meet new social care demands, municipalities often stimulated the creation of new types of non-profit organisations, particularly co-operatives. Co-operatives could easily provide a wide range of services, including home help, while also addressing the increasingly prominent issue of youth unemployment. The outcome of such diverse causal factors appears an intricate web of public–private arrangements, not only where the Christian Democrats held power, but also in leftist regions such as Tuscany and Emilia Romagna, which had originally attempted to create an Italian version of the Scandinavian model. Over the 1980s, even Communist-led regions gradually endorsed a pluralist welfare model shifting from a publicly centred approach to the mixed economy of welfare.

In light of this discussion, timing certainly appears crucial to the contextualisation of Italian social care policies. The causal sequence which brought about the establishment of the regions provided an unexpected opportunity for addressing the 'defamilisation' process, but adverse timing rapidly placed the Scandinavian model well out of reach for regional governments of all political orientations.

But what are the features of the system which emerged out of this process? As Constanzo Ranci insightfully suggests, in the Italian case the evolving relationship between local authorities and the third sector can best be described as 'mutual adjustment' rather than privatisation. Local political elites largely tended to develop clientelistic ties and partisan links with the third sector, thus reinforcing sheltered markets rather than prompting open competition.[26] However, as the 1990s represent a turning point in Italian politics and public administration, they apparently also mark a watershed in this area too. Whereas the national government almost completely ignored social care policies over the 1980s, starting in 1991 parliament issued comprehensive regulations on voluntary associations and co-operatives, and also legislated on the very sensitive issue of tax concessions to non-profit organisations.[27] Although southern Italy continued to lag behind, the new provisions stimulated local authorities to redefine their relations with the third sector. Especially in the centre-north, many municipalities had already undertaken this process which, however, is still largely under way. The issues currently at stake are manifold: service specifications setting out the quantity and quality of inputs and outcomes; staff skills; monitoring and performance requirements; tendering procedures; and, more generally, the degree and openness of the competition among suppliers. Whatever the results of these challenges, the fact remains that until today the Italian third sector has almost entirely relied on public funding by local authorities. But the room for manoeuvre by sub-national authorities is severely limited. As Figure 4 illustrates, local governments recently experienced a sharp drop in state transfers. Increased fiscal autonomy was supposed to counterbalance this trend, but there is no compensating mechanism between national and local fiscal pressure. As a result, local taxation is essentially additional to national taxation. And in the context of high overall fiscal pressure, it becomes increasingly difficult for local authorities to consider expanding their financial obligations. At this time, the increased taxing power granted by the national government to sub-national levels appears more a curse than a blessing.

DEVOLUTION AND FINANCIAL SUPPORT FROM THE CENTRE: THE CASES OF FRANCE AND SPAIN

France and Spain display a different version of the decentralising process unfolding across Europe over the 1980s and 1990s. *Vis-à-vis* the national government, in these two countries sub-national levels do not appear as net losers in a zero-sum game. Figure 5 shows that by the end of the period under consideration, sub-national authorities enjoyed a larger slice of the pie in both countries.

Actually, one can easily identify the main policy measures underlying this upward trend. In the case of France, the 1982–1986 reforms shifted the bulk of responsibilities for *aide sociale* to the *départements*, considerably increasing their budget. Following the introduction of the Revenu Minimum d'Insertion (RMI), departments also took on 20 per cent of the relevant financial burden providing for the insertion component of the programme. In the case of Spain, the substantial rise in the share of regional and local government spending occurred in the second half of the 1980s, and that is exactly when the health reform empowering regional governments started to be implemented. The involvement of the Spanish regions in the provision of minimum income and means tested social care offered a further though smaller contribution.[28]

Yet how is it that sub-national governments managed to strengthen their role and especially their spending capacity relative to other government

FIGURE 5
LOCAL GOVERNMENT CURRENT DISBURSEMENTS AS A PERCENTAGE OF
GENERAL GOVERNMENT CURRENT DISBURSEMENTS IN FRANCE AND SPAIN
(1984–96)

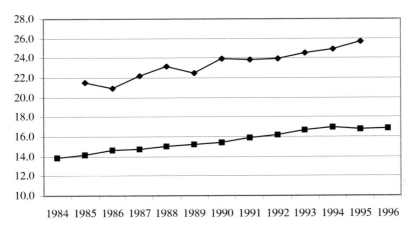

FIGURE 6
DIRECT TAXES AND GOVERNMENT TRANSFERS AS PERCENTAGES OF LOCAL
CURRENT DISBURSEMENTS IN FRANCE (1984–86)

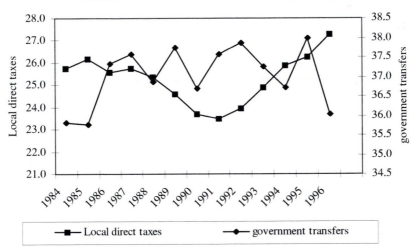

FIGURE 7
DIRECT TAXES AND GOVERNMENT TRANSFERS AS PERCENTAGES OF LOCAL
CURRENT DISBURSEMENTS IN SPAIN (1984–96)

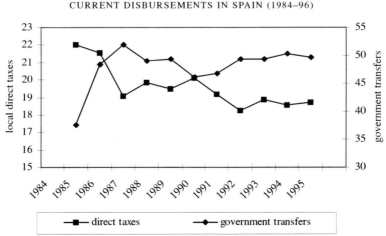

sub-sectors? Part of the answer certainly lies in the different financing strategies pursued by these two countries compared to the Netherlands, Italy and, for that matter, Belgium. As illustrated by Figures 6 and 7, there is no clear-cut drop in the level of government transfers. In short, sub-national authorities in France and Spain faced fewer financial constraints than did their neighbour countries. Despite this financial advantage, not to mention the new emphasis placed on sub-national levels of government in both countries, policy developments in the social care field did not seem to benefit from this relatively privileged position. Nevertheless, the explanation for this common outcome substantially differs in the two cases. Let us begin by considering the French case.

Certainly, over the 1980s and even more during the 1990s, France witnessed growing demands for both childcare and frail elderly care. But at that time the relevant policy arena was already highly structured and densely organised, thereby severely constraining policy choices. The associated implications can best be spelled out by briefly referring to broader concurrent developments in the French welfare state.

Notably, the French social protection system developed over the post-war period was essentially geared to labour market participants. Social insurance funds, which represented the cornerstone of the system, provided highly fragmented and diversified benefits and services to the different occupational groups. It was essentially within this context that social care issues were addressed until the 1980s. Although these issues certainly remained secondary to the management of income maintenance programmes, two of the major insurance agencies, namely the Caisses d'allocations familiales (Caf) and the Caisse national d'assurance vieillesse des travailleurs salariés (Cnavts), were actively involved in financing the provision, respectively, of childcare and home help for the elderly.

However, starting during the Mitterrand presidency in the early 1980s, a second, non-contributory component known as *solidarité nationale* was added to provide a basic safety net for the poor and the socially excluded. Indeed, the most striking change of the last two decades has been the considerable growth of this new component, which has resulted in a highly dualistic social protection system. These 'new social policies' were precisely the ones which became the primary object of the abovementioned decentralising process of 1982–86. In reviewing these new social policies, Bruno Palier emphasises their territorial dimension, which sharply contrasts with the occupational principles underpinning social insurance.[29] But what is most important to our discussion is that whilst the devolutionary policies entrusted municipalities and upper-tier local governments (the *départments*) with prominent responsibilities, they also set local action on a well-defined path. In short, local authorities were supposed to provide a whole range of new benefits and services targeted to the most needy on the basis of stringent means-testing. This clearly ruled out the possibility of creating collective social care services for the population at large; local governments represented an additional actor in a fragmented and extremely diversified network of service providers. A recent OECD comparative study on frail elderly care neatly summarises the consequences of this complex institutional arrangement as follows:

> The diversity of the sources for care funding in France make it necessary for the elderly person and their family to negotiate with a wide range of policy actors to assemble an "income and cost package" ... the sheer complexity of support for home care costs, coupled with the uncertainty whether all the components of the package can be assembled must be an inhibiting factor to choosing home care alternatives when making decisions about care.[30]

To get the full picture, we need to add that the societal and policy trends we are considering intersect with a further independent chain of events, namely the rising problem of unemployment. Claude Martin is correct in calling attention to this aspect when interpreting recent developments in this area.[31] Indeed, within the French debate, '*services de proximité*' are often linked to the revealing expression '*gisement d'emploi*'. Not surprisingly, recent provisions attempting to reconcile family and working life are in tune with creating the widest possible range of job opportunities. In the case of childcare this resulted especially in prompting individual arrangements of home care by childminders (through a series of tax and contributory deductions). But if we extend the analysis to the whole variety of community services, what we find is a mushrooming of non-profit organisations and particularly voluntary associations. In the mixed economy of care the latter are perhaps best equipped to provide flexible and low-cost answers to care needs.[32] Looking ahead, it appears most unlikely that municipalities will take a more active stance, especially considering their extreme fragmentation and the considerable variation in local funds due to significant local reliance on business taxes.

Spain offers yet another worrying scenario. Available studies unanimously describe the level of formal social care as minimal, and there are no signs that the situation will change in the near future. In attempting to explain this outcome, one can hardly blame the weakness of regional and local governments; quite the contrary, the centre–periphery balance of powers is increasingly shifting in favour of sub-national levels. There is instead abundant evidence indicating primarily cultural factors as inhibiting significant public engagement in this field. In reviewing survey data, Elisa Chuliá and Berta Alvarez-Miranda report that four out of five Spanish adults believe caring for the elderly is their children's obligation.[33] However, society is changing very rapidly in Spain and that country might very soon face a social care crisis without being prepared to confront it.

BACK TO THE SCANDINAVIAN COUNTRIES

Turning back to the Nordic countries – where the discussion began – there is abundant evidence that over the last two decades these countries also suffered from the adverse economic and financial conditions affecting the rest of Europe. The negative effects on local government are not surprising, especially 'as they were responsible for the lion's share of public activity.'[34] Figure 8 hardly allows for any misinterpretation. Except for Denmark, which largely recovered the sudden drop in local spending of the mid-1980s, in Norway, Finland and Sweden the proportion of local current spending over total outlays was definitely lower in 1996 compared to a decade earlier, with the biggest drop in Sweden.[35] Yet, despite this relative decline, in the Nordic countries the share of public current outlays controlled by the local level remained considerably higher compared with the rest of Europe.

FIGURE 8
LOCAL CURRENT DISBURSEMENTS AS A PERCENTAGE OF GENERAL
GOVERNMENT CURRENT DISBURSEMENTS IN THE NORDIC COUNTRIES
(1984–96)

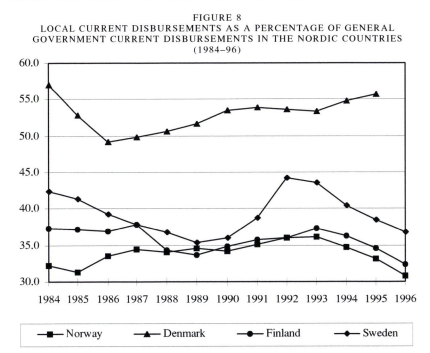

FIGURE 9
LOCAL DIRECT TAXES AS A PERCENTAGE OF LOCAL CURRENT
DISBURSEMENTS IN THE NORDIC COUNTRIES (1984–96)

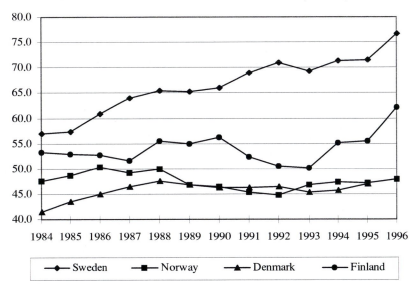

If we turn to the revenue side, we also find an increase in direct taxation as noticed above for other European countries. The evidence presented in Figure 9 is straightforward. Norway is the only country which is not affected by the upward trend in local direct taxation. But we must consider that Norwegian public finances enjoy a very special position because of the country's natural oil resources. Although local-level direct taxation already covered a considerable share of local spending, this strategy was further reinforced to the point that in Sweden today two-thirds of local current budgets are financed through local revenues. Indeed, this is part of a broader political move towards more local discretion as epitomised by the free commune experiment. Such a move inherently implies loosening previously tight national requirements and service standards in a number of areas including social care services.

Nevertheless, the literature documents that the bulk of social care services are still provided by the public sector and coverage levels remain incomparably higher than in any other country. In the case of Sweden, recent studies emphasise that 'political interest on the voluntary sector has remained, to a great extent, at a rhetorical level'.[36] This is not to say that the Scandinavian social care model was immune from reorganisation. In their detailed and informative comparative study, Tine Rostgaard and Torben Fridberg document streamlining measures, phasing out of open-ended care provision and concentration of resources on those most in need of care. But they also illustrate the extent to which all the other European countries lag behind, especially as regards to home help and community care services.[37]

Further, comparing market-oriented reforms in Britain and Sweden, Richard Clayton and Jonas Pontusson state how 'Swedish privatisation has been very limited in scope' and conclude the following: 'the trajectory of change in the Swedish and British cases is clearly different, suggesting that partisan politics still matters.'[38] It does seem that this is the case. Although over the last two decades Scandinavian politics were no longer characterised by uninterrupted Social Democratic rule, and Nordic countries experienced different bourgeois governments, still their political profile remained radically different from that of Britain. However, building on the evidence presented in this article, this line of argument could usefully be integrated by considering inter-governmental relations and their different national dynamics.

In greater detail, high fiscal autonomy allowed Scandinavian local authorities to safeguard the bulk of statutory services, and to hamper any abrupt policy reversal which the central level might have pursued for macroeconomic purposes. In other words, fiscal autonomy offered local authorities a crucial lever in bargaining with central government during the economic downturn, and local governments were in a better position to negotiate retrenchment policies. This was particularly the case in Denmark and Finland, where authoritative centre–local negotiating boards were formally established.[39] Interestingly, recent developments largely appear as the unintended consequence of policy steps taken at an earlier stage rather than the result of long-term rational planning.

Actually, the arguments developed in the literature with respect to the dispersion of powers and the existence of a plurality of veto points generally move in a different direction. As Evelyn Huber and John Stephens suggest:

> constitutional structures that provide multiple veto points are an obstacle to the expansion of public funding and public delivery of welfare state goods and services … the more ambitious any reform attempts are to expand the public role … the more special interests are affected and become potential opponents; and the greater the number of veto points is in the political system, the greater the perceived chances of success and thus the propensity of opponents to mobilise.[40]

The evidence from the Scandinavian experience suggests that, depending on the circumstances, veto points can work the other way round. In detail, a large number of veto points in the political system can block large-scale public service provision just as well as it can prevent its dismantling once it is already in place. The case of Britain offers further support for this view. The extreme weakness of local authorities in the British system, and specifically the legal constraints on their capacity to act, made it possible for the Conservative-led central government to override local-level Labour opposition and to impose the privatisation and marketisation of social care services.[41]

CONCLUDING REMARKS

If just for a moment we contrast our findings with the interpretation usually offered by the literature to describe the development of local government in Europe until the mid-1970s, there is a sense of complete reversal. Prior to the last decade, research indicated progressive increases in local government spending coupled with greater financial dependence on the centre. The more recent trend, however, is for greater local fiscal autonomy but relatively less local spending with respect to total public expenditure. It is against this institutional and financial background that we consider the diffusion of the care needs discussed in the first section. As noted, over the 1980s such needs gradually spread from the centre-north to the southern parts of Europe and are now starting to emerge even in socially and economically backward areas. However, as these increasing demands for elderly care and childcare services came to the fore in virtually all European countries, they inevitably clashed with quite adverse 'confining conditions'.

The evidence presented supports the idea that timing is crucial. Depending on the historical juncture, policy makers are first of all confronted with quite distinct economic constraints and opportunities. In contrast to the Scandinavian experience, the overall level of taxation had largely reached its upper limits when social care issues were addressed in the rest of Europe. Under these circumstances, expansionary options were essentially ruled out; and the central and local levels of government found themselves fighting over the same bit of the cake. But, depending on timing, the possible connections between distinct social realms are also different. And such conjunctural connections are bound to cause distinctive side-effects and unintended consequences as well as influencing the range of available policy alternatives. The particular intersection between unemployment and social care issues discussed for France is a case in point.

Summing up, social care policies in continental and Mediterranean Europe could hardly be expected to follow the Scandinavian path. That path was no longer available. Yet, one can still comment that current efforts appear largely insufficient in the light of the societal changes discussed in the first section, and especially considering future prospects. By the same token, the ideal of an 'inclusive citizenship', as proposed, for example, by feminist scholars Trudie Knijn and Monique Kremer, is more likely to linger in academic debates than be turned into reality.[42] Yet within this apparently gloomy picture, we might also expect locally diverging trends. There is growing evidence that the standardisation process characterising European welfare state development from 1945 to the mid-1970s might be replaced by increasing sub-national variations.

NOTES

This work benefited much from the stimulating and enriching environment that Martin Rhodes and Maurizio Ferrera created as directors of the European Forum at the European University Institute in 1998–99. I wish to express my gratitude to them. I should also like to thank the latter and Paul Pierson for their comments on an earlier version.

1. Data used in the article come from the following sources: Eurostat, *Statistiques en Bref* (various years); Eurostat, *Les femmes dans la Communauté Européenne* (Luxemburg: Eurostat 1992); Eurostat, *Les femmes et les hommes dans l'Union Européenne* (Luxemburg: Eurostat 1995).
2. In the cases of Belgium and France female activity rates are instead slightly higher among married women.

3. The only exception is represented by the Netherlands for which the difference is as high as 20 percentage points.

4. Actually, according to more recent statistical information, the figure for Spain is by now 24 per cent, suggesting that the scenario might change quite rapidly even in southern Europe.

5. European Commission, *Relazione demografica* (Brussels: European Commission 1997).

6. J. Sipilä (ed.), *Social Care Services: The Key to the Scandinavian Welfare Model* (Aldershot: Ashgate 1997).

7. See A. Antonnen and J. Sipilä, 'European Social Care Services: Is it Possible to Identify Models?', *Journal of European Social Policy* 6/2 (1996), p.93.

8. See V. Fargion, 'Current Social Service Regimes in Europe: The Rise and Development', article presented at the ISA RC 19 meetings (Copenhagen, Aug. 1997).

9. See J. Windebank, 'To What Extent Can Social Policy Challenge the Dominant Ideology of Mothering? A Cross-National Comparison of Sweden, France and Britain', *Journal of European Social Policy* 6/2 (1996), pp.147–61.

10. L.Trägårdh, 'Statist Individualism: On the Culturality of the Nordic Welfare State', in O. Soresen and B. Sträth (eds.), *The Cultural Construction of Norden* (Oslo: Scandinavian University Press 1997), p.262.

11. See E. Page, *Central and Local Government Relations. A Comparative Analysis of West European Unitary States* (London: Sage 1987).

12. T. Kröger, 'Local Government in Scandinavia: Autonomous or Integrated into the Welfare State', in Sipilä (ed.), *Social Care Services*, p.97.

13. See Council of Europe, *The Financial Structures of Local and Regional Authorities in Europe*, Vol.I (Strasbourg: Council of Europe 1975).

14. P. Pierson, Not Just What, but When: Issues of Timing and Sequence in Comparative Politics (Studies in American Political Development, forthcoming), p.16.

15. Sipilä (ed.), *Social Care Services*, p.3.

16. See J. Alber, 'A Framework for the Comparative Study of Social Services', *Journal of European Social Policy* 5/2 (1995), pp.131–49.

17. See B. Dente and F. Kjellberg (eds.), *The Dynamics of Institutional Change* (London: Sage 1988).

18. R. Bennet, *Local Government in the New Europe* (London: Bellhaven Press 1993), p.15.

19. A national minimum income programme has just recently been introduced in Italy. However, for the moment the programme is only being implemented experimentally in a very limited number of municipalities.

20. A few words are in order to explain the procedure I followed. As a preliminary step, I first looked at absolute levels of local expenditure and then turned current into constant values (using 1990 prices as a reference point). However, what appears crucial to develop the implications of the 'timing' argument is not how much local government was spending; rather whether and to what extent its spending capacity was expanding as social care issues started entering the policy agenda.

21. Whereas the Netherlands was already a big local spender in the previous decades, in Italy this was primarily the result of the transition in 1978 from an occupational to a national health care system, which empowered regional governments and local health authorities with spending responsibility.

22. J. Bussemaker, 'Rationales of Care in Contemporary Welfare States: The Case of Childcare in the Netherlands', *Social Politics* 5/1 (Spring 1998), p.89.

23. R. Kramer *et al.*, *Privatisation in Four European Countries: Comparative Studies in Government-Third Sector Relationships* (New York: Sharpe 1993).

24. See V. Fargion, 'Social Assistance and the North-South Cleavage in Italy', *South European Politics and Society* 1/3 (1996), pp.135–54; and V. Fargion, *Geografia della sittadinanza sociale in Italia* (Bologna: Il Mulino 1997).

25. For an analysis of the crucial role families have always had in providing care to dependent family members, see R. Trifiletti, 'Restructuring Social Care in Italy', in J. Lewis (ed.), *Gender, Social Care and Welfare State Restructuring in Europe* (Aldershot: Ashgate 1998), pp.175–206.

26. See C. Ranci, *Oltre il Welfare State. Terzo settore, nuove solidarietà e trasformazioni del welfare* (Bologna: Il Mulino 1999).

27. See U. Ascoli, *Il Welfare futuro: Manuale critico del Terzo settore* (Rome: Carocci 1999).
28. See L. Moreno and A. Arriba, 'Decentralisation and the New Logic of Welfare Provision in Spain', article presented at the conference on 'Reforming Social Assistance and Social Services: International Experiences and Perspectives' (Florence, European University Insitute, 11–12 Dec. 1998). Despite the common upward trend, and while over the 1990s the Spanish ratio of local to total public spending came close to the Dutch and Italian middle range value of 25 per cent, France remained around ten percentage points below.
29. See B. Palier, 'La référence au territoire dans les nouvelles politiques sociales', *Politiques et Management Public* 16/3 (1998), pp.13–41.
30. OECD, *Caring for Frail Elderly People: Policies in Evolution* (Paris: OECD 1996), p.135.
31. See C. Martin, 'Reframing Social Policies in France towards Selectivity and Commodification: The Case of Family and Frail Elderly Policies', article presented at the conference 'Reforming Social Assistance and Social Services: International Experiences and Perspectives'.
32. See J. Laville 'Services de proximité: la construction sociale d'un champ d'activités economiques', article presented at the conference 'Third Sector, State, and Market in the Transformation of Social Policies in Europe' (Milan, Oct. 1996).
33. E. Chuliá and B. Alvarez-Miranda, 'Pautas Presentes y Tendencias Futuras en la Prestación de Cuidados a Mayores en España', article presented at the Spanish Political Science Association congress (Granada, Sept. 1999).
34. J. Blom-Hansen, 'Macroeconomic Control of Local Governments in Scandinavia: The Formative Years', *Scandinavian Political Studies* 21/2 (1998), p.134.
35. Notably, most local spending refers to final consumption. In discussing the anti-service bias of recent welfare retrenchment, R. Clayton and J. Pontusson rightly claim that 'final government consumption expenditure continued to grow (in real terms) through the 1980s; it simply grew less rapidly than spending on social security transfers'. See 'Welfare State Retrenchment Revisited. Entitlements Cuts, Public Sector Restructuring, and In-egalitarian Trends in Advanced Capitalist Societies', *World Politics* 51 (Oct. 1998), p.95.
36. See E. Jeppsson Grassman, 'The Voluntary Sector in a Welfare Perspective', article presented at the conference 'Comparing Social Welfare Systems in Nordic Countries and France' (Gilleleje, 4-6 Sept. 1998). Whereas generally voluntary organisations are numerous in the social care field, in Sweden the voluntary sector is dominated by cultural and recreational associations.
37. See T. Rostgaard and T. Fridberg, *Caring for Children and Older People. A Comparison of European Policies and Practices* (Copenhagen: The Danish National Institute of Social Research 1998), which covers the following countries: Sweden, Denmark, Finland, Germany, the Netherlands, Britain and France. For detailed information on legislation and care arrangements in Europe, also see European Commission, *Care in Europe: Joint Report of the 'Gender and Employment' and 'Gender and Law' Groups of Experts* (Brussells: European Commission 1998).
38. Clayton and Pontusson, 'Welfare State Retrenchment', p.91.
39. Blom-Hansen, 'The Macroeconomic Control', provides a historical interpretation of why the central level was able to exert a more prominent role in Norway and Sweden.
40. See E. Huber and J. Stephens, 'Political Power and Gender in the Making of the Social Democratic Service State', Article presented at the ISA RC 19 meetings (Canberra, Aug. 1996).
41. As to this point, Glennerster, for instance, states: 'local authorities are creatures of central government. To pretend otherwise is to confuse the constitutional position.' See H. Gelnnerster, *Paying for Welfare: The 1990s* (Hemel Hempstead: Harvester Wheatsheaf 1992), p.88.
42. See T. Knijn and M. Kremer, 'Gender and the Caring Dimension of Welfare States: Toward Inclusive Citizenship', *Social Politics* 4/3 (Fall 1997), pp.328–61.

Motives, Means and Opportunities: Reforming Unemployment Compensation in the 1990s

JOCHEN CLASEN

At the end of the 1990s the debate about developments in European welfare states looks distinctly different compared with the 1980s, or even the early 1990s. Attempts to explain welfare state change, prominent until the end of the 1980s, gave way to a better understanding of cross-national welfare state diversity, influenced not least by Gösta Esping-Andersen's notion of 'three worlds of welfare capitalism'.[1] The latter was followed by an ongoing debate about the impact of current and potential external pressures on national welfare states, such as European integration, globalisation, demographic shifts and changes in family formation and labour markets. For some time it seemed that commentators were too preoccupied with identifying the degree and direction of potential change to notice actual and significant reforms in some countries, such as the Netherlands, the UK or Denmark. With notable exceptions, the interest in welfare reforms in those countries grew only when policy success began to appear in the form of employment growth and a gradual but significant drop of previously high levels of unemployment without increases in poverty or inequality, excluding the UK. Of course, these outcomes cannot solely be attributed to welfare restructuring, but also have to be related to other changes introduced in macro-economic, fiscal, industrial relation and labour market policy.[2]

Within the European policy debates on welfare systems, aspects of benefit conditionality have moved to centre-stage, as new catch-phrases – such as 'making benefit systems more employment friendly' or transforming passive into active types of social protection – indicate.[3] The fact that the term 'activation' is often applied somewhat loosely possibly reflects conceptual difficulties in distinguishing clearly between active and passive programmes.[4] Furthermore, the debate also tends to ignore the fact that unemployment benefits have never been granted unconditionally, but have always involved requirements on the part of claimants regarding the availability for and willingness to work, as well as demonstrable steps to seek employment. The exact rules which specify those criteria and their administrative application differ considerably across (and even within) countries.[5] These parameters have largely been ignored in cross-national analyses, presumably because they are more difficult to capture than eligibility or entitlement criteria. Yet the specification of conditionality is crucial for the quality of social security benefits and constitutive for their decommodifying effect.[6]

Focusing on increasing benefit conditionality in three countries, the analysis takes as a point of departure the claim that, despite considerable differences in policy design, both Denmark and the UK have substantially altered the balance between rights and obligations, particularly for young unemployed people. The distinguishing feature is not so much a decrease in generosity as the introduction of an obligatory transition from cash benefit receipt to participation in schemes such as training, education, work experience or job creation. These policies were introduced in the UK after 1997 (the New Deal) and in successive labour market reforms in Denmark after 1993 (and earlier, in 1990, for unemployed assistance claimants). While similar requirements might be found in other countries, it is argued here that their introduction in the UK and Denmark indicate significant policy shifts. In other countries, such as Germany, employment offices have the discretion to sanction claimant groups who refuse to take up suitable training opportunities, while local authorities have a legal basis to 'activate' social assistance claimants who are registered as unemployed. It should be noted that this is not the same, since in the other two countries activation programmes are mandatory, setting in after some time spent in unemployment, even though some groups remain exempt, such as lone parents with children below a certain age.

EXPLAINING WELFARE RESTRUCTURING

This whole account might be regarded as an attempt to explore requirements for restructuring social protection. One of the aspects which makes activation policies intriguing in this respect is the reminder that reforming welfare policy is not only about changing rights but also obligations. Moreover, they indicate that it is sometimes difficult to classify a particular policy as an example of either welfare retrenchment or welfare expansion. For instance, the potential expenditure involved in activation programmes is higher than in maintaining passive cash support. In addition, there is an ideological conflict. From the perspective of individual claimants, obligatory activation might be seen exclusively as welfare restriction. If 'activation programmes' are so positive, why do they have to be compulsory? However, within a less liberal approach to welfare rights, programmes are more ambiguous. Activation policies can be designed in different ways and might be aimed at (re)integrating unemployed people into society through the inclusion in the labour market (training, work experience) but also through other spheres such as education, community life or social activities.[7] In other words, activation policies may be regarded as 'compassionate' (tackling social exclusion) or as 'condemning' (tackling anti-social behaviour); as empowering or as forms of social control.[8]

In principle, this ambiguity puts policy makers, intent on restructuring unemployment transfers, in a more favourable position than, say, those keen on reforming pensions or health care systems. Those programmes are not only more popular, but retrenchment is perhaps more easily identifiable, thus requiring skilful political manoeuvres for successful policy implementation. Nevertheless, both Danish and British governments were careful not to stress aspects of compulsion but rather notions of integration and reciprocity. What is more, activation policies were only introduced once centre-left governments had returned to power, suggesting that Conservative governments might have regarded such initiatives as potentially unpopular and thus their implementation was facilitated by governments which have traditionally been welfare state promoters.[9]

With hindsight, as will be shown, these anxieties to avoid blame turned into opportunities to claim credit – not least due to favourable labour market, fiscal and political conditions at and after the time of policy implementation. In other words, while compulsory activation policies *per se* seem difficult to classify, it may not be merely the type of policy but the specific conditions under which policies are implemented which allow 'credit claiming' or require 'blame avoidance'.[10]

Theoretically promising frames of reference for explaining welfare restructuring in the area of unemployment compensation seem to be the concepts of historical institutionalism[11] and social learning.[12] As the following discussion will underline, German unemployment insurance seems an excellent illustration of the relevance of the former. Reforms, as well as reform failures, can be attributed to institutional structures and forms of governance 'setting parameters'[13] both directly and indirectly in terms of providing a normative arena for the formation of interests, preferences and bargaining strategies pursued by collective actors. However, the analysis will also point to the limits of institutionalist frameworks which are generally better at explaining stability than policy change or innovation.

Complementing institutionalist frameworks with a notion of policy learning or adaptation might be useful here. Drawing on Peter Hall,[14] R.H. Cox suggests that the concept of 'social learning' could be applied in order to explain 'paradigm shifts' in Danish and Dutch labour market and social security policy in the 1990s.[15] Put simply, policy makers first tried to adjust to problems with recourse to traditional labour exit instruments. Mounting problems challenged the prevailing policy paradigm and led to 'awkward solutions', but not to a break with fundamental beliefs. Only when the level of tension crosses 'a certain threshold' does the old way of thinking give way to new ideas and better solutions, that is, towards policies of labour market integration.

As discussed below, the development in Danish benefit policies for the unemployed seems to fit this model. However, unless fairly general notions are applied, it is difficult to define stages of social security policy making and to single out parameters which constitute a shift in a given 'policy paradigm'. For example, notwithstanding a shift towards labour market entry programmes, Danish policies continue to include several options for labour market exit. Equally, if the introduction of mandatory activation programmes is used as a more specific indicator for a policy shift, the Netherlands would not qualify since it has not introduced the same compulsory principle as Denmark or the UK.[16]

These shortcomings might be overcome if historical institutionalist and 'social learning' approaches are not treated as theoretical straightjackets but as flexible and potentially complementary frames of reference within which heuristic perspectives can help to shed light on the interdependencies of factors which lead to welfare restructuring. The particular heuristic approach here draws on popular detective novels and the strategies pursued by characters such as Miss Marple or Sherlock Holmes. For them, identifying the murderer involves a rigorous investigation of three aspects: motives, means and opportunities. Applied to the introduction of mandatory activation programmes, this analysis compares motives, means and opportunities which led to significant shifts in welfare policy in two countries but not in the third. It is the interrelation between these factors, it is argued, which makes welfare restructuring more or less probable.

There is some resemblance between the ways in which this discussion conceptualises means, motives and opportunities in relation to policy change and J.W. Kingdon's notion of three 'process streams' of problems (which need to be recognised as policy-relevant), policy proposals (which need to be technically and politically feasible) and politics (for example, change of government or of key policy participants).[17] Put simply, only a particular constellation between these separate three streams, Kingdon argues, provides the opportunity, or 'policy window', for substantial policy change. An analogy might be a slot machine which requires players to align three symbols in a certain way in order to win.[18] However, as will be discussed below, means, motives and opportunities are neither congruent with Kingdon's process streams nor, unlike a slot machine, independent from each other. Before investigating motives, means and opportunities the subsequent section begins with a brief characterisation of benefit systems and major benefit changes in the three countries.

BENEFIT SYSTEMS AND BENEFIT CHANGES – AN ABRIDGED VERSION

International comparisons of replacement and beneficiary rates indicate that Danish support for unemployed people is one of the most generous and British support one of the least generous within the EU, with the German system somewhere in-between.[19] European household panel data (which includes social assistance but not housing allowances) confirms this, placing Denmark and the UK very close to the opposing ends of the spectrum of benefit generosity in Europe.[20] One of the outcomes of this is a significantly lower level of poverty amongst Danish households where the head of the household is out of work compared with most other EU countries, including Germany and the UK.[21] The unemployment compensation systems which produce these outcomes could be characterised as 'comprehensive' or 'solidaristic' in Denmark, as 'differentiated' or 'compartmentalised' in Germany and 'residual' in the UK.[22]

Denmark

The modern Danish unemployment insurance system remains voluntary, trade union-run and highly tax subsidised. It provides a high wage replacement rate, particularly for low-income groups due to a low ceiling which makes earnings-related benefits effectively flat-rate.[23] Measures introduced from the mid-1970s were aimed at easing access to the system. Most important in this respect was the introduction of the so-called job offer scheme, which provided a right to temporary employment after a period of 2.5 years in unemployment. After completion, benefit entitlement was re-established. What is more, work tests were very leniently applied so that, until 1993, 'the unemployed were not too frequently offered a job if they didn't want it'.[24]

Some relatively modest benefit restrictions introduced by the Social Democratic-led government after 1980 have to be seen in the context of mounting fiscal pressure due to rising unemployment from below one per cent in 1973 to over ten per cent in the early 1980s. A Conservative-led coalition government which took over in 1982 initially implemented some more serious cutbacks but backtracked later. As a result, the benefit system remained largely intact during the 1980s and was even improved in some respects so that the beneficiary rate (the proportion of registered unemployed actually receiving benefits) remained at over 80 per cent throughout the decade.[25]

Towards the end of the 1980s, however, thinking about the role and appropriateness of the unemployment insurance system began to change. As a consequence, from the early 1990s onwards, Conservative-led governments introduced a mix of policies which eased temporary and permanent labour market exit, introduced some restrictions and began to put more emphasis on qualification and education. These can be seen as a precursor for a plethora of policies introduced by the Social Democratic government in successive labour market reforms after 1993. Motivated by an upswing in the economy and declining unemployment, including some shortage in skilled labour, leave-of-absence programmes were made less financially attractive and other exit schemes, such as early retirement options, were phased out.[26]

By the late 1990s, activation policies became paramount within both labour market and social policy.[27] Based on individual 'action plans' which try to match the needs and circumstances of individual claimants with local labour market conditions, there are a host of different types of activation programmes, including education, training and work experience schemes.[28] Although in practice perhaps less clearly distinguishable, in principle there is an important difference between programmes for insurance and assistance claimants. Under the supervision of the Ministry of Labour, regional tripartite Labour Market Councils are responsible for labour market policy, which includes activation programmes for recipients of unemployment insurance. By contrast, under the auspices of the Ministry of Social Affairs and therefore considered as social policy, municipalities have an obligation to 'activate' recipients of social assistance benefits. Indeed, it was within social assistance policy that activation first started in 1990 and where programmes still set in earlier in individual unemployment spells than in labour market policy.

Benefit levels have largely remained untouched and a large majority of participants do not regard activation programmes as punitive.[29] Yet it is difficult to argue that benefit policies after 1994 do not indicate a substantial turnaround, with the introduction of significant eligibility restrictions, a maximum period of benefit entitlement and activation periods which set in progressively early in individual unemployment spells and no longer lead to benefit re-qualification. This is consistent with a shift within the overall macro-economic response to high unemployment, which during most of the past two decades had represented a mix between Social Democratic and Conservative policies, that is, increasing public sector employment, raising qualification levels and easing labour market exit.[30] By the end of the decade, this approach seems to have been discredited, although some much less generous temporary labour market exit schemes continue to complement programmes aimed at promoting labour market entry.

Germany

Unemployment insurance transfers in Germany are more strictly earnings-related than in Denmark and reward long-standing contributors over a certain age with longer benefit entitlement. The system is also more compartmentalised, with unemployment insurance providing earnings-related transfers financed by joint earmarked contributions to the unemployment insurance fund which is administered by the tripartite Federal Labour Office (FLO). The same fund also administers unemployment assistance, which is mainly for claimants who have exhausted entitlement to unemployment insurance. It is important to note that while unemployment assistance provides lower earnings-related benefits, those are means-tested and entirely tax funded.

About two-thirds of registered unemployed were in receipt of earnings-related benefits in the mid-1990s, with about equal numbers of insurance and assistance claimants. The remainder were either not in receipt of benefit or relying on locally administered and financed social assistance. Over the past 15 years or so, local authorities have increasingly become a reluctant third source of social security support, particularly for long-term unemployed people. This has led to a range of cost-containment strategies, including a 'recycling' of claimants (by offering limited work contracts which enable participants to re-qualify for insurance benefits), as well as other types of subsidised employment.[31] There has been a significant increase in the number of unemployed social assistance claimants who are 'activated' in this way.[32] However, unlike in Denmark, where half of the costs for local authority activation programmes are being reimbursed by the state, in Germany there is no regular co-funding from the FLO or the state.

Partly responsible for the growing importance of social assistance for the unemployed have been cost containment policies, which began in the early 1980s. At that time, the SPD–FDP (Social-Democratic/Liberal) coalition responded to deficits in the FLO budget, which were due to rising unemployment, by raising contribution rates moderately, introducing selective benefit restrictions and, more severely, curtailing active labour market programmes (which are funded out of the same budget as insurance benefits). This pattern was typical for policies in the 1980s pursued by both centre-left and, after 1982, the centre-right CDU–FDP governments. Required to balance deficits in the FLO budget and reluctant to raise contribution rates, the main victims of cutbacks were active programmes as the structurally weaker type of expenditure,[33] while benefit restrictions were primarily targeted at groups less attached to the labour market.

The collapse of the east German labour market after unification was to a large extent cushioned by easing access to active labour market policies and by benefit transfers, both financed via increased contribution levels. Once unemployment reached extremely high levels in both parts of the country, cost containment programmes introduced substantial benefit restrictions for some groups, while the position of core workers with good contribution records (particularly those with children) remained unaffected. The exceptions were two changes which weakened the 'status protection' for unemployed by significantly watering down the definition of 'suitable job offers' and reducing the level of unemployment assistance over time. So far, the new Social Democratic government has upheld those changes and, at the time of writing, is planning to abolish access to unemployment assistance for groups who were not in previous receipt of unemployment insurance.

The United Kingdom

British unemployment insurance is much more centrally controlled and financed than in the other two countries. There is no earmarked contribution and no separate unemployment insurance fund. Instead, unemployment transfers are financed out of a general National Insurance, which is centrally administered. Means-tested social assistance (Income Support) is also fully centrally controlled. Unemployment benefits have never been overly generous, but unfavourable benefit indexing since the 1970s, the abolition of the earnings-related supplement in the early 1980s and a number of small changes thereafter led to a decline in value in relation to net average wages to less than 25 per cent for a typical blue-collar worker by the mid-1990s.[34] In addition, access to insurance coverage was tightened in the 1980s, contributing to an erosion of social protection based on insurance principles in the UK generally and unemployed people in particular, with more than 80 per cent reliant on means-tested cash support.[35]

Since the end of the 1980s, a main thrust of social security reforms in the UK has been to make conditionality more explicit, tightening controls, prescribing job-seeking behaviour and stiffening sanctions for non-compliance.[36] The new Labour government in 1997 intensified the emphasis on behavioural aspects, which reflects a more general attempt to redefine rights and responsibilities within the British welfare state.[37] In essence, this project involves the propagation of a new 'contract' between citizens and the state, with the latter offering different types of assistance for labour market integration and the former being obliged to accept this assistance.[38] Most prominent in terms of mandatory labour market participation programmes has been the 'New Deal' for young unemployed people.[39] In short, for claimants under the age of 25 individual 'activity plans' are drawn up with the Employment Service, which require the transition from benefit receipt to a subsidised job in the private or public sector or full time education. The focus on labour market integration is also evident in other New Deal programmes (for example, for lone parents) and in range of other social security and tax policies.

Of course, the above is a much simplified and stylised picture of changes in unemployment compensation in the three countries. Yet, three national trends seem clearly identifiable. The Danish policy path was broadly one of improving benefit generosity and coverage as a response to rising unemployment, followed by modest changes under Conservative governments in the 1980s. Policies which indicated a departure from this path became obvious in the early 1990s, but were only implemented once a Social Democratic government resumed office in 1993. In successive steps those substantially changed the balance between rights and obligations on the part of unemployed people, while benefit levels remained largely untouched. British policies under Margaret Thatcher and John Major incrementally whittled away insurance rights for the unemployed and increasingly focused on aspects of job-seeking behaviour which might be seen as a precursor for the 'New Deal' policies introduced by the Labour government after 1997. Unlike under Conservative governments, however, the Labour administration introduced a new element of obligation as an explicit *quid pro quo* for more investment in better labour market integration programmes. As in Denmark, the focus has been on young and long-term unemployed people. By contrast, German policy reforms within unemployment compensation might be characterised as selective rounds of restrictions which particularly hit claimants who are less attached to the labour market. In the 1990s, municipalities and local authorities have been asked to exercise their right to 'activate' unemployed social assistance claimants more regularly. However, unlike in the UK and Denmark, generally applicable mandatory activation policies have been introduced for neither insurance nor assistance claimants.

MOTIVES

Policy changes are often results of complex negotiations and bargaining, rendering the link between motives and policy outcomes rather tenuous at times. What is more, policy interests and preferences are themselves influenced by past policies and by contingent factors, such as changes in economic and labour market contexts. This makes it often difficult to distinguish clearly between motives, means and opportunities. Discussing these aspects separately must therefore remain somewhat artificial and runs the risk of suggesting a goal-oriented rational model of policy making. The following discussion acknowledges this risk, but hopes that it is outweighed by the potential gains of analytically distinguishing and identifying the factors which are important for an understanding of welfare reform in comparative context.

Given the twofold effect of mass unemployment in terms of increasing social security spending and lowering tax revenue, there is no shortage of fiscal motives for making unemployment compensation less expensive. Equally, there are various ways in which spending can be reduced, involving changes in eligibility and entitlement criteria, all of which have been applied by the three countries under investigation after the early 1980s, albeit to differing degrees. However, as discussed earlier, categorising mandatory activation programmes as welfare restriction is questionable, which suggests that motives for their introduction should differ from those which are primarily associated with containing public expenditure. The following two sections explore these aspects for the UK and Denmark.

The United Kingdom: Making Work Pay

Benefit reforms implemented in the UK under Conservative governments in the 1980s and early 1990s were accompanied by free market ideology and the encouragement of individual enterprise, reducing taxation and promoting wage dispersion and labour market deregulation. In social security, emphasis was put on individual provision, the distribution of scarce resources only to 'those in real need' and the reduction of the level of social protection for particular claimant groups. Whether the Thatcherite project was successful or not as a whole,[40] certain policy aims were achieved, such as a substantial weakening of the role of trade unions[41] and the abolition of wage regulating elements which had applied particularly to younger employees in certain industries. Consequently, the relative position of the lowest paid, and those on benefits, declined significantly.[42]

Within this context, neo-Conservative supply-side policies in the 1980s emphasised the need to improve work incentives while policy makers were reluctant to invest in job creation, training or qualification programmes. After successive defeats in general elections, leading Labour Party politicians in the mid-1990s began to accept the need to contain public expenditure. Equally, Conservative social security policies (for example, increased means-testing) were not revoked but (at least implicitly) accepted and continued with reference to the need to improve targeting of social spending.

However, to argue that the Labour government simply continued previous policies would be to ignore substantial differences in the approach towards social security between 'New Labour' and both the previous Conservative government and 'Old Labour'. Alan Deacon[43] has highlighted a number of factors which led to a more authoritarian stance towards some groups of unemployed. Inspired by communitarian and Christian Socialist ideas and influenced by electoral considerations, Tony Blair's New Labour embraced a new centre-left ideology towards the welfare state, with policies informed by a notion of 'moral regeneration' and the need to create a stronger sense of rights and responsibilities. This applies to areas such as community life, parenting and schooling – but perhaps most crucially to the labour market and to paid work as the central source of citizenship. The aim is to 'make work pay' and to provide incentives which allow individuals to pursue an 'enlightened self-interest'. Unlike previous Labour Party policy, the current administration has accepted that the provision of social security can have detrimental effects on individual behaviour. Benefit fraud and unemployment traps, for example, are problems explicitly attributed to the impact of welfare systems on job seekers. This is where the present government has clearly distanced itself from the paradigm of 'non-judgementalism' which was dominant within the British Labour Party until the 1990s.[44]

The problem is, however, that mere positive incentives (that is, higher take-home pay relative to benefits) are unlikely to work for some jobless people because of the effect of long-term unemployment on the behaviour of employers (unemployment functioning as a screening device for recruitment) and on some unemployed (deteriorating work habits, self-esteem etc). Demonstrating a link between lack of skills and long term welfare dependency, empirical research into poverty dynamics in the 1990s[45] has confirmed this notion of hysteresis effects. In addition, labour market research has shown that the rise in employment levels since 1993 has benefited jobless people unevenly, bypassing the relatively high proportion of households with no income earner in the UK.[46] Both types of evidence strengthened the position of those within the Labour Party who advocated a more active and paternalistic approach to social security. A further justification was provided by influential economists who have claimed for some time that stronger benefit conditionality and obligatory training for long-term unemployed would equip participants with new skills, habits and work records. This would make them more 'employable' and thus increase the effective competition for jobs, reducing upward wage pressure.

The shift in centre-left ideology regarding the welfare state appears to have been influenced in part by both conceptual debates on welfare rights and obligations in the US, as well as political strategies adopted by the Clinton administration.[47] While the motives for adopting activation policies must be seen in this context, it is difficult to disentangle those from domestic factors, such as the impact of empirical research mentioned, and electoral expediency in the UK after successive defeats in general elections. Rhetorically, however, the adoption of compulsory programmes for younger claimants has been couched not within an authoritarian but a contractarian terminology, justifying requirements on the part of unemployed with reciprocal obligations on the part of the government to provide better opportunities for training, education and job experience. Here, the difference from Conservative governments of the 1980s and 1990s becomes apparent. While there has been broad implicit agreement with the latter regarding the diagnosis of the problem (welfare dependency), in contrast to its predecessor, the current Labour government has committed itself to increasing expenditure on labour market programmes, which was difficult to justify within a context of one of the central electoral pledges: a commitment to fiscal prudence and to containing public expenditure for some years after the election.

New Deal policies are costly and might require tax increases in the long run. The fact that they were introduced regardless suggests that financial implications were considered less salient than the political profit gained from successfully dealing, or seen to be dealing, with youth unemployment. In addition, three factors helped to justify the financial outlay for activation policies. In the short run, costs were met by revenue from one-off levies on newly privatised companies, which were widely regarded as having unduly profited as a consequence of Conservative governments' drive for privatisation. Secondly, a much improved labour market situation with a steadily decreasing number of young long-term unemployed made policies less expensive and appear successful. Thirdly, singling out young people to participate in activation programmes might have acted as additional legitimation for earmarked increases in public spending. Given the relatively low popularity of social security spending for young unemployed, persuading the broader public to agree with the principle of compulsion for this group was unlikely to be difficult. Within the Labour Party itself, compulsion was much more problematic to justify even until the early 1990s.[48] However, this gradually changed after another defeat in the general election in 1992 and in the wake of party policy changes brought in by Tony Blair since the mid-1990s. In sum, while policy motives are important, the above account gives an indication that their transformation into policies can depend on a range of factors, facilitating motives to become mainstream party policy and providing opportunities for policy implementation.

Denmark: Structural Unemployment and the Problem of a 'Lost Generation'

Several policy strategies can be pursued with the aim of moving people off benefit and into work. The fact that some of those options are much less likely to be applied in some countries than in others indicates the role of unemployment protection systems within the wider political economy of a country.[49] Unemployment benefit levels in Denmark are a good case in point. Although policy rhetoric has suggested otherwise at times, there is a strong motive for any Danish government to maintain a high level of unemployment compensation because of its positive impact on labour mobility. As Jørgen Goul Andersen[50] puts it, Danish unemployment insurance provides 'high protection during unemployment but low protection against unemployment'. In other words, there is a trade-off between generous compensation levels on the one hand and employers' discretion over making workers redundant on the other. As a result, the Danish labour market is highly flexible and unemployment spells, often in the form of temporary layoffs, are fairly common, frequent and dispersed.[51]

Another reason to maintain the generosity of the system is the potential political cost in the face of strong parliamentary and non-parliamentary opposition, particularly from trade unions. Unlike other OECD countries, both the number of trade union members and union density rose rather than dropped when unemployment started to increase in the mid-1970s. Unlike in many other countries, unemployed people retain trade union membership. Not surprisingly, therefore, membership of an unemployment insurance fund is the most important reason for joining a trade union.[52] This gives the latter a strong interest in defending the *status quo*. From this perspective, the acceptance of benefit restrictions and activation policies introduced after 1994 seems surprising. However, the acquiescence in those policies weakened demands for even less palatable policies and might have simply been the price trade unions had to pay for maintaining control over the system.

After having returned to power in 1993, Danish Social Democrats for their part initially did not push for, but reluctantly accepted, demands in favour of more restrictive and directive benefit policies towards the unemployed. To some extent, these can be regarded as the price for deflecting other policies proposed by coalition partners, such as lowering wage levels. However, given the series of labour market reforms and the intensification of activation measures since 1994, it is difficult to assume that policies have merely been imposed, rather than actively pursued, by the strongest government party.

Indeed, by the early 1990s even mainstream Social Democrats seemed to have accepted the need for change. Arguably, the motivation for this can be linked to the 'discovery' of the structural nature of unemployment on the one hand and the growing acceptance of the detrimental effect of long-term unemployment, particularly on young people, on the other. Certainly, the claim that unemployment had become partly structural gained much more credibility in the second half of the 1980s, when a steep rise in employment was only partially reflected in declining levels of unemployment.[53] In addition, social science research in the late 1980s identified tendencies of marginalisation amongst some groups of social security claimants due to a lack of mobility between labour market insiders and outsiders. This applied particularly to younger people who were increasingly portrayed as a potentially 'lost generation' threatened by social exclusion.

This is the context within which a broad consensus gradually emerged across major parties regarding the need to change labour market policies in order to improve the integration into paid work. But how was this to be achieved? Demands by employers and neo-Liberals in favour of lowering wage and benefit reductions were politically unfeasible. Trade unions, for their part, opted for more emphasis on training and education policies. This, however, seemed too much of the same and too little to deal with labour market exclusion. Intense discussions, committee reports and reform proposals in the early 1990s give a clue to the ways in which this *impasse* was overcome.[54] Most indicative was perhaps an early joint report by the Ministry of Finance and Ministry of Social Affairs in 1990, which proposed the activation of passive benefits for all long-term publicly supported persons. Crucially, this was supported by the Social Democrats in opposition at the time and paved the way for labour market reforms implemented after their return to power in 1993. Initially, however, the newly elected Social Democratic government in 1993 responded to high unemployment with improving conditions for permanent and temporary labour market exit and entry (for example, employees taking sabbaticals for childcare or education and being replaced at work by unemployed people). However, once unemployment began to fall, a succession of labour market reforms made exit programmes less financially attractive,[55] restricted unemployment insurance significantly in terms of eligibility and entitlement rights and put an increasingly strong emphasis on mandatory activation policies.

MEANS

It could be argued that Germany has not introduced compulsory activation policies because governments have had little inclination to do so. However, since the early 1980s there have been attempts to abolish (or substantially limit) unemployment assistance and to introduce benefit restriction for younger claimants. What is more, benefit reforms in the mid-1990s restricted suitability criteria and reduced the level of unemployment assistance with the length of unemployment. These could be interpreted as the first signs of a shift from the traditional orientation of a 'status equivalent' social insurance principle towards a system in which benefit and job placement no longer correspond with previous income level and occupational status.[56] However, the reason why this has not been taken further and led towards the adoption of mandatory activation policies has more to do with a lack of means than with a lack of motives. This will be demonstrated with a brief cross-national comparison of institutional capacities for policy making.

In Denmark, policy making is relatively unconstrained except for a potentially major obstacle: governments, which are invariably multi-party and sometimes minority coalitions. At times, this problem has to be overcome by forging majorities on single issues as a result of bargaining with several parties, including those outside the government. More particularly, in the early 1990s the co-operation between centrist parties and the Social Democratic party became much more feasible when the latter moved towards the centre, as indicated with the election of Poul Nyrup Rasmussen as party leader in 1992 and the adoption of a new and more pragmatic party programme.[57] As far as labour market policy is concerned, the adoption of activation policies relied on a broad cross-party consensus which left trade unions as the potentially most powerful obstacle since such a move implied tighter administration of unemployment insurance and enforcement of new rules. However, the (implicit) threat of taking away union responsibility for the system was apparently sufficient to generate compliance. As Jens Lind argued, in order to justify a generous transfer system and its administrative control, trade unions need to demonstrate that unemployment insurance caters exclusively for claimants who are keen to get back into paid work.[58] From this perspective, activation policies can be considered as a compromise. Generous benefit levels were maintained at the cost of conceding more obligations imposed on long-term unemployed persons.

In the UK, a first-past-the-post electoral system and Westminster model of policy making ensures strong central control, which applies particularly to the Labour government due to its substantial majority in the House of Commons after the general election in 1997. A single social insurance fund and central control of both insurance and assistance benefits with no involvement of social partners reduces policy fragmentation. The absence of earnings-related benefits which function as 'deferred wages' in other countries gives very few incentives for trades unions to be involved in matters of social insurance. Other non-parliamentary interest in social security concentrates more on disability or family allowances than on unemployment or insurance-based transfers.

By contrast, the impact of institutional constraints within German policy making is well documented. Important veto points include the independent Central Bank, the Constitutional Court, the bicameral system and the budgetary complexities as a result of the countries' federal structure. More specifically, labour market and security policies are influenced by a compartmentalised funding structure, resulting in apparently perverse policy outcomes at times. For example, because insurance benefits and active labour market programmes are financed out of the same fund, expenditure on the former tends to crowd out the latter whenever unemployment goes up. This leaves depleted resources for re-training or job creation exactly at a time when the need for them increases.[59] Secondly, the disparate funding structure for unemployment compensation can make it rational for a government, intent on curbing public expenditure actually to improve benefit generosity. For example, an extension of the maximum entitlement to insurance benefits prevents, or delays, the transition of claims for unemployment insurance to unemployment assistance, thus shifting some of the fiscal cost of unemployment from general taxation to payroll taxes. This strategy allowed the Kohl government in the 1980s to claim credit for being more generous to (some) unemployed people while at the same time saving (federal) public expenditure.

Two other examples indicate the relevance of institutional structures on reforms in unemployment compensation due to both direct and indirect impacts. As mentioned above, for a federal government intent on cost saving, the tax-funded unemployment assistance rather than contribution-based insurance is the prime target for reform. For example, in 1982 the Social Democratic-led coalition government planned to abolish unemployment assistance for those without prior receipt of unemployment insurance. Such a move would have had adverse financial implications for local authorities due to a much higher uptake of social assistance amongst long-term unemployed. Perhaps not surprisingly, the proposal was successfully blocked by the then Conservative majority in the Bundesrat as the chamber representing the Länder.[60] Interestingly, the same plan resurfaced on two occasions in the 1990s, with the parties proposing and opposing the move having swapped their respective positions. Each time the Bundesrat veto forced the government to either severely reduce the scope for change or abandon plans completely. It is not difficult to see that plans for mandatory (rather than recommended) activation policies, which would have to be implemented and funded at local level, would face the same powerful obstacle.

Secondly, institutional structures categorise claimant groups by type of benefit receipt and thus the relative public support they rely on. For example, the 'equivalence principle' (between contributions and benefits) implies that social insurance transfers function as 'deferred wages', and are thus strongly defended by trade unions. But the notion of quasi-property rights to contributory-based benefits has broad support also within both major parties in Germany. As a consequence, restrictions which are targeted at some claimant groups and not based on insurance-related criteria are very difficult to legislate. A good example is a proposal made by the FDP in 1989. The junior partner in government at the time suggested introducing shorter maximum benefit entitlements for those under the age of 25, differentiated by age. Accused of violating contributory principles, this failed against bitter criticism from opposition parties but also from within the Conservative CDU.

The above examples illustrate the institutional constraints and resistance which mandatory activation policies for recipients of unemployment insurance would face. Activation policies restricted to claimants of means-tested support on the other hand would give rise to considerable budgetary conflicts between federal government, the unemployment insurance fund, other social insurance funds and local authorities. Those would be difficult to negotiate without putting into question the complex system of finance between the different levels of government and para-public organisations.

Of course, demonstrating the role of institutions as constraining policy making is not the same as illustrating their facilitating role. An absence of institutional barriers in Denmark and the UK similar to those in Germany cannot be taken as proof of the significance of institutions for policy formation. In other words, institutional capacities, or means to reform, matter in the sense of facilitating or impeding reform and in terms of making some policies more likely than others. The previous section tried to illustrate this by concentrating on motives for reform. The following section illustrates that motives and means count for little without opportunities for policy implementation.

OPPORTUNITIES

While motives are important, they have to be regarded as dynamic and their strength, and transformation into policy, as dependent on contextual factors. In this case, those factors included Social Democratic parties returning to power at a time when the conditions for introducing activation policies in both the UK and Denmark were favourable in terms of the state of the economy, labour market developments and the incidence of long-term unemployment.

Notwithstanding considerable differences in institutional structures and traditions of labour market and social security policies, there is a degree of commonality surrounding the implementation of activation policies in the UK and Denmark. For example, rhetorically both Social Democratic governments accompanied policies with the portrayal of participation in paid employment as the norm for all in an 'active society' and as the principal means by which to achieve full citizenship.[61] There are also similarities with regard to some policy details (for example, the adoption of individual job seeker and activation agreements). In both countries, policies were justified with reference to high long-term unemployment amongst younger people in particular.

The fact that activation policies were implemented, or significantly reinforced, by centre-left governments points to the relevance of accountability as an important factor for policy reform. While Social Democratic parties have not always and not everywhere been the driving force for welfare state expansion,[62] it is probably safe to argue that the electorates in most European countries associate welfare policies more readily with Social Democratic rather than with Conservative or Liberal parties. At least in principle, this suggests that it might be politically less problematic for a Social Democratic than a Conservative Party to introduce potentially unpopular welfare reforms.[63]

The legitimacy for adopting a more paternalistic stance towards some unemployed groups was further enhanced by labour market conditions.

During the 1980s and early 1990s, high unemployment was characteristic for all three countries, but in the 1990s Germany's position worsened in contrast to substantial improvements in the other two countries (see Table 1). Yet stricter benefit conditionality is more difficult to legitimate and more costly when the availability of jobs is declining. Both Denmark and the UK introduced or intensified activation only after unemployment had begun to drop. The funds initially earmarked for welfare to work programmes for younger people in the UK were not fully required due to much decreased levels of youth unemployment.

Youth unemployment has traditionally been much less of a problem in Germany than in the other two countries. This has only recently changed

TABLE 1
UNEMPLOYMENT RATE AS A PERCENTAGE OF THE TOTAL LABOUR FORCE:
PEAKS AND TROUGHS (1980 TO JULY 1998)

	1980	Peak	Trough	Peak	July 1998*
Denmark	7	9.7 (1983)	6.0 (1986)	10.7 (1993)	4.6
United Kingdom	5.3	11.8 (1984)	6.8 (1990)	10.3 (1993)	6.3
Germany	3.2	7.9 (1985)	5.6 (1991)	10.0 (1997)	9.6

Note: * Eurostatistics (12/1998); seasonally adjusted figures
Source: OECD (1998) Labour Force Statistics 1977–1997.

TABLE 2
YOUTH UNEMPLOYMENT RATE (UNDER 25): PEAKS AND TROUGHS
(1980 TO JULY 1998)

	Peak	Trough	Peak	July 1998*
Denmark	18.9 (1983)	8.1 (1986)	14.6 (1993)	7.5
UK	19.7 (1984)	10 (1989)	17.4 (1993)	6.2
Germany	10.2 (1984)	5.5 (1991)	11.4 (1997)	10.7

Note: * based on Eurostatistics (12/1998); seasonally adjusted figures.
Source: OECD (1998) Labour Force Statistics 1977-1997.

TABLE 3
UNEMPLOYMENT RATE OF THOSE BETWEEN 55 AND 65: PEAKS AND TROUGHS
(1983–97)

	Peak	Trough	Peak	1997
Denmark	6.2 (1983)	5.0 (1986)	8.8 (1993)	5.1
UK	9.4 (1984)	7.2 (1990)	10 (1993)	6.3
Germany	10.8 (1985)	7.3 (1991)**	—	14.5

Notes: * note that unemployment rates in 1997 for those over the age of 65 was 1.1 per cent in Denmark; 3.3 per cent in the UK and zero in Germany; ** break in series.
Source: OECD (1998) Labour Force Statistics 1977-97.

(see Table 2), potentially making a 'lost generation' argument more easily applicable than in the past. On the other hand, long-term unemployment is more concentrated amongst those over the age of 50 in Germany than in the other countries (see Table 3). Empirical data for Germany shows that many above this age are well trained, have long work histories, are out of a job for the first time in their career and many are still in receipt of insurance-based benefits. All of these aspects make mandatory activation programmes harder to justify in Germany than in the other two countries. In addition, the characteristic response to mass unemployment amongst older people in Germany has been to ease labour market exit rather than promote entry. Unemployment insurance has been an important mechanism to achieve this.[64]

In sum, cross-national differences in labour market conditions are crucial constraints on, or opportunities for, claiming policy success. In Denmark, for example, strongly expanding employment meant that many young unemployed were able to find jobs before their activation period was about to begin.[65] Thus, while the effect of activation policies has probably more to do with the state of the labour market than with their design, it is not very difficult for governments to claim that policies have been effective at least to some extent and thus to gain legitimacy for further steps in the same direction.

CONCLUSIONS

As readers of Agatha Christie or Arthur Conan Doyle stories know, the three crucial criteria by which Miss Marple and Sherlock Holmes identify the murderer are motive, means and opportunity. Applied to the introduction of compulsory activation programmes, it could be argued that all three countries have had, in principle, *motives* for improving labour market integration, particularly for younger people. The fact that such policies were actually implemented in the UK and Denmark can partly be attributed to motives of credit claiming. To be seen to be doing something effective against unemployment has remained an important policy objective. By the mid-1990s Social Democratic parties in both Denmark and the UK shared with their predecessors an understanding that traditional social security and labour market policies, and a mere reliance on positive incentives, had failed to overcome problems of labour market integration. Economic and social science research and a general shift in welfare ideology within the centre-left strengthened the acceptance of a more active and, for some groups, paternalistic policy approach.

In Germany, there has been much less agreement regarding both the relevance of structural unemployment or its solution in terms of changing labour market and social security policies. Nevertheless, reform proposals aimed at abolishing unemployment assistance or granting shorter benefit durations for the young unemployed indicate that a lack of motivation was not the only reason for the failure to introduce mandatory activation policies. This is where differences in the *means*, understood as institutional capacity for reform, come in. There are numerous institutional constraints for reforming social security in Germany, both regarding direct impediments (diverse financial implications) as well as normative orientations (the legitimacy of social insurance principles). By contrast, the lack of vested interests in social security (perhaps outside pensions policy) combined with the Westminster system enables relatively straightforward policy formulation and implementation in the UK. In Denmark, the potential obstacle of sometimes volatile minority coalition governments can be overcome by forging broad compromises and shifting issue coalitions even with parties not represented in the cabinet. Trade unions have a strong vested interest in unemployment insurance and activation policies were conceded as the price for avoiding more substantial benefit restrictions.

Finally, *opportunities* are important factors facilitating or impeding reforms in terms of legitimacy. The return to power of Social Democratic governments as traditional advocates of welfare rights at a certain time, that is, when unemployment was in decline, was conducive in both the UK and Denmark. Similarly, a broad, albeit often implicit, party consensus of policy problems provided the ground for the adoption of compulsory activation policies which Conservative parties found difficult to oppose. Relatively low financial outlays and a decline in unemployment – and thus an apparent success of early policies – eased the legitimacy of these policies and their further development. None of the above factors applies to Germany, where youth unemployment has become a serious problem only recently and restricting benefit rights based on non-contributory criteria such as age are difficult to legislate.

Of course, the reference to motives, means and opportunities has limits. Neatly separated for literary purposes, in policy making the picture becomes messy with means and opportunities affecting motives and the latter changing means and influencing opportunities in turn. Besides, the introduction of activation policies is not a criminal act and it is not yet clear whether the 'committing' governments will 'get away with it', maybe even with lasting success, being able to claim credit for achieving both social inclusion and labour market improvement. If this is to be the case, it might be the German government which will be punished for having failed to 'commit' reforms in time. At present, both the Danish and the British governments can be seen as claiming success (rather than avoiding blame), since there are few who currently regard activation policies as welfare retrenchment and young people as 'victims' of the latter. However, if labour market conditions should seriously deteriorate, activation policies will become not only much more expensive but also potentially less successful, and thus more likely to be perceived as welfare retrenchment than merely restructuring.

NOTES

I should like to thank Giuliano Bonoli, Daniel Clegg, Bob Cox, Markus Haverland and members of the European Forum 1998/99 at the European University Institute for critical comments on an earlier version of the article. I am grateful to Jørgen Goul Andersen, Alan Deacon, Hubert Heinelt and Jon Kvist for comments regarding the questions of motives for the introduction of activation policies.

1. G. Esping-Andersen, *the Three Worlds of Welfare Capitalism* (Oxford: Polity Press 1990).
2. H. Ganssmann and M. Hass, 'Flexibilität und Rigidität auf den Arbeitsmärkten in den Niederlanden, Schweden und Dänemark' (mimeo, Free University of Berlin: Department of Sociology 1998); A. Hemerijk and M. Schludi, 'Policy Adjustments under International Constraints: Sequences of Challenges and Responses', *Conference Article Ws/46*, European Forum (Florence: European University institute 1999).
3. European Commission, *Social Protection in Europe 1997*, Employment and Social Affairs, DG V (Luxembourg: Office for Official Publications of the European Communities 1998); OECD, *The OECD Jobs Study: Evidence and Explanations; Part 1: Labour Market Trends and Underlying Forces of Change; Part 2: The Adjustment Potential af the Labour Market* (Paris: OECD 1994).
4. See A. Sinfield, 'Blaming the Benefit: The Costs of the Distinction Between Active and Passive Programmes', in J. Holmer and J.C. Karlsson (eds.), *Work – Quo Vadis? Re-Thinking the Question of Work* (Aldershot: Ashgate 1997); J. Clasen, 'Unemployment Compensation and other Labour Market Policies', in J. Clasen (ed.), *Comparative Social Policy: Concepts, Theories and Methods* (Oxford: Blackwell 1999).
5. H. Bolderson and D. Mabbett, *Delivering Social Security: A Cross-National Study*, Department of Social Security, Research Report 59 (London: The Stationery Office 1997).
6. J. Kvist, 'Complexities in Assessing Unemployment Benefits and Policies', *International Social Security Review* 51/4 (1998), pp.33–55.
7. D. Geldof, 'New Activation Policies: Promises and Risks', in European Foundation (ed.), *Linking Welfare and Work* (Dublin: European Foundation for the Improvement of Living and Working Conditions 1999).
8. R.H. Cox, 'From Safety Net to Trampoline, Labor Market Activation in the Netherlands and Denmark', *Governance* 11/4 (1998), pp.397–414; B. Hvinden, 'Activation: A Nordic Perspective', in European Foundation (ed.), *Linking Welfare and Work*.
9. F. Ross, 'A Framework for Studying Unpopular Policies: Partisan Possibilities, Institutional Liabilities and the Anti-State Agenda', *Seminar Article Ws/9*, European Forum (Florence: European University Institute 1998).
10. R.K. Weaver, 'The Politics of Blame Avoidance', *Journal of Public Policy* 6 (1986). pp.371–98.
11. S. Steinmo, K. Thelen and F. Longstreth (eds.), *Structuring Politics. Historical Institutionalism in Comparative Perspective* (Cambridge: Cambridge University Press 1992).
12. P.A. Hall, 'Policy Paradigms, Social Learning, and the State: The Case of Economic Policymaking in Britain', *Comparative Politics* 25/3 (1993), pp.275–96.
13. P. Pierson, 'Irresistible forces, Immovable Objects: Post-industrial Welfare States Confront Permanent Austerity', *Journal of European Public Policy* 5/4 (1998), pp.539–60.
14. Hall, 'Policy Paradigms'.
15. Cox, 'From Safety Net to Trampoline'.

16. W. Van Oorschot, 'Work, Work, Work: Labour Market Participation Policies in the Netherlands (1970–2000)', *Conference Article Ws/70*, European Forum (Florence: European University institute 1999).
17. J.W. Kingdon, *Agendas, Alternatives and Public Policies*, 2nd edn (New York: Harper Collins 1995).
18. I owe this suggestion to Richard Freeman.
19. See Ministerie Van Sociale Zaken En Werkgelegenheid, *Unemployment Benefits and Social Assistance in Seven European Countries*, Werkdocumenten No. 53 (Den Haag: Ministerie Van Sociale Zaken En Werkgelegenheid 1995); OECD, *The OECD Jobs Study*.
20. See European Commission, *Social Protection in Europe 1997*; OECD, *The OECD Jobs Study*.
21. J. Goul Andersen, 'Marginalization, Citizenship and the Economy: The Capacities of the Universalist Welfare State in Denmark', in E.O. Eriksen and J. Loftager (eds.), *The Rationality of the Welfare State* (Oslo: Scandinavian University Press 1997), p.169.
22. See also N. Ploug and J. Kvist, *Social Security in Europe* (The Hague: Kluwer Law International 1996).
23. PLS Consult and P. Jensen, *Labour Market Studies – Denmark* (European Commission, Luxembourg: Office for Official Publications of the European Communities 1996), p.51.
24. Goul Andersen, 'Marginalization, Citizenship and the Economy', p.162.
25. J.E. Larsen, *The Welfare State and Unemployment Policies in Denmark and Other European Countries*, Research Report (Copenhagen University: Institute of Political Science 1991).
26. J. Goul Andersen, 'Welfare Crisis and Beyond: Danish Welfare Policies in the 1980s and 1990s', in S. Kuhnle (ed.), *The Survival of the European Welfare State* (London: Routledge, 2000, forthcoming).
27. P. Jensen, 'Activation of the Unemployed in Denmark since the Early 1990s: Welfare or Workfare?', Centre for Comparative Welfare State Studies (CCWS), *Working Article 1/1999* (Aalborg: Aalborg University 1999).
28. J. Torfing, 'Workfare With Welfare: Recent Reforms of the Danish Welfare State', *Journal of European Social Policy* 9/1 (1999), pp.5–28.
29. Ibid.
30. Goul Andersen, 'Welfare Crisis and Beyond'.
31. J. Clasen, A. Gould and J. Vincent, *Voices Within and Without: Responses to Long-Term Unemployment in Germany, Sweden and Britain* (Bristol: Policy Press 1998).
32. Deutscher Städtetag, *Kommunale Beschäftigungsförderung* (Cologne: Deutscher Städtetag 1997).
33. G. Schmid and B. Reissert, 'Do Institutions Make A Difference? Financing Systems of Labor Market Policy', *Journal of Public Policy* 8/2 (1988), pp.125–49.
34. Ploug and Kvist, *Social Security in Europe*, p.65.
35. A. Erskine, 'The Withering of Social Insurance in Britain', in J. Clasen (ed.), *Social Insurance in Europe* (Bristol: Policy Press 1997).
36. D. Finn, 'The Stricter Benefit Regime and the New Deal for the Unemployed', article presented at the Social Policy Association, 31st Annual Conference (University of Lincolnshire and Humberside, June 1997).
37. R. Plant., 'So You Want to Be A Citizen', *New Statesman*, 6 Feb. 1998.
38. See Cm 3805, 'New Ambitions for Our Country: A New Contract for Welfare' (London: The Stationery Office 1998).
39. A. Deacon, 'Benefit Sanctions for the Jobless: "Tough Love" Or Rough Treatment?', *Employment Policy Institute Economic Report* 11/7 (London: Employment Policy Institute 1997); R. Warton, R. Walker and S. McKay, 'Implementing "Welfare to Work" in Britain: Evidence from Applied Research' (mimeo, Loughborough University, Centre for Reseach in Social Policy 1998); D. Finn, 'From Full Employment to Full Employability: New Labour and the Unemployed', *Conference Article Ws/69* European Forum (Florence: European University Institute April 1999).
40. A. Graham, 'The UK 1979–95: Myths, and Realities of Conservative Capitalism', in C. Crouch and W. Streek (eds.), *Political Economy of Modern Capitalism* (London: Sage 1997).
41. P. Edwards, 'Great Britain: From Partial Collectivism to Neo-Liberalism to Where?', in A. Ferner and R. Hyman (eds.), *Changing Industrial Relations in Europe* (Oxford: Blackwell 1998).

42. A. Goodman, P. Johnson and S. Webb, *Inequalities in the UK* (Oxford: Oxford University Press 1997).
43. See Deacon, 'Benefit Sanctions for the Jobless'; Warton *et al.*, 'Implementing '"Welfare to Work" in Britain'; Finn, 'From Full Employment to Full Employability'; and A. Deacon, 'The Green Article on Welfare Reform: A Case for Enlightened Self Interest?', *Political Quarterly* 69 (1998), pp.306–11; A. Deacon, 'But Not Just America: the influence of European and American Ideas Upon "New Labour" Thinking on Welfare Reform', Article Presented to the Conference on 'Global Trajectories: Ideas, Transnational Policy Transfer and 'Models' ofWelfare Reform', European Forum (Florence: European University institute March 1999).
44. Deacon, 'But Not Just America'.
45. for an overview, see L. Leisering and R. Walker (eds.), *The Dynamics of Modern Society: Poverty, Policy and Welfare* (Bristol: The Policy Press 1998).
46. P. Gregg and J. Wadsworth, 'It Takes Two: Employment Polarisation in the OECD', *Discussion Article No 304*, Centre for Economic Performance (London: London School of Economics 1996).
47. Deacon, 'But Not Just America'; D. King and D. Wickham-Jones, 'From Clinton to Blair: The Democratic (Party) Origins of Welfare to Work', *Political Quarterly* 70/1 (1999), pp.62–74.
48. King and Wickham-Jones, 'From Clinton to Blair'.
49. J. Clasen, 'Beyond Social Security: the Economic Value of Giving Money to Unemployed People', *European Journal of Social Security* 1/2 (1999), pp.151–79.
50. Goul Andersen, 'Welfare Crisis and Beyond'.
51. T. Boje and P.K. Madsen, 'Wage Formation and Incomes Policy in Denmark', in R. Dore, R. Boyer and Z. Mars (eds.), *The Return of Income Policy* (London: Pinter 1994).
52. J. Lind, 'Trade Unions: Social Movement or Welfare Apparatus?', in P. Leisink, J. Van Leemput and J. Vilrokx (eds.), *Challenges to Trade Unions in Europe* (Cheltenham: Edward Elgar 1996).
53. Boje and Madsen, 'Wage Formation and Incomes Policy in Denmark'; J. Lind, 'Social Chapters and the Regulation of the Labour Market', Discussion Article (Aalborg: University of Aalborg 1997); P.K. Madsen, 'Das Dänische "Beschäftigungswunder"', *Die Mitbestimmung* 5 (1998), pp.36–8.
54. K. Nielsen, 'Learning to Manage the Supply Side: Flexibility and Stability in Denmark', in B. Jessop *et al.* (eds.), *The Politics of Flexibility. Restructuring State and Industry in Britain, Germany and Scandinavia* (Aldershot: Edward Elgar 1991).
55. Madsen, 'Das Dänische "Beschäftigungswunder"'; P.K. Madsen, 'Labour Market Policy Reform in Denmark. From Rules and Regulations to Worksharing and Decentralisation', in I. Hamsher and J. Stanyer (eds.), *Contemporary Political Studies*, Vol. III, PSA (Oxford: Blackwell 1996).
56. H. Heinelt and M. Weck, *Arbeitsmarktpolitik. Vom Vereinigungskonsens Zur Standortdebatte* (Opladen: Leske und Budrich 1998).
57. S. Marklund and A. Nordlund, 'Economic Problems, Welfare Convergence and Political Instability', in M. Kautto *et al.* (eds.), *Nordic Social Policy* (London: Routledge 1999).
58. Boje and Madsen, 'Wage Formation and Incomes Policy in Denmark'; Lind, 'Social Chapters and the Regulation of the Labour Market'; Madsen, 'Das Dänische "Beschäftigungswunder"'.
59. G. Schmid, B. Reissert and G. Bruche, *Unemployment Insurance and Active Labour Market Policy. An International Comparison of Financing Systems* (Detroit: Wayne State University Press 1992).
60. J. Clasen, *Paying the Jobless. A Comparison of Unemployment Benefit Policies in Great Britain and Germany* (Aldershot: Avebury 1994).
61. W. Walters, 'The "Active" Society: New Designs for Social Policy', *Policy and Politics* 25/3 (1997), pp.221–34.
62. P. Baldwin, *The Politics of Social Solidarity. Class Bases of the European Welfare State 1875–1975* (Cambridge: Cambridge University Press 1991).
63. Ross, 'A Framework for Studying Unpopular Policies'.
64. M. Oppen, 'Concerted Cooperation and Immobilism: Labour Policy in Germany and the Regulation of Early Exit', in M. Muramatsu and F. Naschold (eds.), *State and Administration in Japan and Germany* (Berlin: Walter De Gruyter 1997); P. Manow and E. Seils, 'Globalization and the Welfare State: Germany', Workshop Article, European Forum (Florence: European University institute October 1998).
65. Goul Andersen, 'Welfare Crisis and Beyond'.

'Defrosting' the French Welfare State

BRUNO PALIER

Since the mid-1970s, the Western welfare states have found themselves in new circumstances. After a period of analysis of the welfare state crisis during the 1980s, more and more studies have focused during the 1990s on the actual welfare state changes that have occurred (or not) during the last 25 years. Probably under Anglo-Saxon influence – Ronald Reagan and Margaret Thatcher had explicit anti-welfare agendas – the early analyses were phrased in terms of retrenchment (after the golden age of growth). They sought to discover how far governments had reduced social expenditure since the late 1970s. In 1994, Paul Pierson emphasised the stability of welfare arrangements when comparing Reagan's or Thatcher's ambitions to the actual outcomes of their reforms. He explained this resistance to change by the force of past commitments, the political weight of welfare constituencies and the inertia of institutional arrangements which all engender a phenomenon of path dependency. He concludes that: 'Any attempt to understand the politics of welfare state retrenchment must start from a recognition that social policy remains the most resilient component of the post-war order.'[1] Broadening the scope to other developed countries to analyse 'national adaptation in global economies',[2] Gøsta Esping-Andersen came to a similar conclusion, depicting a generally frozen landscape and emphasising the rigidity of the continental welfare state arrangements. He concluded that 'the cards are very much stacked in favour of the welfare state status quo'.[3] Even though the conclusion was again that no dramatic changes could be (fore)seen, analyses of different welfare regime's developments did allow a differentiation of the general notion of retrenchment into different processes linked with the specific institutions of each welfare system.

However, John Myles and Gill Quadagno demonstrated that things were not so rigid. Some changes could be identified, specifically in pension reforms,[4] even if, as Pierson and Myles have recently argued, these changes were always path-dependent. For while they often reduce the level of benefits, all pension reforms are framed by past commitments and specific institutional arrangements. They operate differently and each perpetuates (and sometimes even reinforces) the historical logic in which the pension system has developed.[5] Thus, to date, welfare state analyses have concluded that the last 25 years have shown either little retrenchment and great stability or path-dependent changes. Even if they partially reduce its expenditure on certain programmes, recent reforms do not change the *nature* of post-war welfare states.

In another field of state intervention, analyses show that policy changes can be more diverse and much more profound. When analysing economic policy changes, Peter Hall has shown that policy making usually involves 'three central variables: the overarching goals that guide policy in a particular field, the techniques or policy instruments used to attain those goals, and the precise settings of these instruments'.[6] Building on these distinctions, he has identified three distinct kinds of changes in policy: first order changes, that is, changes in the levels (or settings) of the basic instruments while the overall goals and instruments of policy remain the same; second order changes, when the instruments of policy as well as their settings are altered in response to past experience but the overall goals of policy still remain the same; and third order changes, when simultaneous changes in all three components of policy ('the instrument settings, the instruments themselves, and the hierarchy of goals behind policy') occur.[7]

If we apply this framework of analysis to recent work on welfare state changes, we can say that the reduction of the level of benefits, the most commonly analysed retrenchments, are first order changes; that path-dependent changes (that is, the introduction of new calculation rules, new kinds of entitlements or benefits) are second order changes since they remain within the same historical and political logic; and, apparently, no third order changes can be identified in recent welfare reforms. This raises the question of whether the welfare state is so resistant that no structural or 'paradigmatic' changes (implying new instruments and new goals, a new logic) can be introduced in this field?

France is a good case study for addressing this question since, among the 'frozen' continental European welfare states, the French social welfare system is often seen as one of the most 'immovable'.[8] This study will analyse most of the welfare system changes that have occurred in France during the last 25 years, and will argue that during this period French governments have implemented all three orders of change to cope with their welfare state problems. During the late 1970s and the 1980s, they have dealt with social security deficits mainly by raising the level of social contributions; these policies, which simply changed the level of the available instrument, introduced first order changes. In the early 1990s there appeared second order changes with the sectoral reforms – new medical agreements in health care, a new benefit in unemployment insurance and new modes of calculation for retirement benefits. They introduced new instruments, but remained within the traditional (historical and institutional) logic of French welfare system. Since these two kinds of changes appeared insufficient and since the French welfare system itself appeared to create economic and social problems (unemployment, social exclusion), governments have also decided to act indirectly in reforming the institutional causes of these problems. The French welfare state was felt to be so resistant to changes that governments decided to introduce structural reforms so that it would become less immovable. These structural reforms – new means-tested re-insertion policies (RMI), new financing mechanisms (CSG) and a new role for the state – imply both new instruments and a new logic of welfare, that is, third order changes. The conclusion is that the eurosclerosis or the path-dependent continuity theses neglect certain reforms which may imply profound welfare state changes.

After a rapid sketch of the main traits of French social protection system, an analysis will be offered of the first governmental reactions (late 1970s and 1980s) to social security deficits, which implied no real changes of the French system. We will then focus on the sectoral reforms of the 1990s, which introduced limited retrenchment, and then show that, because of the limitations of these two kinds of reforms, the welfare system has been perceived not only as a victim, but also as a cause of economic and social problems. This new perception explain the occurrence of structural reforms implying a change of instruments and goals within some part of the system, which will be analysed afterwards. The final section will present the main political condition for the appearance of such structural reforms.

SOCIAL PROTECTION IN FRANCE: A FRAGMENTED SOCIAL
INSURANCE SYSTEM, APART FROM THE STATE

If one looks at its institutions (techniques or policy instruments) and its general goals, the French social protection system is an illustration of the continental Christian Democratic way of providing welfare. Its general aim is income maintenance, much more than poverty alleviation (as in a liberal welfare regime) or universalistic redistribution (as in social-democratic one). The main component of the French welfare system clearly reflects the Bismarckian tradition of social insurance: in France, entitlement is conditional upon a contribution record; most benefits are earnings-related; financing is provided mainly by employers' and employees' contributions; and the social partners are greatly involved in the management of the system.

The French social welfare system is mainly based on a specific set of non-state agencies, called *la Sécurité sociale*, built up from 1945 to the 1970s. This system is divided into a number of different sectors (*branches*): health care, old age, family and unemployment insurance, and highly fragmented into different schemes (*régimes*) covering different occupational groups. There is a set of compulsory basic schemes, to which anyone working must be affiliated, and a further set of complementary schemes (improving the coverage level), which may be compulsory or not. Schemes are made up of different funds (*Caisses*) organised at national, regional and local levels. Their staff is neither paid by the state, nor under its authority. Each fund is headed by a governing board comprising representatives of employers and employees, with a chairman elected from their ranks, and a director of the fund, who is appointed by the governing board in liaison with the Ministry of Social Affairs. The system is supposed to be managed by those who pay for it and have an interest in it, subject to only limited control by the state, which is supposed to have only a supervisory role called *la tutelle*. In the French welfare system, the state is thus characterised by a very low level of autonomy, even though it generally decides the level of benefits and contributions, since the social partners did not want to do so, especially when these decision became difficult to take in the early 1970s.

THE SOCIAL SECURITY DEFICIT

This section examines the first government reactions to social security problems and emphasises that the difficulties encountered by the French welfare state are quite different from those faced by the liberal or the Scandinavian ones. It then shows that, until the late 1980s, the main public response was to raise the level of social contributions, which implied only first order changes. This preference for raising resources instead of cutting benefits can mainly be understood in reference to the financing mechanisms, which are based on social contribution and not taxes.

Like anywhere else, France has encountered important economic difficulties since 1973. However, the consequences of these difficulties in the social protection area took a particular form. The first consequence for the social insurance system was the appearance in 1974 and the development thereafter of a 'social security deficit' (*trou de la Sécurité sociale*). As the social insurance system is not part of the state in France, its budget is presented separately. It is therefore possible to isolate a specific deficit which is not treated as a public deficit but as a specific problem of *la Sécurité sociale*. This deficit is understood as a consequence of both decreasing resources (less economic growth, that is, lower wage increases, more inactive or unemployed people who do not pay social contribution) and increasing expenses (more unemployed people, more demands in health and old age).

After years of positive balance, the deficit of the main social insurance scheme[9] budget was 2.8 per cent of its resources in 1974, four per cent in 1978, around two per cent from 1981 to 1987, between 0.9 per cent and 1.8 per cent from 1988 to 1992, and around five per cent from 1993 to 1996. It has progressively diminished since to 0.3 per cent in 1999 (various reports of the *Commission des Comptes de la Sécurité Sociale*). To deal with this problem, from 1975 to 1995, French governments all adopted the same approach: a dramatisation of the situation of *la Sécurité sociale*, emphasising – and sometimes exaggerating – the importance of the deficit[10] and the need to save the system by finding new resources and reducing the expenses. The rhetoric is based on the idea that the system is in danger and must be rescued, and not, as when the welfare system is part of the state, that it is too costly and ineffective. Following up on this rhetoric, there appeared a series of measures aimed at increasing resources and diminishing expenses. As the state is not supposed to interfere in the system, and as its decision will inevitably be unpopular (either in increasing social contributions or in lowering benefits), dramatisation is very important for justifying the decision.

The French population is very attached to its social insurance system, and any attempt to reform it is perceived as an attack. And the more the system is threatened, the more the population is attached to it. During the 1980s, all polls showed that more than 80 per cent of the French population would consider it very damaging if the *Sécurité sociale* was dismantled. This is similar to the situation portrayed by Pierson in his analysis of the UK and USA.[11] But, beyond this general similarity, the politics are not the same since the legitimacy of French social protection as well as its constituencies are quite different from those associated with the liberal welfare states.

Since the early 1970s, each member of the population is supposed to be covered by one social insurance fund and actually receives quite generous benefits from it. Meanwhile, its fragmented corporatist organisation guarantees each social group that its specific interests are protected. The French social insurance system has therefore created a large constituency among all salaried workers. In the UK or USA, the interest groups associated with social policies (retired people, patients, doctors, social worker and so on) are much more limited. The French salaried workers' constituency is represented by the trade unions, who are legitimate participants in the debate on welfare reform since social security is financed by social contributions paid by labour, and because they take part in its management. This particular institutional setting generates a tension between governments (regardless of political persuasion) and the trade unions. Trade unions are widely regarded as those who defends the current system against governments who are suspected of dismantling it when trying to cope with its deficit.[12] This is in sharp contrast to the British or American cases, where welfare state problems do not appear to concern trade unions.

These differences in politics partly explain why the reaction of French governments is different from those of the British or American. First, instead of developing a rhetoric against the welfare state which would provoke the whole population and trade unions, they recognise the importance of the *Sécurité sociale*, but underline its dangerous current situation (because of the deficit) and the deficiency of existing measures which are not aimed at reforming the system but only at restoring it to viability. Until the early 1990s, no French government, left or right, even the most neo-liberal one (when Jacques Chirac was Prime Minister, 1986–88), aspired to dismantle the system, or even to change it. Second, as they have to justify their intervention in the public's eyes by dramatising the situation, they focus the attention on their intervention and do not try to hide it. If they tried to avoid blame, the French governments do it less by 'obfuscating' retrenchment measures[13] than by avoiding any decision which could appear as unnecessarily changing the system.

Increasing Resources rather than Retrenching Benefits

From 1975 to 1993, unless an election was on the agenda, each time a deficit of the *Sécurité sociale* was announced this was followed by the presentation of different measures gathered in a *plan de redressement des comptes de la Sécurité sociale* (programme for balancing the social insurance system's budget), consisting typically of increases in contributions paid by employees and economising measures, mainly in health.

The content of these plans show that when they try to 'square the welfare circle',[14] French governments prefer to increase revenue than to reduce expenditure. If one refers to Vic George's list of eight different methods used by European governments to reduce social expenditure,[15] one can only find two of them within all the plans implemented in France: the progressive introduction of an annual budget for the French hospital system during the 1980s, and change of the indexation method from wages to prices for family allowances (one of the rare universal flat-rate benefits in the French system). To save money, between 1975 and 1992, these plans have mainly increased users' charges, through a gradual lowering of the level of reimbursement of health care expenditure. In 1980, 76.5 per cent of health expenditure paid by the insured person was reimbursed by the basic social insurance funds, falling to 74 per cent in 1990 and 73.9 per cent in 1995. During the same period, all contributory benefits like sickness pay, old age pensions and unemployment insurance benefits have increased or at the

TABLE 1
THE DEVELOPMENT OF SOCIAL PROTECTION SPENDING
(IN BILLION FRANCS – CURRENT PRICES – AND IN % PER YEAR)

	Total spending	Old age	Health care insurance	Family benefits	Unemployment insurance	Evolution of prices
1981	820.643	332.097	207.065	117.872	44.316	
1982	982.833	389.738	243.528	139.454	55.668	+ 11.79 %
	+19.76 %	+17.36 %	+17.61 %	+18.31 %	+25.62 %	
1983	1 104.971	437.362	270.433	158.504	53.707	+ 9.64 %
	+12.43 %	+12.22 %	+11.05 %	+13.66 %	-3.52 %	
1984	1 225.303	484.063	304.865	173.216	62.747	+ 7.41 %
	+10.89 %	+10.68 %	+12.73 %	+9.28 %	+16.83 %	
1985	1 325.306	530.811	325.868	181.940	65.634	+ 5.84 %
	+8.16 %	+9.66 %	+6.89 %	+5.04 %	+4.60 %	
1986	1 416.907	568.161	352.379	190.837	73.189	+ 2.64 %
	+6.91 %	+7.04 %	+8.14 %	+4.89 %	+11.51 %	
1987	1.473.808	595.850	363.988	199.341	79.501	+ 3.14 %
	+4.02 %	+4.87 %	+3.29 %	+4.46 %	+8.62 %	
1988	1 570.661	639.714	389.748	210.137	86.324	+ 2.69 %
	+6.57 %	+7.36 %	+7.08 %	+5.42 %	+8.58 %	
1989	1 669.736	683.435	426.174	217.063	89.769	+ 3.64 %
	+6.31 %	+6.83 %	+9.35 %	+3.30 %	+3.99 %	
1990	1 773.818	732.280	454.857	224.801	95.309	+ 3.37 %
	+6.23 %	+7.15 %	+6.73 %	+3.56 %	+6.17 %	
1991	1 886.936	779.586	484.000	232.346	111.956	+ 3.21 %
	+6.38 %	+6.46 %	+6.41 %	+3.36 %	+17.47 %	
1992	2 007.868	831.895	518.008	242.938	125.205	+ 2.33 %
	+6.41 %	+6.71 %	+7.03 %	+4.56 %	+11.83 %	
1993	2 136.365	878.285	545.346	261.411	133.681	+ 1.80 %
	+6.40 %	+5.58 %	+5.28 %	+7.60 %	+6.77 %	
1994	2 202.247	910.472	561.657	269.164	129.375	+ 1.40 %
	+3.08 %	+3.66 %	+2.99 %	+2.97 %	-3.22 %	
1995	2 287.462	954.474	587.952	280.438	125.417	+ 1.65 %
	+3.87 %	+4.83 %	+4.68 %	+4.19 %	-3.06 %	

Sources: SESI, Comptes de la Protection sociale and Ministère du Budget, Direction de la prévision.

TABLE 2
TRANSFORMATION OF THE STRUCTURE OF TAXATION IN FRANCE (%)

	Average 1970–75	Average 1981–85	Average 1988–92	1992	1995
State taxation (VAT, income tax, on companies, assets, oil tax…)	59.2	53.4	51.4	50.1	51.5
Social contribution	39.0	44.8	46.1	47.4	46.2
European tax	1.8	1.8	2.5	2.5	2.3

Source: INSEE, Tableaux de l'économie française 1996–1997.

very least been stabilised. Consequently, social expenditure has continue to increase rapidly until the mid-1980s, and more slowly ever since (see Table 1). The ratio of social protection expenditure to GDP grew from 19.4 per cent in 1974 to 27.29 per cent in 1985 and 27.75 per cent in 1992.[16]

However, between 1975 and 1991, these plans gradually achieved their goal. From one year to the next, the deficit did not accumulate so as to form a debt. Increases in expenses have always been compensated for by an increase in resources. During the 1980s, while they were decreasing the level of direct income taxation, French governments were simultaneously raising the level of social contributions paid by employees. Thus, within taxation, the share of social contributions has increased dramatically (see Table 2) as well as in terms of their proportion of GDP. In 1978, the volume of social contributions was less than 20 per cent of French GDP, and almost 23 per cent in 1985, from which point it stabilised.[17]

In France – as well as in other continental or southern countries, governments have long preferred raising social contributions to cutting social benefits. This is counter-intuitive from an Anglo-Saxon (and even a Scandinavian) point of view, where the most politically risky thing to do is to raise taxes, which the population much prefers some cuts in social programmes. This is due to differences in the type of benefits and, moreover, in the ways they are financed. In France, most of the cash benefits are contributory earnings-related benefits. And the bulk of social expenditure, around 80 per cent, is financed through employment-related contributions.

On the benefits side, it is more feasible to reduce flat-rate or means-tested benefits than earnings-related ones. Since earnings-related benefits are expressed as a proportion of a salary, there is a form of 'automatic' indexation on earnings, which tends to be the most generous form of indexation. In this respect, the strategy of incremental reduction of the relative value of a benefit through a shift in indexation to consumer prices, which has been used in Britain, is *de facto* not available to French policy makers.[18] When benefit indexation mechanisms are based on consumer prices, the residualisation of cash benefits occurs automatically, without the need for active government intervention.[19] In contrast, in the French case, benefits remain constant in terms of replacement rates unless cuts in the benefit formula are adopted. These are highly visible and politically difficult to implement, especially because, as they are contributory, people think that they have 'bought' their own social benefits through the social contribution they have paid. In France, each *branche* (health, old age, unemployment insurance, family benefits) has its own contribution which appears on every French employee's pay slip. The link between payment and entitlement is very visible. When you pay health insurance contribution, for instance, you 'buy' your right to health care which guarantees that you will be protected whenever sick.

The difference in the financing mechanisms is essential. Whereas taxation goes to the state, social contribution is perceived as a 'deferred wage' which will come back when the insured person will be sick, unemployed or aged. When Reagan, Thatcher or Major could denounce the excessive weight of taxes and the excessive cost of the social benefits delivered to those who do nothing, it was much more difficult for French politicians to attack social insurance rights acquired by all the working population through the payment of social contribution. It was much easier to raise social contributions, as long as it was to preserve the social rights of all and the level of their benefits. Social enquiries show that, during the 1980s, the French preferred to pay more contributions than to see cuts in their benefits.[20]

Until the early 1990s, there were no real incentives in France to retrench social expenditure since, as described above, its growth has been financed through an increase of social contribution. None of the *plans de redressement des comptes de la Sécurité sociale* – the main form of governmental intervention in social protection during the 1980s – have introduced important changes within the French system. They have only changed the settings of the disposable instruments (raising the rate of social contributions, lowering certain benefits levels). It is only when the social security deficit has become too great to be financed through another social contribution rise (after 1992) in a context of economic recession (especially in 1993) and when the economic constraints of the European Single market and single currency became stronger, that the French government decided (felt obliged) to opt for retrenchment in the social protection system.

SECTOR AL REFORMS

We now turn to the main sectoral reforms, which imply the introduction of new instruments within the French social protection system: a new unemployment insurance benefit (AUD), new rules of calculation in the retirement pension system and the development of 'medical agreements' in health care. These path-dependent reforms imply continuity in the historical and institutional logic as well as in the rate of growth of the social expenditure.

Unemployment Compensation

In 1945, building an unemployment insurance scheme was not seen as a priority since the country was short of workers. Unemployment insurance was created in 1958, outside the state, through an agreement between the representatives of employers and employees, who were responsible for setting rates of contributions and benefits. The system provided various benefits which were periodically increased from 1974 to the early 1980s. Before 1982, the wage replacement rate was 80 per cent for half of the unemployed during the first year. In 1982, the benefits were reduced to 75 per cent for the following nine months.[21] From 1982 to 1992, there were several attempts to rationalise the system and to stabilise the level of the benefits, which remained, however, very generous. During the 1980s, the main problem was the number of different unemployment insurance benefits (at least five) and the difficulty of controlling and rationalising the evolution of the system: it was beyond the control of the state and difficult to manage through agreements between the social partners.

The second trend in the policies towards the unemployed during the 1980s has been called *le traitement social du chômage* (social treatment of unemployment). As has been well described for Germany or Italy by Esping-Andersen,[22] the aim of these policies is to remove the oldest workers from the labour market. In 1981, the legal age for retirement was lowered from 65 to 60. There has been a massive use of early retirement: from 84,000 early retired people in 1975 to 159,000 in 1979, 317,000 in 1981 and 705,000 in 1983.[23] Governments also created 'assisted jobs' (*emplois aidés*) for the young and the long-term unemployed. With the numerous contracts proposed to the unemployed, the state assumed more and more a role of employer of second resort.

It was only in the late 1980s that problems in this area began to be phrased in terms of necessary retrenchment. Since the late 1980s, early retirement has been seen as too expensive an instrument and has been limited in its use (the number of early retired people fell from 705,000 in

1983 to 433,000 in 1988[24]). The main reform of the unemployment insurance system was adopted in 1992 through an agreement between employers and some employees' representatives (the CFDT union[25]). The reform involved the replacement of all the different unemployment insurance benefits by only one 'digressive' benefit (which decreases with time) known as the *Allocation Unique Dégressive* (AUD).

The new unemployment insurance benefit is payable only for a limited period of time, which depends on the contribution record. The amount of the benefit depends on the level of contribution and decreases with time. For instance, a person who had worked at least 14 months of the last 24 would receive full benefit for nine months, then lose 17 per cent of the benefit at six-monthly intervals (the intervals were four months between 1992 and 1996). While entitlement to the main unemployment insurance benefit runs out after 30 months, a variety of measures exist to extend the cover provided by the unemployment insurance funds. Most important of these is the *Allocation de Solidarité Spécifique* (ASS), which is subject to a means test, but is still contributory. The level and the volume of unemployment benefits started to decrease after 1992 (see Table 1). As the AUD was delivering less money for a shorter period, the means-tested benefits played a more important role.

In unemployment compensation, the 1990s are thus characterised by second order changes: the introduction of a new instrument (the AUD) allowed the insurance system to become less costly. The balance on its account was actually positive after 1993, in a period of rising unemployment! However, the very logic of social insurance is still preserved, since the majority of the unemployed are still covered by the unemployment insurance scheme. The contributory dimension of the benefit is even reinforced with the new mode of calculation.

Old Age Pensions

The French pension system is very fragmented, since each 'professional category' is covered by a particular pension scheme. However, anyone with earnings below a ceiling on social security contributions, can expect a pension of around 75 per cent of final gross earnings. The basic pension is earnings-related, while second tier provision (also compulsory) is a defined contribution, even though it works on a pay-as-you-go basis. The system also provides a means-tested benefit for pensioners with incomes below a given threshold: the *Minimum vieillesse*. The number of recipients of the *Minimum vieillesse* has decreased constantly since the 1960s, as a result of the expansion of social insurance.

In France, the 1980s have seen a growing concern over the issue of financing pensions. Between 1985 and 1993 a series of government-mandated reports were published. All of them take a rather pessimistic view of the future of pension policy in France, and call for savings measures to be adopted. The reform of pensions, though, is widely perceived as a politically sensitive issue, so that throughout the 1980s, governments were inclined to procrastinate. In France, due to the institutional design of both basic and supplementary pension schemes, governments have to negotiate their reforms with the trade unions for each of the different professional schemes. They also have to confront strong popular opposition to any retrenchment proposal. It was only in 1993 that the newly elected right-wing government managed to adopt a reform of the main basic pension scheme, covering private sector employees. This was made possible by a carefully designed reform package, which included both cuts and concessions to the trade unions with regard to their role in the management and control over pensions. It was only through political exchange that the government was able to reform pensions.[26]

With the 1993 reform, a *'fonds de solidarité vieillesse'* has been created, which has the task of funding non-contributory benefits through state resources. This *fonds* appeared as a concession to trade unions against some retrenchments: the qualifying period for a full pension has been extended from 37.5 to 40 years; the period over which the reference salary is calculated has been extended from the best ten years to the best 25. These are being introduced gradually over a ten-year transition period. Finally the indexation of benefits has been based on prices (as opposed to earnings).

According to projections by the administration of the old age insurance scheme (CNAVTS), without the 1993 reform contribution, rates in 2010 would have had to be increased by around ten percentage points. With the reform, this figure could be between 2.73 and 7.26 percentage points. The 1993 reform will have an impact on the amount of pensions as well as on actual age of retirement. Because of the extension to 40 years of the qualifying period, it is expected that some employees will delay their retirement in order to receive a full pension despite the reform. The extension of the period over which the reference salary is calculated will have an impact on the level of pensions. The impact of this measure is a reduction in benefits by 7–8 per cent for high salaries, but does not affect those on the minimum wage, as they receive the minimum pension (*minimum vieillesse*), which has not been modified by the reform.

In 1995, the Juppé government attempted to extend these measures to the pension schemes of public sector employees. Contrary to Prime Minister Eduard Balladur's approach with the private sector reform, this measure was kept secret, with no negotiations with the trade unions. The result was a massive protest movement, led by a rail workers' strike, which forced the government to abandon its plans. The current Jospin government is still studying the best way to reform the public sector schemes. A recent report written for the Prime Minister and published in April 1999 (*rapport Charpin*) has suggested that all employees (including the public sector) should contribute during 42.5 years to be able to obtain a full pension. Simply proposing this change has provoked the strong opposition of the trade unions, which shows that further reform of the pension system is still controversial. Yet the government is announcing a formal proposition for 2000, which will probably prolong the period of contribution and include the creation of voluntary fully funded pension schemes, managed by the social partners.

In the area of pensions, France shows a strong resistance to the (non-state) contributory pension schemes and a stabilisation of the (state-controlled) minimum pension. No one could say that the French resistance to change is due to a better financial situation of pensions than in Britain, for instance, which introduced a reform in 1986. In contrast, it is strong public support for the social insurance system combined with the great involvement of the social partners in the management and defence of the pension schemes that can explain the different timing of reform and the less profound cuts in France.

Health Care

The government has no direct control over health expenditure. French health insurance is managed by the social partners; services are provided by public and private hospitals, and by independent doctors. The fees for medical care and treatment are decided through agreements negotiated between the social security funds and medical practitioners' professional organisations. There is no limited budget, but a system of reimbursement of health care expenditure first paid by the insured person. For medical and pharmaceutical expenses, the insured person initially settles the bill out of his/her pocket and is then partly reimbursed. Medical care and treatment are reimbursed at up to 75 per cent of the charge at maximum. The remainder (co-payment), known as the *ticket modérateur*, varies between 20 and 60 per cent of the total expense; it has to be paid by the patient. This system is supposed to encourage people to moderate their demands. However, complementary insurance (*Mutuelles*) very often reimburses the cost of the *ticket modérateur*. Today, 85 per cent of people pay for a complementary health care insurance.

The rise in health expenditure is seen as one of the main reasons for the social security deficit. The proportion of health care expenditure to GDP has increased from 7.6 per cent in 1980 to 9.7 per cent in 1994 (compared with 5.8 per cent in 1980 and 6.9 per cent in 1994 for UK[27]). During the 1970s and 1980s, governments relied on plans for balancing the *Sécurité sociale* budget to cope with the difficulties. Since the early 1990s, a new tool has been elaborated: agreements with the medical professions in order to contain health care expenditure.

The numerous 'plans' implemented during the late 1970s and the 1980s (see above) have not been successful in limiting the unstoppable growth in demand for health care. After 1990, it was decided to force the medical professions, the Health Insurance Funds and the state to elaborate a *'convention médicale'* (medical care agreement) which could help to control the evolution of expenditure. The medical care agreement is an instrument for budgetary control, as it sets a provisional target for the evolution of health care spending, practitioners' remuneration and additional expenses. The agreement has to be negotiated and signed by the social partners, but the 1995 *plan Juppé* established that the state can replace the social partners when the latter are not able to reach an agreement.

The new instruments (medical agreements) developed in the early 1990s were not sufficient to prevent health expenditure increases (see Table 1). In 1999, sick pay, for instance, has increased by seven per cent. In 1999, the deficit of the health care insurance fund is still FF12 billion (around two per cent of its resources) while the deficit of the whole of *Sécurité sociale* is 0.3 per cent of its resources. In order to introduce a real control, the state is intervening more and more in this area, as the analyses of the structural reforms below will show.

France has introduced sectoral reforms which imply 'second order changes' in the social protection system: new instruments, but following the same logic of social insurance. As far as the sectoral developments are concerned, the French case confirms recent analyses of welfare state changes which emphasise path-dependent continuity. In accordance with the links the system has with the realm of employment, the only changes which have been possible were those that the representatives of employees and employers accepted to negotiate. As a result, the new instruments reinforce the very logic of the system: all these reforms are based on a 'rationalisation' process[28] which separates insurance benefits (kept by the social partners) and assistance benefits (given back to the state). The social insurance system is governed even more than before by a contributory logic: the new employment insurance benefit AUD as well as the new calculation rules of pensions strengthen the links between contributions and benefits.

FROM VICTIM TO CAUSE OF THE PROBLEMS

The following section will show that the social security system, which was thought to be a victim of the economic crisis, has progressively been understood as one of its main causes, because of its insurance basis and its financing and management arrangements.

The reforms presented above did not allow a real containment of social costs. The *Sécurité sociale* deficit still exists and some important areas of social expenditure (in pension and health care) are still increasing faster than GDP (see Table 1). No real change in the structure, poor improvement in the results – this frozen landscape can be analysed as an effect of the institutional arrangements, which create obstacles to serious change: entitlements (earned by work) have a high degree of public support and thus these benefits are more difficult to reduce than others; the social insurance benefits are more generous than others and their reduction is more visible; the financing mechanism (social contributions) is more legitimate than taxes and thus easier to raise; the management rules create a specific political configuration, where the government parties (left or right) appear as the system breakers and where the trade unions appear as the system defenders and are able to mobilise strong opposition to government reforms.

The institutional configuration of social insurance systems thus appears to be an obstacle to adaptation. Furthermore, the social insurance system has also been accused of being partly the cause of some economic, social and political problems through three broad mechanisms: the weight of social contributions prevents job creation; the contributory nature of most social benefits reinforces social exclusion; and the joint management of the system by the social partners engenders irresponsibility and a management crisis of the system.

Since the late 1970s, France has experienced a significant increase in unemployment. The social insurance system set up in 1945 was not made to tackle mass unemployment. This predominantly contributory system is unable to deal with those who have never been involved in the labour market or who have been removed from it for a long period. Because they have not contributed to social insurance, or because they are not contributing any more, young unemployed or long-term unemployed have no access to social insurance rights. Therefore, social insurance is seen as compounding labour market exclusion and reinforcing social exclusion. The number of 'excluded people' has continued to increase during the 1980s, so that it became one of the most pressing social issues in the late 1980s.

The system was not only seen as reinforcing social exclusion, but it was said to be *producing* unemployment. We know that in France, 80 per cent of social protection is financed through employment-related contributions. We know that the weight of social contributions has been increased during the 1980s. The high level of contributions is seen to have an overall negative impact on the country's economic competitiveness and to be responsible for the high rate of unemployment. The argument is that social insurance contributions inhibit job creation, since they have a direct impact on the cost of low-skilled labour. Consequently, the weight of 'charges sociales' has become a central issue in the French debate. Any report on the financing of the French social protection system stresses the need to lower labour costs by decreasing the level of social contributions.[29]

The management arrangements have also been criticised. In 1945, the management of the social insurance system was given to the social partners in the name of democracy (démocratie sociale) and in order to avoid bureaucratisation and the subordination of social policy efficiency to purely budgetary considerations. As budget control has become an important issue during the 1980s, the devolution of the management of social insurance to the social partners has become problematic: the government is accusing the social partners of having hijacked the social security funds, of abusing their position within the system at the expense of the general good and of not taking seriously their responsibility to contain cost increases. We know that the strongest opposition to changes are not coming from political confrontation, but from trade unions and social mobilisation when governments try to implement important reforms. Within the sphere of government, the social partners' involvement in social insurance is nowadays considered a source of inefficiency whereas the state would be better at containing expenditure increases.

The basic institutional settings of the French social protection system accumulate problems, they impede important reforms, they cause economic and social difficulties. These accusations served to support a change in the political discourse and agenda around the late 1980s–early 1990s: from rescuing the Sécurité sociale, the aim of governmental intervention became that of transforming it. This has been done through several structural reforms which are most often neglected in the analyses of welfare retrenchments. These are incremental reforms aimed at changing the politics of social protection, often marginal at the beginning.[30] After several years of development, we can now assess the importance of these structural changes.

STRUCTURAL REFORMS

This section will focus on the development of three main structural reforms: a re-insertion policy (RMI), a new social tax and the new distribution of power within the system. These no longer marginal reforms introduce both new instruments and a new logic into the French welfare system: means tests, taxation and more state autonomy.

Structural Change in Entitlements and Types of Benefit

A number of new programmes designed to cover those who did not have access to the labour market and therefore to social insurance have been introduced since the early 1980s in response to growing social exclusion. The first were employment policies where the state proposed specific contracts for those excluded from the labour market. As their number grew even more by the late 1980s, it appeared necessary to create specific social benefits, delivered through new social policies, aimed at re-insertion (*politiques d'insertion*). These policies contrast with the traditional features of social insurance, emphasising the inadequacy of the former system. While the social insurance system is centred on employees, these new policies target the socially excluded. Instead of treating all sorts of situations with the same instruments, social re-insertion policies are geared towards specific groups and are designed according to local needs, with a high degree of devolution to local authorities. In addition, instead of treating social risks separately (old age, sickness, unemployment), re-insertion policies address a whole range of relevant social problems in an integrated manner (poverty, housing, vocational training).[31]

The creation of the RMI (*Revenu Minimum d'Insertion*) is the most important of these new social benefits. This new non-contributory scheme, meant for those having no or very low income, was introduced in December 1988. Its main features are the guarantee of a minimum level of resources to anyone aged 25 or over, which takes the form of a means-tested differential benefit. The basic rates in January 1999 were FF2,502.30 for a single person, and FF3,753.45 for a couple, plus FF1000.92 per child. In addition, the RMI has a re-insertion dimension, in the form of a contract between the recipient and 'society'. Recipients must commit themselves to take part in re-insertion programme, as stated in a contract, signed by the recipient and a social worker. Such programmes can be either job-seeking, vocational training or activities designed to enhance the recipient's social autonomy.

When it was created, this new benefit was supposed to be delivered to 300–400,000 people. But by December 1998, 1,112,108 persons were receiving RMI. Including spouses and children of recipients, 2,117,000 million people were covered by this scheme, that is, 3.5 per cent of the French population.[32] Since unemployment insurance benefits have become more contributory, more people are depending on RMI, which has been more and more playing the role of income support in the UK. Besides RMI, France now has seven other minimum social incomes. In 1995, 3.3 million households, more than six million people, that is, more than ten per cent of the French population, were receiving one of these minimum.[33] This means that through the development of new social policies and the development of minimum income benefits, part of the French social protection system is now targeting specific population in using new instruments (means-tested benefits delivered according to need, financed through state taxation and managed by national and local public authorities), with reference to a new logic (to combat social exclusion instead of guaranteeing income and status maintenance).

Structural Changes in Financing

We have seen that in order to cope with financing difficulties, different French governments have often raised the level of contributions paid by employees – while the rate of contribution paid by the employers has decreased over the last 25 years. The rate of contributions (below the ceiling) paid to the general scheme by employees went up from 17.2 per cent in 1970 to 44.4 per cent in 1992.[34] Meanwhile, since the late 1970s, governments of different political orientations have adopted contribution exemptions for employers in order to encourage job creation. These measures are usually targeted on some particularly disadvantaged groups, such as the long-term and young unemployed, or on small companies, which are considered to be the most affected by the relatively high cost of unskilled labour.

In order to generalise this movement of lowering labour costs by reducing the level of social contributions, governments have progressively replaced some contribution by taxation. A new tax was created in December 1990: the *Contribution Sociale Généralisée* (CSG) originally aimed at replacing the social contribution financing non-contributory benefits. Unlike insurance contributions, it is levied on all types of personal income: wages (even the lowest ones), but also capital revenues and welfare benefits. Unlike income tax in France, CSG is strictly proportional and ear-marked for non-contributory welfare programmes. In the early 1990s, the CSG appeared to play a marginal role in the system. When it was introduced, the CSG was levied at 1.1 per cent of all incomes. In 1993, The Balladur government increased the CSG to 2.4 per cent of incomes. In 1995, the *plan Juppé* set it at 3.4 per cent of all income, and, since 1998, the rate has been at 7.5 per cent, replacing most of the health care contribution paid by employees. In 1999, CSG provided more than 20 per cent of all social protection resources and represented 35 per cent of those of the health care system.[35]

The introduction of this ear-marked tax has enabled a shift in the financing structure of the system towards more state taxation. This new instrument has two main general consequences, which means a partial change in the logic of the system. First, since financing comes not only from the working population, the CSG breaks the link between employment and entitlements. Access to CSG-financed benefits cannot be limited to any particular section of society. The shift in financing is thus creating the conditions for the establishment of citizenship-based social rights, especially in health care. Meanwhile, it weakens the strong legitimacy of the financing mechanism, as well as the expenses associated with it. It may be that through this reform it will be less possible to increase the resources of the system, and more necessary to reduce the expenses. Second, this shift means less legitimacy for the social partners to participate in the decision and the management of the provision financed through general taxation since in France there is a fairly strong normative perception, according to which joint management of employers and employees is only acceptable if schemes are financed through employment-related contributions. In this respect, a shift towards taxation constitutes pressure for a transfer of control from the social partners to the state. This evolution corresponds to more important political changes which occurred since the mid-1990s in the distribution of power within the system.

Structural Changes in the Distribution of Power

The difficulties in containing social expenditure are partly interpreted by French politicians and civil servants as a consequence of the lack of state control over the system. Therefore, some reforms have been implemented in order to empower the state within the system, at the expense of the social partners' position. New instruments have been invented to reinforce the autonomy of the state within the system. These reforms have mainly been implemented since the Juppé Plan of 1995. This plan had three principal objectives. First, as a traditional plan for balancing the *Sécurité sociale* budget, imposing some savings and increasing resources.[36] Second, it planned to reform old age insurance for the public sector and public companies, applying to it the same rules as those decided in 1993 for the private sector. This was one of the key measures against which the mass protest of December 1995 was directed, and Prime Minister Alain Juppé had to remove it. Third, a number of the proposed measures were meant to modify the organisational structure of the social insurance system.

New institutions have been created to achieve this third goal. The health care system has been restructured through the creation of regional bodies in charge of the planning of health care provision and budgets. Half of the members of these *Agences Régionales de l'Hospitalisation* are representatives of the state. State representatives are also present in the new *Unions Régionales des Caisses d'Assurance Maladie*, in charge of co-ordinating and harmonising health care policies of the different social insurance funds. More generally, each social insurance fund is now supervised by a *Conseil de Surveillance*, composed essentially of MPs and state representatives, in charge of controlling the proper implementation of the agreements on objectives and management decided each year between the state and the social partners. The composition of the governing board of each social insurance fund has been changed, giving the same number of representatives to employers and to employees and involving more state representatives. The nomination of each director of each fund is controlled more than in the past by the Ministry of Social Affairs. These changes do not mean that the system has gone from a corporatist to a statist one, but that the state has more disposable instruments for controlling the evolution of expenditures.

The most important reform is the vote of a constitutional amendment (in February 1996) obliging parliament to vote for a social security budget every year. For the first time in France, parliament is taking part in the debate on the *Sécurité sociale* budget, which before was seen as not being part of the state budget. Every year, the parliament decides what should be the total amount of resources and expenses of the *Sécurité sociale* in a *loi de financement de la Sécurité sociale*. The use of this new parliamentary responsibility helps the government to control the social policy agenda. Instead of having always to legitimise its intervention in a field originally belonging to the realm of labour and employers, with the institutionalisation of a parliamentary vote, it is now able regularly to plan adaptation measures, especially in cost containment.[37] This new instrument also introduces a new logic of intervention. Instead of trying to find resources to finance social expenditure which are driven by demand from insured persons, the vote of a *loi de financement* implies that a limited budget should be allocated for social expenditure. As most of the social benefits are still contributory, it is impossible totally to define *a priori* a limited budget, but governments are entering this new logic, and the parliament has voted for new instruments for achieving this goal, such as limited global budgets for hospitals and for ambulatory doctors, ceilings and rates of growth for social expenditure.

WHEN POLICIES CHANGE HISTORICAL PATHS

These structural reforms all contribute to changing the original Bismarckian nature of the French social security system, and a move towards a state-run, tax-financed logic and practice, at least in the area of health care, family benefits and poverty alleviation, which were alien to the French post-war tradition of welfare. The traditional way of providing social protection in France has been fiercely criticised and destabilised; the new instruments aimed at coping with the structural difficulties of the French social system belong to another logic than the Bismarckian/Christian Democratic one. After several years of implementation, one can see that these reforms are not marginal, but concern a significant proportion of the population, an important share of the financing and have given the state more possibilities to intervene within the system. Whereas the landscape seemed frozen in the 1980s in France, the conclusion must be less categorical at the end of the 1990s.

One question remains open: how did these structural changes occur? There is not enough room here to detail the political processes of each reform,[38] but it is possible to characterise the general patterns of adoption of these reforms and the political conditions that made them possible.

First, two important changes in the context seem essential to acknowledge: the end of Keynesianism in the late 1970s–early 1980s and the new European constraints. Through Jacques Chirac's failure in 1974–76 and that of Pierre Mauroy in 1981–82, the Keynesian use of social benefits has been definitely delegitimised for both left- and right-wing governments.[39] The economic role of social protection could not be thought of in the same way anymore, and this has been very important for the development of the critics of social insurance mechanisms: they appeared to have become a cost rather than a social investment. The second contextual element – European constraints and commitments – are also important for understanding the changes in perception of social protection in France: lowering 'social charges' appeared necessary in order to render French companies competitive within the single market, retrenching social expenditure had to be included in the strategy of reducing public expenditure and public deficits in order to meet the Maastricht criteria.

Second, an important political change has been the new position of one of the trade unions during the late 1980s. The CFDT was outside the management of social insurance funds since 1967, but recently has changed in economic and social position. This trade union has been one of the most active proponents of re-insertion policies, and above all of CSG (and nowadays 35 working hours). On the contrary, FO or CGT[40] appeared to remain very much on the defensive, opposing any kind of reform proposal.

After 1995, the head of each social insurance fund has changed. FO has lost all of its important positions (especially at the head of the National Health Care Insurance fund) to the benefit of the CFDT, which made alliances with the employers' representatives. It is probable that the change in the position of at least one of the employees' representatives is one of the most important political conditions for policy changes in a 'corporatist-conservative' social insurance system.

Third, a large majority of the actors concerned with social protection problems agreed to the new measures (RMI, CSG, parliamentary vote). Like Pierson,[41] we find that a very large majority of the actors is necessary to allow for welfare change to proceed. However, a precise analysis of the different position of the actors *vis-à-vis* the new measures described above show that the reason why they agree on them are very different, and sometimes contradictory.[42] An important element seems to be the capacity of the new measures to aggregate different – even contradictory – interests, through different – even contradictory – interpretations of it. This leads to the conclusion that structural changes are made through ambiguous measures rather than via a clear ideological orientation.

Finally, these changes have been introduced very progressively, as if they were very marginal, before they begin to play a major role within the core of the social protection system. It is probably because they are seen as marginal that few analyses focus on these changes and that the common analysis of welfare state changes (and especially on continental welfare systems) emphasise path dependency and continuity. The latter focus on the processes of adaptation of the welfare states. They are closed to an evolutionary perspective, emphasising the inertia of internal dynamics of institutions. They do not credit public policies with having much structural impact. Yet, the recent developments in the social protection systems are not only due to their own evolutionary dynamic, but also to the implementation of public policies. Therefore, the analysis should also focus on the impact of public policies, which sometimes have structural force.

NOTES

This text owes a lot to John Myles and to Giuliano Bonoli. Parts were presented with G. Bonoli in July 1998 in Montreal in the session 'Restructuring Welfare States' organised by Jens Alber during the World Congress of the International Sociology Association. I also benefited greatly from the discussions within the European Forum, 'Recasting the European Welfare State', in the EUI, particularly with Maurizio Ferrera and Paul Pierson.

1. P. Pierson, *Dismantling the Welfare State? Reagan, Thatcher and The Politics of Retrenchment* (Cambridge: Cambridge University Press 1994), p.5.

2. G. Esping-Andersen (ed.), *Welfare States in Transition, National Adaptations in Global Economies* (London: Sage 1996).

3. Ibid., p.267.

4. Myles and Quadagno show that retrenchment means targeting for universal benefits, reinforcing selectivity and adding conditions to already targeted benefits, and tightening the links between contribution and benefits for the contributory benefits. J. Myles and J. Quadagno, 'Recent Trends in Public Pension Reform: A Comparative View', in K. Banting and R. Boadway (eds.), *Reform of Retirement Income Policy. International and Canadian Perspectives* (Kingston, Ontario: Queen's University, School of Policy Studies 1997), pp.247–72.

5. J. Myles and P. Pierson, 'The Comparative Political Economy of Pension Reform', forthcoming in P. Pierson (ed.), *The New Politics of The Welfare State* (Oxford: Oxford University Press 2000).

6. P. Hall, 'Policy Paradigm, Social Learning and the State, the Case of Economic Policy in Britain', *Comparative Politics* (April 1993), p.278.

7. Ibid., pp.278–9.

8. P. Pierson, 'Irresistible Forces, Immovable Objects: Post-industrial Welfare States Confront Permanent Austerity', *Journal of European Public Policy* 5/4 (Dec. 1998), p.558, n.8.

9. *Régime général* covering 60 per cent of the population.

10. This *trou de la Sécurité sociale* was usually at least ten times less important than the state budget's deficit, but much more publicised.

11. P. Pierson, 'The New Politics of the Welfare State', *World Politics* 48/1 (Jan. 1996), pp.162, 165.

12. G. Bonoli and B. Palier, 'Reclaiming Welfare. The Politics of Social Protection Reform in France', in M. Rhodes (ed.), *Southern European Welfare States* (London and Portland, OR: Frank Cass 1996), pp.240–59.

13. Pierson, *Dismantling the Welfare State?*.

14. V. George and P. Taylor-Gooby (eds.), *European Welfare Policy – Squaring the Welfare Circle* (London: Macmillan 1996).

15. V. George, 'The Future of the Welfare State', in ibid., pp.20–22.

16. Source, SESI, *Comptes de la protection sociale*, various years.

17. *Comptes de la protection sociale*, SESI, various years.

18. A similar observation is made by Pierson, *Dismantling the Welfare State?* p.71, with reference to a comparison between the British and the US basic pensions

19. M. Ferrera, 'Modèles de solidarité, divergences, convergences: perspectives pour l'Europe', *Swiss Political Science Review* 2/1 (1996), pp.55–72.

20. D. Gaxie *et al.*, *Le 'social' transfiguré* (Paris: PUF, 1990), p.145.

21. M.-T. Join-Lambert, *Politiques sociales* (Paris: Dalloz, 1997), p.575.

22. Esping-Andersen, *Welfare States in Transition*, Chapter 3.

23. J. Bichot, *Les politiques sociales en France au 20ème siècle* (Paris: Armand Colin 1997), p.132.

24. Ibid.

25. Confédération Française Démocratique du Travail.

26. G. Bonoli, 'Pension Politics in France: Patterns of Co-operation and Conflict in Two Recent Reforms' *West European Politics* 20/4 (1997), pp.160–81.

27. Join-Lambert, *Politiques sociales*, p.510.

28. Myles and Pierson, 'The Comparative Political Economy of Pension Reform'.

29. J.B. de Foucauld, *Le financement de la protection sociale* (Paris: La documentation française, 1995).

30. G. Bonoli and B. Palier, 'Changing the Politics of Social Programmes: Innovative Change in British and French Welfare Reforms', *Journal of European Social Policy* 8/4 (Nov. 1998), pp.317–30.

31. B. Palier, 'La référence aux territoires dans les nouvelles politiques sociales', *Politique et Management public* 3 (1998), pp.13–41.

32. CNAF, 'Revenu Minimum d'Insertion au 31 décembre 1998', *Recherche, prévisions et statistiques* (May 1999).

33. CERC, 'Les minima sociaux', *les dossiers de Cerc-association* 2 (1997).
34. Join-Lambert, *Politiques sociales*, p.339.
35. *Libération*, 22 Sept. 1999, p.15.
36. Family benefits were frozen in 1996, and it was planned to make them taxable in 1997 and means-tested in 1998 (the Jospin government means-tested them in 1998, but removed the measure for 1999). Resources have been raised through the increase in health insurance contributions for unemployed and retired people by 2.4 per cent in 1996; and the introduction of a new tax, levied at the rate of 0.5 per cent on all revenues, earmarked for the repayment of the debt accumulated by the social security system.
37. This has been done regularly in autumn 1997, 1998 and 1999.
38. See B. Palier, 'Réformer la Sécurité sociale' (Ph.D. thesis, IEP de Paris 1999).
39. In both cases, these Prime Ministers tried to raise social benefits in order to boost private consumption and then economic activity. They both ended up with large public deficits, negative trade balances and increases in interest rates. In both 1976 and 1982, their economic policies had to be switched to a restrictive monetarist one.
40. Force Ouvrière, Confédération Générale du Travail.
41. Pierson, 'The New Politics of the Welfare State'.
42. All these reforms have been made in the name of the distinction between insurance and assistance (called 'national solidarity' in French). Trade unions wanted this rationalisation in order to preserve their realm of social insurance, whereas governments and civil servants expected more responsibilities in social protection through these changes. RMI was seen by the left as a means to deliver money *and* social help (vocational training for instance) through the contract, while the right supported the RMI since it was money given *in return for* an effort made by the contracting beneficiary. The left supported CSG because it was a fairer tax than social contributions for employees, whereas the right supported this as means for lowering social charges for employers; civil servants supported CSG because it was leading to state control over the expenses financed by this new tax, whereas employers and the CFDT argued that it would allow the social partners to preserve the purity of social insurance, non-contributory benefits being financed by this new tax.

The Employment Crisis of the German Welfare State

PHILIP MANOW AND
ERIC SEILS

How did the German welfare state fare in the 1990s and what are its prospects for the near future? If one were to follow recent accounts of two influential German social scientists there does not seem to be reason for much concern. By looking at a wide range of comparative data, Jens Alber[1] finds that the German welfare state in almost all dimensions is located at or very close to the OECD or EU median. Welfare entitlements are not overly generous in Germany, nor is the welfare state especially expensive when compared with its European counterparts. Nor are social programmes particularly inefficient. According to Alber, it is rather its 'lack of distinctiveness' which makes the German welfare state distinctive. Given that the German welfare state appears to be almost a 'median on all dimensions', Alber finds no empirical support for the rhetoric of crisis that is so pervasive in the current debates about 'Standort Deutschland'.[2] In a similar vein, Manfred Schmidt[3] holds that Germany is still following the 'politics of the middle way' because a multi-veto point polity prevents extreme swings of both the economic or political pendulum from occurring. While the overall performance of German capitalism may have suffered after unification, Schmidt's general message is that Germany still performs astoundingly well in economic terms and that its institutional order still reveals a remarkable stability. In fact, since unification has not led to a profound alteration of the way in which the German model functions, for many, unification is both the cause of a temporal crisis and the proof of the basic health of the German model. The economic costs of this dramatic 'shock to the system', so the argument goes, only overshadow the still impressive international performance of the German economy and the notable robustness of its political order. Hence, a fundamental critique of the German model is largely unjustified and would – if followed up – cause more harm than good.[4]

The following analysis argues that the current widespread feeling of crisis in Germany is indeed much better founded than these accounts concede – at least if one focuses on the welfare state and the closely related performance of the German labour market. We claim that the economic slumps since the early 1970s – including the unification crisis after 1992 – have regularly triggered a pathological response pattern of the German economic and political system leading to ever higher levels of unemployment, to a low level of total employment, and to steadily increasing non-wage labour costs, in particular continuously rising social insurance contributions. In turn, high non-wage labour costs have adverse effects on job growth in the low wage (service) sector and on the competitiveness of German industry in world markets.

What do we mean when we speak of a 'pathological response pattern' in the German economic and political system'? The pathology of economic adjustment to recessions takes roughly the following course. Both the independence of the German central bank and the federalist fragmentation of the 'public purse' prevent the use of strategic depreciation or expansionary fiscal or monetary policies to maintain high levels of employment in times of economic crisis.[5] Real wage flexibility is also not sufficient to prevent large-scale job losses. Consequently, it is the welfare state that becomes the main instrument of economic adjustment. Germany's prime response to economic crises is the reduction of labour supply with the help of various social insurance schemes. Given the real-wage resistance in the German wage bargaining system, an increase in labour taxation translates into higher wage costs. While this burden already puts both the system of social protection and the labour market under stress, the response pattern of the German political economy to economic crises has yet another pathological side to it. Given that the Bundesbank's tight monetary policy forces the government to pursue strict fiscal discipline – a pressure that is especially felt in times of economic slump – the financial autonomy of the social insurance schemes' budgets provides the government with a strong incentive to shift financial obligations out of the general budget into these budgets or to reduce the state's overall financial involvement in social spending. Thus, economic crises trigger a dual process of cost shifting: firms seek to externalise their adjustment costs onto the welfare state, and the government tries to ease budgetary pressures by reducing its contribution to welfare finance.

The steady increase in non-wage labour costs endangers the competitiveness of German industry in world markets and at the same time impedes the growth of the domestic service sector. Declining employment, in turn, is particularly problematic within a social policy model that relies almost exclusively on revenue stemming from dependent employment. The resulting financial crisis of the welfare state and the labour market distortions caused by the exaggerated cost burdens imposed on wages were seriously aggravated by German unification, but have in fact been noticeable since the mid-1970s.[6]

The discussion proceeds as follows. Since the pathology of adjustment is the result of the strategic interaction of economic and state actors within the German economic and political system, we first give a brief account of the basic functioning of this broader political-economic framework, before describing the emergence of a pattern of pathological adjustment after the high growth/full employment period had come to an end. We then discuss in greater detail the policy responses in the 1980s and 1990s before considering the impact of unification on the welfare state and the German labour market. In the final section we briefly discuss the adverse effects of the resulting welfare-without-work equilibrium on structural change and the competitiveness of German firms.

A SKETCH OF THE GERMAN POLITICAL ECONOMY

Central to the German social market economy (*Soziale Marktwirtschaft*) is a high degree of autonomy of the German Bundesbank, strong unions and employers' associations, which jealously defend their constitutionally guaranteed right to free collective bargaining without any state intervention (*Tarifautonomie*). The welfare state comes close to Richard Titmuss' industrial achievement/performance model. It emphasises occupational status and transfer payments rather than the direct provision of services. Public employment is low. Apart from central bank independence, federalism is the second most severe source of restriction on government independence in fiscal, monetary and economic policies and grants the Länder (states) a say in almost all matters of federal legislation. Thus, negotiation is the dominant mode of decision making and conflict resolution. Policy co-ordination between the federal government and the Länder, if it happens at all, is the end-result of protracted processes of political compromising. Blockages and political stalemate occur frequently and sweeping reforms are rare due to the meshed jurisdictions between central and state governments and the strong legislative veto-position of the states in the upper house (creating a 'joint-decision trap').[7] The potential for political obstruction is aggravated by the competitive character of the German party system. Over time the political parties have learned well how to exploit the opportunities that the German multiple veto-point polity offers to them.[8]

State intervention in the economy is not absent, but rare, since business associations have shown a very high capacity for efficient self-governance[9] and the German collective bargaining system has functioned smoothly for most of the post-war era. The strike rate is low, while the coverage rate of collective agreements remained high and stable – despite medium and, since the 1980s, steadily decreasing union density. Wage bargaining takes place in a mainly voluntary framework, but the Bundesbank's credible threat instantly to punish inflationary wage agreements has had strong disciplinary effects.[10] The high binding force of collective agreements is due, first, to the high organisational density of employers; second, to legal provisions that endow voluntary agreements between unions and employers with quasi-official, authoritative status;[11] and, third, to the joint interest of employers to avoid wage competition and to protect the high-skill, high-wage production regime that crucially depends on the banning of *sectoral* wage competition.[12]

The German system of industrial governance can be labelled corporatist. German corporatism, however, is different from the central corporatist concertation of the Austrian, Swedish or Dutch variety. German industrial relations are rather an example of horizontal or 'covert' co-ordination.[13] To exaggerate only slightly, one might label the German industrial relations system not as 'corporatism without labour',[14] but rather as 'corporatism without the state'. The German welfare state primarily covers risks associated with a loss of income of the male industrial wage earner, such as sickness, old-age and unemployment. Each risk is dealt with by a separate social insurance scheme. The relatively strict adherence to the insurance or equivalence principle means that entitlements follow very much the income distribution generated by the market. Hence, the welfare state puts a premium on steady working careers and therefore benefits workers with relatively high skills and thus high incomes, while it discriminates against part-time work and, as a consequence, also against female labour force participation. These welfare-induced rigidities support the so-called 'standard employment relationship' (*Normalarbeitsverhältnis*), that is, full-time, life-long employment.

The main beneficiary of this welfare state model has been the male, skilled, unionised worker in the manufacturing sector. With respect to financing, the overwhelming part of social spending is financed from social insurance contributions. The sickness fund budgets are entirely autonomous, so contribution rates have to increase whenever a deficit appears. The pension scheme receives a subsidy from the government. Nevertheless, the lion's share is financed by contributions of employees and employers. The share financed from the government's budget declined from 31.9 per cent in 1957 to around 19 per cent in 1970 and has slowly risen since (today it is at approximately 24 per cent). Contribution rates rose from 14 per cent of gross wages to 19.5 per cent today. Whenever the revenue from contributions and the state subsidy (as a fixed share not linked to outlays but to revenue) were insufficient to meet the expected expenditures, the contribution rates had to be raised by law. Unemployment insurance is also subsidised. The system is run by the Federal Employment Office (Bundesanstalt für Arbeit) and, once again, is mainly contribution-financed. Deficits must, however, be covered by the federal budget. Means-tested social assistance as the ultimate safety net of the German welfare state is run and financed by local authorities under national legislation. This also represents an in-built incentive for the central government to shift costs out of programmes where it is financially involved in social assistance.

THE END OF THE ECONOMIC MIRACLE

With the end of the German economic miracle in the early 1970s, the reduction of labour supply became the dominant 'solution' to German labour market problems. Foreign workers, so indispensable during the boom of the 1960s, were the first to be affected. At about the same time, the use of the social insurance schemes as a means of reducing the supply of labour rose to prominence. The use of early retirement was of particular importance.

About a year before the onset of the first OPEC crisis, the pension reform of 1972 had opened up the possibility of 'flexible retirement' at the age of 63 without an actuarial reduction in benefits. The introduction of this measure was completely unrelated to considerations about using early retirement to ease labour market pressure in economic downturns. On the contrary, after very high wage increases and considerable economic growth in the years between 1969 and 1971, the budgets of the social insurance schemes showed a surplus, and the faith in the effectiveness of Keynesian deficit spending that still prevailed at that time led politicians to extrapolate the present growth rate and budget surplus for the entire decade.[15] However, the substantial welfare state expansion brought about by the pension reform of 1972 took place against the background of the first oil crisis. It is clear that, with the deteriorating economic situation, flexible retirement became increasingly attractive among older workers. While the introduction of flexible retirement caused a decline in the take-up rates for disability pensions as the second pathway into early retirement, in the years following the recession the number of entrants increased again. This was also due to two important court rulings (in 1969 and 1976) that held that the definition of 'inability to work' must also take the situation on the labour market into consideration, that is, the probability for a less than fully employable, but not fully disabled person to find adequate part-time employment in his or her respective profession. Since the German labour market regime offers only few part-time positions, older workers regularly qualify for a full disability pension even if they have only a partial ability to work. The third variant of early retirement is the so-called 59er rule. The practice makes use of a regulation that establishes the right for those aged 60 or older to claim a pension if they have been unemployed for more than one year. This provision was used especially by large companies to reduce staff in times of slack business. Companies urge workers at 59 or even younger to leave the firm by offering to top up their unemployment benefits to the level of their last net earnings until the employee can draw a pension at 60. Apart from overtime reduction, this became the most important strategy for reducing staff in a comparatively 'painless' or peaceful way in large firms with more than 5,000 employees.[16]

As for the reaction of the government to the stagflation of the 1970s, we witness a mixture of cost-cuts and cost-shifting. The net result was a reduction in social spending as a share of GDP, but a simultaneous rise in the share of social expenditure financed from social insurance contributions. The consequence was an increasing cost burden on labour.

One of the major factors responsible for the increasing cost burdens on wages has been the federal and state governments' retreat from financing welfare expenditures. This is shown in Table 1, which presents sources of welfare revenue over the last three decades. The shift in the financial shares can be the result either of the redefinition of programme responsibilities (for example, if benefits for the very long term unemployed are paid not by tax-financed social assistance but by contribution-financed unemployment insurance), or by simply cutting transfers from the federal budget to the social insurance budgets or by the introduction of new programmes or the extension of entitlements which are primarily or entirely financed out of contributions (for example, the introduction of long term care insurance which substitutes for social assistance payments to the frail and elderly; see below). Finally, it is possible that programmes without government participation grow more costly due to increasing demand or above average inflation.

The effect of German federalism can also be read from Table 1 since it shows quite clearly that not only the federal government, but the Länder as

TABLE 1
SOURCES OF THE SOCIAL BUDGET, 1970–97

Year	Federal government	States	Local authorities	Private households and others
1970	23.6	13.7	6.7	56.0
1975	24.5	12.3	7.2	56.0
1980	22.4	11.5	7.2	59.0
1985	20.4	11.1	7.7	60.9
1990	18.7	10.2	7.8	63.3
1991	19.7	10.1	8.0	62.2
1995	19.9	9.9	8.9	61.4
1997	19.5	10.8	8.6	61.1

Notes: The data given refer to West Germany until the first half of 1990, thereafter to Germany. Data for 1995 are estimated and for 1997 forecasts.

Source: Bundesministerium für Arbeit und Sozialordnung, *Statistisches Taschenbuch. Arbeits- und Sozialstatistik* (Bonn: Bundesministerium für Arbeit- und Sozialordnung 1998), Table 7.4, own calculations.

TABLE 2
FINANCING STRUCTURE OF THE SOCIAL BUDGET, 1970–97

Year	Contributions	General taxation	Other
1970	58.4	39.7	1.9
1975	58.8	39.2	1.9
1980	62.8	35.9	1.4
1985	64.9	33.5	1.5
1990	67.5	30.9	1.7
1991	66.3	32.0	1.7
1995	65.9	32.6	1.4
1997	65.2	33.2	1.6

Notes: see Table 1.

Source: Bundesministerium für Arbeit und Sozialordnung, *Statistisches Taschenbuch. Arbeits- und Sozialstatistik* (Bonn: Bundesministerium für Arbeit- und Sozialordnung 1998), Table 7.3, own calculations.

well were successful in reducing their share of social spending. The states apparently did not use their veto position in the German upper house, the Bundesrat, to advocate and protect the interests of local authorities, which have come to bear an ever increasing part of social spending. However, the shifts in the relative shares of welfare state financing have been most unfavourable for employers and employees, as shown in Table 2.

The same response pattern of the German political economy that was observable in the wake of the first oil crisis occurred again at the beginning of the 1980s when another oil-price shock led to declining employment in industries and rising inflation. Again, the welfare state became the prime means of economic adjustment and the Bundesbank, as in the early 1970s, stuck to a hard currency policy and urged the Federal Government to consolidate its budget in the midst of the economic slump. Again, as ten years before, the strict monetarist course of the Bundesbank was provoked by the fact that the recession met with an expansionary fiscal policy. The G-7 Bonn summit in 1978 had ascribed to Japan and Germany the role of economic 'locomotives' that were to pull the world economy out of recession. When in 1980 the ensuing expansionary fiscal policies met the increasing oil bill in the wake of the OPEC II crisis, Germany had its first current account deficit for 14 years. The Bundesbank soon considered the 'locomotive experiment' as a failure and tried to maintain a strong external value of the DM despite Germany's deteriorating current account balance. The bank stuck to its restrictive policy until the trough of the recession had been passed in 1983.

The restrictive policy of the German central bank in a time of high real interest rates encouraged the government to follow a course of budget consolidation. Finally, the Social Democratic/Liberal coalition encountered irreconcilable positions with regard to the 'right' budgetary policy and to the necessity of further cuts in social spending. Nevertheless, it was still under Chancellor Schmidt that the shift to a more restrictive fiscal policy took place.[17] The best known package of cuts was the so-called 'Budget Operation 82'.[18] When the Kohl government came to power it shelved expansionary policies altogether and embarked on a policy of consolidating the budget with the intention to reduce taxation thereafter. It claimed that it would do so mainly by curbing public and especially social expenditure. Furthermore, the new government wanted to reduce public ownership in industry and deregulate labour markets.

With the help of revenue from privatisation and transfers from the Bundesbank, the centre-right government under Chancellor Kohl was quite successful in reducing the public deficit. Revenue from privatisation and the central bank's transfers were clearly helpful, but not enough to achieve both lower taxes and a balanced budget at the same time. Therefore, the government sought simultaneously to cut especially social spending – both through 'real' cuts and through cost shifting. Cost shifting led to a further increase in contribution rates, which grew even after the economy had gained strength again in the second half of the 1980s. This is explained by the fact that the government in the second half of the 1980s used the better financial situation of the social insurance budgets to expand programmes again. These were now especially designed to take care of those who had been left unemployed by the previoust crisis and had very poor prospects for re-employment, in particular older workers.

With the budget deficit decreasing, tax reform became a political priority towards the end of Kohl's second term, in the late 1980s, for which the CDU/FDP coalition was even prepared to accept somewhat higher deficits.[19] Most unfavourably, the revenue losses caused by the tax reforms occurred at the time when additional layouts for the GDR became necessary.[20] The resulting deficit further fuelled the boom that had developed in the late 1980s and led to an overheating of the economy.[21] Clearly, the Kohl government had departed from its consolidation policy of the 1980s in the face of the demands resulting from the fall of the Berlin Wall and the forthcoming general elections in December 1990.

In its effort to balance its budget and later to provide taxpayers and the electorate with tax relief, the government had largely neglected the financial problems of the welfare state. There is no doubt that cost containment did happen and that it was relatively successful in keeping social expenditure as a share of GDP more or less constant.[22] Yet cost containment did not prevent a further rise in social insurance contribution rates. This was because the federal state had increasingly reduced its financial share since the onset of the crisis. In fact, this was a secular trend from the mid-1970s on, but which accelerated during the crises of the early 1980s and 1990s (see Table 1). The gap caused by the federal and state governments' steady withdrawal from its share of funding the welfare state finally had to be made up from other sources, primarily social insurance contributions. In Figure 1, the actual development of social insurance contribution rates is shown against what they would have been if the share of contributions in overall welfare financing had remained at the 1970 level. Until 1975, actual and counterfactual contribution rates grew in line. At the eve of unification in 1990, however, the share financed from contributions had risen from 58 per cent in 1970 to 67 per cent. Had shares stayed the same, contribution payers would have saved an aggregate of DM70 billion and the contribution rate could still have basically remained at its 1975 level.

Shifting costs on to the insurance schemes results in higher non-wage labour costs for the individual. Looking at the income level of an average production worker, we indeed find that social insurance contributions and other taxes have made up a rapidly increasing share of total labour costs. According to Figure 2, Germany ranks second in this respect, only

FIGURE 1
ACTUAL AND COUNTERFACTUAL CONTRIBUTION RATES (1970–97)

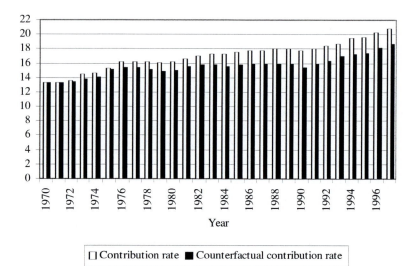

☐ Contribution rate ■ Counterfactual contribution rate

FIGURE 2
TAX WEDGE IN GERMANY, BELGIUM, AND THE OECD (1979–97)

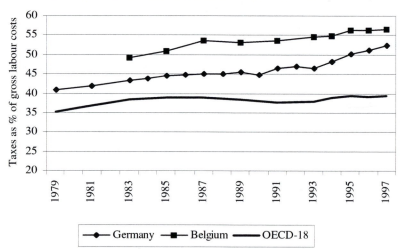

◆ Germany ■ Belgium ▬ OECD-18

TABLE 3
TAX WEDGE AT LOW EARNINGS (1997)

Belgium	49.5	France	41.6	Canada	27.9
Sweden	49.2	Austria	41.1	Switzerland	27.3
Italy	48.8	Netherlands	38.8	Ireland	24.9
Germany	47.7	Norway	34.3	New Zealand	20.3
Finland	44.2	USA	29.2	Australia	19.4
Denmark	41.7	UK	28.4	Japan	19.4

Notes: Employees' and employers' social security contributions and personal income tax less transfer payments as a percentage of gross labour costs, single individual at 67 per cent of average production worker wage level, 1997.

Source: OECD, *The Tax/Benefit Position of Employees, 1997. Edition 1998* (Paris: OECD 1999).

surpassed by Belgium. Table 3 shows that this finding also holds at lower income levels. At an earnings level of 67 per cent of the average production worker, the tax wedge, that is, the difference between gross labour costs and net wages, is also among the highest in the OECD. This is especially so for lower wages, where social insurance contributions are salient since they are usually levied from the first unit of earnings, but only up to a certain ceiling. Income taxes, by contrast, often have personal allowances but tax all income beyond this level. High tax burdens at low incomes are even more problematic for employment than at higher levels, a point we will come back to.

In the following section we will give a more detailed account of the various social policy measures enacted in the 1980s and 1990s that made up for most of the pathologic adjustment from which the German economy suffers today. The particular impact of unification on the welfare state and the German labour market will be described subsequently.

FIRMS, THE STATE AND THE REDUCTION OF LABOUR MARKET SUPPLY

The *prima facie* highly contradictory course of social policy in the 1980s that saw both the attempt to retrench social spending *and* the substantial expansion of entitlements appears less incoherent if interpreted against the background of the business cycle. The government's response to economic recessions follows two partly conflicting objectives, namely to contain the growth of social spending and to help firms to cope with the economic crisis by offering them the opportunity to lay off workers 'painlessly' via welfare state programmes. The trade-off between both objectives was partly solved by 'policy sequencing'. This leads to the same pro-cyclical policy profile that we can also observe in the area of active labour market policy (see below): cutbacks in times of economic slump – in order to ease the financial pressures on the public budget – were followed by the considerable extension of entitlements and eligibility during booms, in order to help those that were left unemployed by the last recession. These latter extension measures then become especially important for the response to the next crisis.

Thus it is no surprise that it was the social entitlements which had been granted in the past in times of brighter economic prospects which came to be especially important for the response of the German welfare state to the recession in the first half of 1980s. The first policy reaction to the second OPEC crisis comprised the enactment of a number of cutback measures that either sought simply to contain costs (for example, reduction of the unemployment benefit levels in 1983) or that sought to make the entry into early retirement less attractive for workers and firms (for example, the introduction of more restrictive qualifying criteria for the disability pension in the budget law of 1984). Also in the last category falls the introduction of the Early Retirement Act (*Vorruhestandsgesetz*, 1984),[23] which was enacted with the intention to substitute it for the more costly 59er rule – that is, pensions linked to long-term unemployment.[24] Already in 1982 the government had forced firms to pay back unemployment benefits that the Labour Office paid to formerly long-term employed workers who had been dismissed at the age of 59. Two years later employers were also forced to repay pension and health insurance contributions that the Labour Office had paid on behalf of these unemployed. However, firms were quick to challenge this new provision before the courts and in the end employers' repayments turned out to be rather insignificant. Thus, while the 59er rule is still a frequently used pathway into retirement, the Early Retirement Act expired in 1988 and has been succeeded only by an even less successful programme. The employers' obligation to pay back social insurance contributions paid by the Labour Office was abolished altogether in 1991. The numbers of unemployment pensions steadily increased from the mid-1980s and sky-rocketed in the wake of the unification crisis in the early 1990s. The meagre results of the fight against an ever earlier exit from the labour market reflects the ambivalence of the government's position. On the one hand, the use of pension policy as an instrument of labour supply control promised to ease labour market pressures and was in the foremost interest of both unions and employers. On the other hand, pensions because of long-term unemployment were a very costly instrument of 'passive labour market policy'. Moreover, efforts to restrict access to early retirement were pursued only half-heartedly since the economy seemed slowly to pick up again in 1984.

While the attempts to reverse the trend of an ever earlier exit from work did not add up to much, the extension of entitlements introduced once the crisis seemed to be over and once social insurance budgets were in surplus again had much more of a long-term impact.[25] In the second half of the 1980s, in an economically more favourable period, one of the more important measures was certainly the considerable extension of the period in which unemployment benefits for workers of 54 and over were paid out. From 1987, these workers have been eligible for the regular unemployment insurance benefit (unemployment benefit – *Arbeitslosengeld*) for up to 32 months. Ever since 1927 and until as late as 1985, the maximum duration had been only 12 months. Given the longer eligibility for unemployment benefits, workers could now exit the labour market at the age of 57 and then draw a pension because of long-term unemployment from the age of 60. The 59er rule effectively became a 57er rule.[26] Moreover, workers aged 58 and over did not have to be at the Labour Offices' permanent disposal. These workers did not appear thereafter in the unemployment statistics.

The overall effect of these various measures was a decline in the labour force participation of the 55–65 age group. When we look at the more active attempts to deal with the labour market problems of the 1980s, we observe the same pro-cyclical logic as with early retirement.[27] Since active labour market policies in Germany are financed from unemployment insurance contributions, the fund quickly runs into financial difficulties in a recession: the payment of unemployment benefits increases while at the same time revenue deteriorates. The government then faces the choice of either subsidising the insurance fund or cutting expenditure. Since there are no legal entitlements to training or work creation measures, and given the Bundesbank's disciplinary pressures towards the consolidation of the public budget, these programmes become a natural candidate for cost cuts. This was clearly the case when the Social Democrats curbed spending in the 1975 Budget Act. Once the recession is over, the financial situation of the insurance fund improves again and those still unemployed exhaust their insurance benefits and have to rely on unemployment assistance, which is financed from the federal budget. This turns the incentive structure around as the government can now shift part of the financial burden back into the insurance fund by introducing new work-creation schemes.

The same pro-cyclical policy pattern was observable in the early 1980s in the wake of the OPEC II crisis. Active labour market measures were scaled down with the 1981 amendment to the Employment Promotion Act. After unemployment insurance was back in surplus and the recession seemed to have passed in 1985, the cuts were partly reversed. Nonetheless, labour market policy was quite active during this time and clearly contributed to the lowering of unemployment. But since training is contribution-financed, the pro-cyclical shifts from programme contraction to programme expansion prevented social insurance expenditures from decreasing and contribution rates from falling once the economic crisis was over. The business-cycle responsiveness of the German welfare state is thus skewed, asymmetric: economic downturns and the accompanying deficits provoke semi-successful programme cutbacks, cost shifting as well as instant contribution rate increases. During booms the contribution rates remain high and stable. The resulting revenue surplus is either used for post-crisis welfare expansion, especially targeted at the long-term unemployed who have exhausted their benefits in the meantime, or to finance the federal government's retreat from funding the welfare state. With this higher level of spending and revenue, but also with more generous welfare entitlements, the welfare state then enters the next crisis. Thus, we witness a ratchet-effect that parallels the rise in unemployment. In each recession, insurance contributions are raised but do not fall back to their initial level with the recovery.

Although it represented an extraordinary and unique 'external shock', German unification triggered the same, by now familiar, policy sequence: initial fiscal expansion is brought to a rather abrupt halt by the monetarist intervention of the German central bank. In the ensuing crunch, the social partners and the federal government use the welfare state as a buffer for both the financial and labour market pressures with which they are faced. In the following section we show how this sequence unfolded – and with what consequences – in the early 1990s.

A ROUTINE RESPONSE TO A NON-ROUTINE SITUATION: GERMAN RE-UNIFICATION

The two decisions that proved to be most significant for the fate of the east German economy were the fixing of an unrealistic conversion rate between the east German currency and the D-Mark and the attempt of the social partners to replicate the west German high wage/high productivity regime in the east. Fierce party competition due to the numerous state and general elections in 1990 combined with the intensive efforts of west German corporate actors to preserve the western *status quo* resulted in a straightforward transfer of the west German institutional setting to the east.[28] As was soon to become clear, this strategy had devastating consequences.

In spite of widespread warnings, the DM replaced the east German currency at a conversion rate largely out of line with purchasing power parities. Literally overnight, eastern industries became uncompetitive. The immediate result was a drastic surge in unemployment.[29] At a time when the effects of this disastrous decision were already being felt, the metal workers union pressed for an agreement aimed at the rapid reduction of wage differentials between east and west. As a consequence, unit labour costs in the east shot up to levels that were way above those prevailing in the west.[30] Considering that even the west German manufacturing sector had severe competitiveness problems at the beginning of the 1990s, this can explain the ensuing terrible employment losses in the manufacturing sector in the former GDR. Employment began to decline sharply as early as 1990 in all sectors that were exposed to western competition. Between 1991 and 1993, total employment shrank by 15 per cent and manufacturing employment fell by some 45 per cent. Of course, an economic catastrophe of these dimensions affected public finances and the welfare state. Budget deficits rose quickly and added to public debt, which had already grown substantially, given that the debt of the former GDR was absorbed by the united Germany.

Even in the face of such an extraordinary challenge as unification, the Bundesbank continued to follow its tight monetary policy. The bank had been already very uneasy about the rate at which the GDR's currency was converted into Deutsche Mark,[31] but was unable to do more than voice its

TABLE 4
BUDGET DEFICITS AND PUBLIC DEBT AS A SHARE OF GDP (1991–98)

Year	Deficit	Debt
1991	−3.3	41.3
1992	−2.6	44.4
1993	−3.2	50.1
1994	−2.4	50.2
1995	−3.3	60.5
1996	−3.4	63.0
1997	−2.6	63.6
1998	−2.0	63.1

Notes: Deficit (-) refers to general government financial balances as a percentage of nominal GDP. Debt refers to general government gross financial liabilities as a percentage of nominal GDP. From 1994 onwards it includes the debt of the German Railways Fund and the Inherited Debt Fund from 1995.

Sources: OECD, *Economic Outlook* (Paris: OECD July 1999), pp.254 and 258.

concerns. From the very beginning, the German central bank had also signalled that it would not accept deficit financing of the unification process beyond a level that could be justified by initial 'unexpected burdens'.[32] Furthermore, the bank was worried about the high wage increases that were struck in the immediate post-unification boom. It signalled to the federal government and to the unions that it was unwilling to accommodate their expansionary policies.[33] In December 1991 the bank rate and the Lombard rate were raised to a new post-war record level and about half a year later the bank rate was raised even further.[34] The Bundesbank raised interest rates at a time when recession was already in sight[35] and thereby hardly cushioned the downturn. The unification boom in the west ended in a deep recession at a time when the eastern economy had hardly recovered from the immediate post-unification recession. With the Deutsche Mark as the anchor of the European Monetary System, the Bundesbank's policy also had international repercussions. Other European countries had either to raise their interest rates to German levels or were forced out of the system. Eventually, major European countries that had pegged their currency to the DM had to defend parity or suspend it. Consequently, the DM appreciated even further. The high wage increases aggravated the competitiveness problem of German industry, leading to major employment losses in the west German export industries. Finally, the Bundesbank started to reduce interest levels, albeit in many small steps.

The federal government had strongly underestimated the costs of unification and overstated revenue especially from the sale of the Treuhand[34] companies, that is, the privatisation of the formerly state-owned companies in the east.[36] This was a mixture of wishful thinking and 'strategic optimism' related to the approaching general elections in 1990. Things turned out quite differently. Instead of a renewed economic miracle, a depression devastated the east and the public budget went deep into deficit. The privatisation of the Treuhand companies became a burden rather than a boon for the federal budget.[37] To make things even worse, the government had committed itself just before the elections to a no tax-raise policy in an attempt to make the public believe that current income would suffice to cover the costs of unification. In 1991, expenses could still be covered partly through additional tax revenues from the boom in the west. The remainder had to be financed out of borrowing. Given the policy of the Bundesbank, however, this quickly came up against difficulties. The government had to renege on its 'no tax-rise' commitment: the Solidarity Law and the Tax Amendment Act as of June 1991 introduced a temporary 7.5 per cent surcharge on personal and corporate income tax, increased some excises and provided the new Länder with temporary special tax expenditure allowances. However, these allowances, which were intended to promote investment in the new Länder, reduced the price of capital in relation to labour. In consequence, western companies placed highly capital-intensive production sites in the new Länder, which, of course, did not make a substantial impact on unemployment. Moreover, the tax allowances[38] became a major fiscal loophole that decreased revenue from assessed income tax.

The public deficit increased again to 3.2 per cent of GDP in 1993 as economic growth turned negative; but even after economic recovery in 1994 the deficit remained high since tax revenue did not grow in line. It was only in 1995 that the underlying erosion of the tax base became apparent. Despite the solidarity surcharge, tax revenue grew less than nominal GDP[40] due to the rapid decrease of assessed income tax and the corporate tax. The former declined between 1992 and 1996 from DM41.5 billion to DM11.5 billion! This was mainly due to the above mentioned generous tax exemptions for investments in the new Länder. The decline of corporate income tax was less pronounced but developed against a background of increased company profits. In this case tax competition may well have played a role.[41]

At a time when increased deficits were ruled out and revenue from corporate and personal income taxes stagnated or even decreased, while a reduction in the expenditure for the east was impossible as well, it became tempting to finance unification via social insurance. This is exactly what happened. It has already been pointed out that the social insurance schemes were financially in pretty good shape at the beginning of the 1990s. Initially, they could support the increased burdens imposed by unification without immediately running into deficits. Unemployment insurance was most rapidly hit by the collapse of the east German labour market. The government raised the contribution rate by 2.5 percentage points in 1991. The additional expenditure for the east in that year amounted to some DM30 billion, of which only DM5 billion could be met out of the federal subsidy. The remaining deficit of DM25 billion had to be financed by contributions in the west.[42]

Health insurance was also, albeit indirectly, used to cover expenditures which otherwise would have to be paid for by the federal budget. Cutting payments from unemployment insurance to the sickness funds which provide health insurance for the unemployed helped reduce the deficit in the unemployment insurance that had to be covered out of the central budget. This again saved the government money. Finally, the government shifted the burden onto the pension scheme. In 1992, the pension scheme of the GDR was integrated into the western system, two years in advance of the date that had initially been agreed upon. This meant that west German contributors now covered deficits in the east that resulted from the gap between pension revenue and spending under the all-German pension scheme.[43] It has been calculated that the west German pension schemes would have run surpluses that could have even made a reduction in contribution rates possible if the money had not been spent on the revenue gap in the east. The same goes for unemployment insurance.[44] While the government was successful in shifting the burden into other budgets, the money had to come from somewhere. The consequence was rapidly rising contribution rates.

This trend was not counteracted by the Health Reform Act of 1993 (Gesundheitsstrukturgesetz), which could no more than flatten the slope of the growth trend in expenditures and contribution rates. However, despite the precarious state of public finance and the poor labour market performance, even expansionary steps in social policy appeared possible. The introduction of Long-Term Care Insurance (LTCI) in 1994 seemed to go against the trend to cut back welfare spending and to lower entitlements and coverage of welfare programmes. The introduction of LTCI appears to be less surprising, however, if one considers that the main financial burden was once again placed on contribution payers. In fact, the LTCI even reduced public social spending because the insurance partially replaced social assistance payments to the old and frail that were previously covered by the local authorities.[45] While LTCI had some positive employment effects (creating an estimated 67,000 new jobs[44]), the net effect is significantly smaller due to the detrimental impact of increased non-wage labour costs.

The welfare schemes had to bear the brunt of adjustment in the labour market as well. In the west we basically find the familiar adjustment pattern: new cohorts of older workers continued to leave the labour market. The pension reform of 1989, which took effect in 1992, did not substantially restrict access to early retirement: the introduction of a higher retirement age was to be only slowly phased in from 2001. Hence the impact of the reform was marginal and early retirement remained the most important response to the crisis. Work creation in the west never regained the importance that it had in the late 1980s, despite increasing unemployment in the recession. This seems to be a consequence of the large shift of resources to the east. Vocational training, by contrast, has remained quite stable.

Turning to the east, it is clear that the huge west German welfare state had to buffer the economic shock. Once a functioning labour market administration had been established in 1991 in the five new states, early retirement became widely used. The first pre-retirement provision had already been introduced by the last Communist Modrow government and was included in the Unification Treaty. About 400,000 older workers in east Germany made use of this pre-retirement provision. The Unification Treaty replaced this scheme – which had to be financed out of the federal budget – by a new scheme (*Altersübergangsgeld*) with very similar benefits but financed by the Federal Employment Office. Around 600,000 workers used this scheme. As an effect of these and other early retirement programmes, the labour force participation of older eastern workers fell to extremely low levels.

However, given the scale of the labour market disaster in eastern Germany, early retirement programmes alone could not do the job. Active labour market policy was extended to unprecedented lengths. Employment in work-creation schemes has been at least twice as high in the east as in the west in every year since 1991, although the working-age population in the new Länder is only about a fifth of that of the west. In contrast to the situation in the old Länder, work creation schemes were often used to improve eastern infrastructure. Since such investments are quite expensive, the federal government subsidised these schemes in the first two years of their existence. When budgetary pressures intensified, the government curbed spending. Consequently, employment in these schemes fell by 60 per cent in the following years, interrupted only by a short-lived upturn just before the 1998 elections. The expansion of both active as well as passive labour market policy led to a further increase in social insurance contributions. In the following final section we briefly discuss the effects this had on labour market performance and economic competitiveness.

WELFARE AND WORK: SOCIAL INSURANCE AND EMPLOYMENT

It has been pointed out repeatedly that in Germany the fate of social insurance is closely linked to the development of employment, since gross wages are the financial base of the German welfare state. Although less obvious, the reverse is also true. Employment in Germany began to decline in the early 1990s and has continued to do so in both parts of the country. While this has clearly put social insurance under financial strain, the very same schemes may well be part of Germany's unemployment problem.

Rising insurance contributions do not affect employment as long as employers are able to turn over the burden to the employees (or to consumers), which are then faced with a (real) net wage decline.[47] If employees or the unions successfully defend (real) net wage levels, labour costs rise. This, of course, has adverse employment effects. As Tyrväinen[48] has shown, real wage resistance is indeed very high in Germany. Another study conducted by Bauer and Riphahn[49] also concludes that the rise in social security contributions has led to higher real wages and consequently had negative employment effects. These findings explain why employers and employees increasingly search for legal loopholes that would free them from the obligation to pay the ever higher social insurance contributions. An increasing number of companies try to avoid paying contributions by classifying their workers as 'self-employed'. This practice is particularly widespread among workers with average or above-average wages (for example, journalists or marketing experts), but also increasingly used in home-delivery, cleaning or transportation. The impact of rising social insurance contributions at this lower end of the wage scale is even more problematic. Here, the net wage often cannot fall in response to higher non-wage labour costs, given that wages would then fall below the level of unemployment benefits or social assistance. One consequence is that many low-productivity jobs become unprofitable and are either replaced with more capital-intensive production methods or are not created in the first place. The upshot is poor job growth and below-average employment in the German service sector. Until recently, employers and employees could also avoid paying insurance contributions through the use of a special provision that exempted employment contracts of less than 15 hours a week and DM 630 a month from paying contributions. There is considerable uncertainty as to how widespread this non-regular form of employment has become, with estimates ranging from 1.6 to 5.4 million jobs. But all available empirical evidence shows that there has been a sharp increase in the number of these non-standard jobs since the early 1990s. This again indicates that increasing non-wage labour costs, in particular rising social insurance contributions, do pose a serious problem. It is our contention that Germany's unemployment problem is closely related to the steady upward trend in non-wage labour costs caused by the increase in the welfare cost burden put on labour. The increase in labour's cost share, in turn, is a consequence of the tendency of both firms and the state to externalise the costs of economic and financial adjustment to economic crises onto the contribution-financed welfare state.

In putting our argument in perspective, two final remarks are in order. First, when assessing in comparative terms how pathological Germany's 'pathological adjustment' really is, it is necessary to make certain implicit normative judgements explicit. In fact, we do not think a basic shortcoming of the contemporary German *Standort* debate is that it ignores the fact that mass unemployment occurs in other European countries as well. That many other countries of continental Europe share Germany's problem of very poor labour market performance provides little comfort in our view for 'the median' (Germany) within this miserable group. Mass unemployment is not less of a social scandal if it also occurs somewhere else.

In this study we have confined ourselves to identifying the basic mechanisms that have prime responsibility for the German 'welfare-without-work' dilemma. We have tried to explain why high structural unemployment might be a strategic equilibrium given the incentives of Germany's political and economic order and the interests of the key actors: employers, unions and the state. Yet, it should be clear that we do not think the cost-shifting game we have described has been inevitable or is irreversible. Quite the contrary. A number of political initiatives, some of which were already undertaken by the former CDU/FDP government, have tried to lower social insurance contribution rates mainly by increasing again that part of welfare spending financed from the central budget, that is, out of general taxation. Yet, in showing how long the shifting of welfare costs to the expense of labour has been going on, our analysis can help highlight how problematic and politically difficult a trend reversal will be – especially in times when taxation has become pretty much a depleted resource. In our view, the current turmoil in German politics indicates that while the traditional strategies of economic adjustment have become disadvantageous for the key actors responsible, the search for alternatives remains costly and conflict-ridden.

NOTES

1. See J. Alber, 'Der deutsche Sozialstaat im Licht international vergleichender Daten', *Leviathan* 26/2 (1998), pp.199–227.
2. Translation: 'business location Germany'.
3. M.G. Schmidt, 'Immer noch auf dem "mittleren Weg"? Deutschlands Politische Ökonomie am Ende des 20. Jahrhunderts', *ZeS Arbeitspapier* 7 (1999).
4. See W. Carlin and D. Soskice, 'Shocks to the System: The German Political Economy under Stress', *National Economic Institute Review* 159 (1997), pp.57–76; R. Czada, 'Vereinigungskrise und Standortdebatte. Der Beitrag der Wiedervereinigung zur Krise des westdeutschen Modells', *Leviathan* 26/1 (1998), pp.24–59.
5. F.W. Scharpf, *Crisis and Choice in European Social Democracy* (Ithaca: Cornell University Press 1991).
6. See with more detail P. Manow and E. Seils, 'Adjusting Badly: The German Welfare State, Structural Change, and the Open Economy', in F.W. Scharpf and V.A. Schmidt (eds.), *From Vulnerability to Competitiveness. Welfare and Work in the Open Economy* (Oxford: Oxford University Press 2000, forthcoming); A. Hemerijck, P. Manow and K. van Kersbergen, 'Welfare without Work? Divergent Experiences of Reform in Germany and the Netherlands', in S. Kuhnle (ed.), *The Survival of the European Welfare State* (London: Routledge, forthcoming).

7. G. Lehmbruch, *Parteienwettbewerb im Bundesstaat. Regelsysteme und Spannungslagen im Institutionengefüge der Bundesrepublik Deutschland* (Opladen: Westdeutscher Verlag 1998).
8. W. Abelshauser, 'Ansätze "korporativer Marktwirtschaft" in der Korea-Krise der frühen Fünfziger Jahre', *Vierteljahreshefte für Zeitgeschichte* 30 (1982), pp.715–56; A. Shonfield, *Modern Capitalism* (Oxford: Oxford University Press 1965).
9. P.A. Hall, 'Central Bank Independence and Coordinated Wage Bargaining: Their Interaction in Germany and Europe', *German Politics and Society* (Spring 1994), pp.1–23; W. Streeck, 'Pay Restraint without Incomes Policy: Institutionalized Monetarism and Industrial Unionism in Germany', in R. Dore, R. Boyer and Z. Marn (eds.), *The Return of Incomes Policy* (London: Pinter 1994), pp.118–40.
10. For instance, acceptability criteria in German unemployment insurance hold that unemployed persons have to accept only those jobs whose pay does not fall below the level that has been agreed upon by unions and employers in collective bargaining. See K.-H. Paqué, 'Unemployment and the Crisis of the German Model: A Long-Term Interpretation', in H. Giersch (ed.), *Fighting Europe's Unemployment Problem* (Berlin: Springer 1996), pp.123–55.
11. D. Soskice *et al.*, 'Wage Bargaining, Labour Markets and Macroeconomic Performance in Germany and the Netherlands', in L. Delson and E. de Jong (eds.), *The German and Dutch Economies. Who follows Whom?* (Berlin: Physica 1998), pp.39–51.
12. See OECD, *Employment Outlook* (Paris: OECD July 1994), p.175.
13. T.J. Pempel and K. Tsunekawa, 'Corporatism without Labor? The Japanese Anomaly', in J. Ravenhill (ed.), *Japan Vol. 1 (The Political Economy of East Asia)* (Aldershot: Elgar 1995), pp.31–75.
14. H.G. Hockerts, 'Vom Nutzen und Nachteil parlamentarischer Parteienkonkurrenz. Die Rentenreform 1972 – ein Lehrstück', in K.-D. Bracher *et al.* (eds.), *Staat und Parteien* (Berlin: Duncker & Humblot 1992), pp.903–34.
15. See H. Russig, 'Sozialversicherungs- und arbeitsrechtliche Rahmenbedingungen für die Ausgliederung älterer und leistungsgeminderter Arbeitnehmer aus dem Betrieb', in K. Dohse, U. Jürgens and H. Russig (eds.), *Ältere Arbeitnehmer zwischen Unternehmensinteressen und Sozialpolitik* (Frankfurt: Campus 1982), pp.237–82.
16. M.G. Schmidt, 'Staatsfinanzen', in K. von Beyme and M.G. Schmidt (eds.), *Politik in der Bundesrepublik Deutschland* (Opladen: Westdeutscher Verlag 1990), pp.53–5 and 60.
17. See Sachverständigenrat zur Begutachtung der gesamtwirtschaftlichen Entwicklung, *Gegen Pessimismus. Jahresgutachten 1982/83* (Stuttgart: Verlag W. Kohlhammer 1982), p.98.
18. R. Sturm, 'Die Wende im Stolperschritt – eine finanzpolitische Bilanz', in G. Wewer (ed.), *Bilanz der Ära Kohl: christlich-liberale Politik in Deutschland 1982–1998* (Opladen: Leske+Budrich 1998), p.186.
19. See Sachverständigenrat zur Begutachtung der gesamtwirtschaftlichen Entwicklung, *Auf dem Wege zur wirtschaftlichen Einheit Deutschlands. Jahresgutachten 1990/91* (Stuttgart: Metzler-Poeschel 1990), pp.136–7.
20. Alber, 'Der deutsche Sozialstaat'; J. Alber, 'Recent Developments in Continental European Welfare States: Do Austria, Germany and the Netherlands prove to be Birds of a Feather?', paper presented at the 14th World Congress of Sociology, 29 July 1998, Montreal.
21. The Pre-Retirement Act introduced the opportunity for employers to lay workers off at the age of 58 (the so-called 58er rule) and to pay them for between two (women's retirement age: 60) and five years ('flexible retirement' age for men: 63) at least 65 per cent of their last net wage. At the same time, the law provided a public subsidy of a maximum 35 per cent of the retirement wage if the vacant position was filled by a registered unemployed or a trainee for at least two years. However, early retirement did not stir up a lot of excitement among employers and workers since it was more costly for employers and offered less generous benefits for workers. The take-up rate was rather modest, with about 165,000 workers between 1984 and 1988 when the act expired. The substitution rate has been estimated to have been about 80 per cent, thus producing a maximum of 135,000 new jobs. See K. Jacobs, M. Kohli and M. Rein, 'Germany: The Diversity of Pathways', in M. Kohli, A.-M. Guillemard and H. van Gunsteren (eds.), *Time for Retirement. Comparative Studies of Early Exit from the Labor Force* (New York: Cambridge University Press 1991), pp.181–221. J.

Frerich and M. Frey, *Handbuch der Geschichte der Sozialpolitik in Deutschland bis zur Herstellung der deutschen Einheit* (München: Oldenbourg 1993), report even lower numbers.

22. See I. Mares, 'Business (Non-)Coordination and Social Policy Development: The Case of Early Retirement', in P. Hall and D. Soskice (eds.), *Varieties of Capitalism* (Cambridge: Cambridge University Press, forthcoming).

23. The Federal Office of Labour had a budget surplus of 3.1 and 2.3 billion DM in 1984 and 1985 and a marginal deficit of 0.2 billion DM in 1986. In the years between 1983 and 1988 the government did not need to cover deficits of the Federal Office with state subsidies.

24. See Jacobs *et al.*, 'Germany: The Diversity of Pathways', p.203.

25. F.W. Scharpf, 'Optionen der Arbeitsmarktpolitik in den achtziger Jahren', in F.W. Scharpf *et al.* (eds.), *Aktive Arbeitsmarktpolitik. Erfahrungen und neue Wege* (Frankfurt: Campus 1982), pp.18–19.

26. G. Lehmbruch, 'Die deutsche Vereinigung. Strukturen und Strategien', *Politische Vierteljahresschrift* 32/4 (1991), pp.585–604.

27. W. Seibel, 'An Unavoidable Disaster? The Germany Currency Union of 1990', in P. Gray and P. 't Hart (eds.), *Public Policy Disasters in Western Europe* (London: Routledge 1998), pp.96–112.

28. See Sachverständigenrat zur Begutachtung der gesamtwirtschaftlichen Entwicklung, *Vor weitreichenden Entscheidungen. Jahresgutachten 1998/99* (Stuttgart: Metzler-Poeschel 1998), p.80.

29. Deutsche Bundesbank, 'Ein Jahr deutsche Währungs-, Wirtschafts- und Sozialunion', *Monatsbericht der Deutschen Bundesbank* 43/7 (July 1991), pp.19–20.

30. Deutsche Bundesbank, 'Die westdeutsche Wirtschaft unter dem Einfluß der Vereinigung Deutschlands', *Monatsbericht der Deutschen Bundesbank* 43/10 (Oct. 1991), p.21.

31. Deutsche Bundesbank, 'Überprüfung des Geldmengenziels 1991', *Monatsbericht der Deutschen Bundesbank* 43/7 (July 1991), p.17.

32. Deutsche Bundesbank, 'Überprüfung des Geldmengenziels 1992 und Anhebung des Diskontsatzes', *Monatsbericht der Deutschen Bundesbank* 44/8 (Aug. 1992), pp.15–21.

33. Deutsches Institut für Wirtschaftsforschung, 'Deutsche Geldpolitik wirkt prozyklisch', *Wochenbericht* 10/93 (1993), p.96.

34. A holding owned by the federal government that comprised a large part of the GDR's economy.

35. R. Czada, 'Der Kampf um die Finanzierung der deutschen Einheit', *MPIfG Discussion Paper* (Cologne: Max Planck Institute for the Study of Societies 1995), p.5.

36. Deutsche Bundesbank, 'Die Finanzen der Treuhandanstalt', *Monatsbericht der Deutschen Bundesbank* 46/4 (April 1994), pp.22–31.

37. Bundesministerium der Finanzen, *Finanzbericht 1991* (Bonn: Bundesministerium der Finanzen 1991), pp.103–10.

38. Deutsche Bundesbank, 'Neuere Entwicklungen der Steuereinnahmen', *Monatsbericht der Deutschen Bundesbank* 49/8 (Aug. 1997), p.87.

39. Ibid., pp.92–3.

40. Deutsche Bundesbank, 'Aktuelle Finanzentwicklung der Sozialversicherungen', *Monatsbericht der Deutschen Bundesbank* 49/11 (Nov. 1991), p.34.

41. Moreover, in some cases the recalculation of east German pensions in line with west German law led to lower pensions as compared to the old entitlements in the GDR. The difference was then made up by an additional transfer (*Auffüllbetrag*) until 1995. According to the Deutsche Bundesbank, 'Die Finanzentwicklung der gesetzlichen Rentenversicherung seit Beginn der neunziger Jahre', *Monatsbericht der Deutschen Bundesbank* 47/3 (March 1995), p.22, it amounted to DM6 billion a year. This sum again had to be covered mainly by contributions.

42. See Deutsches Institut für Wirtschaftsforschung, 'Vereinigungsfolgen belasten Sozialversicherung', *Wochenbericht* 40/97 (1997), p.729; Deutsches Institut für Wirtschaftsforschung, 'Gesetzliche Rentenversicherung: Senkung des Rentenniveaus nicht der richtige Weg', *Wochenbericht* 24–25/97 (1997), pp.433–4.

43. J. Alber, 'Paying for Long-Term Care in a Social Insurance System: The Example of

Germany', paper presented at a meeting on 'Caring for Frail Elderly People: Policies for the Future' (Château de la Muette, Paris, 5–6 July 1994).

44. See Bundesministerium für Arbeit und Sozialordnung, 'Erster Bericht zur Lage der Pflegeversicherung', *Bundestags-Drucksachen* 13/9528 (1997), p.38; S. Pabst, 'Mehr Arbeitsplätze für Geringqualifizierte nach Einführung der Pflegeversicherung?', *WSI-Mitteilungen* 4/52 (1999), pp.234–40.

45. The increasing internationalisation, or in the case of Germany, Europeanisation of markets has made it near impossible simply to add national increases in production costs to prices.

46. T. Tyrväinen, 'Real Wage Resistance and Unemployment: Multivariate Analysis of Cointegrating Relations in 10 OECD countries', *Jobs Study Working Paper* No.10 (Paris: OECD 1995), p.19.

47. See T. Bauer and R.T. Riphahn, 'Employment Effects of Payroll Taxes – An Empirical Test for Germany', *IZA Discussion Paper* No.11 (Bonn: Institute for the Study of Labor 1998).

Desperately Seeking a Solution: Social Democracy, Thatcherism and the 'Third Way' in British Welfare

MARTIN RHODES

With the arrival of the Blair government in Britain and the subsequent hype surrounding the 'Third Way', there has been much media debate and academic argument about the nature of New Labour and the fate of the economy and the welfare state in its hands. While the media have simultaneously been charmed by the novel amalgam of policies embraced by the Blair government and irritated by the 'spin' with which their presentation has been managed, academics can be divided between those who have picked their way through the policy detail so as to specify what is really new and those who seek to assess New Labour in terms of the social democratic tradition. The latter, in turn, can be divided between those who find a complex combination of neo-liberal continuity and social democratic change,[1] those who criticise New Labour for accommodating the preferences of 'capital' and repudiating its social democratic inheritance,[2] and others still who see New Labour in power as a party facing a genuine set of dilemmas created by globalisation, a fractured domestic production system and fragmented national identities.[3] All would argue that New Labour could push much further than it has with policies that revive the social democratic agenda, both in terms of enhancing competitiveness and reconnecting politics with the interests and collective aspirations that were marginalised under Thatcher and Major.

This normative view is grounded in a critique of New Labour's rightward march since the late 1980s and is linked to a set of analytical arguments concerning the scope for social democratic innovation at a time when many argue that sovereignty has been severely eroded by globalisation. The aim of the discussion which follows is to engage tangentially with that debate by considering, in historical perspective, the problems faced by British governments of both right and left in building and reforming the welfare state, culminating with a brief and schematic consideration of New Labour in this context. Like some of the authors cited above, the analysis accepts that the loss-of-sovereignty argument has been heavily overstated and that room for manoeuvre remains substantial for national governments in selecting and promoting priorities in the trade-off between social equity and growth. Nevertheless, some nations – and their political representatives in government – enjoy more autonomy than others; the weight of the past is more constraining in certain countries, depending critically on the availability of both material and institutional resources and the capacity to mobilise them.

In the British case, an understanding of the welfare state under New Labour must begin by considering the history of post-war welfare state policy, the nature of the British social democratic project for welfare, and its failings, and the extent and depth of the legacy of the Conservative government. Although much has been written on these subjects, this article seeks to reinterpret that literature in terms of the problematic nature of the welfare state in relations between governments and the labour movement and its contribution to the fractured history of British social democracy. Several main points will be emphasised below: (1) the distinct – and perhaps unique – failure of social democracy in Britain to internalise a consensus on the social wage and broader welfare priorities; (2) the contribution of this failure to the problems of economic management from the 1950s to the 1970s, to which the welfare state frequently fell victim; (3) that Thatcherism, for all its faults and failures, provided a solution to this problem, to which British social democracy could not respond given its own internal contradictions; and (4) that rather than globalisation and the purported arrival of the 'knowledge society', it is this legacy – of the welfare state as problem rather than resource for British social democracy – that explains the nature of New Labour and its 'Third Way'.

THE HISTORICAL LEGACY: SOCIAL DEMOCRACY AND THE SOCIAL WAGE

In the British case, it is not so much a question of accepting or repudiating the preferences of capital – or even the constraints imposed by 'globalisation' – that is at issue with New Labour. It is rather one of coping with the complex policy interdependencies and embedded assumptions about taxation and social expenditure created by almost two decades of radical, market-oriented reform under the Conservatives in the absence of an alternative, legitimising 'success story'. Whereas other European countries are recasting their welfare states within a modified tradition of social corporatism (Scandinavia, apart from Sweden) or revived or newly created structures of concertation (the Netherlands, Italy, Portugal, Ireland), the UK's legacy of failed concertation in the 1960s and 1970s, the 'demonisation' of corporatism by the Conservatives after the truly disastrous experience of the 'Winter of Discontent' and the massive loss of power suffered by the unions under Thatcherism makes such experimentation unlikely in Britain. Whereas numerous new 'Third Ways' in Europe consist of making expensive welfare states with heavy long-term pension liabilities and funding problems more employment-friendly and sustainable (a process in most cases inaccurately described as neo-liberal),[4] the UK under New Labour is engaged in a different process: making a highly deregulated and increasingly polarised economy with much less generous welfare buffers a little more compassionate; and countering the most severe failings of the system within the limits set by the Thatcherite legacy and the precarity of its new electoral base.

At the same time, whereas the welfare state is a solid and undeniable achievement of European Social and Christian Democracy, in Britain it is one that has been far less complete and universal (and for that reason less costly) than in continental Europe, and one that is less solidly entrenched in the social democratic movement and its aspirations. This has its origins in the inter-war period. Although the introduction of social insurance against unemployment and sickness in 1911 led to union involvement in running the state's insurance schemes alongside their own limited occupational regimes, the unions withdrew from social insurance management under the pressure of recession and high unemployment in the 1930s. One of the peculiarities (at least in the European context) of the British system was the consequent divorce between the labour movement and the social insurance system.[5] Combined with 'voluntarism' and organisational fragmentation in industrial relations, this helped prevent the development of the notion of the 'social wage' in Britain and would contribute to the more general problems of economic management in the post-war period.

Thus, in the British case it makes analytical sense to separate clearly the 'formal' welfare state – the core programmes of social provision – from the 'informal' welfare of employment and incomes policy.[6] On the formal side were the programmes introduced by the major pieces of legislation in the 1940s, providing universal rights of access to equal standards of health care, family income support, comprehensive social insurance (including pensions), public housing and education. Compared to many of its continental counterparts, however, this was to be a rather 'austere' welfare state – due to the 'reluctant collectivism' of the system's architect, William Beveridge, as well as resistance from the Treasury to a more generous system of National Insurance, pessimism about the state of the post-war economy and a reluctance to antagonise industrialists with high social costs. While often seen as the cradle of British social democracy, the Attlee government's innovations were in reality rather cautious, reflecting a mix of influences and involving a large dose of pragmatism and continuity with pre-war policies and institutions.[7] On the 'informal' side of the welfare state lay the commitment to a full and stable level of employment. But therein lay one of the biggest flaws in the post-war settlement. For successfully stimulating growth and full employment via demand management depended on the predictable behaviour of employers and trade unions. Inflationary pressures in a seller's market for labour could only be contained if distributional conflict was controllable.[8] However, in the absence of a consensus on the social wage and an acceptance of trade-offs between wage gains and social policy advances, organised labour could not easily be 'encompassed' within a broader structure of economic management.

Thus, the formal and informal sides of the welfare state, broadly defined, would constantly come into conflict. Social democracy in Britain was consequently unable to consolidate welfare as a major foundation of its own project for social transformation for its expansion was always to be problematic. Thus welfare – which has always been a victim of rather than contributor to Britain's economic problems[9] – became closely caught up in the unfolding pathology of permanent post-war economic crisis. The maintenance of full employment in an uncompetitive industrial system and in the absence of a sustainable incomes policy strongly contributed to the 'stop–go' cycle of the 1950s and 1960s. When demand was expanded to sustain employment, imports increased, potential exports were diverted to the home market, and a balance of payments crisis threatened (frequently also provoking a sterling crisis and higher interest rates, indicating that 'globalisation' has always been problematic for Britain). Given that devaluation was often resisted to protect the trading and reserve roles of sterling, the response was always the same: reduce demand, increase unemployment and create the conditions for another 'go' phase in the cycle; and, in turn, the revenue and spending policies used to regulate these fluctuations frequently also hit formal welfare provision.[10]

As a result, neither party in power was fully capable of controlling the social policy agenda or of successfully managing the economy in classical Keynesian fashion. Of course, governments were not just victims of this process; they directly contributed to it, not just by excacerbating the cycle by poorly timed expansionary policies and unrealistic assumptions about their capacity to end 'stop–go', but also because their commitment to the so-called 'welfare consensus' was much more fragile than often assumed –

and, according to some historians, a myth.[11] Thus, there was an early
'Thatcherite' critique of the burden of welfare in the Conservative Party in
the 1950s (and successful attempts to claw back social spending and reduce
the state's contribution to National Insurance), while, on the Labour side,
the image of a solid and unassailable commitment to full employment and
a high-spending universal welfare state should be modified. By the mid-
1960s, many Labour ministers, including Jim Callaghan, also accepted the
'burden approach' to welfare, while, as Bale argues:

> the story of social policy between 1964 and 1970 is the story of a
> Labour government trying – often by moving more or less
> successfully from "universalism" to "selectivity" – to control
> increases in expenditure originating in both its own promises in
> opposition and the pre-election profligacy of its Conservative
> predecessors, while at the same time hoping to retain its electoral
> image as defender of the welfare state.[12]

This not only raises questions about the actual commitment of Labour
governments in power to universal welfare, but also about the strength of
the commitment in British social democracy to Marshall's concept of
citizenship and unconditional entitlements. Even if a central part of the
Labour Party's own mythology, it has frequently been overridden to meet
the exigencies of policy making.

Romanticisation of the Attlee years should also be tempered. Although
the Attlee government was doubtless more committed to building a strong,
universal welfare state than subsequent Labour administrations (its ministers
had yet fully to comprehend the difficulties of doing so in British conditions),
in fact the late 1940s saw the first breakdown between Labour in power and
the trade union movement over the issue of the social wage. Despite the
credit gained with the labour movement from building the welfare state,
nationalising a substantial proportion of the economy and leaving in place a
raft of cost-of-living subsidies, wages policy quickly led to breakdown when
Britain was forced into its first major currency devaluation in 1949. Attempts
to offset the impact of subsidy reductions and price increases with more
social spending met with union opposition.[13] When, in spring 1950, Stafford
Cripps, the Chancellor of the Exchequer, offered budgetary concessions in
return for wage restraint, the TUC General Secretary advised that 'he did not
believe the unions would recognize the notion of the social wage'.[14] At the
same time, the beginnings of bargaining fragmentation had already appeared,
with a powerful shop stewards movement in the car industry and unofficial
dockers' strikes. So too had the external constraint on welfare spending: the

1947 sterling convertibility crisis reduced the availability of dollars for timber imports (hitting the government's housing programme), while expenditure cuts after the 1949 devaluation reined in spending on health and education. Per capita health spending was static between 1948 and 1954 (it fell as a proportion of GDP), capital expenditure on hospitals fell to a third of pre-war levels and, in May 1951, a divided government beset by economic difficulties introduced charges for dental and ophthalmic care – breaching the principle of a free health service and provoking the resignation of the Health Minister, Aneurin Bevan.[15]

This example is only the first of many to suggest that one of the most important constraints on social democracy in government in Britain has had less to do with 'capital's fear of and opposition to socialism' (although employers will always be wary of constraints on their freedom and resist them) than the internal divisions of social democracy as a movement and the contribution this has made to economic mismanagement. Elsewhere, more coherent social democratic projects and productive links between social democratic parties and labour movements succeeded in accommodating employers to welfare expansion and the costs that implied. In Britain, the absence of a strong cross-party consensus on welfare obviously exacerbated matters. In the 1950s, attacks by the Conservatives on universal welfare provision united the trade unions in their defence of free collective bargaining and against the introduction of new incomes policy measures. The government then became caught between two contradictory policies: it used rising wages and full employment to justify the removal of universal social welfare, while also using the welfare state to justify appeals for wage restraint.[16] At the same time, the external constraint continued to operate and the failure of incomes policy initiatives made it all the more unmanageable. Policy lurched between contracting the economy when a failure to achieve balances, above all in foreign payments, threatened sterling, and expanding it when unemployment started to rise. The excessive use of monetary and fiscal instruments to engineer deflation was highly damaging to investment – both public and private. The manipulation of current and capital social expenditure had damaging effects on social provision.

Labour should have been better placed than the Conservatives to confront this set of contradictions. But while it did not provoke industrial strife by directly attacking the social wage, nor could it underpin it with sustainable advances in welfare and a workable incomes policy or use it as a means of rendering the external constraints less debilitating. Ironically, it was the last years of the Conservative government in the early 1960s that witnessed a more or less successful, if 'tacit', alliance with the unions in which wage moderation was exchanged for welfare expansion – in hospitals, higher education and council housing. But the conditions for an enduring and explicit bargain did not exist, as revealed by the crises of the 1964–70 Labour government. Labour under Harold Wilson planned a state-led modernisation strategy, linking planning with industrial policy, and a revival of incomes policy; but both were completely overwhelmed by economic problems. By 1965/66, the economy was over-heating and inflation threatened competitiveness. After many years of current balance surplus, a large deficit was recorded in 1964 and low reserves and a weak payments position exposed sterling to crisis on three occasions between 1965 and 1967. The consequent combination of cuts and tax increases diverted nearly £1bn (or three per cent of GNP) from consumption. 'Globalisation' was arguably more problematic then than now. Greater international competition increased the import propensity of the economy and prevented producers from passing on increasing unit wage costs; and, as revealed by the financial disasters of 1965–68, the confidence of overseas bankers and speculators had become at least as important as the state of the real economy.[17]

Against this background – and supporting the interpretation of Bale above – not only were ambitious reforms of pensions, local government and the NHS abandoned, but means-tested claimants and benefits increased enormously after a promised 'income guarantee' and upgrade in universal benefits were jettisoned. Plans for a complete overhaul of the training system were undermined by the absence of consensus among firms on training delivery and a failure to override union control of the apprenticeship system. Prescription charges – which Labour had withdrawn on its return to office – were reintroduced.[18] Nor was there any new consensus on the social wage. Labour was unable to use demand-management to draw the unions into a voluntary and long-term incomes policy commitment. A fractured labour movement, in any case, provided an unlikely partner in such a project, for there were by now 200,000 or more workshops, sections or groups into which 2,000 or so plants had fragmented for pay decisions. In 1965/66, wage rates and hourly earnings rose at twice the norm due to plant-level pay increases and wage drift. After devaluation, attempts to introduce a zero norm, deflationary policies, unemployment at over two per cent and attempts by employers to recoup profitability all led to the strikes and wages explosion of 1969–70 that brought the Conservatives back to power.

In terms of the underlying dynamic of discontinuous economic policy
making, there is no sharp break between the experiences of recurrent 'mini-
crises' in the 1960s and the major crises of the 1970s. 'Globalisation', it is
true, became more pernicious. Competitive and sterling reserve problems
were longstanding features of the economy and short-term capital flows had
always had a strong influence on exchange rate policy and the balance of
payments. But in the 1970s the foreign exchange market became much
more important in determining the exchange rate, reflecting both long-term
factors, such as the internationalisation of capital markets, and short-term
factors, including the inflow and outflow of OPEC oil revenues after the oil
price hikes of the mid-1970s. Nevertheless, the essence of Britain's problem
remained the same: the failure to maintain productive efficiency in industry,
which led to export losses, an increased import propensity, balance-of-
payments problems and short-term, knee-jerk government responses which
further damaged investment and productivity. Incomes policies increasingly
became attempts (though rarely successful) to bring prices into line with the
weakened condition of the economy as export markets became more
competitive. But the competitiveness problem itself remained untackled:
Britain's major competitor countries (France, West Germany, Italy and
Japan) were able to absorb higher wage costs by productivity gains that
British industry failed to generate.[19] Social democracy in Britain had failed
to find any answer to this problem, regardless of a series of industrial policy
and planning initiatives during the 1960s and 1970s.

Against this background, the welfare state continued to be the victim
rather than a cause of recurrent crisis. Conflict around the issue of the social
wage remained central to problems of economic management and renewal.
Like other Conservative governments before it, the Heath administration in
the early 1970s failed to appreciate the importance of the social wage.
While health and education were ring-fenced, alternatives to state provision
were actively sought in housing and income maintenance and the 1973
Pensions Act sought to wind down National Insurance and introduce greater
reliance on private occupational pensions.[20] Nor did its industrial relations
policies enamour it to an increasingly militant labour movement: the
Industrial Relations Act of 1971 – which sought to bring greater coherence
and responsibility to wage bargaining – was rejected outright by the unions.
Most reprehensible for the latter was its attack on the closed shop. Through
1972, the unions consciously sought to develop the issue of the social wage
and demanded radical welfare concessions to any new wage accord. The

collapse of these talks led to an initially successful statutory pay freeze but ultimately helped create the circumstances in which the Heath government toppled in the face of a large miners' wage claim and strike.

By contrast with the Conservatives' refusal to make large social spending concessions in return for wage moderation, Labour came back to power in 1974 with the social wage placed very firmly at the centre of its drive to innovate in economic management and welfare reform. It was its total failure to do so – in an ignominious culmination of successive preceding attempts – that sounded the death knell of British-style social democracy, as much as the heavily symbolic 'Winter of Discontent' that concluded Labour's four troubled years of 'power'. By invoking the social wage, the Wilson government hoped to be able to bind the unions to government policy without surrendering its freedom to govern. However, as it turned out, inflexibility in domestic policy at a time of unprecedented external pressures meant that, in 1974–75, Labour prioritised full employment while relying on an insubstantial incomes deal. In Germany and the US, by contrast, a tough combination of fiscal and monetary constraint in the face of the first oil price shock was followed by a return to expansionary policies in 1975. Thus, Britain went into Europe's deepest recession in 1974–76, with zero growth (compared with 3–5 per cent growth in France, Italy and Germany), stagnant productivity and a collapse of industrial profitability. Both prices and unemployment rose faster in Britain than elsewhere.[21]

Welfare policy advanced and retreated as the desperately sought consensus on improvements in the social wage failed to hold. 'Real wages' – that is, pay after tax, social security and benefits – was to be at the centre of the Labour's new incomes policy, backed by industrial relations reform. Fulfilling its side of the bargain, Labour repealed the Conservatives' industrial relations laws, strengthened dismissals protection and the closed shop, bolstered union recognition, guaranteed pay during lay-offs and extended mandatory notice periods for redundancies. Pensions reform sought to end the massive dependency on means-tested, supplementary benefits by introducing a state earnings-related pension (SERPS). Earnings-related contributions for National Insurance were also introduced.[22]

On the labour side, however, the unions failed to deliver – despite the desire of many of the labour movement's leaders to sustain concertation. Wages spiralled out of control in 1975 – the year the social wage innovations were introduced – and, despite some success in Phase 1 of the incomes policy, the story of the next three years is one of policy conflict and disaster, compounding the problems created by a difficult external situation.

Decentralised, plant-level bargaining made local shop stewards pivotal and union leaders could not deliver restraint. The wages and prices explosion of 1975 led to tax increases and cuts and cash limits in all spending programmes. A growing fiscal crisis forced the government into heavy borrowing to meet increased demands for welfare as unemployment rose, undermining foreign confidence and forcing the value of sterling to historically low levels. By spring 1977, unemployment was rising less rapidly, inflation was falling and the pressure on the exchange rate had eased after market confidence was restored by the negotiation of the $3.9 billion loan from the IMF. But now the unions felt less constrained and attacked the government for abandoning full employment and over IMF-induced cuts and spending limits. Labour had lost control of the situation, and a miscalculated and over-restrictive pay norm for the last phase of the incomes policy provoked its collapse – and with it that of the Callaghan government.

The casualties of the 1974–78 period were not just the welfare advances made in Labour's first year in power (in the 1978 Supplementary Benefit Review, a renewed emphasis on means-tested benefits was explicitly made[23]), but also any possibility of a productive relationship, based on a social-wage consensus, between the Labour Party and the unions. The death of traditional British social democracy can be dated from this point – a demise due not to globalisation or the collapse of the Keynesian paradigm (elsewhere in Europe, social democracy has adapted and survived) – but to the dysfunctions and contradictions generated by the basic flaw at its heart: the failure to make the welfare state a resource rather than a problem for its project of social and economic transformation. By the 1970s this had become a structural constraint, rather than one just of attitudes and ideology.

As Nina Fishman has argued, the relationship between the unions and the Labour Party had long been troubled by a dysfunctional union world view that prevented even pragmatic and flexible labour movement leaders from engaging in constructive social partnership. She describes this world view as one in which those unionists socialised into the activist 'rank and file' tradition saw 'the state' as alien to workplace matters:

> The cultural composition of this view is dense and complex. It contained elements of true-born Englishness, the denser mythology of British trade union triumphalism and disingenuous Leninist obfuscation. What is crucial is that no Labour intellectual, from Tony Crosland to Dick Crossman, made any serious attempt to combat it.[24]

At the same time, combating this world view had become increasingly difficult given the manifest problems facing successive Labour governments in delivering on their promises and the fact that, despite its many achievements, the British welfare state had fallen short in many respects. Thus, three decades of development in which continuity had been overridden by crises, short-term policy switches and budgetary fluctuations undermined the government's powers of raising revenue, distributing income and meeting new needs. Coupled with technical and organisational inefficiencies, this had affected the quality of provision in all services. Long and growing waiting lists in the health service, deficiencies in education and literacy problems among school leavers and the proliferation of social problems in areas of slum rehousing all attested to these problems. There were persistent gaps in coverage of social need (affecting the long-term unemployed, the low paid with inadequate income support, the disabled, single-parent households and pensioners), alongside poverty and unemployment traps. By the end of the 1970s the social security system was struggling to deal with the consequences of an increasingly regressive tax system and the expansion of means-tested benefits – to which Labour in government had contributed.[25]

The financing of welfare and the operation of the tax system had become caught up in the pathologies of the industrial relations system. Years of increasing benefits and funding them from higher taxes and National Insurance contributions produced heavy distortions in the social wage, with detrimental consequences for incomes – amongst the working poor as well as higher wage earners. Thus, while trade union militancy was fuelled by an obstructionist world view, empowering legislation, rising membership, the growth of the closed shop and the fragmentation of the bargaining system, it was also driven by genuine frustration with the decline of freely disposable incomes. This was due to the incidence of standard tax rates at low levels of income and the rapid rise in additional costs per employee in National Insurance contributions and taxes (which rose from 21 to 47 per cent of net earnings between 1960 and 1980). While taxes on income and capital, including net insurance contributions, rose only from 20.8 per cent of GNP in 1950 to 23.8 per cent of GNP in 1980, taxes on spending – which are regressive in effect – rose from 14.7 to 19.3 per cent. It has been calculated that between 1949 and 1975/76, the proportion of post-tax income received by the bottom 50 per cent of income earners rose hardly at all – from 25.6 to 27.4 per cent.[26]

In sum, from the 1950s on, the two dimensions of the British welfare state – the formal programmes of social provision and the informal welfare of employment and the labour market – were kept in separate spheres, and when and where they interacted the result was often dysfunctional. As in other European countries, welfare could be used as part of an ensemble of public interventions to sustain demand and full employment and compensate for risks over the life cycle. But in Britain, Keynesian policies were always problematic in practice, especially in reconciling full employment with wage demands and growth with the balance of payments and exchange rate stability. In turn, the lack of consensus on the social wage – fed by and feeding into a dysfunctional union 'world view' – triggered a level of industrial relations conflict that exacerbated the cycle of macro-mismanagement and decline. Thus, in its disjointed mix of formal social programmes and labour market income delivery, both the 'accumulation functions' and 'legitimation functions' of welfare in British capitalism were flawed. As the system worked its way steadily towards breakdown in the mid to late 1970s, so its contradictions also ripped apart what remained of 'real existing' social democracy in Britain.

Rather than destroying social democracy in Britain, Thatcherism simply put the twisted, distorted and broken being it had become out of its misery, helping New Labour by the mid-1980s to seek a renewal of its tradition, but in radically changed political and economic circumstances. This is not a normative statement in favour of Thatcherism, but simply to stress that although there may have been alternatives to the subsequent programme of New Right-inspired reform, it is difficult to find one in the tradition and practices of Labour governments in power in the 1960s and 1970s. Reviving corporatism was not an answer in the late 1970s and early 1980s given the fragmentation of bargaining and the hostility of an unstable but conservative coalition of union activists and leaders to anything other than 'the historic, democratic working-class traditions of "free" British trade unionism'.[27] Even if the will and organisational capacity had existed on both sides, a new Labour government in power after 1979 would have had little to exchange in return for a union commitment to concertation.

THE THATCHERITE SOLUTION: BREAKING THE CIRCLE

Understood broadly in both its formal and informal dimensions, and the relationship between them, the story of the British welfare state until the 1980s was one in which political debilitation combined with economic decline to create what Glennerster calls 'welfare with the lid on'.[28] That is, a constrained welfare state in which, despite periods of spending expansion, there was little scope for building on the basic foundations put in place in 1945 or indeed to protect them from steady erosion, as manifest, for example, in the steady shift from universal to means-tested benefits. Debilitation and decline can be attributed in part to the failure of both Labour and Conservative governments to find a means of establishing autonomy from either trade unions or producer groups or forging a consensus on distributional issues. As demonstrated above, distributional conflict during the not-so-golden 'Golden Age' of British welfare fed into a vicious circle of industrial maladjustment, macro-economic mismanagement and social strife.[29]

Only Thatcherism succeeded in breaking this circle. This, it is true, was only after a further 15 years of economic turbulence and much unnecessary damage to Britain's industrial base; but therein lies the power of its legacy. It is commonplace to stress that Thatcherism combined a political with an economic strategy and that creating a strong market required a strong state.[30] Yet it is worth reiterating that, in contrast to the understanding of many not acquainted with the history of post-war economic policy, the Conservatives did not simply avail themselves of an institutional structure (the 'Westminster model') to radically transform the country. To wield power as she saw fit, Margaret Thatcher had to demolish, then rebuild, with demolition firmly centred on Britain's collectivist institutions. Some see this as the only consequence of her policies – with little being put in their place, or even much success in refounding the British economy.[31] But coming at the question from the above analysis of distributional conflict, the rather brutal institutional 'fix' achieved by Thatcherism had a number of important effects, with far-reaching implications for economic management, the welfare state and the future of the Labour Party.

In abandoning the attempt of governments since 1946 to forge a negotiated link between the formal and informal welfare states around the notion of the social wage, the power of unions to influence government policy was radically reduced – indeed eliminated – and a new and instrumental linkage could be forged between the social security system and the labour market, by 'activating' benefits and making welfare a tool of employment policy. To that extent, the welfare state had ceased to be a problem of economic management; if effective trade-offs between incomes and the social wage could not be achieved, then abandoning the attempt to do so removed a perennial source of conflict from the policy-making agenda. As a result, even if welfare spending remained at roughly the same level in 1997 as 20 years earlier (a key component in arguments about the failure of the Conservatives to retrench in welfare), its role changed fundamentally. The most important long-term results would be a new subservience of social policy to the interests of the economy (and where possible subject to market competition), the division of welfare purchasers from welfare providers, the decentralisation of responsibilities for benefit delivery (to local government and in some cases businesses) and the concentration of formal powers of control in the hands of central government – trends largely continued, and indeed reinforced under New Labour in the late 1990s.[32]

This is not to suggest, however, that there was a clear blueprint for change in the hands of the Conservatives in 1979 and that they proceeded to implement it with unerring determination and foresight. But privatisation, new restrictive industrial relations laws, the diminution of the powers of local government and the massive sell-off of public housing all simultaneously strengthened the institutional capacity of central government, sapped the electoral strength of Labour and helped to build a new pro-market social coalition. In formal welfare provision, as many acknowledge, public spending on welfare changed little as a proportion of GDP between the mid-1970s and the mid-1990s, and spending on health and social security actually increased while that on education stagnated and that on housing fell. Julian Le Grand noted that welfare remained critical throughout the 1980s and 1990s in cushioning the impact of economic restructuring on incomes and social stability.[33] Nevertheless, Britain did move over this period from being a relatively high spender and taxer to being relatively low on both counts. The impact could be found in the deteriorating quality of many programmes, reductions in capital investment (which affected public housing, infrastructure and education, in particular) and a large reduction in the size of the public sector workforce. There were also the long-term effect of cuts and the break in the linkage between earnings and benefits, the new managerialism in the NHS, the political and economic consequences of greater social divisions and changes in citizenship rights as explicit and implicit disentitlement hit vulnerable sections of the population.[34]

Then there is the long-term impact of these changes on the ideology of the left and the prospects of responding to Thatcherism with a revitalised social democratic agenda. So successful was Thatcherism as a 'hegemonic' project – and so weak by contrast was the social democratic alternative on offer between the early 1980s and the late 1990s – that, regardless of one's judgement of the long-term success in transforming Britain's economic prospects, its anti-inflation, low tax and liberal labour market policies became socially and politically embedded. In making itself electable, Labour has therefore been forced to embrace the same macro- and micro-economic policy orientation and engage with the 'Thatcherite' electoral coalition, while also striving to differentiate itself from Conservative neo-liberalism and bring its own traditional supporters on board. Again, particularly as regards welfare and economic management, there was little that it could revive in the way of a counter-plan from its own experiences in government. This – at least as much as the residue of traditional Labour Atlanticism – explains its attempts in the 1990s to borrow elements from the US Democrats' employment and social policy agenda, mingled with some suitably modified components of its own dirigiste tradition.[35]

Of course, in attempting to innovate in policy, New Labour has also had to deal with the very real transformation of the British economic model produced by Thatcherite social and employment policy and the economy's roller-coaster ride in the 1980s and 1990s. It is difficult to disentangle the consequences of macro-economic policies, a secular process of tertiarisation, purposive policy objectives and the knock-on effects of a high level of foreign direct investment (attracted in part by the low levels of corporation tax and employers' contributions allowed by the lean UK welfare state). Changes in legislation and labour law dovetailed neatly with other influences to create a liberal market economy with a strong bias in employment-creation towards both the high-paid and low-paid ends of the service sector and growing income inequality. On the policy side, without entering into all of the details, it is worth noting the following general orientations: trade unions were placed in a legal straightjacket which overturned the tradition of 'labour immunities'; labour market reregulation re-empowered employers and facilitated non-standard forms of employment; benefit changes provided 'incentives' to find work and remove employment traps; and in the 1990s they were increasingly integrated with work or training requirements. This reform mix interacted with the labour shakeout and manufacturing crises induced by the cycle of boom and bust to hasten the process of socio-economic change.

This was arguably an unnecessarily drastic and painful way of unblocking the system. Rowthorn argues that Britain under the Conservatives has been a clear and distinctive case of 'negative de-industrialisation' in which manufacturing labour has been shed against the background of a stagnant manufacturing output and a much less than full absorption of the unemployed into services.[36] But unblock the system it did. Tough new industrial relations laws, recession and the massive reduction in manufacturing employment all contributed to the decline in trade union power, the reassertion of employers' prerogatives over pay and conditions of work and the parallel decline of collective bargaining. The transformation of the labour market has been extensive. Jobs lost in manufacturing and other non-service sectors were concentrated in the middle range of the earnings distribution, while the increase in employment has been concentrated in sectors like banking, finance and business services where earnings are relatively high and in hotels, catering and other services where pay is low, contributing to growing income inequality.[37] Welfare benefits, meanwhile, took on a 'stick and carrot' character. In the 1980s there was a shift away from insurance benefits towards income-tested benefits for the unemployed, while their generosity was reduced by taxation and de-indexation from earnings.[38] If this was the 'stick', the 'carrot' was the appearance of 'in-work benefits' (Family Credit), which sought to remove the unemployment trap by increasing incomes for those in work while also reducing the replacement rate without major cuts in benefits. Meanwhile, combining the stick with the carrot, new education and training schemes to improve employability were married to a set of benefit changes to coerce the young unemployed into taking up places.

If alongside tax reform one takes into account the combination of industrial relations law, labour market re-regulation and the restructuring and reorientation of social security, one becomes aware of the scale of the transformation that has taken place in the way in which welfare interacts with the economy – regardless of many continuities in spending levels and even institutions in certain areas. Moreover, this is a welfare system reconfigured to match a new economic trajectory. Given the return of Britain to economic stability, non-inflationary growth and employment creation since 1992, it can be argued that these changes have recreated a functional compatibility between the institutional infrastructure and essential individualism of a liberal market economy, when past attempts to build relationship capitalism so dismally failed. This is not a normative argument in favour of Thatcherism but an attempt to grasp – from a long-term perspective – the nature of the change that has occurred. For several interlocking components of a new 'model' can be discerned in the new configuration created by nearly 20 years of neo-liberal social and employment policies, macro-economic (mis)management and a more advanced degree of tertiarisation than elsewhere in Europe.

First, by breaking the link between state pensions and earnings in 1980, the Conservatives have penalised those solely dependent on such pensions, but also freed subsequent governments from the accumulated pensions liabilities that other European countries are struggling to deal with. This will also allow a forecast decline in employer and employee National Insurance contributions – an important advantage in a low-productivity, service-based economy. Second, if, as argued by Desmond King and Stewart Wood,[39] Conservative policies transformed training partly into a means of providing firms with temporary, low-cost labour rather than creating incentives for investment in employable skills, 'in work' means-tested social security benefits arguably subsidised employers so that they could create more low-wage employment.[40] This dovetailing of the social security system and the deregulated labour market with the demands of the large low-wage, low-skill sector of the economy, has become simultaneously a source of employment creation in sectors where other European countries perform poorly and a contributor to greater income inequality. If New Labour's thinking is partly mid-Atlantic, this is not just because of a tradition of Atlanticism on the British centre-left, but because there are many similarities between the UK and US labour markets and the way they now function.

Bringing relatively low levels of taxation and easy access to credit into account, a further key component of this model is sustained demand by high levels of personal disposable income (by European standards) for the supply of low-wage, low skill (increasingly service sector) labour. Demand for higher skilled service sector and manufacturing labour has been driven by success in certain high technology sectors and an internationalisation strategy creating considerable dependence on FDI for investment, employment and exports, sustained by low corporation taxes and employers' social charges and a compliant workforce.

Britain's formal and informal welfare systems are now locked into a particular form of competitiveness and economic growth which – for all its faults (in particular high levels of income inequality) – represents a form of 'success'. Moreover, one can argue that the 'new functionality' between welfare and the economy must be conformed with, for on this will depend the growth and employment creation that might allow for more equitable policies in the long run. As argued below, rather than the accommodation of the preferences of capital, or the subversion of social democracy in the global era, it is this legacy of complex policy linkages and institutional transformation that explains – and constrains – New Labour.

TURNING VICE INTO VIRTUE: NEW LABOUR'S 'THIRD WAY'

We live in a world of trade-offs which are difficult to avoid. In the case of welfare the systemic trade-off appears to be between high levels of social protection and low levels of employment versus high levels of employment and inequality. But to borrow a term from Jonah Levy, it is possible to turn 'vice into virtue'.[41] In the case of many continental European economies, this requires a complex process of recasting social security systems to facilitate the type of employment creation which Britain enjoys – without, however, creating a mass of working poor. In doing so they have to negotiate a course among powerful vested interests wedded to their system's structure of transfer payments and income support. In the British case, creating greater equity alongside economic growth will involve the opposite strategy. Having avoided many of the pitfalls of Europe's expensive, transfer-heavy welfare states, Britain – in moving closer to the European mainstream – will have to resolve its problems of inequality while retaining its capacity for employment creation, in both highly paid and low-paid services. It, too, must avoid alienating entrenched interests. Yet in the British case it is much less the usual array of welfare constituencies that count on the continent, but rather the resistance of the general public to paying higher taxes – regardless of the willingness oft-recounted in opinion polls. This appears to be the course on which New Labour has embarked.

The challenges are considerable. For as well as finding itself in charge of a welfare model which has some advantages over those of its continental counterparts, New Labour has also inherited a host of problems – not just from the Thatcher/Major years but from the long-term inadequacies of the British welfare and broader economic systems. Thus, there are a number of question marks over Britain's economic performance. On the one hand, according to the OECD, by 1996 the 'natural rate of unemployment' was below many European countries, as was the 'non-accelerating wage rate of unemployment' (NAWRU), reflected in five to six years of recovery with very little wage pressure since 1993. Meanwhile, from 1985 to 1995, UK relative labour productivity levels rose by five percentage points per person and ten percentage points per hour worked *vis-à-vis* the United States. Nevertheless, UK labour productivity is still the weakest of the G7 along with Canada, due to a lower level of per capita investment in physical assets and skill acquisition than elsewhere in the OECD. Spending on education, research and development as share of GDP has fallen from above the OECD average to about the median level and the stock of qualifications lags behind countries with significantly higher living standards – a difficult gap to bridge unless the arrival of the 'knowledge economy' truly does prioritise generic education and skills in which Britain performs less badly.[42]

The most important legacy of Thatcherism is inequality and its broader effects in terms of poor social cohesion, poverty and crime. Despite a real increase in social security spending of more than 50 per cent between 1979 and 1993/94, the number in poverty (on less than half the average national income) more than doubled to ten million. By 1997, 14 million people were officially classified as poor.[43] Almost one-fifth of all working age households are jobless – a threefold increase since the late 1970s – while one-third of all children live in poor families, more than in any other EU country. The increase in the number of *working* poor is the down-side of Britain's apparent success in job creation in the 1990s. Between 1978 and 1992 there was a rapid growth in the polarisation of income distribution with virtually no real wage growth for the lowest income earners. By 1995, the share of income distribution for the tenth decile was eight times that of the first decile, compared with 4.5 times in 1979. At the same time, recent studies report a decline in income mobility, with growing numbers stuck in a low-pay-no-pay cycle.[44] In the mid to late 1990s, nearly ten million people in 5.7 million families (20 per cent of the population) were dependent on means-tested Income Support, compared with 4.4 million in 2.9 million families receiving the equivalent in 1979.[45] This poses a no less considerable problem than the flaws in the British economy, but neither are susceptible to easy solutions.

Meanwhile, certain sectors of the welfare state remain under strain, with a constant call for new resources – and in many areas this is a problem which pre-dates Thatcher. As pointed out above, the Conservatives were responsible for stagnant investment in education, but increased spending in social security and health where there are constant demands for new resources. The British NHS may be efficient in comparison with other European countries, but there are major shortfalls – and this is has been true for decades – in terms of access to specialist treatment, the availability of hospital beds and a relative paucity of doctors and nurses. As *The Economist* recently reported, although the $1,454 per head spent by Britain on health in 1997 compared with the European average of $1,684 does not show up in life expectancy figures, survival rates for certain diseases are poor. British women under 65 diagnosed with breast cancer have one of the worst survival rates in Europe, and a woman with heart disease in Britain is four times more likely to be killed by it than her counterpart in France.[46]

At the same time, the arrival of a new Labour government in power has naturally triggered demands for progression in other areas towards European best practice, for example in the provision of good-quality, affordable child care.[47] Of course, all of this is expensive, and while New Labour has set out a number of proposals in a series of Green Papers, commitments have been kept to a minimum given its desire to prove itself a competent economic manager and the knowledge that higher taxation as an open strategy is unavailable in Britain. An exception to aversion to large-scale spending promises has been in health, for this – as discovered by Margaret Thatcher – is an area that no government interested in re-election can afford to neglect. Thus, in response to opinion poll concern with the state of the NHS, compounded by the strains placed on hospital care by the flu epidemic in 1999/2000, the Blair government has promised to spend five per cent extra a year on health between 2000 and 2002, although its aim to bring health spending up to the European average would require the extension of those increases through until 2005.

This is just one indication that there is something 'new' under New Labour, alongside another initiatives, that render attempts to characterise what is happening in terms of 'neo-liberal convergence' too blunt and imprecise, although there are certainly elements of continuity between Major and Blair.[48] Nor are other approximations to either traditional British liberalism or a more 'capitalist version of liberalism and one-nation, paternalistic conservatism' any more adequate as descriptions.[49]

In favour of the 'neo-liberal convergence' argument, there was the pledge to hold public spending for the first two years to previous Conservatives targets, with the exception of the 'New Deal' for employment (see below) to be financed by a £5.2 bn 'windfall tax' on the privatised public utilities. Spending was set to rise by a real 2.8 per cent per annum between 1998 and 2002, leaving total spending at 40.6 per cent GDP in 2001/2 and *below* the 41.1 per cent of the Conservatives' last year in government.[50] Efforts at budgetary consolidation made under the Conservatives were also continued, including the Private Finance Initiative (PFI), which brings private sector funding and management into public infrastructure projects via competitive tendering. The 'New Deal' and 'Welfare to Work' initiatives also seem to follow closely the logic and method of Conservative employment and benefits policy, by linking 'in work' benefits even more closely to coercive instruments for labour market insertion.

Nevertheless, a number of initiatives indicate that, alongside the 'Third Way' rhetoric on a 'new contract' in welfare and its stress on 'a modern form of welfare that believes in empowerment not dependency',[51] one does find elements of an older, social democratic concern with redistribution and social justice. Rather than announcing grand spending plans, New Labour has been increasing expenditure and taxation by stealth. 'Stealth taxes' have included a £5bn per annum tax on pension funds and future pension incomes and the abolition of mortgage tax relief and the married couple's tax allowance. 'Stealth spending' has included the new working families tax credit (see below), a guaranteed minimum income of £175 per week to unemployed older workers (aged 50 to 64) finding work and a £40 per week top-up to part-timers. They will also be offered a £750 grant if they find work to help with training and a personalised advice service if unemployed for more than six months. Child benefits have been given above inflation increases. A new minimum income guarantee for pensioners adds £75 a week for singles and £121 a week for couples to their annual incomes, and future increases will be indexed to earnings. Also operating with redistributive effect is a lower tax band of ten per cent introduced in the 1999 budget to benefit low-income earners. The same budget also reduced the standard rates of tax to 22 per cent, but increased National Insurance contributions. The increases in the health and education budgets may prove quite substantial, with a combined increase of £5 billion per annum by 2002, although there is concern that a significant proportion of this sum will be absorbed by salaries and capital spending.

As Colin Crouch has pointed out in his analysis of reforms in the labour market, innovations such as these bear the hallmarks of classical social democracy, British-style, while others mix social democratic aims with neo-liberal instruments.[52] A third category of initiatives – manifest in public services reform – mix the Thatcherite legacy with pure New Labour concerns with community and partnership.

On the social democratic side of the scale, the introduction of the new £3.60 per hour minimum wage (for adults aged 22 and over) in April 1999 provided more than two million workers with wage rises of up to 40 per cent. There have been enforcement problems, with employers seeking to evade the new regulations, and criticism of the absence of social partner involvement in ensuring effective pay structures. But, together with the implementation of the EU's Working Time Directive by New Labour, the minimum wage has been described as representing a 'quantitative shift in the role of employment legislation in the creation of rights for workers at least as important as that brought about by the Equal Pay Act of the 1970s'.[53] New rights to trade union recognition fall into the same camp. Under the 1999 Employment Relations Act, workers in firms with more than 20 employees will be entitled by law to union representation if at least 40 per cent of their number vote for it, while in firms where at least 50 per cent of workers are already union members, recognition is awarded as of right. The Act also extends protection against dismissal to all employees after 12 months' service and all employees involved in a grievance procedure will have the right to representation by a union official.[54]

As in the new statutory redundancy consultation procedures (another example of legislation introduced to comply with EC law), there remain problems with the nature of representation given New Labour's opposition to statutory frameworks for information and consultation with employee representatives. British labour law is still not fully in line with the ILO Conventions breached by Conservative reforms in the 1980s, even if this new legislation considerably closes the compliance gap,[55] but alongside

New Labour's emphasis on 'partnership projects' in the workplace, such innovations may lay the foundations for a more solid system or permanent consultative arrangements.[56] While the Conservatives opposed all such measures on the grounds of their supposed threat to competitiveness, for New Labour they are important for underpinning a flexible labour market with fair minimum standards. To that extent, while the methods may be described as 'social democratic', the objectives reveal an effort to render a deregulated (neo-liberal) labour market less iniquitous.

Those initiatives linking neo-liberalism with a social democratic ethos include, most explicitly, as Crouch argues, the New Deal and Welfare to Work. New Labour's pensions' policy can also be placed in this category. The New Deal moves people from social security benefits to work through new resources for training, subsidies for employers taking on workers for more than six months (or older people for two years). There is also a commitment to guaranteeing work for all 18–24 year olds unemployed for six months or more.[57] In a clear example of how New Labour marries compulsion with obligation in its 'contract for welfare', young people have four options: training, subsidised private sector work force, voluntary sector work or work with the new Environmental Taskforce. There is no fifth option of benefit receipt for unemployed young people under 25 years beyond six months.

Other benefit changes seek to reinforce the 'in-work' welfare initiatives of the Conservatives. Thus, welfare payments to lone mothers without jobs have been reduced, and their workforce participation encouraged by the provision of both childcare and occupational training. The Working Families Tax Credit is more generous than the Family Credit that preceded it and is linked to a new child care tax credit; together, they are intended to combat the unemployment trap, although there is some doubt about their potential impact on poverty.[58] As for pensions, New Labour is creating a three-tier system, in which the existing flat-rate contributory pension, which is indexed to prices, is complemented by a State Second Pension, which provides those earning less than £9,000 per annum with state-funded contribution credits which effectively bring them up to £9,000 for purposes of entitlements, while those earning between £9,000 and £18,500 receive tapered credits of the same type. The 'neo-liberal' or 'market' element is the third tier of 'stake holder' pensions, which will be privately administered retirement income protection plans competing with other such schemes in the private pension market and relying on a new partnership with private pension companies.[59]

Other initiatives mix the Thatcherite inheritance with something new altogether, seeking to balance the legacy of Thatcherite marketisation with a new emphasis on partnerships and community and 'network governance' that is pure New Labour. Thus, in health care there is a retention of the Conservative's purchaser-provider principle alongside a step back from the quasi-market system introduced by the Conservatives. New Labour will create local partnerships that consolidate family doctors and community nurses into Primary Care Groups to work with hospitals and care services, while an attempt is being made to resurrect national health dentistry, which has all but collapsed in recent years. More generally in the public services, the stress is on new collaborative structures that retain the Conservative's centralised control over services, while encouraging their delivery via local authority–agency–private sector partnerships.[60]

In sum, this is a complex and in some respects imaginative amalgam of policy reforms representing important innovations, even if they are much less extensive than many welfare professionals and traditional Labour supporters would like.[61] But then this is the 'Third Way', not the 'old way'.

CONCLUSION

In effect, New Labour has to contend with two historical legacies. The first, identified by many commentators both inside and outside the party, is the legacy of the 1970s and the tarnishing of the Labour Party with a reputation for incompetence in economic management. As the first part of this article stressed, the inheritance is in reality much more complicated than responsibility for the 'Winter of Discontent', an episode inflated and exaggerated by years of right-wing and media demonology and in itself a considerable constraint on the resurrection of social concertation. The real legacy is one of 30 years in which conflict over the social wage undermined both Labour and Conservative administrations. This was arguably much more important for Labour since it cut to the heart of its social democratic project and identity and eventually ripped it out. None of this makes progressive, centre-left politics impossible in contemporary Britain, but it makes the revival of anything resembling the old social democratic (perhaps one should say Labourist) tradition not just difficult but politically suicidal.

The second is the legacy of the Thatcher/Major governments, which might not be so profound had New Labour in the late 1990s found itself instead in the economic circumstances of 1990/91, when recession, high unemployment, low growth and the ERM debacle had all discredited the Conservatives (if not yet making them unelectable). Labour came to power with a fundamentally transformed economy delivering high rates of growth and job creation compared with its European neighbours, a situation quite different from that encountered by the Attlee government in 1945 and one in which, as argued above, there are many new and complex, interlocking policy linkages – created over two decades – which are highly resistant to radical reform. This is neither a 'preference accommodation' nor a structural dependence argument, nor even one suggesting that 'there is no alternative'.[62] However, it does seek to allow for the possibility that there is now a degree of functionality between the formal and informal dimensions of the contemporary British welfare state and the country's current economic trajectory which, in comparative perspective, has both its manifest problems and its undeniable successes. If it is committed to any degree of progressive reform, New Labour must of necessity tackle the former while building on the latter – while also maintaining its new electoral base. Such is the art of politics.

NOTES

This article is based on wider research on internationalisation and welfare states carried out for the Max Planck Institute for the Study of Societies in Cologne. The findings of that project will be published in *Work and Welfare in Open Economies* (Oxford: Oxford University Press 2000), edited by Fritz Scharpf and Vivien Schmidt. I should like to thank Ian Gough and Des King for their comments on an earlier draft.

1. E.g. C. Crouch, 'A Third Way in Industrial Relations?', in S. White (ed.), *Labour in Government: The 'Third Way' and the Future of Social Democracy* (London: Macmillan 2000, forthcoming); and D. King, *In the Name of Liberalism: Illiberal Social Policy in the United States and Britain* (Oxford: Oxford University Press 1999).
2. See, e.g., C. Hay, *The Political Economy of New Labour: Labouring under False Pretences?* (Manchester: Manchester University Press 1999).
3. E.g., J. Krieger, *British Politics in the Global Age: Can Social Democracy Survive?* (Oxford: Oxford University Press 1999); and M. Kenny and M.J. Smith, '(Mis)understanding Blair', *Political Quarterly* 68/3 (1997), pp.220–30.
4. For a useful discussion on the character of Social Democratic welfare reform in Europe, see P. Pennings, 'European Social Democracy between Planning and the Market: A Comparative Exploration of Trends and Variations', *Journal of European Public Policy* 6/5 (1999), pp.743–56.
5. C. Crouch, 'Employment, Industrial Relations and Social Policy: New Life in an Old Connection', *Social Policy and Administration* 33/4 (1999), pp.437–57; C. Toft, 'State Action, Trade Unions and Voluntary Unemployment Insurance in Great Britain, Germany and Scandinavia, 1900–1934', *European Economic Review* 39 (1995), pp.565–74.
6. This formulation – and the centrality of the notion of the 'social wage' in the argument which follows – owes much to the influence of Herman Schwartz and Noel Whiteside.
7. J. Tomlinson, 'Why so Austere? The British Welfare State of the 1940s', *Journal of Social Policy* 27/1 (1998), p.72; N. Barr and F. Coulter, 'Social Security or Problem?', in J. Hills (ed.), *The State of Welfare: The Welfare State in Britain since 1974* (Oxford: Clarendon Press 1990), pp.274ff..
8. D. Marquand, *The Unprincipled Society: New Demands and Old Politics* (London: Fontana Press 1988), p.44.
9. See, e.g., R. Bacon and W. Eltis, *Britain's Economic Problem: Too Few Producers* (London: Macmillan 1976).
10. For details, see R. Lowe, *The Welfare State in Britain since 1945* (London: Macmillan 1993), pp.109ff; and M. Stewart, *The Jekyll and Hyde Years: Politics and Economic Policy since 1964* (London: J.M. Dent & Sons Ltd 1977).
11. See B. Pimlott, 'The Myth of Consensus', in L.M. Smith (ed.), *The Making of Britain: Echoes of Greatness* (London: Macmillan 1988).

12. T. Bale, 'The Logic of No Alternative? Political Scientists, Historians and the Politics of Labour's Past', *British Journal of Politics and International Relations* 1/2 (June 1999), pp.192–204.
13. N. Whiteside, 'Creating the Welfare State in Britain, 1945–1960', *Journal of Social Policy* 25/1 (1996), pp.90ff.
14. R. Jones, *Wages and Employment Policy, 1936–1985* (London: Allen & Unwin 1985), pp.30ff.
15. Lowe, *The Welfare State in Britain since 1945*, p.180; J. Tomlinson, 'Welfare and the Economy: The Economic Impact of the Welfare State, 1945–51', *Twentieth Century British History* 6/2 (1995), p.212.
16. Whiteside, 'Creating the Welfare State in Britain', p.98.
17. See N. Woodward, 'Labour's Economic Performance, 1964–1970', in R. Cooper, S. Fielding and N. Tiratsoo (eds.), *The Wilson Governments, 1964–1970* (London: Pinter 1993), pp.74–5; and S. Pollard, *The Development of the British Economy 1914–1990* (London: Edward Arnold 1992), p.360.
18. S. Vickerstaff, 'Industrial Training in Britain: The Dilemmas of a Neo-Corporatist Policy', in A. Cawson (ed.), *Organized Interest and the State: Studies in Meso-Corporatism* (London: Sage 1985), pp.45–64; Lowe, *The Welfare State in Britain since 1945*, p.143.
19. Pollard, *The Development of the British Economy*, pp.366–7.
20. H. Glennerster, 'Welfare with the Lid On', in H. Glennerster and J. Hills (eds.), *The State of Welfare: The Economics of Social Spending* (Oxford: Oxford University Press), pp.18–20.
21. K. Burk and A. Cairncross, *'Goodbye, Great Britain': The 1976 IMF Crisis* (New Haven and London: Yale University Press 1982), pp.221–4; K. Middlemas, *Power, Competition and the State: Volume 3 – The End of the Post-war Era: Britain since 1974* (London: Macmillan 1991), pp.10–12
22. Barr and Coulter, 'Social Security or Problem?', pp.277–9; R.J. Flanagan, D.W. Soskice and L. Ulman, *Unionism, Economic Stabilization and Incomes Policy: European Experience* (Washington, DC: Brookings Institution 1983), pp.418–24.
23. Lowe, *The Welfare State in Britain since 1945*, p.324
24. N. Fishman, 'Reinventing Corporatism', *Political Quarterly* 68/1 (1997), pp.31–40.
25. R. Parry, 'United Kingdom', in P. Flora (ed.), *Growth to Limits: The Western European Welfare States since World War II* (Berlin and New York: Walter De Gruyter 1986), pp.202–8; Lowe, *The Welfare State in Britain since 1945*, pp.280–97.
26. Lowe, *The Welfare State in Britain since 1945*, p.282; Parry, 'United Kingdom', pp.200–201
27. Fishman, 'Reinventing Corporatism', p.36.
28. Glennerster, 'Welfare with the Lid On'.
29. Marquand, *The Unprincipled Society*; J. Wolfe, 'State Power and Ideology in Britain: Mrs Thatcher's Privatisation Programme', *Political Studies* 34 (1991), pp.237–52.
30. See A. Gamble, *Britain in Decline: Economic Policy, Political Strategy and the British State* (London: Macmillan 1994).
31. E.g. ibid., p.212.
32. C. Pierson, 'Continuity and Discontinuity in the Emergence of the 'Post-Fordist' Welfare State', in R. Burrows and B. Loader (eds.), *Towards a Post-Fordist Welfare State* (London and New York: Routledge), pp.95–113.
33. J. Le Grand, 'The State of Welfare', in J. Hills (ed.), *The State of Welfare: the Welfare State since 1974* (Oxford: Clarendon Press 1990), pp. 359-360.
34. P. Wilding, 'The Welfare State and the Conservatives', *Political Studies* 45 (1997), pp.716–26.
35. Hay, *The Political Economy of New Labour*; D. King and M. Wickham-Jones, 'From Clinton to Blair: The Democratic (Party) Origins of Welfare to Work', *Political Quarterly* 70/1 (Jan. 1999), pp.62–74. On Labour Atlanticism, see D. Sassoon, 'European Social Democracy and New Labour', in A. Gamble and T. Wright (eds.), *The New Social Democracy* (Oxford: Blackwell Publishers 1999), pp.19–36.
36. R. Rowthorn, *The Political Economy of Full Employment in Modern Britain* (The Kalecki Memorial Lecture, Department of Economics, University of Oxford, 19 Oct. 1999).
37. J. Michie and F. Wilkinson, 'Inflation Policy and the Restructuring of Labour Markets', in J. Michie (ed.), *The Economic Legacy, 1979–1992* (London: Academic Press 1992), pp.195–217.
38. A. Atkinson and J. Micklewright, 'Turning the Screw: Benefits for the Unemployed

1979–1988', in A. Dilnot and I. Walker (eds.), *The Economics of Social Security* (Oxford: Oxford University Press 1989), pp.39–40

39. D. King and S. Wood, 'The Political Economy of Neo-Liberalism: Britain and the United States in the 1980s', in H. Kitschelt *et al.* (eds.), *Continuity and Change in Contemporary Capitalism* (Cambridge: Cambridge University Press 1999), pp.371–97.

40. C. Grover and J. Stewart, '"Market Workfare": Social Security, Social Regulation and Competitiveness in the 1990s', *Journal of Social Policy* 28/1 (1999), pp.73–96.

41. J. Levy, 'Vice into Virtue? Progressive Politics and Welfare Reform in Continental Europe', *Politics and Society* 27/2 (June 1999), pp.239–74

42. OECD, *OECD Economic Surveys: United Kingdom* (Paris: OECD 1998).

43. D. Piachaud, 'Changing Dimensions of Poverty', in N. Ellison and C. Pierson (eds.), *Developments in British Social Policy* (London: Macmillan 1998), pp.233–46; D. Piachaud, 'Wealth by Stealth', *The Guardian*, 1 Sept. 1999.

44. R. Gurumurthy, 'Tackling Poverty and Extending Opportunity', *Political Quarterly* 70/3 (July 1999), pp.335–40.

45. S. Machin, 'Wage Inequality in the United Kingdom', *Oxford Review of Economic Policy* 12/1 (1996), pp.47–64; P. Johnson, 'The Assessment: Inequality', *Oxford Review of Economic Policy* 12/1 (1996), pp.1–14; and OECD, *OECD Economic Surveys: United Kingdom*.

46. 'The Doctor's Dilemma', *The Economist*, 22–28 Jan. 2000, pp.35–6.

47. See L. Harker, 'A National Childcare Strategy: Does it Meet the Childcare Challenge?', *Political Quarterly* 69/4 (Oct. 1998), pp.458–63.

48. Cf. C. Hay, 'Blaijorism: Towards a One-Vision Polity?', *Political Quarterly* 68/4 (Oct. 1997), pp.372–8.

49. M. Freeden, 'True Blood or False Genealogy: New Labour and British Social Democratic Thought', in Gamble and Wright (eds.), *The New Social Democracy*, pp.151–65.

50. J. Hills, 'Thatcherism, New Labour and the Welfare State' (CASE paper No. 13, Centre for the Analysis of Social Exclusion, London School of Economics, Aug. 1998).

51. From New Labour's 'Green Paper on Welfare Reform', cited by A. Deacon, 'The Green Paper on Welfare Reform: A Case for Enlightened Self-interest?', *Political Quarterly* 69/3 (July 1998), p.307.

52. Crouch, 'A Third Way in Industrial Relations?'

53. B. Simpson, 'A Milestone in the Legal Regulation of Pay: The National Minimum Wage Act 1998', *Industrial Law Journal* 28/1 (March 1999), p.30.

54. See Crouch, 'A Third Way in Industrial Relations?'

55. K.D. Ewing, 'Freedom of Association and the Employment Relations Act 1999', *Industrial Law Journal* 28/4 (Dec. 1999), pp.283–98.

56. M. Hall and P. Edwards, 'Reforming the Statutory Redundancy Consultation Procedure', *Industrial Law Journal* 28/4 (Dec. 1999), pp.299–318.

57. Crouch, 'A Third Way in Industrial Relations?'; Grover and Stewart, '"Market Workfare"'.

58. OECD, *OECD Economic Surveys: United Kingdom*.

59. M. Hyde, J. Dixon and M. Joyner, '"Work for Those That Can, Security for Those That Cannot": The United Kingdom's New Social Security Reform Agenda', *International Social Security Review* 52/4 (1999), pp.77–8.

60. C. Painter, 'Public Service Reform from Thatcher to Blair: A Third Way', *Parliamentary Affairs* 52/1 (Jan. 1999), pp.94–112, and OECD, *OECD Economic Surveys: United Kingdom*.

61. For a broad critique of the emphasis on obligations and compulsion in New Labour reforms, and a plea for a 'robust interventionist approach to welfare', see Hyde *et al.*, '"Work for Those That Can, Security for Those that Cannot"', pp.69–86.

62. See Hay, *The Political Economy of New Labour*, who critiques the 'structural dependence' argument and advocates one based on 'preference accommodation' prior to presenting an alternative – based on developing a new regionally based investment culture – which he appears to equate with a revival of the British social democratic tradition. Krieger, *British Politics in the Global Age*, by contrast advises New Labour to build a new 'rainbow coalition' amongst women and ethnic communities to achieve the same end. Each view echoes sentiments found on various parts of the British Left, and links its arguments with the nature of contemporary economic change. But although they mention it in passing, neither takes full account of the problematic nature of welfare politics in Britain, nor its centrality for understanding the contradictions of social democracy in the UK and the nature of New Labour.

Reforms Guided by Consensus:
The Welfare State in the Italian Transition

MAURIZIO FERRERA AND
ELISABETTA GUALMINI

For Italy, the 1990s may be considered an important 'season of reform' in the field of social and labour policy. Between 1992 and 1998 there were numerous innovations in both policy sectors. As regards social insurance, the reforms introduced by Prime Ministers Giuliano Amato and Lamberto Dini have substantially altered the mechanism for calculating pension benefits. These reforms have moreover redesigned the system of seniority pensions (*pensioni di anzianità*) and the relation between the various occupation-based regimes. As regards the labour market, the agreements made by the Amato and Ciampi governments have given rise to radical innovations in the area of industrial relations and incomes policy, in job placement and in policies to promote new employment.

There is a clear *leitmotiv* underpinning this wave of reform: the negotiated nature of the measures, in the shape of consensual agreements between the government, the trade unions and the business associations, which only subsequently received the blessing of the Italian parliament. The negotiations on the reform of the social security system begun by Amato in 1992, the agreements introduced by Amato and Ciampi on employment and incomes policy in 1993, the 'pact for work' (*patto per il lavoro*) approved by Prodi in 1996, and the more recent 'Christmas pact' (*patto di Natale*) of 1998 on socio-economic development of the D'Alema government are the main stages of this new process. Consensus among the social partners has once again become, as in the period of emergency at the end of the 1970s, the vital ingredient in any recipe for reform, and the failure of the Berlusconi government (1994), in the face of a sudden wave of social unrest, to approve an ambitious pension reform proves this point. This consensus must be understood as the fruit of a more or less explicit political exchange between the government and the social partners, in particular the trade unions, which have accepted sacrifices and losses in the short term (the abolition of the system of wage indexation, wage moderation, benefit freezing and the subsequent reform of the pension system, and so on), in exchange for specific medium- to long-term promises (the redistribution of those resources thus recovered for new initiatives to develop and relaunch employment, particularly in the *Mezzogiorno*).

The 1990s provide us with further proof of the singularity of the Italian case. In contrast to other European countries, in Italy concertation, after the hesitations and the uncertainties of the past, seems to occupy an ever broader space and to play an ever more crucial role in national policy making. The Italian case would appear to be close to the Dutch example, where, as of the late 1980s, the rebirth of concertation was accompanied by processes of political learning and policy change which developed into measures of innovation and flexibility.[1]

There is an extraordinary and evident synchronicity between the return of concertation and the politico-institutional changes which occurred in Italy following the collapse of the post-war party system in 1992/93. It was this period of transition – with a growing delegitimation of political parties and a corresponding reinforcement of the executive – which afforded the social partners an excellent opportunity to side-step party mediation and to deal with government directly. In addition to the transformation of the political system, we must add the pressure generated by the process of European integration, which in a certain way 'obliged' the government and the social partners to embark on a rigorous reform of the welfare state and a clear path of incomes policy to keep inflation under control. The 'virtuous' interlinking of the endogenous dynamics of the politico-institutional transition and the exogenous dynamics of the European integration produced a new scenario, and it is here that the constellation of actors favouring the reform of social and employment policies has found a different and arguably more stable footing.

This examination of the reform of the Italian welfare state has two objectives. The first is a reconstruction of the process of reform in the social insurance sector and the labour market in the course of the 1990s. The second is the description of the ways in which the reforms have been introduced, and the characteristics of the constellation of actors which have made them possible.

THE INTERNAL IMBALANCES OF THE BREADWINNER MODEL

Between the late 1940s and the late 1970s, Italy built a welfare system that was highly skewed in favour of male breadwinners located in the core sectors of the labour market.[2] The beneficiaries of this system enjoyed generous protection not only during their working lives (through a defensive wage policy based on the heavily entrenched principle of indexation), but also in the case of temporary redundancy or unemployment through replacement benefits (*integrazioni salariali ordinarie*), and at the end of their working lives through the pension system. Earnings (linked to the cost of living), unemployment benefits (earnings replacement, early retirement, solidarity contracts and mobility benefits) and finally old age pensions – conceived of as a sort of 'deferred wage' – guaranteed full social protection for these workers and allowed them, in turn, to extend this protection to their family dependants.

The social insurance system was substantially completed at the end of the 1960s through the extension of coverage and the raising of benefit levels. Between 1968 and 1969, the 'defined benefit' formula was introduced whereby pensions were linked to the level of earnings received in the last five years of employment. The value of the benefit leaped to 80 per cent of earnings after 40 years' employment at the age of 60 for men and 55 for women. It was moreover possible to claim a pension after only 35 years of service, irrespective of age, with benefits equivalent to 70 per cent of last earnings (the so-called *pensione di anzianità*).

In the case of labour policies too, the end of the 1960s is the period in which the various instruments of protection were strengthened and completed. Until that time, state intervention generally took the form of ordinary allowances for total unemployment and the ordinary earnings replacement fund (*cassa integrazione guadagni*) for partial unemployment. Both these instruments rested on a contribution-based mechanism and both were purely 'passive policies'. In contrast to other European countries, such as Sweden and then Germany, active policies for job-creation were largely unknown. In 1968, special earnings replacement benefits were introduced (*integrazioni salariali straordinarie*), making Italian unemployment benefits the most generous in Europe. The latter functioned according to the same logic as the ordinary benefits, but the motives for intervention differed in so far as they were linked to situations of crisis, restructuring and the reorganisation of firms.

The obligation to pay contributions reflected the primary tenet of public intervention, that is, the safeguarding of existing levels of employment. To obtain benefits it was necessary to have paid contributions and therefore to have benefited from an employment relationship, something that still held good for the great majority of workers. Neither those seeking first-time employment nor the long-term unemployed were entitled to benefits.

A similar mechanism of 'discrimination' was also inherent in the functioning of the system of job placement established in 1949 and placed under complete public control. Anyone seeking employment was required to register at the local employment office and this registration was automatically classified by professional sector, productive category, skills and specialisation. Entry into the labour force took place by means of a 'guaranteeist' mechanism in the form of an anonymous 'numerical call' (*chiamata numerica*). A potential employer was not free to choose the worker to hire, but could only give the employment office an indication of the number of workers needed and the skills required. The principle of the numerical call-up was not, however, valid for workers who moved from one place of employment to another: they did not respect the rule of the 'call by lot' (the numerical order of the list), but they simply responded to the employers' 'nominative call' (job offer *ad personam*).[3]

Social insurance and labour policies thus shared the same objective: the hyper-protection of the already employed worker. While this system could be efficient and function well in a period marked by the 'economic miracle' and favourable international circumstances, this was certainly not the case with the onset of the serious economic crisis of the 1970s. In the face of the massive increase in the numbers of those excluded from the labour market, and hence from the system of social protection (women, young people, precarious workers and the unemployed), the imbalances and distortions inherent in the traditional, protected breadwinner model became evident.

The 1980s did witness some policy reform, but this fell short of resolving or correcting the contradictions inherent in the original model. At the beginning of the decade, proposals for a restrictive reform of the pension system began to be discussed in parliament and to be included on the agenda of various governments. However, the reform process did not make marked progress until the early 1990s.

In the case of the labour market, starting from the end of the 1970s and more thoroughly in the 1980s, some active policies of job-creation were added to the existing menu of passive policies. However, partly on account of the scarce availability of public financing, and partly due to the insufficient technical preparation of the national and regional administrations, these active policies did not succeed in reducing the predominance of passive policies. Between 1977 and 1984, key innovations were introduced (on-the-job-training contracts, vocational training, measures to encourage job mobility, solidarity contracts and part-time work),[4] to provide incentives for the employment of the weakest categories of the labour market (such as young people and women), but the level of implementation of these new and positive measures remained rather low. With the exception of on-the-job training contracts, which experienced a genuine expansion, training initiatives and contracts for atypical work did not have a marked impact on the existing employment regime. The familistic model thus looked out onto the new decade with its contradictions intact, making the need for structural reforms more urgent than ever.

THE REFORMS OF THE 1990s

The Social Insurance System

In the case of social insurance, the reforms began in 1992. The Amato reform of that year introduced significant innovations after decades of marginal adjustments. In the first place, the retirement age was raised by five years for both men and women: from 55 to 60 years for women and from 60 to 65 years for men (employees in the private sector), though with a gradual process of phasing in. Secondly, the length of minimum contributions for old age pensions was extended from 15 to 20 years. Thirdly, the reference period for calculating average earnings was prolonged from five to ten years, and to the entire working life-cycle for new entrants. Furthermore, the period of required contributions for seniority pensions was increased to 36 years for all workers, including those in the public sector, for whom 20 years had previously been sufficient (though, again, with a very gradual phasing in). Finally, contribution levels were increased.

A year after the Amato reform, but closely linked with it, a new regime for supplementary pensions was introduced. In Italy, second-tier social insurance schemes have always been relatively underdeveloped precisely on account of the entrenched and generous nature of public social insurance and of the rules governing severance payments (*trattamenti di fine rapporto*). The new measures outlined a co-ordinated system for the establishment of integrative second-tier schemes and introduced tax incentives. In the same year, the Ciampi government stipulated new penalties for seniority pensions and stepped up checks on those receiving invalidity pensions so as to limit their misuse. But the persistent crisis in public finances, the growth of social expenditure – irrespective of the cuts and corrections made – and the pressure of international bodies pushed policy makers to find new and more incisive solutions. In its budget for 1995, the government, led by Silvio Berlusconi, attempted to make radical changes to seniority pensions, which would effectively have led to their disappearance, but was faced by fierce trade union protest and had to limit itself to speeding up the entry into force of the higher retirement age and temporarily blocking access to seniority pensions.

The trade unions promised to renegotiate the entire system of social insurance in the first six months of 1995, but by that time the Berlusconi government had already been replaced by a new government headed by Lamberto Dini. The task of finding an accord with the social partners on the single points of the reform thus fell to Dini and an agreement was approved in parliament in August the same year. The Dini reform constituted a truly 'revolutionary' innovation for the Italian social insurance system. The substitution of the 'defined benefit' method (that is, the linking of pensions to earnings), with 'defined contributions' (which re-establish a tight link between contributions made and benefits received) – to come into effect gradually starting from 2013 – put an end to the mechanism which was the main cause of the irresponsible 'buoying up' of benefits.

The Dini reform also introduced a flexible retirement age (57–65 years) and a minimum age threshold for entitlement to pension benefits (57 years) for all workers, to be phased in by the year 2008. The rules governing retirement in the public and private sectors were standardised and made homogeneous. An income test was introduced for survivors' pensions and, finally, stricter norms were introduced regarding the accumulation of benefits and the entitlement credentials of beneficiaries.

The 1992–95 pension reforms represented major breakthroughs with respect to the institutional legacies of the past. They were also, however, the result of social and political compromises in which the government had to make a number of concessions (for example, on the phasing in of the reforms) with respect to its own original plans. But the approximation of the EMU deadlines kept the Italian authorities under acute budgetary pressures: so, soon after each of these compromises, the government relaunched its reformist efforts, even widening the scope of its ambitions. In this vein, the new centre-left 'Olive-Tree' coalition, led by Romano Prodi and voted into office in spring 1996, made a comprehensive reform of the *stato sociale* one of its highest priorities. In January 1997, Prodi appointed a commission of experts to draft a broad plan for reform. A report was submitted by this commission (known as the Onofri Commission, after its chairperson, Paolo Onofri, an economist from Bologna), which was centred on the idea of re-equilibrating and containing (though not reducing in the aggregate) social expenditure.

The Onofri report was the subbject of a rather heated debate in the summer and autumn of 1997. In the budget law for 1997, the Prodi government tried to adopt many of the Commission's recommendations, but the fierce opposition of the *Rifondazione comunista* (Refounded Communists) – whose votes were crucial for reaching a majority in parliament – and the difficult negotiations with the social partners, forced the government substantially to scale down its ambitions. In the field of pensions, Prodi was able to introduce some cuts to seniority pensions, especially for public employees: their contributory requirement for claiming a seniority pension was aligned with that applying to private employees. Contributions for the self-employed were raised and a temporary freeze on the indexation of higher pensions introduced. However modest (with respect to the government's original ambitions), these cuts had the advantage of being immediately effective and thus made a small contribution (0.2 per cent of GDP) towards reaching the budgetary targets for 1998. The most important recommendation of the Onofri plan – a much faster phasing in of the new pension formula introduced in 1995 – could not be adopted and, by creating a government crisis, *Rifondazione comunista* was able to obtain the exemption of blue-collar workers from the cuts in seniority pensions. The government was also able to push through some important innovations in the field of social assistance. More transparent rules for the financing of this sector were introduced and the budget law for 1998 – which was approved in December 1997 – empowered the executive to take measures in two important directions: (1) the introduction of a new 'indicator of socio-economic conditions' (ISE), based on both income and asset criteria, to be used as a yardstick for all means-tested benefits; and (2) the introduction of a new (experimental) scheme of 'minimum insertion income' (RMI) as a last resort, guaranteed safety net administered by local governments. Both the ISE and the experimental RMI were introduced in the course of 1998.

This sequence of reforms has not fully eradicated the distributive and allocative distortions of the Italian welfare state which have already been described. They have, however, made significant steps in this direction. More importantly, they have created promising institutional mechanisms that may trigger a spontaneous and self-sustaining dynamic of internal re-equilibration in social expenditure. On the one hand, the setting of more transparent and clear-cut boundaries between social insurance and social assistance, as well as the consolidation of new instruments such as the ISE and the RMI, will work to strengthen that safety net of means-tested and needs-based benefits and services which has been historically lacking (or very weak) in Italy. On the other hand, the new architecture of the pension system will work gradually to scale down (or at least contain the further expansion of) a sector which has been historically hypertrophic. It is true that, in spite of the reforms, at the end of the 1990s Italy still displays one of the highest ratios of pension expenditure/GDP in the whole OECD area and that the situation is likely to worsen. However, the significance of the 1992/95/97 reforms must be appreciated by contrast with the *status quo ante*. In the absence of reform, pension expenditure would have reached the impressive peak of 23.2 per cent of GDP in the year 2040, before beginning to decline. After the reforms, the peak is expected to be 'only' 15.8 per cent of GDP in the year 2032. The virtual stabilisation of pension expenditure may not have been enough to cure fully the long-standing disease of Italy's unbalanced welfare state, but it has certainly contained its fatal aggravation.

Labour Market Policies

In the 1990s the biggest problem facing the Italian economy was the drop in the employment rate after more than 20 years of positive growth. The drop in employment was, moreover, accompanied by a steep increase in the level of unemployment which in the second half of the decade (until 1998) remained unchanged at around 12 per cent. In the meantime, the dualism between the north and the south of Italy became more accentuated (in 1998 the unemployment rate amounted to 22.8 per cent in the south against 7.5 per cent in the centre-north) and the share of youth unemployment reached a European record (32.1 per cent in total, but beyond 50 per cent in many southern regions).[5]

It was in this context that employment policies developed in two distinct directions: on the one hand, a return to concertation and the experimentation with co-operative and consensual solutions to combat unemployment; on the other hand, the introduction of a structural reform of the labour market which reorganised the entire system of job placement, creating new space for private actors in the regulation of the labour market and promoting new active policies for local development.

The Amato and Ciampi agreements of 1992 and 1993 redesigned the entire system of collective bargaining and incomes policy. The system of wage indexation was abolished 50 years after its creation, thus accommodating the requests of the business community which had, as of 1983, called on governments and trade unions to review the mechanisms of indexation, perceived as an accelerator of inflation. The new structure of collective bargaining has been organised on two distinct levels of negotiation: the national level, and the territorial or company level. In this way, the chaotic superimposition of multiple levels of bargaining has been averted and homogeneous standards have been fixed for the regulation of wages in all categories. Finally, a stable system of incomes policy has been established, organised through two distinct sessions of tripartite meetings between the government and the social partners to discuss the main goals of macro-economic and budgetary policies.

The Ciampi agreement also included the objective of a broad reform of labour policies. This reform was actually launched with the 'pact for work' approved by the Prodi government and the interest organisations in September 1996 and in its main enacting measure, the Treu Law of June 1997 (after the name of the Labour Minister, Tiziano Treu). This law was the first measure to sanction the dismantling of the public monopoly of the system mediating labour supply and demand, instituted in 1949, through the introduction of temporary work which until then has been prohibited in Italy. It moreover contains provisions for the reform of the system of vocational training, the introduction of grants for job-creation (*borse lavoro*) in the *Mezzogiorno* and the reorganisation of public job schemes (*lavori socialmente utili*).

A second form of labour market innovation in the 1990s is that of policies for local development, introduced between 1995 and 1997. We refer in particular to the territorial pacts (*patti territoriali*) and area contracts (*contratti di area*). These instruments have a prevailingly 'pro-active' nature and are specifically designed to promote the creation of new employment for those excluded from the labour market. They are based on local concertation between public and private subjects which pool programmes, resources and structures to promote economic growth, create employment opportunities and reduce social exclusion.

The new policies for local development mark a complete overturning of the regulatory paradigm of the Italian labour market – from protection centred on 'passive' income support for the employed (the insiders) to attempts to encourage economic growth and employment opportunities for the unemployed (the outsiders). This paradigm change is even more accentuated if one considers the most recent labour market innovation – the decentralisation of employment services (*servizi per l'impiego*) introduced in 1997. This reform defines *ex novo* the distribution of responsibilities for the regulation of the labour market between the centre (state) and the periphery (regions) of the national territory and definitively abolishes the state job placement monopoly. The criteria guiding the distribution of the functions between the state and the regions appear to be highly innovative. The tasks which remain the responsibility of the state are those relative to control, certification and delegation, whereas two fundamental groups of functions – job placement and the promotion of pro-active (employment) policies – are instead devolved to the regions. Responsibility in matters of active policies covers the planning, co-ordination and management of programmes to promote the participation of the weakest categories in the labour market. The decentralisation of responsibilities in matters of job placement and pro-active policies for the regions and provinces constitute a radical innovation in the nature and style of the public regulation of the labour market, now based on the performance and participation of local and private actors.

The 'season of reform' in Italy's labour market policy has not yet come to an end. The objectives of decentralisation, privatisation and concertation at both the national and local levels have been forcefully confirmed by the 'pact for development' approved by D'Alema and by over 30 interest organisations on 22 December 1998. Finally, in the 1999 Budget Law we find a provision for the – long awaited but repeatedly postponed – reform of the 'social shock absorbers' (that is, the panoply of passive unemployment cash benefits). The near future will provide an opportunity to verify whether the path of reform is being effectively followed up, or whether it will be interrupted by events more or less contingent on politics, as has been the case in the past.

WHY REFORM?

What explains this new wave of policy innovations in the sector of labour and social insurance during the 1990s? In searching for an explanation, it is useful to distinguish between these factors that have had a *direct* impact and those that have conditioned policy *indirectly*. The examination of the explanatory dimensions needs to be carried out on two different levels. The first is that of the *actors* and of their *mode of interaction*: in short, we need to ask who promoted the reforms and how the necessary consensus has been reached to approve them. The second level is defined by the institutional context in which actors are embedded. In our case, the institutional context is constituted by two distinct arenas: the arena of domestic policy making, and therefore the politico-institutional transition of the 1990s; and the supranational arena, characterised by the processes of European integration and of increasing economic internationalisation. The two arenas have not had a direct impact on the solution of policy problems contained in government agendas, but have facilitated the emergence and consolidation of a new network of actors inclined towards reforms (see Figure 1).[6]

The Actors: Concertation and Political Learning

In the 'classical' literature on neo-corporatism, Italy has always been considered the 'Cinderella of Europe'. It has been perceived as a case of would-be corporatism and systematically relegated to the bottom of international rankings because of the absence of the classical functional requirements, such as the existence of strong, cohesive and centralised

FIGURE 1
THE EXPLANATORY FACTORS OF REFORM

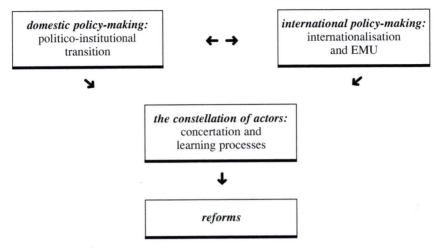

interest organisations with a monopoly of representation and the presence of a pro-labour government.[7] A second generation of studies, however, has sought to rehabilitate the cases of would-be corporatism by demonstrating how concertation can also develop where the functional requirements stipulated in the literature appear to be absent, as in the UK at the end of the 1970s or in Italy in the 1970s and 1980s.[8]

The exchange relations observed in Italy between social actors and the state have been interpreted in terms of specific variants within the general category of 'neo-corporatism', such as 'micro-corporatism', or 'corporatism by default'. The first term refers to those exchanges between interest groups, the administrative apparatus, the political parties or government, designed to obtain reciprocal advantages in terms of fringe benefits and distributional policies, a variation of the so-called pressure politics.[9] With the second concept the focus shifts to the characteristics of functioning (or rather, dysfunctioning) of the Italian parliamentary arena and to its chronic inability to provide efficient and problem-oriented decision-making processes. The consensual mediation of interests and the formulation of public policies thus emerge for want of a better alternative. The Italian version of neo-corporatism clearly belongs to the second group studied by Crouch,[10] who makes a useful distinction between neo-corporatism with a strong state (the Scandinavian example), and neo-corporatism with a weak state (the continental variety).

What, then, has changed in the 1990s with respect to the corporatist agreements of the so-called First Republic (that is, the period 1948–92)? If the consensual practices of interest mediation were not alien to the Italian political system of the 1970s and 1980s, what are the innovations ushered in by the transition? Our hypothesis is that, as of 1992 – from the collapse, that is, of the party system that characterised the post-war period – a consensual mediation of interests began to emerge which was closer to the formal model of neo-corporatism described in the literature and which tended to institutionalise itself and to acquire legitimacy as the main mode not only of settling interests, but also of formulating public policies. As of the early 1990s, concertation in Italy assumed those characteristics of stability and solidity that had previously seemed so difficult to achieve.

Concertation has in a way helped (re)create itself. Starting with the Amato and Ciampi agreements on labour costs and the system of social security and ending with the D'Alema agreement, increasingly precise and formalised rules have regulated the development and consolidation of the concertative model of policy making. The keyword is now 'consensus' with the social partners, as if only those reforms guided by co-operative strategies, held together by an amalgam of public and private interests, are to be considered feasible and legitimate.

But how was it possible to reach such a consensus? In what way did Amato, Ciampi and Dini manage to convince, in particular, the trade unions to embark on a path of reform? It was first and foremost Ciampi who put into action a constant and effective policy of persuasion geared to spreading an understanding of the costs of non-adjustment. In the absence of a rapid and radical reduction of interest expenditure (*spesa per interessi*), not only would entry into Europe become more of an illusion, but it would also mean sizeable losses for both the business community – in an exponential acceleration of labour costs – and for the trade unions in the draining of the resources available not only to promote new social programmes, but also to sustain existing commitments. The resistance of trade unions has been overcome through an open and negotiated policy style ready to make substantial concessions on the phasing-in of the reform, but also by persuading them of the long-term advantages connected with the *risanamento* (that is, the restoration to health of public finances) and the entry into EMU (that is, revived growth and lower interests on public debt). This latter point has played a crucial role in the reform process, for the *risanamento* could also be presented as a 'fight against the rent', involving possible gains for all workers. With interest rates at 9.5 per cent, in the early 1990s a relatively modest bank deposit of 260 million Lire (about 135,000 euros) invested in state bonds would generate a 'rent' equal to the yearly wage of a metal worker.[11] The challenge proposed by the government to the social partners (and repeatedly explained publicly and privately by such figures as Amato, Ciampi, Dini and Prodi) was thus to accept sacrifices (especially benefit cuts and wage restraint) with a view to abating a huge and unproductive debt service, diverting the resources thus liberated to other purposes and triggering off a virtuous circle of revived growth, new public investment and 'healthier' redistribution.[12]

That Ciampi was correct became clear in the first six months of 1995 when the *Banca d'Italia*, at the time of the fall of the Berlusconi government, increased interest rates twice and the value of the national currency reached 1,400 Lire against the DM (starting from about 800 Lire in early 1992). The trade unions quickly became convinced of the risks of non-adjustment and of the importance of co-operating with government. They also accepted that the sacrifices of the preceding years had been vital in sparking off a dynamic of virtuous reform.

The participation of the trade unions in the agreements of the period 1992–95 can therefore be interpreted as a learning process and a reorientation of their strategies of action based on the mechanism of 'serial equity':[13] that is, the acceptance of sacrifices in the short term in exchange for the promise of future benefits (represented by the 'pact for work' of September 1996 and the 'social pact' of December 1998). This mechanism has indeed functioned effectively and the promises made have been maintained. Between 1992 and 1998, interest on public debt fell from 10.2 per cent to 6.4 per cent of GDP and the trend is destined to continue through the convergence of Italian interest rates with respect to German ones. In this way, the resources thus released are earmarked for activities to relaunch employment in depressed areas and to provide production incentives for firms.

Turning to a more detailed analysis of the contents of the agreements drawn up in the period 1992–98, the year 1992 marks the return to concertation in Italy, when the climate of national emergency generated by the scandals of *Tangentopoli*, by the consequent turnover of the entire national political class and the dramatic fiscal and monetary crisis threw Italy into a state of flux. The government headed by Amato called on the trade unions and the business organisations to formulate solutions and programmes to respond to the crisis. Within a few months, Amato had undertaken one of the most striking financial manoeuvres to reform public finances in the post-war period (amounting to 93,000 billion Lire or about six per cent of GDP). Thanks to this, for the first time in many years, the accelerating debt service was brought to a halt. In September 1992, the Lira suffered a steep devaluation (dropping by 30 per cent), and the government and the social partners approved a broad agreement to reduce inflation and to 'cool off' wage dynamics. The most striking results of the agreement were the abolition of wage indexation introduced in the immediate post-war period, and the freezing of company-based bargaining on wages for the years 1992 and 1993.

The Amato agreement was taken up again a year later by the Ciampi agreement which – albeit in a less critical situation – confirmed the abolition of the system of wage indexation, instituted a structured system of incomes policy and completely reformed – as illustrated above – the structure of bargaining. It was the introduction of incomes policy (never actually practised in the preceding years) that constituted the additional element with respect to the Amato agreement in the direction of the institutionalisation of concertation as the 'normal' mode of interest mediation. Incomes policy was presented as a genuine instrument of economic policy designed to achieve a 'growing equity of income distribution by containing inflation and nominal incomes, to encourage economic development and the growth of employment by means of the enlargement of the productive base and a greater competitiveness in the system of enterprises'.[14] Incomes policy is tightly linked to budgetary policy, which is in turn designed to secure an inflation rate aligned with the average for the most 'virtuous' European countries, and therefore to the reduction of the public debt and deficit.

However, the labour market was not only the object of concertation. It was precisely in 1992 and 1993 that the negotiations on the reform of pensions took shape, designed to correct the severe imbalances in the Italian system of social expenditure. As illustrated above, the Amato law of 1992 did introduce some key corrections, but these were not enough to halt the runaway spending dynamics. Ciampi therefore embarked on a path of dialogue and mediation with the social partners in order to reach a consensus on a more incisive reform. But the Ciampi government only lasted a short time and its successor, the Berlusconi government, opted for an alternative strategy to that of consensus by trying to push through provisions that would have led to the abolition of seniority pensions in the budget for 1995, with no previous consultation with the social partners. The trade unions mobilised against these provisions, and after a general strike – which enjoyed considerable support – the measures were (eventually) scrapped. It thus became the job of the new Dini government to pick up the threads of the negotiations with the social partners. The consensus wrested by Dini on the reform of social insurance was still partial in so far as the *Confindustria* did not sign the agreement. The proposed law was, however, approved by parliament and the trade unions' proposals were voted for by a majority in the workplace.[15]

If the negotiations on pensions appeared to come to a halt in the post-Dini period (also because of the great difficulty and complexity of intervening in benefits which the greater part of citizens consider their 'due') the same did not apply to the problems of employment and incomes policy, which were the central focus of two key social pacts, that of Prodi in September 1996 and that of D'Alema in December 1998. The latter agreements differed with respect to those of the period 1992–95. In contrast to the sacrifices of the past, we are now at the 'paying up of accounts' stage. The government started to 'pay back' the social partners for their support of the *risanamento* strategy: on the one hand, the new pacts introduced policies of employment promotion, warmly supported by the trade unions; on the other, they included measures of flexibility and de-regulation of the labour market, particularly favoured by the business community.

The main objective of the 'pact for work' of September 1996 was the launching of new strategies to reform employment policies.[16] The document is divided into four distinct parts. The first covers the reform of the employment services, based on three principal imperatives: the institutional decentralisation of the employment offices, the dismantling of the public monopoly, and the new role of supervision and control exercised by the Ministry. The second part is dedicated to the reform of the system of vocational training, the most important innovation being the link-up with the education system. The third part of the pact introduces temporary work, along the lines discussed above. Finally, the last part of the agreement introduces the new policies for local development, in particular the 'territorial pacts' and the 'area contracts', described earlier.

The agreement stipulated by Prodi was followed two years later by the social pact on development, approved under the aegis of the D'Alema's government, and which may be interpreted as the 'final balance' of the long series of negotiations of the 1990s. D'Alema moved explicitly in the direction of redeveloping and entrenching the triangular mode of policy making inherited from the transition. In the 'Christmas pact', concertation emerged as the formal and institutional model for the mediation of interests. The explicit aim of the agreement is to reinforce concertation, in accordance with the characteristics already outlined in the agreement of 23 July 1993 and to link it, arguably drawing lessons from the 'Dutch miracle', to measures of flexibility and deregulation. Concertation was not only consolidated, but was also extended horizontally and vertically, and it is these changes which give it its 'modern' character with respect to the practices of the 1970s and 1980s.

Indeed, for the first time in Italian history the approval of the pact on development involved a very high number of interest organisations, and was not limited to accommodating the positions of the three main national unions (CGIL, CISL and UIL) and the *Confindustria*. Moreover, the agreement explicitly encouraged the development of concertative arrangements at the local and decentralised levels.

The pact distinguishes three distinct levels of concertation. The first refers to those social policies that require outlays of expenditure by the state and that therefore need to be discussed by all three components of the triangle: trade unions, government and the business community. The second level concerns those relations between enterprises and workers that do not imply burdens for the state, and which can be regulated without the direct intervention of government. Finally, the third level deals with the transposition of Community directives into Italian law.

The pact moreover reinforced the dual – national and decentralised – structure of bargaining provided for by the Ciampi agreement, and introduced a great many innovations and concessions for both business and labour, such as the reduction of income taxes (using for this purpose the revenues recovered from the fight against tax evasion), a reduction of social charges, the acceleration of the process of administrative reform and the establishment of a multi-year plan for the integrated reform of the system of education, training and research.

Not surprisingly, the reactions and comments on the signing of the agreement were unanimously positive: both the business associations and the trade unions underlined the many innovative elements contained in the pact, implicitly recognising it as the 'compensating' round in the long sequence of exchanges begun in 1992.

Domestic Policy-Making: The 'Technical' Governments and the Transition
The original welfare model presented in the first part of this discussion, heavily skewed in favour of pension protection and based on micro-distributive policies and interventions, may be considered a reflection of some of the more deeply rooted characteristics of the political system of the First Republic, in particular the dynamics of polarised pluralism,[17] and the spoils system of government (*governo spartitorio*).[18] The fragmented and pluralistic nature of political representation constituted an especially fertile ground for the development of an occupationally segmented (and often clientelistic) system of social insurance. The extensive presence of the main political parties (DC, PSI and PCI) inside the public organisations responsible for the delivery of benefits (INPS, the committees of the

Ministero del Lavoro, and the old job-placement offices) guaranteed direct contact with citizens. The choice of agreeing to a preferential track for (male) heads of households, and considering pensions as a deferred wage, was shared by both the Catholic and Marxist doctrines (whose paradoxical 'co-presence' is a distinguishing feature of Italy's political culture).

The distributional character of social insurance and employment policies (in particular the social shock absorbers) could, moreover, be considered the result of a national policy-making which, beyond being fragmentary and reactive, was in the hands of unstable executives based on broad and unwieldy coalitions. These executives not only did not enjoy the sort of duration or internal cohesion necessary to formulate far-reaching reforms, but were forever engaged in the settling and mediation of conflicts among their many internal components. The result of all this could only be, on the one hand, broad and general measures that in order to satisfy everyone actually contented no one, and, on the other, a panoply of micro-measures supported by one or other member of the political alliance. The spoils system of government was facilitated by a system of interest representation which was also highly fragmented and lacking in cohesion, and organised along the same ideological divisions as the party system.

In the early 1990s the Italian political system underwent a number of serious upheavals caused by the scandals of *Tangentopoli*, the almost total turnover of the political elite, the disappearance of the main parties of government (DC and PSI) following the introduction of the new quasi-majoritarian electoral system and the reinforcing of the role of the President of the Republic. In politico-institutional terms, the most important consequence of these upheavals was the progressive 'autonomisation' of the executive from the political (parliamentary) parties.[19] The reinforcement of the executive, which began with the 'technical' governments of Amato and Ciampi, translated into a greater capacity on the part of the Prime Minister to direct his ministers, a greater co-ordination among the ministries and a generally more cohesive government – all characteristics favouring the introduction of the reforms.

The delegitimisation of the party system, moreover, created spaces and opportunities for the system of representation of interests and enabled the latter to enter into direct relations with government. On the one hand, it was the government which sought a consensus among the interest groups as a surrogate of party-parliamentary legitimacy[20] and as a means of passing the 'emergency' measures. On the other, it was the interest groups that recognised in the collapse of the entire political elite and in the decline of the main political parties an opportunity to move into spaces which were traditionally inaccessible and to actively participate in policy making.

It is interesting to note how concertation emerged in a politically exceptional context and above all as the sum of two 'weaknesses': a system of government in transition with an increasingly delegitimised parliament; and a system of interest groups suffering a severe crisis of representation, and whose visibility and legitimation far outstripped their actual strength.

Even if born as a sort of emergency solution, concertation has now established itself as an almost 'routine' mode of policy making. Under the D'Alema government, the authority of parliament has continued to be eroded in terms of its formal functions and the silence of the parties on social and employment issues (beyond their purely symbolic implications) persists. Political parties have indeed continued to demonstrate a weak capacity for policy making in these areas of policy: in simplistic terms their positions can be reduced to the clash 'for and against flexibility' and 'for and against cuts in the welfare state', easily superimposed on the left–right cleavage. Real, substantive decisions and the sorting out of technical problems would appear to have been delegated to the *Ministero del Lavoro* and to the interest organisations themselves. The transition from the 'First' to the 'Second' Republic is not over yet and it is therefore premature to speculate about the institutional robustness and future prospects of concertation within Italy's political system. But for the medium term it can be safely predicted that further reform in the field of welfare and labour policy will either be 'concerted' or doomed to fail.

Supranational Constraints: Internationalisation and the Process of Monetary Union

The financial readjustment and the progress of policy reform embarked upon in Italy in the early 1990s have been heavily conditioned by the events marking the process of European integration in general and of economic and monetary union in particular.

The deadlines fixed at Maastricht in February 1992 forced Italy to make an immediate and radical effort to reform and correct its public finances in order to halt the growth of public debt, which had risen steeply throughout the 1980s. Furthermore, growing internationalisation and the liberalisation of markets obliged Italian governments to embark on programmes to deregulate a labour market regime which had, until the 1980s, been one of the most rigid and protective in Europe. The 'external constraint' has therefore acted as a stimulus to, and a motor of the processes of reorganisation and reform.[21]

The impact of the process of European integration has been most direct in the case of social insurance policies. Indeed, the need to respect the parameters of Maastricht was immediately translated into a drive to rationalise and reorganise welfare schemes. In order to join Monetary Union with the first group of countries, Italy was called on to deal seriously with its problems of public deficit and public debt. The room for manoeuvre for raising taxation was very limited, given that taxation levels had been constantly on the increase since the 1980s, putting Italy at the top of the European division. Indeed, in the early 1990s the increasing fiscal pressure and its inequitable distribution provoked clear signs of a tax revolt especially among the business community of northern Italy (a protest immediately taken up and exploited by the *Lega Nord*).

Given the impracticability of increasing revenues, cuts in social expenditure appeared to be the sole policy strategy able to contain the deficit, and social insurance benefits became the first target of the financial reform. In actual fact, looking at the data from other European countries, the volume of Italian welfare was not, and is still not, alarming. In 1993, social expenditure amounted to 25.8 per cent of GDP and was the sixth lowest in Europe (the average value amounted to 27.7 per cent), while in the same year per capita GDP in Italy was the fourth highest.[22] Three years later, in 1996, social expenditure was more or less the same (24.8 per cent of GDP). However, in the national debate on public welfare policies social expenditure was unanimously singled out as the main cause of the country's financial problems.

There are a series of reasons which help account for such a generally held belief. Notwithstanding its modest aggregate size, social expenditure constituted the single largest item of state expenditure. Second, it is not hard to define the organisational and financial characteristics of the pension system in the early 1990s as disastrous, and demographic forecasts predicted even more alarming scenarios, so that without the necessary social insurance reforms expenditure would have grown from around 14 per cent to around 23 per cent of GDP between the early 1990s and the year 2040.[23]

The 'meshing' of fiscal obligations imposed by Community decisions, and the contradictions inherent in the organisation of welfare effectively opened up the way for the reforms guided by three main imperatives: financial reorganisation, social equity and the reinstatement of efficiency and legality. These imperatives were first accommodated by the Amato reform in 1992 and then, more completely, by the Dini reform of 1995, already discussed.

By contrast to the welfare sector, the impact of the process of European integration on labour market policies was less direct. The reduction of expenditure was not an item on the agenda of the various governments, in so

far as Italian expenditure on employment policies is amongst the lowest in
Europe (2.1 per cent of GDP in 1993, as against 3.8 per cent in the
Netherlands, 3.4 per cent in France and 4.2 per cent in Germany),[24]
particularly as regards active policies, where spending is particularly low.

Domestic policy making was mainly conditioned by the push to
deregulate the labour market. The opening up of the markets placed the
Italian economy in a new context, characterised by transactions of a global
nature. The flows of goods, capitals and labour into and out of the country
intensified, and the stepping up of transactions inevitably put the Italian
labour market in contact with the experiences and regulatory regimes of
other countries, first in Europe and then in the rest of the world. The rigidity
of the Italian labour market – its most significant inheritance from the
welfare model of the past – emerged in its entirety. The difficulty of firing,
the confused and confusing nature of the procedures for hiring workers, the
hyper-bureaucratic functioning of the old job-placement offices and high
labour costs became the main targets for protest by the business community.
The strategies of deregulation in the UK, the massive move towards flexible
and deregulated employment contracts in Spain and the 'Dutch miracle'
based on the flexibility of labour market conditions thus became
'importable' experiences. It was, above all, the business associations which
had, as of the 1980s, embraced the struggle for the deregulation of the
labour market; and the measures dealing with atypical contracts of the
1980s (law 863/1984), the liberalisation of job placement (law 56/1987),
and the recognition of collective redundancies (law 223/1991) opened the
door to the structural reforms of the 1990s.

CONCLUSION

We have described the main reforms that have significantly modified the
characteristics and goals of Italian social insurance and labour policy in the
1990s. We have highlighted how these reforms have been generated within
the sphere of interest intermediation and consensual policy-making. In Italy,
the return to concertation is linked to the transformations and changes that
have marked the shift from the First to the Second Republic. Concertation
would indeed appear to be one of the main fruits of this transition. The
delegitimisation of the entire political class and the main political parties of
the First Republic created an opening for the trade unions which thereby
regained a vital space in the decision-making arena. But the return to
concertation in Italy is also traceable to other factors that help explain its
specificity. It has also been the outcome of the pressures exercised by

international bodies (especially the EU) for the reform and correction of the many imbalances inherent in Italy's public sector (especially public finances). In response to such pressures, and in order to promote financial reform, policy makers and representatives of organised interests have been prompted to initiate processes of policy learning and change by means of co-operative agreements. These co-operative agreements have been based on a mechanism of 'serial equity', that is, on a sequence of trade-offs between immediate sacrifices and future benefits. The social partners committed themselves to the path of adjustment outlined by the Amato and Ciampi agreements in view of future benefits, subsequently delivered with the Prodi and D'Alema 'pacts'.

This has generated the high level of continuity and institutionalisation of concertation witnessed in the period 1992–98. Even if not all of the measures contained in the various pacts have been fully implemented, the consensus surrounding this form of policy making is high. Paradoxically, at the beginning of the new millennium, Italy could find itself retracing its steps along the well-trodden, but apparently abandoned, road of neo-corporatism. Were this to be the case, the repercussions on the characteristics and functioning of the Italian democratic system would clearly demand further analysis.

NOTES

This article is based on a wider research carried out for the Max Planck Institute of Cologne. The findings of this wider research will be published in a collected volume edited by Fritz Scharpf and Vivien Schmidt, *Work and Welfare in Open Economies* (Oxford: Oxford University Press 2000). A more detailed Italian version of the research has already been published in M. Ferrera and E. Gualmini, *Salvati dall'Europa?* (Bologna: Il Mulino 1999). The authors wish to thank the MPI, all the project participants and – especially – the project directors, Fritz Scharpf and Vivien Schmidt for the precious advice given in all the phases of their research.

1. J. Visser and A. Hemerijck, *A Dutch Miracle: Job Growth, Welfare Reform and Corporatism in the Netherlands* (Amsterdam: Amsterdam University Press 1997).
2. On the 'familistic' model of welfare, see M. Ferrera, *Modelli di solidarietà* (Bologna: Il Mulino 1993), M. Ferrera, *Le trappole del welfare* (Bologna: Il Mulino 1998); G. Esping-Andersen, *The Three Worlds of Welfare Capitalism* (Princeton: Princeton University Press 1990); G. Esping-Andersen, *Welfare States in Transition, National Adaptions in Global Economies* (London: Sage 1996); E. Gualmini, *La politica del lavoro* (Bologna: Il Mulino 1998). For a more detailed discussion of the Italian model of welfare, cf. M. Ferrera, 'Italy', in P. Flora (ed.), *Growth to Limits. The Western Welfare Since World War II* (Berlin: De Gruytier 1987), vol. II, pp.385–499); and M. Ferrera, 'The Uncertain Future of the Italian Welfare State', *West European Politics* 20/1 (1997), pp.231–49.
3. On the functioning and the many damaging effects of the Italian system of job placement, at least until the reform of legislative Decree 469 of 1997, see P. Ichino, *Il collocamento impossibile* (Bari: De Donato 1982), and P. Ichino, *Il lavoro e il mercato* (Milan: Mondadori 1996).
4. Law 285/1977 on youth employment, Law 675/1977 on industrial conversion, Law 748/1978

on vocational training, and Law 863/1984 on training and work contracts, part-time work and solidarity contracts.

5. ISTAT, *Forze di lavoro* (Rome: Istituto Nazionale di Statistica 1990–98).

6. Our analysis is clearly inspired by the so-called 'actor-centred institutionalism' developed within neo-institutional theory. See P.A. Hall and R.C.R. Taylor, 'Political Science and the Three New Institutionalism', *Political Studies* 5 (1996), pp.936–57; E.M. Immergut, 'The Theoretical Core of the New Institutionalism', *Politics and Society* 1 (1998), pp.5–43; J.G. March and J.P. Olsen, *Democratic Governance* (New York: The Free Press 1995); and especially F. Scharpf, *Games Real Actors Play. Actor-Centered Institutionalism in Policy Research* (Harper: Westview Press 1997).

7. Cf. P. Schmitter, 'Still the Century of Corporatism?', *Review of Politics* 36 (1974), pp.85–131; G. Lehmbruch and P. Schmitter, *La politica degli interessi nei paesi industrializzati* (Bologna: Il Mulino 1984), and W. Streeck and P. Schmitter, 'Comunità, mercato, stato e associazioni?', *Stato e mercato* 13 (1985), pp.47–85.

8. Cf. J.H. Goldthorpe (ed.), *Ordine e conflitto nel capitalismo moderno* (Bologna: Il Mulino 1989); M. Regini, 'Le condizioni dello scambio politico. Nascita e declino della concertazione in Italia e Gran Bretagna', in Goldthorpe (ed.), *Ordine e conflitto*, pp.191–221; M. Regini, *Confini mobili. La costruzione dell'economia tra politica e società* (Bologna, Il Mulino 1991); E. Gualmini, *Le rendite del neo-corporativismo* (Soveria Mannelli: Rubbettino 1997); P. Schmitter and J.R. Grote, 'Sisifo corporatista: passato, presente e futuro', *Stato e mercato* 50 (1997), pp.183–215; and H.J. Wiarda, *Corporatism and Comparative Politics. The Other Great 'Ism'* (New York and London: M.E. Sharpe Inc. 1997).

9. Cf. P. Lange and M. Regini, *Stato e regolazione sociale* (Bologna: Il Mulino 1987).

10. C. Crouch, *Industrial Relations and European State Traditions* (Oxford: Clarendon Press 1993).

11. See L. Pennacchi, 'La moneta unica europea fra risanamento, sviluppo e crescita dell'occupazione', *Info/Quaderni* Special Issue (1998), pp.8–30.

12. See C.A. Ciampi, 'Risanamento e sviluppo, due momenti inscindibili della stessa politica', *Info/Quaderni*, Special Issue (1998), pp.198–203.

13. Cf. J.B. Barney and W.G. Ouchi, 'Information Cost and Informational Governance', *Management Science* 10 (1984), pp.35–63.

14. Presidenza del Consiglio, *L'intesa sul costo del lavoro* (Rome: Vita Italiana 1993).

15. I. Regalia and M. Regini, 'Sindacati, istituzioni, sistema politico', in G.P. Cella and T. Treu (eds.), *Le nuove relazioni industriali* (Bologna: Il Mulino 1998), pp.467–94.

16. The 'pact for work' approved by the Minister for Labour, Treu, and by the main interest organisations was, moreover, preceded by another social agreement stipulated by the Treu and by the Minister for Education, Berlinguer, in July 1996 on the theme of training and education.

17. Cf. G. Sartori, *Teoria dei partiti e caso italiano* (Milan: Sugarco 1982).

18. Cf. S. Vassallo, *Il governo di partito in Italia (1943–1993)* (Bologna: Il Mulino 1994).

19. S. Fabbrini and S. Vassallo, *Il governo. Gli esecutivi nelle democrazie contemporanee* (Rome and Bari: Laterza 1999).

20. G. Amato, 'Un governo nella transizione: la mia esperienza di presidente del consiglio', *Quaderni costituzionali* 14/3 (1994), pp.355–71.

21. See K. Dyson and K. Featherstone, 'Italy and Emu as a "Vincolo esterno": Empowering the Technocrats, Transforming the State', *South European Society and Politics* 2 (1996), pp.272–99.

22. CEC, *Social Protection in Europe* (Luxembourg 1995).

23. Ministero del Tesoro, *Convergenze dell'Italia verso l'UEM* (Rome: Ministero del Tesoro 1998).

24. OECD, *Social Expenditure Statistics* (Paris: OECD 1996).

The Scandinavian Welfare State in the 1990s: Challenged but Viable

STEIN KUHNLE

STEIN KUHNLE

HISTORICAL PREREQUISITES

Historical, cultural and institutional attributes influenced Scandinavian political choices for social insurance institutions and welfare policies at the time of the Bismarckian 'conception' of national social insurance on a grand scale in the 1880s. Although not realised at the time, the modern European welfare state was born. This idea of national social insurance dawned on European countries at different stages of social and economic development and political institution-building, and the basis for 'four social Europes'was laid.[1] In Norway, the concept of a 'people's insurance' was coined in political debates already at the beginning of the twentieth century, and soon Swedish social democrats adopted the term a 'people's home' to market the vision of the welfare society to be developed. The terms embody an inclusiveness that characterises the Scandinavian welfare states to this day. More than elsewhere in Europe 'peasants were carriers of freedom and equality' in Scandinavia.[2] The combination of relatively egalitarian pre-industrial social structures and homogenous (and small) populations in terms of language, religion and culture, was conducive to the gradual development of comprehensive, principally tax-financed, redistributive and universal social and welfare policies. That the state came to be the prime welfare provider can probably be attributed to the observation that no major competing welfare provider existed. The secular state did not have to relate to a supra-national church with its separate institutions for education and health services. Thanks to the Lutheran Reformation during the first half of the 1500s, church and state bureaucracies were fused under the mantle of the state. 'The market' was not much of an alternative for social insurance in Scandinavia when the German idea quickly spread northwards in the 1880s,[3] and the 'civil society' of voluntary non-governmental organisations was of limited scope. For historical reasons, the role of the state is seen as legitimate, perhaps more so than elsewhere in Europe. Scandinavian societies are more 'state-friendly'; indeed, 'state' and 'society' are sometimes used to mean the same thing.[4]

The Scandinavian (or more precisely the 'Nordic') welfare states share a number of common characteristics, such that researchers tend to group them into one specific category of 'welfare regime',[5] 'family of nations',[6] or 'type of welfare state'.[7] Concepts and classifications of various 'social Europes' are based on different sets of more or less precise indicators of institutional characteristics and/or institutional and public policy outcomes. The concept of 'type of welfare state' used here suggests that countries and welfare states can be classified by characteristics of the 'welfare mix' of four major providers of welfare in society: the state, the market, the civil society and the family. Thus, although all four possible providers have been and are active (and interactive) in Scandinavian countries as elsewhere in Europe, the dominant role of the state is paramount in the Scandinavian setting.

In 1985, between 22 (Norway) and 28 per cent (Denmark) of the labour force in Scandinavian countries were employed in the 'welfare state sector' (social insurance, welfare, health, education), and more than 90 per cent of all 'welfare state employees' were publicly employed,[8] putting Scandinavian countries clearly 'at the top' of the Western leagues of both total and public welfare state employment.

Since the early 1980s there has been growing attention from politicians, international organisations, the media and economists to the actual and potentially increasing welfare role played by the market, the family and voluntary organisations. Somewhat paradoxically, this new attention, frequently based on sharp criticism of the allegedly bureaucratic, inefficient and, not least, costly welfare state, emanated from political leaders of the 'less advanced' or 'less expensive' Western welfare states: Margaret Thatcher in Britain and Ronald Reagan in the USA. But this paradox serves to emphasise the importance of political rather than economic factors for policy initiation and change. Just as the birth of the modern welfare state more than 100 years ago was politically rather than economically motivated, so did the anti-state rhetoric and ideology in the 1980s appear politically motivated. But it was not just ideologues of the political right who were in favour of more non-state rather than state welfare provision. The OECD generally legitimised welfare state scepticism and criticism through its widely spread book on *The Welfare State in Crisis* based on analyses and projections of demographic and economic challenges: 'new agents for welfare and well-being [must be] developed; the responsibilities of individuals for themselves and others reinforced'.[9]

International winds of welfare state criticism and warnings quickly reached Scandinavian shores, but hardly seemed to rock the solid historical position of the state (meaning both central and local government; the public sector) in the welfare state. Despite some significant economic problems, especially at the beginning of the 1990s in Sweden and Finland, Scandinavian countries have fundamentally maintained, and even to some extent also strengthened, their welfare states during the last decade. In the Scandinavian case, economic rather than ideological factors drove reforms. The 'stateness' of the welfare states was fundamentally preserved. Political solutions were tempered by institutions and normative legacies. The following study presents a broad outline of what has happened in the fields of social security and welfare in the 1990s in Scandinavia and offers an interpretation of reform activities and reforms. It ends with an assessment of the status and prospects of the 'Scandinavian type of welfare state'. But let us begin with some background data on trends of economic development.

ECONOMIC CHALLENGES: THE WELFARE STATE PUT TO TEST

Among the Nordic countries, Sweden and Finland experienced the most critical economic problems in the early 1990s – especially Finland. The Finnish economy suffered a severe backlash. This was a result of the combined effect of international recession, the effect on trade of the fall of the Soviet Union, and of the political decision to link the Finnish Mark to the Deutschmark at a time when the latter was extremely solid.[10] Finland was no longer 'Europe's Japan', as viewed by some commentators in the late 1980s when the economy grew rapidly (but given the remarkable recovery in the latter half of the 1990s perhaps Japan one day might like to become 'Asia's Finland'). Gross domestic product declined during each of the three years 1991–93, in 1991 by close to eight per cent. From an average unemployment rate of 4.8 per cent during the 1980s, the figure during 1991–97 averaged 15 per cent,[11] with a top figure of 17.7 per cent as an average for 1993,[12] up from 3.4 per cent in 1990. This is a Nordic post-Second World War record: Denmark reached its peak rate of unemployment, 12.4 per cent, in 1993;[13] the rate in Sweden jumped from 1.3 per cent in 1989 to a post-war peak of 8.2 per cent in 1993 (not counting those on labour market training programmes); while the rate in oil-rich Norway peaked at about six per cent in 1993.[14] Unemployment rates have been falling across the Nordic countries since the mid-1990s. The Finnish budget deficit peaked at 70 per cent of GDP in 1995.[15] A declining GDP combined with high unemployment pushed social expenditure as a proportion of GDP up to 37.8 per cent in 1993. It is no wonder that the dramatic economic turn of events affected the politics of welfare. As shown below, Finnish politics in the 1990s is the politics of cuts and retrenchment in the area of social security. The struggle to regain control of public finances led to more radical policy changes than in the other Nordic country in some trouble, Sweden.

Sweden lived through its worst economic recession since the 1930s in the early 1990s. The unemployment figures soared in a short time, and GDP declined during each of the three years 1991–93. Central government budget deficits increased substantially, and government debt as a percentage of GDP reached the level of 83–85 per cent during the period 1993–96.[16] Primarily because of unemployment and a declining GDP, social expenditure as a proportion of GDP peaked at 40.3 per cent in 1993. The Swedish economy started to grow again in 1994, resulting in increased exports, large and growing surplus on foreign trade and on the balance of payments.[17]

Denmark has had quite high unemployment figures since the 'first oil crisis' in the 1970s, and started restructuring public finances and the welfare state in the 1980s. It achieved solid economic growth during the mid-1980s and again from 1992 to 1993,[18] and has been described as experiencing an 'economic miracle'.[19] Denmark did not endure years of negative economic growth. During Europe's economic *'annum horribilis'* in 1993, the Danish economy showed a solid balance of payments, foreign trade surpluses and ultra-low inflation. Since 1993, unemployment has fallen consistently, to about seven per cent in 1999. For the first time in ten years the state budget showed a surplus in 1997.

Although Norway was affected by the international recession and experienced an economic setback around 1990, the economy has grown persistently every year since 1989. Large revenues from the oil and gas sector makes Norway a unique case, and, naturally, the economically solid position has motivated less pressure for welfare reforms to reduce expenditure. The average annual GDP growth rate was 3.5 per cent during 1990–96, compared to an OECD average of 2.5 per cent, and the EU average of 1.7 per cent.[20] Unemployment has fallen to about three per cent in 1999 from its peak of six per cent in 1993. For the first and only time since 1950, the general government financial balance was in the negative in 1992–93, but is well back on the plus side – with the biggest surplus (estimated at 6.8 per cent of GDP) in Europe in 1997.[21]

All four nations were affected by the international recession around 1990, but to a greatly varying degree. Judging from indicators of economic development, one should expect Sweden and Finland to be much more active in welfare reform activities – and in efforts to cut back on welfare spending – than Denmark and Norway. This has also been the case. All have striven to reduce spending by the public sector, but government final consumption per capita has increased rapidly since the early 1980s through the mid-1990s in Norway, while the trend in Sweden has been the opposite. Denmark was by 1995 the most costly Nordic country, and also overtook Sweden in terms of public spending,[22] although public expenditure as a percentage of GDP has also declined in Denmark during the latter half of the 1990s.[23] In all four countries, trade surpluses have been growing in the 1990s, thus indicating that the economies have recuperated and are strong at the end of the 1990s.

WELFARE REFORM ACTIVITIES IN THE 1990s[24]

All four Nordic countries under review had universal coverage of old age pension systems, sickness insurance, occupational injury insurance, child allowance and parental leave schemes at the time of the international recession around 1990. The unemployment insurance was in principle compulsory only in Norway, and only for union members in the other three countries, but with unemployment cash assistance available for the non-insured (non-unionised). The same institutional pattern existed at the end of the 1990s, although the introduction of a partial income-test of the 'pensions supplement' part of the basic old age pension in Denmark in 1994 can be seen as a potentially significant change towards some element of means-testing. The same is true for the pension reform passed in Sweden in 1998, to be implemented in 2001, which restricts the payment of the previously universal basic amount to people with no, or low, employment-derived pension. Similarly in Finland, the pension reform of 1996–97 limits the hitherto universal minimum national pension to pensioners with employment-derived pensions below a certain limit. But in all countries, all citizens/residents are still entitled to an old age pension. With the exception of Denmark, all countries had an earnings-related supplementary pension schemes for all employees and self-employed both at the start and end of the 1990s. In Denmark, with the most generous basic pension of the Nordic countries,[25] all employees (only) have been entitled to a modest non-earnings-related supplement, but a labour market pension scheme agreed between the labour market partners in 1989 has given Denmark a *de facto* earnings-related pension system. In all four countries, some reduction of pension benefit levels or income replacement rates has been decided in the

1990s, most marked in Finland and Sweden. In Norway, the earnings-related part was modified in 1992, while the basic minimum pension was substantially increased in 1998. In Finland, the old age pension system has seen several changes in the 1990s: index-linking and cuts in the employment-derived part; lowering of the age limit for part-time pensions, and the increase of retirement age for some groups in the public sector. The pension reform of 1996–97 implies a stronger link between contributions and pensions, and a greater importance of work history. The Swedish parliament initiated a reform process in 1994 through a solid and broad cross-party effort, and passed a law in 1998 which implies a move from a 'defined benefit' to a 'defined contribution' system, thus also creating a closer link between contributions and payments.

There has been no change in the principle of universal coverage of sickness insurance in any of the countries during the 1990s, but a tightening of the qualifying conditions has been made in Finland and Sweden, although not in Denmark and Norway. Only in Norway has the replacement rate remained stable (100 per cent up to a maximum of six times the so-called 'basic amount' in the insurance scheme), while it has been significantly reduced in the three other Nordic countries. Only Denmark and Norway have maintained a system free of waiting days. The sickness cash benefit scheme is the most frequently and extensively reformed area of the Swedish social security system in the 1990s. This has been partly induced by rising sickness absenteeism and rising costs in the 1980s, and by a dramatic rise in the number of persons receiving permanent and temporary disability pensions (a 33 per cent increase between 1981 and 1994).

All four countries have introduced stricter qualifying conditions for unemployment insurance during the 1990s. The income replacement rate has been significantly reduced in Sweden, which has also introduced waiting days. Denmark has now the only scheme without waiting days; on the other hand, the maximum period for which benefits could be paid has been reduced from very generous nine to a still rather generous five years. All countries offer support for the education of unemployed and active labour market programmes have been improved in the 1990s. In Finland, a partially means-tested benefit known as labour market support was introduced in 1994 to secure the basic livelihood of the long-term unemployed and young people with no job experience.

All countries have held on to their universal child allowance schemes, and had, in a European comparison, relatively generous schemes for maternity benefits and maternity/parental leave. The parental leave period has been significantly extended in Norway, from 28/35 weeks to 42/52 weeks leave at 100 per cent/80 per cent wage compensation from the beginning to the end of the decade, but Sweden has kept its 'leading' position with 64 weeks of parental leave, although the wage compensation level has, as in Finland, been reduced markedly (as for sickness insurance). In all four countries the schemes allow for a father's period of leave, and this period was increased in Denmark and Norway during the 1990s.

Kindergarten coverage was already relatively high in 1990, especially in Denmark and Sweden (64 and 48 per cent coverage for children aged 0–6 years, but in Norway only 33 per cent). By 1995 the coverage had increased in all four countries, in Norway and Sweden in particular, indicating a real and important welfare priority during a period of economic downturn.

Almost all health and social care services are funded from tax revenues and provided by public authorities in Scandinavia. The principle of universalism covers not only social security schemes, but also access to health and social care services, with the partial, but important, exception of dental treatment for adults. In the health sector, user charges for services have gradually been introduced in Finland, Norway and Sweden, but with rules which set a defined maximum payment of user charges. Medical treatment is still free of charge in Denmark, and, as is to be expected, there are more medical consultations per capita in Denmark than in the other countries (in 1994: 4.8 consultations per capita, in Sweden 3.0[26]). Hospital service is still mainly a public issue as there are few private hospitals in Scandinavia, but, partly as a response to the problem of 'health queues', there has been a trend of development of private health centres with out-patient clinics/policlinics which charge market prices for treatment. The organisation of the health sector is otherwise primarily the responsibility of the municipal and/or county authorities. In all countries, dental treatment of children and young people has remained completely or partly free of charge, while the rest of the population generally pay all costs for treatment, or are reimbursed a small part of the cost. Public expenditure on health per capita was significantly higher in Sweden than in the other Nordic countries in the early 1980s, but by 1994 Norway was top.[27] Expenditure per capita increased during the first half of the 1990s in Denmark and, especially, Norway, but declined in Finland and Sweden. Expenditure on services for the elderly and handicapped has increased enormously in Norway since the early 1980s and during the 1990s, and also markedly in the temporarily 'crisis-ridden' Finland and Sweden during the first half of the 1990s. Denmark has had only a small increase, but had the most expensive system of social care services in place by the early 1980s. A major comparative study of health and social care services in the Nordic countries concludes that the Nordic model of social and health services has not significantly weakened in the 1990s. As a matter of fact the model is providing even better childcare. The differences between the Nordic countries decreased in the 1980s. There are some areas where the economic hardships of Sweden and Finland in the 1990s seem to have led to an increase in differences between them and the better off Norway and Denmark.[28]

All countries, except Sweden, spent substantially more public resources per capita in real terms on social welfare in 1995 than in 1990 (see Table 1). The increase in absolute terms was about 22 per cent in Denmark and Finland, 15 per cent in Norway, and the slight decline in Sweden was about one per cent. In both years Sweden spent the highest share of GDP on social purposes. By 1995, Norway spent the lowest share. These data illustrate the ambiguity of interpretations, but whether figures are expressions of (persistent) welfare state generosity, and/or persistent or changing social needs and entitlements, and/or stronger or declining economies, they at least indicate that social expenditure makes up an increasing share of GDP in all Nordic countries from 1990 to 1995. Despite substantial cuts in social security cash benefits for individual beneficiaries, a declining share of social expenditure was on services in Finland and Sweden. In Denmark and Norway, with little or no cuts in cash transfer benefits, the share of expenditure for services went up, particularly markedly in Norway. The interpretation of these aggregate figures must be that rapidly rising unemployment levels caused a sharp increase in cash transfer benefits in Finland and Sweden, and that Denmark and Norway expanded services as responses to persistent or increasing needs.

Table 2 shows the breakdown of social expenditure by main purposes in 1990 and 1995. It indicates that unemployment takes a much larger share of expenditure in Finland and Sweden in 1995 than five years earlier, and health and illness a smaller share. Changes in overall expenditure patterns were minor in the more stable welfare states Denmark and Norway.

Table 3 confirms the dramatic effect on expenditure of the sudden rise in mass unemployment in Finland and Sweden, showing a rise in aggregate expenditure by far more than 300 per cent for this purpose over the five-year period, while expenditure in Denmark and Norway grew by only 30 and 12 per cent, respectively. On the other hand, put differently, it also shows the budgetary effects of having a comprehensive welfare state based on individual entitlements in place when a crisis in the economy occurs, and indicates, perhaps, the political effect of the normative legacy of 'full employment' in Scandinavia with more emphasis also on a number of labour

TABLE 1
THE NORDIC COUNTRIES: SOCIAL EXPENDITURES*

| | Social expenditure | | Share of expenditure (%) | |
	As % of GDP	Per inhabitant	Services	Cash transfers
Denmark				
1990	29.7	51,104	34	66
1995	33.7	62,288	35	65
Finland				
1990	25.7	28,988	37	63
1995	32.8	35,322	30	70
Norway				
1990	26.4	50,503	35	65
1995	27.4	58,181	42	58
Sweden				
1990	34.8	67,481	41	59
1995	35.8	66,692	39	61

Notes: * as a percentage of GDP; social expenditure per inhabitant, 1995-prices, in national currencies (Kr/Fm); relative share of expenditures on services and cash benefits/transfers, 1990 and 1995.

Sources: Nososco, 'Sosial trygghet i de nordiske land. Omfang, utgifter og finansiering 1990', *Statistical Reports of the Nordic Countries No. 58* (Copenhagen: Nordic Social-Statistical Committee 1992); Nososco, *Social Protection in the Nordic Countries. Scope, Expenditure and FInancing 1995* (Copenhagen: Nordic Social-Statistical Committee 1997) No. 7.

TABLE 2
THE NORDIC COUNTRIES: SHARE (%) OF SOCIAL EXPENDITURE FOR MAIN PURPOSES (1990 AND 1995)*

| | Denmark | | Finland | | Norway | | Sweden | |
	1990	1995	1990	1995	1990	1995	1990	1995
Families/children	12.2	12.4	14.3	13.3	12.1	14.1	14.9	11.4
Unemployment	15.4	14.7	5.5	14.3	7.1	6.7	4.2	11.1
Health & illness	20.0	17.8	28.7	21.2	31.2	26.3	33.9	21.7
Old age, disabil. & surv.	48.3	48.2	49.8	47.6	47.5	48.4	45.1	49.5

Notes: * Housing and 'other social benefits' not included.

Sources: See Table 1.

TABLE 3
THE NORDIC COUNTRIES: UNEMPLOYMENT 1990 AND 1995*

	Denmark	Finland	Norway	Sweden
1990	35,624	7,101	13,442	19,162
1995	46,573	25,093	16,683	64,606
Increase (%)	30.7	325.2	12.4	337.2

Notes: * Expenditure at current prices in national currencies (million Kr/Fm).

Sources: See Table 1.

market measures. The Nordic governments spent more resources on active labour markets measures in the early 1990s, with a remarkable growth in the volume of activation measures in terms of participant inflows.[29] In both years, health and pensions make up the two by far 'heaviest' items on the welfare budget in all countries – between 65 and 80 per cent.

To put Scandinavia in some perspective, a comparison with the other group of most expensive European welfare states shows that, in 1990, social expenditure as a proportion of GDP was on average slightly lower in the Nordic countries (28.1 per cent) compared with the average for continental European countries (29.6 per cent).[30] Yet, by 1995, the Nordic average had reached 32.1 and the figure for continental Europe was 30.1.[31] But 'Scandinavian exceptionalism' really stands out in terms of one indicator of the 'stateness' of the welfare states: in 1990, government employment as a percentage of total employment was on average 26.9 per cent, while 18.7 per cent on average in continental Europe. By 1995, after the phase of severe economic downturn in Finland and Sweden, the average Nordic figure had increased to 29.4 per cent, while it was still only 18.8 per cent in continental Europe.[32] Not only government employment, but employment levels as a whole are higher in Scandinavia, with the highest levels of female employment (mostly for welfare state provision of services) in the OECD area.[33] Contrary to the general recipe proposed by the OECD crisis report from 1981, that is, stimulate non-state welfare provision, Scandinavian countries have consolidated state welfare solutions and employment. This has happened whether countries have been through periods of serious economic turmoil or not in the 1990s, and the four countries have all entered a new period of steady economic growth in the latter half of the 1990s.

THE POLITICS OF WELFARE REFORM ACTIVITIES

Public support for the welfare state in Scandinavia has traditionally been high. New studies show no declining long-term trend in support for the welfare state,[34] but with some slight variations in short-term developments in the 1980s and 1990s. Universal welfare schemes are in all countries more popular than selective ones. The big, expensive, welfare programmes, health care and health-related income transfers and old age pensions, are the most popular welfare programmes. Programmes for social assistance, housing benefits and unemployment benefits are less popular.[35] These stable patterns of public support for the welfare state influence the support and willingness of parties and governments to maintain universal and generous welfare states. At the level of the voters, it appears that divisions between the political left and right are very small in Norway and most pronounced in Sweden. Such contrasts reflect historical differences between the more polarised 'class politics' in Sweden and the more 'consensual' politics in Norway in the post-Second World War period.

The politics of welfare reform in Scandinavia in the 1990s is characterised by efforts to create compromises across competing parties and across the government–opposition division. This may be seen as joint efforts of 'blame avoidance': governments tend to want to share with the opposition the political price of cuts in benefits and services, and most opposition parties must be prepared to form or be invited into a government. Politics in general has been pushed towards more compromises simply because majority coalition governments or minority governments have become the order of the day. The era of one-party (Social Democratic) majority government (in Norway and Sweden only) seems to be gone forever: not since 1961 (Norway) and 1970 (Sweden) have one-party majority governments existed in Scandinavia.[36] More governmental 'instability' has given parliaments and opposition parties more power. Thus, changes in the way the main political institutions function work against any government proposals for radical change in policies, unless support from at least part of the parliamentary opposition is secured. The situation invites compromises over welfare policies, and trade-offs between various policy areas. More 'unstable' governments and parliamentary majorities may hinder major 'unpopular' cuts in public programmes of any kind. The political cost of taking the blame is higher than it used to be in the 1950s–1970s (but at that time of steady and 'eternal' economic growth governments were mostly blamed for building the welfare state too slowly). No major political party or political actor in any of the Nordic countries has called for state withdrawal from central spheres of health and social security, although some parties on the right are favourable to more private alternatives or, rather, supplements to state welfare. In short, both at the elite level and among voters, there exists widespread political consensus for continued public responsibility for welfare provision. There are also signs in the 1990s that welfare reforms to a greater extent are being achieved through compromises across traditional political cleavage lines. In Sweden, the Social Democrats have intensified their close co-operation with the agrarian Centre Party on social security issues, and the 1996 decision to reform the pension system resulted from a controversial compromise with the Conservatives, the Liberals and the Christian Democrats.[37] The Social Democratic government has also implemented a number of cutbacks and legislative changes since taking office in October 1994, after three years in opposition. For example, even though the party opposed the general reduction of replacement rates of social insurance benefit schemes to 80 per cent under the Conservative-led government in 1993, it was the Social Democratic government that decided to lower the sickness benefit compensation rate to 75 per cent in 1996. In Finland, Paavo Lipponen's 'Rainbow coalition' government (Conservatives, Greens, Left-wing Alliance, Swedish People's Party and Social Democrats) has had to deal with one of the deepest economic crises in Finland's modern history.

The remedy has been unpopular cuts in a whole range of key social security benefits, only made possible through broad political compromises. Even in affluent Norway – 'the Scandinavian Kuwait' – the fear of inflation and an 'overheated economy' has brought the Social Democrats and the Conservatives closer together in matters concerning government spending in general, and expenditure on welfare in particular. Thanks to the popular support of the welfare state, the non-socialist minority government of three small parties (without the Conservatives and the Progress Party) achieved parliamentary majorities in favour of a law that ensures significant cash benefits to families with small children not sending their children to kindergartens, and significant increase in the level of the minimum old age pension.

Political debate over state welfare has increasingly been influenced by those advocating incentives to work. There has been a shift in focus from receiving passive benefits to active participation through rehabilitation, training and education. This shift stems partly from the experience with large budget deficits during the 1990s (except in Norway), a lot of which was accumulated through mass unemployment and the financing of social security schemes. But it also reflects the acknowledged need to keep people in, or move them into, regular employment. Stricter employment criteria, tightening of eligibility, and shortening of benefit periods all illustrate this shift of focus, manifested *inter alia* through the Danish labour market reform (1994), the recommendations of the 'Incentives Trap Working Party' in Finland (1996), and the various Swedish reforms in the unemployment and sickness benefit schemes. Some aspects of the incentives debate seem ideologically motivated by a neo-liberal orientation towards the comprehensive welfare state. This orientation seems to have been most evident in Finland, where the economic crisis was most severely felt, and where politicians and researchers expressed fears over the risk of developing a state-based 'dependency culture'.[38] A further general characteristic of the Nordic politics of welfare in the 1990s is the strong welfare populism evident with the smaller parties on both the left and the right of the political spectrum. On the right, it has not been unusual for parties to favour substantial increases in public spending on health and pensions (at the same time as they strongly advocate tax reduction). On the left, the rule has been to 'outbid' government proposals for more generous welfare, or to accept no cuts or smaller cuts than those proposed by governments.

Some general impressions of Nordic welfare politics in the 1990s can be elaborated. In Sweden, the need for reform was acknowledged by all important parties, and the reform process which has taken place has enjoyed support from both the political left and right, although, naturally, there existed disagreement on exactly what kind of measures to take.[39] After three years with a non-socialist government led by the Conservatives, the entire election campaign of 1994 was fought over the welfare state, the public deficit and the economy. There has been general agreement on the need for state intervention in the spheres of social security, but also louder voices for the increased responsibility of both the family and the market. The Conservatives have wanted less public insurance because they view the general level of taxation as harmful to the rate of investment and economic growth. But the party abandoned in practice the idea of major tax cuts. The Conservatives have argued for greater family responsibility for welfare and for greater individual choice of insurance from a set of private insurance companies.

Somewhat similar arguments were heard in the Norwegian election campaign in September 1997, especially from the Conservatives and the Christian People's Party, but in practice more public expenditure for families with children and for old people on minimum pensions were agreed upon. The Swedish Liberal Party, a government coalition partner during 1991–94, changed its views on social security issues during that period. In opposition it favoured tax cuts, while in power it argued in favour of the maintenance of tax levels in order to protect the earnings-related basis of the social security system. Yet, the party agreed on the necessity of reforms and advocated a system with a stronger link between contributions and benefits, and stronger incentives for work participation. These principles were incorporated into the cross-party reform of the pension scheme in 1998. The (originally Agrarian) Centre Party is a traditional defender of flat-rate benefits, since the farming population has had little to gain from earnings-related benefits. The party has called for the strengthening of the basic security elements of the social security system and for reducing costs through a general lowering of benefit ceilings.

The Swedish Christian Democrats, who entered parliament for the first time in 1991, are a strong advocate of cash care allowances for families with children, in order to permit a greater degree of family choice of child care solutions (kindergartens, mothers/fathers, au-pairs, mixed or other solutions). In Norway, its sister party has argued strongly along similar lines for several years, and such a scheme was implemented in 1998 after a budget compromise with the two parties on the right not participating in the government. The Swedish Centre Party defends cuts in public spending and the need for work incentives, but wants to maintain major public responsibility in the area of social security. The short-lived (an interesting observation in itself) right-wing populist party, New Democracy, which may have influenced public opinion but otherwise played a marginal political role, favoured tax cuts, more means-testing, and a general reduction of earnings-replacement rates to 70 per cent. These ideas match those of its politically more entrenched populist cousin in Norway, the Progress Party.

The Swedish Social Democrats, traditional defenders of welfare state universalism, have altered their views on a number of social security issues since financial problems made their impact in Sweden in 1990–91. The party has on several occasions implemented cutbacks in schemes it previously protected from changes, as was the case with the unemployment and the sickness benefit schemes in 1996. Since 1995, its most stable parliamentary ally has been the Centre Party, and their common aim is to balance public finances and, by 2000, halve unemployment levels. By implication, the possibilities for expanding social expenditure are clearly constrained. Beyond the parties, the Swedish employers' federation has strongly argued in favour of lower replacement rates, more private providers of social insurance, and a financial system that gives economic incentives to individual employers to reduce health hazards. Still, there is no doubt that Swedish voters prefer a comprehensive welfare state, even to the extent of favouring tax and contribution increases to tax cuts in order to finance social expenditure.[40]

The Danish Conservative-led government of 1983–93 pursued the overriding goal of keeping inflation down. Debate before and after the 1994 election was dominated by the topic of the future of the welfare state,[41] as in the Swedish election campaign in 1994 and in the Norwegian in 1997. There was a difference though. In Denmark the premise was how to deal with the unemployment problem and the growth of social expenditure, in Sweden how to cut benefits and expenditure, while in Norway the focus was on how much more of public finances ('oil money') should go into the health system, old age pensions and care for the elderly. As in Sweden, the Danish welfare state enjoys strong popular support, and there is widespread consensus on public responsibility for welfare. Yet there is some evidence of declining welfare state support in the Danish case, mainly because of concerns over the problem of future financing.[42]

Finnish politics in the 1990s is the politics of cuts and retrenchment in the area of social security. The struggle to regain control of public finances led to more dramatic policy changes than in Sweden. But although the crisis in the public finances brought forth a number of critics, popular support for the welfare state – for primary public responsibility for welfare – is still strong.[43] Two phases can be singled out regarding reform measures that have been implemented to regain control of public finances and expenditure.[44] The centre-right government (1991–94) introduced cuts in the earnings-related sickness and unemployment benefit schemes. Public expenditure was reduced, taxes increased and tighter fiscal policies introduced in 1991. Cuts in social benefits were spread to all schemes, and techniques of cutting varied: modification of benefit levels, of compensation levels, of indexation of benefits, of eligibility to benefits. Thanks to these reforms, the growth of social expenditure in real terms decreased from 9.3 per cent in 1991 to 1.6 per cent in 1993. The economy gradually improved as of 1994, but still the 1995 budget reaffirmed the decision of 1992 to restore expenditure at 1991 level. While the centre-right government avoided cutting into minimum security benefits, the 'Rainbow coalition' government under Social Democratic leadership since 1995, added minimum social security benefits (pensions, sickness, family, labour market support) to the 'cutting list'. A government committee advocated a system of basic public services combined with private supplements, and, based on its recommendations, the government implemented reforms in 1996 that put an end to health insurance indexation, tightened eligibility criteria and reduced levels of compensation. All key benefits were subject to cuts during 1992–97, but the original structure of the benefit system has been preserved. The most radical changes were made in publicly funded unemployment and health insurance benefits, and in means-tested housing support.

Norway parts company with its Nordic neighbours – and European countries in general – when it comes to welfare cuts. The booming Norwegian oil economy in the 1990s created opportunities for maintaining and developing a welfare state which was not the most expensive from the outset. Reforms in Norway are very limited in scope. Some schemes have been modified slightly, others have been made more generous. The government and parliament have set up a 'Petroleum Fund' – to be used for investments abroad – to guarantee future financing of pensions and welfare. A government White Paper on welfare submitted to parliament in 1994 ('*Velferdsmeldingen*') concluded that the public system of social security was to be maintained in basically the same form as before. But it also emphasised a stronger work orientation. It was argued that without a high level of employment and improved schemes for rehabilitation, job training, and so on, it would be difficult to preserve the structure of the welfare system in the future. This view enjoys full support from the major parties represented in parliament. The Conservatives, the Centre Party and the Liberal Party want to promote private pension arrangements as a supplement to public pension schemes, while the Christian People's Party – which has held the premiership since September 1997 – is primarily concerned about care for the elderly, increased minimum pensions and family-oriented policies. The Labour Party emphasises 'work orientation' in social security matters – the importance of moving people from passively receiving benefits to active work through measures such as job training, education, and so on, and the tightening of eligibility/lowering of compensation in regular transfer schemes. Special efforts should be made for the young, sick, disabled, and suchlike, who are especially exposed to the risk of social marginalisation and exclusion. The Socialist Left Party is mainly concerned with the principle of fair distribution of resources in society. It advocates a strong public sector and counters all proposals to privatise welfare. Among the Nordic welfare states, the Norwegian one is the least threatened at the dawn of the new century. Unless the price of oil drops dramatically and consistently, Norway will remain the strongest Scandinavian welfare state for years to come.

THE VIABILITY OF THE SCANDINAVIAN TYPE OF WELFARE STATE

Despite the assessment that 'the Nordic welfare states had truly "grown to limits", be it in terms of comprehensiveness, universalism, or benefit generosity',[45] it has been shown above that Nordic welfare states, with the exception of Sweden, continued to grow significantly in terms of real social expenditure per capita in the 1990s. The Norwegian welfare state definitely grew both in comprehensiveness (parental leave scheme) and benefit generosity (minimum pensions, child allowances), while expenditure growth in Finland typically, even with substantial cuts in benefit levels, reflected increases in the number of beneficiaries with entitlements. If one should extract a single denominator for welfare development in the Nordic countries in the 1990s, it would be a *less generous welfare state*, but Norway does not fit the picture. The basic structure of the welfare systems has been preserved, with the partial exception of the pension reforms in Finland (1996) and Sweden (1998). Not necessarily valid for all four countries, and not for all schemes, there are at least five factors justifying the interpretation of decreased generosity in the field of public welfare. Firstly, benefit levels have been reduced, most markedly in Finland and Sweden across all social security schemes. Secondly, benefit periods have been shortened and waiting periods introduced or prolonged. Thirdly, eligibility has been tightened through a whole range of different measures. Fourthly, a much stronger emphasis on rehabilitation, activation, education and training is evident. Finally, structural reforms in the old-age pension systems in order to handle the increase in old-age pensioners in the next century (from about 2010) have been introduced.

Reform activities have been motivated by socio-structural, economic or financial considerations, and much less by political visions of an alternative type of welfare state or society. Voters seem to prefer this type of welfare state. Governments and politicians do their best to lower expectations towards the state in order to balance their budgets. Public deficits, public indebtedness, (temporary) falls in gross domestic product and high unemployment have all induced substantial retrenchment of social security benefits in Sweden and Finland, and to a lesser extent in Denmark, but hardly at all in Norway (only the earnings-related component of the old-age pension scheme was adjusted downwards in 1992). Although all of the Nordic countries are now more open for private initiatives in the fields of health services, social care services and social insurance than before – a trend which not only reflects strained public budgets but also large, well-to-do middle classes preferring more diversified responses to welfare needs of various kinds – no political party (and very few voters) favour a deconstructed welfare state. The observation that the Nordic countries seem to have overcome the 'crisis' or dramatic economic challenges of the early 1990s with reasonable economic success towards the end of the decade, and with welfare state institutions and programmes largely intact, makes it less likely that the Nordic type of welfare state is fit for the dustbin of history. The Nordic welfare states stood the test.

The Finnish case is illustrative. As shown, Finnish politics in the 1990s is the politics of cuts and retrenchment in the area of social security. Nearly all key social benefits were subject to cuts during 1992–97, but cuts were made in such a way that broad political compromises secured their legitimacy and in such a way that income distribution was barely affected.[46] The economic downturn did not create large-scale new poverty or dramatic new social and economic inequalities in society. The institutional characteristics of the Scandinavian type of welfare state were preserved. The Finnish economy began to pick up again in the latter half of 1993, and has shown steady growth since then. Unemployment is still high, but the rate was brought down to 11–12 per cent by 1999 from a peak of 17.7 per cent in 1993. The Nordic countries in general, but perhaps the Finnish experience in particular, may teach other governments a lesson: an advanced, universalistic, welfare state is not a handicap when a sudden, unexpected economic crisis occurs. On the contrary, the type and format of the welfare state may have helped these countries, and Finland especially, more rapidly through the crisis than a welfare state of another, less comprehensive, type might have and with considerably less social damage. The politically and socially controlled cuts and policy adjustments made it easier to recuperate economically and to recuperate fast. As shown by both the Finnish and Danish experiences, the Scandinavian type of welfare state was well equipped for crisis management and economic recovery. The Nordic experience in the 1990s shows that the universal and comprehensive welfare state can be a vital shock absorber which stabilises the economy and social conditions so that the economy can recuperate fast and well.

If the experience of the Nordic countries suggests that the comprehensive, universalistic and redistributive Nordic or Scandinavian type of welfare state is viable in times of serious economic challenge, this does not mean that it is invulnerable to other challenges. The affluence of Scandinavian societies and social structures with large, well-to-do middle classes may be factors which in the longer term will limit the demand for state welfare simply because many more people will demand more private and non-governmental welfare to meet their diversified welfare needs. Welfare is a high priority for people and affordable for many. The combination of individual welfare priorities, affluence and demand will surely stimulate the supply of non-state welfare provision, both for pension insurance, health insurance and personal and institutional social care. Greater space for private or non-governmental welfare – also from international, mostly European, providers within the rules of the European Economic Area – will lead to a more differentiated welfare state (and society). New generations will become more accustomed to a mix of welfare providers and institutions and will more naturally expect to pay for welfare services. Expectations for the state to ensure welfare provision will decline. This may be a good thing for the future viability of a universal welfare state when, if everything else is constant, changing demographic profiles may increase social needs and result in a stronger pressure for welfare state provision (both cash transfers and services). The Scandinavian type of welfare state may be adjusted, restructured and made less generous, but, given the welfare state history of Scandinavian countries through economic growth and recession, it seems rather unlikely that the institutional characteristics of the welfare state will be challenged in the foreseeable future. It will remain universal, comprehensive, redistributive and employment-oriented.

NOTES

1. M. Ferrera, 'Four Social Europes Between Universalism and Selectivity', in Y. Meny and M. Rhodes (eds.), *The Future of European Welfare: A New Social Contract?* (London: Macmillan 1997).
2. Ø. Sørensen and B. Stråth, 'Introduction: the Cultural Construction of Norden', in Ø. Sørensen and B. Stråth (eds.), *The Cultural Construction of Norden* (Oslo: Scandinavian University Press 1997), p.8.
3. S. Kuhnle, 'The Growth of Social insurance Programmes in Scandinavia: Outside Influences and Internal Forces', in P. Flora and A.J. Heidenheimer (eds.), *The Development of Welfare States in Europe and America* (New Brunswick: Transaction Books 1981).
4. E. Allardt, 'The Civic Conception of the Welfare State in Scandinavia', in R. Rose and R. Shiratori (eds.), *The Welfare State: East and West* (New York: Oxford University Press 1986).
5. G. Esping-Andersen, *The Three Worlds of Welfare Capitalism* (Cambridge: Polity Press 1990).
6. F.G. Castles (ed.), *Families of Nations: Patterns of Public Policy in Western Democracies* (Aldershot: Dartmouth 1993).
7. S. Leibfried, 'Towards a European Welfare State?', in C. Jones (ed.), *New Perspectives on the Welfare State in Europe* (London: Routledge 1993); Ferrera, 'Four Social Europes'; S. Kuhnle and M. Alestalo, 'Introduction: Growth, Adjustments and Survival of European Welfare States', in S. Kuhnle (ed.), *Survival of the European Welfare State* (London: Routledge 2000).
8. J.E. Kolberg and G. Esping-Andersen, 'Welfare States and Employment Regimes', in J.E. Kolberg (ed.), *The Study of Welfare State Regimes* (Armonk: M.E. Sharpe 1992), p.23.
9. OECD, *The Welfare State in Crisis* (Paris: OECD 1981), p.12.
10. M. Heikkilä and H. Uusitalo (eds.), *The Cost of the Cuts. Studies on Cutbacks in Social Security and their Effects in the Finland of the 1990s* (Helsinki: Stakes, 1997).
11. OECD, *Economic Outlook* (Paris: OECD 1997), No.61.
12. N. Ploug, 'Cuts in and Reform of the Nordic Cash Benefit Systems', in M. Kautto *et al.* (eds.), *Nordic Social Policy. Changing Welfare States* (London: Routledge 1999), p.82.
13. Nososco, *Social Protection in the Nordic Countries. Scope, Expenditure and Financing 1995* (Copenhagen: Nordic Social-Statistical Committee 1997), No.7, p.8.
14. S. Marklund and A. Nordlund, 'Economic Problems, Welfare Convergence and Political Instability', in Kautto *et al.* (eds.), *Nordic Social Policy*; Ploug, 'Cuts in and Reform of the Nordic Cash Benefit Systems'.
15. OECD, *Economic Surveys: Finland* (Paris: OECD 1996).
16. OECD, *Economic Surveys: Sweden* (Paris: OECD 1997).
17. Nososco, *Social Protection in the Nordic Countries*, p.17.
18. OECD, *Economic Surveys: Denmark* (Paris: OECD 1997).
19. J. Goul Andersen, 'Welfare Crisis and Beyond: Danish Welfare Policies in the 1980s and 1990s', in Kuhnle (ed.), *Survival of the European Welfare State*.
20. OECD, *Economic Outlook* (Paris: OECD 1997), No.61.
21. OECD, *Economic Surveys: Norway* (Paris: OECD 1997).
22. Marklund and Nordlund, 'Economic Problems', pp.24–5.
23. Goul Andersen, 'Welfare Crisis and Beyond'.
24. The summary review of status and reforms of welfare programmes is based on Nososco (*Social Protection in the Nordic Countries*), and P. Eitrheim and S. Kuhnle, 'Nordic Welfare

States in the1990s: Institutional Stability, Signs of Divergence', in Kuhnle (ed.), *Survival of the European Welfare State*.

25. Nososco, *Social Protection in the Nordic Countries*, p.103.
26. Ibid., p.88.
27. J. Lehto, N. Moss and T. Rostgaard, 'Universal Public Social Care and Health Services?', in Kautto *et al.* (eds.), *Nordic Social Policy*, pp.102–3.
28. Ibid., p.130.
29. J.A. Drøpping, B. Hvinden and K. Vik, 'Activation Policies in the Nordic Countries', in Kautto *et al.* (eds), *Nordic Social Policy*, pp.142ff.
30. By Continental European countries we are referring to Austria, Belgium, France, Germany, the Netherlands.
31. Kuhnle and Alestalo, 'Introduction'.
32. Ibid. Note that the figures indicate unweighted averages of proportions. The OECD definition of government employment is used and stems from the system of national accounts. The definition covers 'producers of government services', those who are employed by central or local bodies in administration, defence, health, education and social services. The definition excludes most public enterprises: See M. Alestalo, S. Bislev and B. Furåker, 'Welfare State Employment in Scandinavia', in Kolberg (ed.), *The Study of Welfare State Regimes*, pp.37–45).
33. OECD, *Historical Statistics 1960-1995* (Paris: OECD 1997), p.41.
34. J. Goul Andersen *et al.*, 'The Legitimacy of the Nordic Welfare States: Trends, Variations and Causes', in Kautto *et al.* (eds.), *Nordic Social Policy*, pp.255–6.
35. Ibid., p.256.
36. O. Petersson, *Nordisk Politik* (Stockholm: Norstedts Juridik 1998).
37. J. Palme and I. Wennemo, *Swedish Social Security in the 1990s: Reform and Retrenchment* (Stockholm: Ministry of Health and Social Affairs 1998).
38. M. Heikkilä, 'Justifications for Cutbacks in the Area of Social Policy', in Heikkilä and Uusitalo (eds.), *The Cost of the Cuts*.
39. J. Palme, 'Recent Developments in income Transfer Systems in Sweden', in N. Ploug and J. Kvist (eds.), *Recent Trends in Cash Benefits in Europe* (Copenhagen: the Danish Institute of Social Research 1994).
40. Ibid.
41. O. Borre and J. Goul Andersen, *Voting and Political Attitudes in Denmark* (Århus: Århus University Press 1997).
42. Gould Andersen *et al.*, 'The Legitimacy of the Nordic Welfare States'.
43. Heikkilä, 'Justifications for Cutbacks in the Area of Social Policy', p.22.
44. V. Kosunen, 'The Recession and Changes in Social Security in the 1990s', in Heikkilä and Uusitalo (eds), *The Cost of the Cuts*.
45. J. Stephens, 'the Scandinavian Welfare States: Achievements, Crisis, and Prospects', in G. Esping-Andersen (ed.), *Welfare States in Transition: National Adaptations in Global Economies* (London: Sage 1996).
46. Heikkilä and Uusitalo (eds.), *The Cost of the Cuts*.

Change and Immobility:
Three Decades of Policy Adjustment in the Netherlands and Belgium

ANTON HEMERIJCK AND
JELLE VISSER

TWO NEGOTIATED ECONOMIES

With ten and 15 million inhabitants, respectively, Belgium and the Netherlands are two of the smaller members of the European Union. Bordering on Germany and hosting the two largest seaports and one of the largest airports, they are transit economies. Imports and exports make up three-quarters or more of GDP. Small domestic markets encourage trade liberalisation and a search for competitive advantage through product specialisation and economies of scale in export markets. As the oldest industrial nation of continental Europe, Belgium developed a strong position in the production of raw material, coal and steel, and related industrial products, until decline began in the 1960s. Since then, the economic axis has shifted to light industry and services, with a strong impact on the port of Antwerp and the inward investment of multinational, mainly US, firms. The Netherlands industrialised late and never became an industrial nation, despite its post-1945 efforts. The Dutch economy is specialised in transport and logistics, international finance, business services, agro-industry and foreign trade. The country is home to large indigenous and Anglo-Dutch multinational firms, like Philips, Unilever, Shell, Heineken and some of Europe's largest banks.

In small countries a sense of vulnerability is usually engraved in the minds of policy makers. How well they work together to manage economic progress and social conflict depends as much on institutional features as on preferences, strategic goals, power resources and control over their constituencies. External shocks tend to induce policy actors to play down their divisions, but it usually takes time to understand the nature and implications of such shocks. Policy making is critically dependent on the agreement of different coalition parties and support from social partners. None of the actors is autonomous and free to choose its most favoured response to new conditions or external pressures. This is particularly true for the government, whose role under the rules of corporatism and consociationalism is constrained both from without and within.[1] By incorporating multiple parties in coalition governments and integrating the social partners into the administrative structures of public policy making, the state can mobilise more resources and rally support for policy change. But consociationalism and corporatism can also inhibit change, precisely because of the need for extensive compromises and coalition formation. All negotiated systems are vulnerable to so-called 'joint-decision traps'.[2] Where the state is weak and its powers are 'hollowed out', this may create prolonged immobility.

Both countries experienced the slow-down in output and productivity growth that has characterised all advanced economies since 1973. In the wake of the 1973 oil-price shock, policy makers in Belgium and the Netherlands tried to combine a hard currency policy with Keynesian demand stimulation. The failure to organise wage restraint in support of fiscal reflation accelerated cost-push inflation (see Figure 1), caused a loss of competitiveness, a sharp fall in manufacturing employment, a rise in unemployment and higher public debts. Thus, both countries began the 1980s with a very deep crisis, with unemployment rates reaching double digits. In both countries the crisis triggered a rather similar U-turn in policies, restoring external competitiveness (see Figure 2). However, outcomes were rather different. This is most strikingly visible when we look at our indicators for employment (Figure 3) and unemployment (Figure 4). Output growth over the full period 1983–97 was slightly higher in the Netherlands, especially in the 1990s, but many more jobs were created for each point of output growth in the Netherlands. Employment was more or less stagnant in Belgium, whereas its northern neighbour experienced one of the most spectacular employment booms in its history, and in Europe. The question, therefore, is why. How can we explain the difference? What happened in the Netherlands that was prevented from happening in Belgium? Is the explanation to be found in the nature of these jobs, in the preferences, the policy legacies, or in the institutions?

Belgium and the Netherlands are 'Bismarckian', or Christian-Democratic welfare state.[3] Protection is based upon the principle of industrial insurance against occupational risks, financed by earmarked payroll contributions from employers and workers. Employment-related social security programmes revolve around income replacement and are targeted at the male breadwinner in order to preserve traditional family patterns. In contrast to the Nordic welfare state model, social services are underdeveloped. Instead, the system

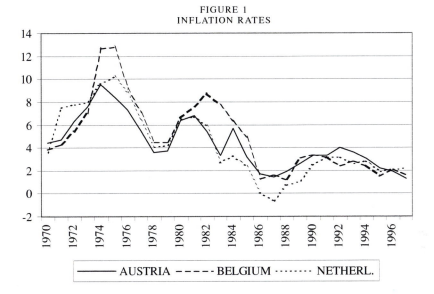

FIGURE 1
INFLATION RATES

FIGURE 2
REAL GROWTH

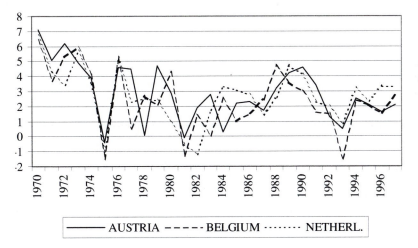

FIGURE 3
UNEMPLOYMENT RATES

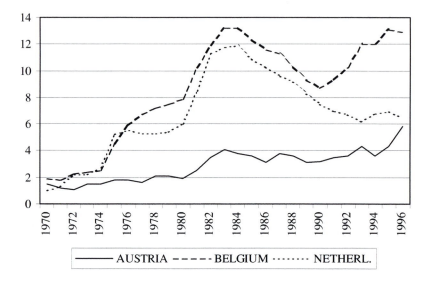

FIGURE 4
EMPLOYMENT POPULATION RATIO

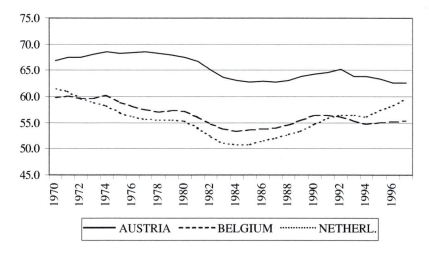

is highly transfer-oriented. Active labour market policies are of recent discovery. Both countries reveal similar trends in terms of total government outlays, resources spent on social expenditure, the share of social transfers, or taxation in general. In 1995, total government outlays were 55.3 per cent in Belgium and 54.5 per cent in the Netherlands in 1995. Social transfers as a proportion of GDP were 24.3 per cent and 25.1 per cent respectively and very stable. Almost three-fifths was paid from social security contributions of employers and workers. In terms of the share of non-wage labour costs in total labour they fell into the mid range. Considering the whole tax structure, taxes fall heavily on labour.

Many authors, for instance Peter Katzenstein,[4] Gerhard Lehmbruch[5] or Philippe Schmitter[6] have classified Belgium and the Netherlands under the label of 'democratic corporatism'. But, unable to exert control over external events, post-war policy elites had favoured co-operation across class cleavages through tightly knit networks of consultation and negotiation. The Central Economic Council (CCE, 1948) and National Labour Council (CNT, 1952) in Belgium and the Foundation of Labour (STAR, 1945) and Social-Economic Council (SER, 1950) in the Netherlands embodied the idea that organised capital and organised labour, together with state representatives, central bankers and experts, shoulder the responsibility for the welfare of the nation.

In Belgium, the Social Pact of 1944 and the Productivity Agreement of 1954 became the basis for a 'Golden Age of Planning and Growth'.[7] In wage policy, labour legislation and social security, the main decisions were taken by trade unions and employers, codified in seven major central agreements between 1960 and 1974. Unions and employers maintained a high level of autonomy. In 1975 this development came to an abrupt halt. From 1975 state involvement increased in all three areas – wage bargaining, social security and labour market policies – and Belgium moved from a bipartite to a tripartite system in which the social partners were frequently taken into 'preventive custody' or placed 'under house arrest'.[8]

In the Netherlands, the Agreement of 1943, negotiated between employers and union leaders in illegal wartime talks, became the basis for national concertation. A distinctive feature of Dutch post-war economic policy was its state-led wage policy. Between 1945 and 1963 the Netherlands ran a statutory wage policy controlled by the state-appointed Board of Mediators.[9] In social security, however, unions and employers retained a large measure of autonomy. Labour market policy was non-existent. In the 1960s and 1970s, responsibility for wage policy reverted to unions and employers. But since they were unable to agree among themselves, actual negotiations frequently ended with state intervention. Thus, in the 1970s we observe a similar shift towards tripartism in both countries, though from a different direction.[10] Because of its growing costs and implications for non-wage labour costs and the income of a large number of people outside the labour market, social security increasingly becomes an issue in wage negotiations. But the role of unions and employers in supervising and governing employee insurance funds is at first unchallenged. In labour market policy, the state has the difficulty of redefining its traditional passive role.

In structural terms, union–management relations in the two countries are rather similar, but with some significant differences.[11] The main bargaining level is sectoral, though in the Dutch case large (multinational) companies bargain separately. Coverage is relatively high and affects four out of five employees. In both countries, the mandatory minimum wage is comparatively high, but in the Netherlands, unlike Belgium, the gap between minimum and average wage has widened by almost 20 percentage points since 1983. In both countries, the minimum wage serves as the anchor for the calculation of minimum social benefits. Employers are well organised, with 80 per cent or more joining an association. The central organisation of employers in Belgium (VBE) appears to have less authority over its affiliates than its Dutch sister organisation (VNO-NCW). The level of unionisation in Belgium (53 per cent) is twice that of the Netherlands (28 per cent). The difference has been attributed to workplace presence and involvement in the individual case handling of unemployment insurance in the Belgian case.[12] The Dutch unions witnessed between 1979 and 1987 a sharp drop in unionisation, but have since recovered somewhat. In both countries unions are divided in different currents.

The political systems of Belgium and the Netherlands, together with Austria and Switzerland, have been considered the clearest examples of consociational democracies and typical 'segmented' or 'pillarised' societies.[13] Party elites are encouraged to co-operate under a spirit of non-competitive power sharing. The Reformation and Counter-Reformation had divided the Netherlands between Protestants and Catholics, who in the process of developing mass democracy and worker mobilisation emerged as self-contained communities or vertical 'pillars', alongside the Socialists and Liberals, each with their own parties and associations. This system experienced its maximum strength in the 1950s, but began to disintegrate after the mid-1960s. Class division in Belgium was cross-cut by the division between Catholics and anti-clerical forces over the role of church and state, and by the language conflict between Dutch- and French-speaking Belgians. Within 100 years of the foundation of Belgium as an independent state in

1830, hopes for having French as its sole, unifying language had vanished. Neither was there a basis for generalised bilingualism. Eventually Belgium became divided in three linguistic territories: a Dutch one, a French one and a bilingual one in Brussels – the French-speaking capital of Flanders. The linguistic conflict was contaminated by differences of class and the reversal in the economic position of the regions. The solution that was eventually found was a double federation into three language communities and two regions, producing five sub-national parliaments and governments. In 1993 Belgium was formally declared a federal state.

THE NETHERLANDS: REINVENTING ITSELF

The 1970s: The Dutch Disease

When the Bretton Woods system collapsed, the Netherlands joined the European currency 'snake', reflecting a tradition of defending a strong currency and the placement of financial before industrial interests. This choice meant that if Dutch unions would prove unable to hold wages back, competitiveness would decline in the case of an appreciating currency. This is exactly what happened. As labour costs in manufacturing were rising faster than in competing countries, all relevant policy actors agreed on the desirability of some form of income policy, but no agreement was reached. On the eve of the first oil crisis, a left-of-centre government led by Joop Den Uyl (PvdA) had taken office. Impressed by the recession but expecting the crisis to be temporary, he opted for a Keynesian strategy of fiscal stimulation, setting the stage for a corporatist policy package, exchanging fiscal reflation for wage restraint. But the radicalised Dutch unions wanted more reforms in economic policy and corporate governance than the government, with the reluctant support of its Christian coalition parties, could offer. In 1974 the government imposed a wage and income stop, but its effect was undone when the ban was lifted.

Thanks to its gas exports, the Netherlands experienced no balance-of-payments problems. Hence an expansionary course seemed feasible and appropriate. The main rise in government spending was directed at expanding welfare programmes, reflecting in part a concession to the egalitarian and solidaristic preferences of the unions. In 1974, the minimum wage and, indirectly, public sector salaries and social security benefits were index-linked to private sector wage increases. Youth minimum wages sharply increased and were indexed as well. Most collective agreements contained automatic price escalators. The result was that pay increases in the private sector automatically translated into a rise in public sector outlays. It made the government a prisoner to the outcome of negotiations in the private sector and an interested party in wage negotiations, which, unavoidably, became tripartite.[14]

The main problem with an elaborate system of indexation is that it limits the room for manoeuvre in case of external shocks and tends to increase real wage stickiness. It makes 'inflation less painful and socially disruptive, but faster and more difficult to brake'.[15] The employer offensive to revise the system in 1977 failed after a brief but massive strike. The penalty paid by the unions for their successful defence of indexation was government intervention and ever smaller scope for negotiated nominal wage increases.[16]

In this context, natural gas turned out to a mixed blessing, culminating in the infamous 'Dutch disease'. Export revenue and import savings from natural gas resulted in a current account surplus, which put upward pressure on the guilder. Moreover, the Dutch Central Bank (DNB) pursued its hard-currency policy with ever more zest when it realised that the government was losing control over wage setting and public finance. By the end of the decade, the inconsistencies in the Dutch policy mix grew to self-defeating proportions.[17] From 1976, Finance Minister Wim Duisenberg tried to moderate public sector growth and make room for private sector investment. Den Uyl resigned the next year (over the issue of land-ownership), won the largest ever victory for his party in the general elections, but failed to attract the Christian Democrats into a new government. Dries Van Agt, the leader of the newly formed Christian Democratic Party (CDA), brokered a coalition with the Conservative Liberals (VVD). Like its predecessor, this government tried to talk trade unions into restraint, but it had even less to offer. Unable to bring public finances under control, it felt obliged to intervene in wage setting in 1979, 1980 and 1981. The wavering position of the government was epitomised by internal conflict between the two CDA Ministers of Social Affairs and Finance.[18]

Worried by continued decline in manufacturing jobs and the collapse of shipbuilding, the main union in industry made a U-turn and came to support wage moderation in combination with working-time reduction. Late in 1979 there was even a draft central agreement in the Foundation of Labour. But the leader of the Dutch Federation of Trade Unions (FNV), Wim Kok, withdrew his signature at the last minute when opposing affiliates' threatened revolt. After this failed accord, carefully arranged by Social Affairs Minister Wil Albeda, his Finance colleague, Koos Andriessen, called for an extended wage freeze for two years. As even the VVD considered this outlandish, Andriessen decided to resign. The commitment to concertation had triumphed over the objective of fiscal restraint, but not for long.

The 1980s: The Crossroads at Wassenaar

The restrictive macroeconomic policies of the US, UK and Germany in the wake of the second oil shock increased the financial liabilities of Dutch firms, squeezed profits and caused a spate of bankruptcies and factory closures. Unemployment soared at a rate of 10,000 to 15,000 per month to a record 800,000 in 1984. Against the background of strong labour force growth, forecasts were extremely gloomy. Within five years trade unions lost 17 per cent of their members. The public deficit peaked at 6.6 per cent in 1982. Slowly but surely the relevant policy actors in the Dutch political economy began to understand the disastrous consequences of the perverse spill-over between a hard currency, high real wages, indexation, lower profits, less investment, growing unemployment and fiscal crisis.

The general elections of 1981 had resulted in a patched-up coalition between the Christian and Social Democrats, but the new administration immediately fell back into deadlock and lasted only nine months. New elections in 1982 brought an austerity coalition of CDA and VVD to power, thanks to gains for the Liberals. This coalition, led by Ruud Lubbers (CDA), committed itself to a 'no-nonsense' strategy of economic recovery through improved business profitability, fiscal consolidation and cost-neutral work-sharing in order to alleviate the unemployment problem. Unveiling its plans in November 1982, the new cabinet declared that 'it is there to govern'. Two days later, the leaders of the main union and employers' confederation, Kok and Van Veen, announced that they had struck a deal, prepared in the Foundation of Labour since the summer. The social partners were in a hurry to prevent another intervention. The government had already announced that it would suspend indexation in 1983.

With unemployment running at double digits, the trade union movement was in no position for a wage conflict. Employers saw a chance to rid themselves of recurrent state intervention. The Wassenaar agreement was a recommendation only, but one that carried authority. With this agreement, Dutch unions acknowledged that 'for a higher level of investment, essential for job growth, a higher level of profitability was required'.[19] The response to the Wassenaar agreement was swift. In less than a year two-thirds of all collective agreements were renewed, mostly for two years, during which the payment of price compensation was suspended and a five per cent reduction of working hours took place. By 1985, cost-of-living clauses had virtually disappeared; average real wages fell by nine per cent in real terms.[20]

Assured of restraint, the government had its hands free to regain control over public sector finance. In 1983 salaries, minimum wages and related benefits were frozen and for 1984 the government cut public sector wages by three per cent. This brought the public sector unions to arms, but after a strike of three weeks they found themselves isolated. Special measures were taken for the poor and families living on only one minimum income. As the most influential CDA power broker behind Lubbers, Social Affairs Minister Jan De Koning had convinced him, against the advice of DNB and the Finance Ministry, not to follow the Germans in the EMS currency realignment of 1983. The guilder devalued two per cent against the D-Mark – a decision that was soon regretted when financial markets demanded an extra risk premium. In March 1983, Dutch monetary authorities announced that henceforth the guilder was to be pegged to the D-Mark.

Helped by the international economic upswing, investments and jobs benefited from the recovery of profits in the second half of the decade. The reduction of working hours had an additional work-sharing effect, but the largest contribution came from the rapid expansion of part-time jobs, mainly among married women and young people.[21] The growth in part-time jobs, however, was not the result of policy changes, but originated in the behavioural changes of women. In the absence of day-care facilities, part-time work became the dominant 'coping' strategy of working mothers. In health, education and social services, but also in central and local government, part-time employment was a welcome means for employers to adjust to budget restrictions.

Lubbers' austerity policy paid off politically. In 1986 the centre-right coalition was re-elected with gains for his CDA party. Two governments of the same persuasion meant a clear break with the immobilism of the 1970s. Inflation decreased to almost zero in the mid-1980s. The strict exchange rate policy exerted disciplinary influence on wage developments, while, in turn, wage moderation enabled the DNB to stick credibly to its non-inflationary policy. Low inflation allowed unions to forget about indexation. The new mix of macro-economic policy and wage setting also changed the institutional relations between unions, employers and the state. The new pattern became a central dialogue over a wide range of policy issues combined with sectoral wage bargaining, based on the primacy of industrial self-regulation. The role of the central organisations was confined to redirecting sectoral contracting towards tacit, economy-wide wage restraint and public-regarding behaviour.[22]

The second Lubbers administration promised a further reduction of the deficit, not to increase taxes and social premiums and lower unemployment. The new policy challenge was to curtail the costs of social security and reduce the number of welfare recipients, which had continued to rise throughout the 1980s. Under the increased competitive pressures of the

1980s, many firms had channelled less productive and expensive, mostly older, workers out of the labour market into unemployment or disability benefits. Here there was a clear moral hazard, since the insurance costs were borne by all firms and, should funds run out, by the taxpayer. The rising insurance premiums resulted in higher social security contributions, while the wedge between total (wage and non-wage) labour costs and take-home pay increased. This engendered a vicious circle of employment destruction, of firms seeking to match rising costs by increasing productivity through lay-offs, leading to higher costs, and so forth.

It became increasingly obvious that firms, with the complicity of social security administrators, were reducing slack while externalising the costs of adjustment, leading to an ever-growing volume of claimants. The so-called 'system reforms' in social security, implemented in 1987, had tightened eligibility and lowered guaranteed benefits from 80 to 70 per cent of last-earned wages, but it had not altered the bipartite governance structure. After the reforms, Lubbers had promised 'peace on the social security front', but it was not to be. The route through sickness and disability was the way of least resistance for Dutch employers. In the 55–64 year age group, recipients of a disability benefit outnumbered workers with a job already in 1986. Leo Aarts and Philip De Jong[23] list four features that may explain the Dutch disability crisis. First, no distinction was made between occupational and social causes of disabilities. Second, entitlement was based on an assessment of a worker's incapacity to find a job similar to his former job. Third, since the administration of the sickness and disability schemes was separate, workers could first spend a year on sickness leave, almost unsupervised, and then move on to disability. Fourth, under collective agreements, most firms topped up sickness benefits to 100 per cent of previous earnings and supplemented disability benefits. The scheme produced a harsh welfare trap: once officially recognised as (partially) disabled, workers acquired a permanent labour market handicap. All these factors conspired in a seemingly unstoppable rise in the number of claimants, approaching, by 1990, one million in a working age population of seven million.

The 1990s: From Fighting Unemployment to Increasing Participation

In the late 1980s, policy makers became aware that the low level of labour market participation was the Achilles' heel of the extensive but passive Dutch system of social protection. This diagnosis inspired the CDA–PvdA administration (1989–93) and subsequent Lib–Lab administrations to recast the balance between active and passive policies. In 1993, the social partners followed suit in their embrace of higher levels of participation in the New Course agreement.

Lubbers had exchanged his Liberal coalition partners for the Social Democrats after a break in the old coalition (over environmental policy) and new elections in 1989. Lubbers III, now with the PvdA, led by ex-union leader and Wassenaar negotiator Kok as Finance Minister, began in an optimistic mood. Index-linking between contractual wages, minimum wages and benefits was restored, albeit contingent upon the ratio of active to inactive people. Soon after the formation of the Cabinet a tripartite common policy framework, with promises of growth, employment, tax relief and wage moderation was agreed between the government and the social partners. But in early 1991 the employers withdrew their signature and stepped up their campaign for tax relief, lower non-wage labour costs and a cap on government spending. To drive their point home, they decided to stay away from the customary spring meeting of the Foundation of Labour with core ministers from the Cabinet. Employers favoured one-to-one exchanges with the unions or with the government above trickier tripartism.

At around this time German unification boosted economic growth, but soon high interest rates dampened economic activity. The decline in unemployment was immediately reversed. The government was preoccupied with the lack of a quick response from wage negotiators and prepared intervention on the basis of the 1970 wage law. Since its revision in 1986, this law entitled the government to intervene in wage setting in case of a severe economic setback. Under pressure, the Foundation of Labour recommended a two-month stop on wage negotiations in early 1993. Later in the year, while the government formally prepared a stop, unions and employers concluded a new agreement, called 'A New Course'. This was a true follow-up of Wassenaar, going further down the path of organised decentralisation and flexibility.[24] Employers gave up their blanket resistance to shorter working hours, unions promised further wage restraint. Both parties agreed to work together in improving the unfavourable employment/population ratio and recommended flexible working time patterns and part-time work as a solution.

In the course of Lubbers III, the exchange logic behind organised wage restraint changed character. Increasingly wage moderation was matched by lower taxes for workers and social contributions for employers, made possible by improved public finances and a broader tax base. This was supported by the tax reform of 1990, which integrated taxes and social security charges, and lowered the overall and highest rate, while limiting deductions. Since the reform was sugared by a tax break for most households, consumer spending surged by four per cent in real terms, with highly favourable employment effects.[25]

Lubbers I and II had exhausted the 'price' policy of bringing social expenditures under control through the freezing and lowering of benefits. Moreover, the PvdA opposed any further measures of this kind. The emphasis therefore shifted to a so-called 'volume' policy aimed at reducing the number of benefit recipients. Unavoidably, the political crisis of the Dutch welfare state came to revolve around disability pensions. When in 1990 the politically unacceptable number of one million disability claimants seemed near, Lubbers dramatised the issue and shocked viewers of the TV evening news with the message that the country was 'sick' and required 'tough medication'. The next summer, after long agony, the government decided to tighten the sickness and disability programmes. In response, the unions organised the largest post-war protest march in The Hague. This episode had far-reaching political consequences. PvdA went through a deep crisis and Kok nearly resigned. Popular and party resistance notwithstanding, the reforms were enacted. They included a reduction of replacement rates for all workers under age 50. After some time, benefits would decrease to 70 per cent of the statutory minimum wage plus an additional age-related allowance. Below 50, those in the system would furthermore be subjected to new medical examinations, on the basis of stricter rules.

The 1994 elections were those of popular discontent. The Lubbers–Kok coalition was effectively voted out of power, losing 32 of its 103 seats in parliament, which is four short of a majority. This was a political earthquake:[26] no single Dutch coalition had ever lost so much support in one election. The extraordinary loss of the CDA (from 54 to 34 seats) was caused by a leadership crisis and the untimely publication of a party document that future retrenchment might include a freeze of basic pensions. Ironically, PvdA, losing 12 of its 49 seats, became the largest party. A restored PvdA–CDA coalition was now only possible with the help of the progressive Liberals (Democrats 66). This party persuaded the historical enemies, PvdA and VVD, to form a coalition and form the first government since 1917 without a confessional party.

The new 'purple' coalition did not slow down in its reform effort, but PvdA had a bottom-line condition for its co-operation: the level and duration of social benefits would not be tampered with. From this very defensive position, the party was committed to the 'job, jobs and more jobs' approach as the only way out. This explains its support for reforms aiming at efficiency improvements, by means of the introduction of financial incentives through a partial re-privatisation of social risks and a managed liberalisation of social policy administration. The latest government plans are likely to bring all insurance under one public service. The unions, supported by employers, oppose these plans which would further reduce their involvement, but the government appears determined to have its way. The welfare reforms of the 1990s were helped, politically, by the results of some alarming inquiries into the causes of the social security crisis. A parliamentary inquiry in 1993 revealed what was already common knowledge, namely that the social partners had made 'very liberal use' of social security for purposes of industrial restructuring and social peace. The government limited the self-governing autonomy of social partners and set up an independent supervisory board. A separate National Institute for Social Insurance became responsible for contracting the administration of social security out to privatised delivery agencies. A final string of measures concentrated on the introduction or intensification of activation obligations for the long-term unemployed.

The new policy priority of 'jobs, jobs and more jobs' made its imprint on all kinds of labour market policy initiatives. There was a new focus on active labour market policies, an underdeveloped area in post-war policy-making. The public employment service was reorganised and in 1991 brought under tripartite control, financed by the government but run independently. There was also devolution of responsibility to regional employment boards. A critical evaluation after four years led to another overhaul in 1996 and provided a policy window for issue linkage between labour market and welfare policy. As a result of the strengthening of 'activating' measures in unemployment insurance and social assistance, municipalities and social insurance organisations have a budget to buy placement and training activities from the employment service. From 2000 the employment service is expected to compete with private providers, like the temporary work agencies. Including the 40,000 permanent jobs in the public sector for unemployed youth and the long-term unemployed, additional job programmes absorb around 1.5 per cent of total employment. In addition, the government has introduced several kinds of employment subsidy schemes based on a reduction of social security contributions paid by employers. Employment subsidies can add up to 25 per cent of the annual wage. Subsidy schemes cover as many as one million workers.

Labour market flexibility is an integral part of the new labour market policy mix. Legislation removing constraints on shop opening hours, business licences, temporary job agencies, working time, and dismissal law consolidate this development. In 1995 unions and employers signed the first collective agreement for temporary workers, introducing a right of continued employment and pension insurance after four consecutive contracts or 24 months of service. It prepared the ground for the central agreement on 'Flexibility and Security' of 1996, which, in turn, paved the way for an overhaul of Dutch dismissal protection law in 1999. This 'flexicurity' law is a compromise, not just between employers and employees, but also within the unions between workers with and without stable jobs. The incremental individualisation of the tax system since 1984, the improved possibilities to switch from full-time to part-time jobs, and the removal of all remaining elements of discrimination on the basis of working hours, have contributed to a 'normalisation' of part-time employment.[27]

BELGIUM'S IMMOBILISM

The 1970s: Hard Currency plus Keynesianism without Restraint

The shocks of the 1970s had a powerfully disturbing influence on the Belgian economy. During the recession, unemployment doubled from 100,000 in mid-1974 to 228,000 two years later. By the end of the decade, Belgium had the highest unemployment rate in Europe except for Spain. Employment contracted by almost six per cent between 1974 and 1983. Comparing the six years before and after 1973, GDP growth halved; export growth fell from 11 to three per cent per year; inflation rose to eight per cent, whereas unemployment trebled.[28] The public sector debt, fuelled by costly settlements of the linguistic conflict and steeply rising deficits in the social security funds, reached alarming proportions by the end of the decade and required perennial austerity in the next. In 1981, the public deficit stood at -12.7 per cent of GDP, which was the record in the OECD. Debt servicing alone had risen to almost one-fifth of government revenue. At the end of 1981, net external liabilities were larger than the foreign exchange reserves of the Belgian National Bank (BNB). In 1981, the economy contracted by more than a full percentage point and unemployment rose to 500,000, or 700,000 (16 per cent) if people in various early retirement schemes are included.

When the Bretton-Woods system collapsed, Belgium also joined the European currency 'snake'. It stayed in until the very end, despite the defection of France and other initial participants. It did so for broadly the same reason as the Netherlands; with wage negotiators unwilling or unable to control cost-push inflation, a hard currency policy was its main protection against imported inflation. As explained in the case of the Netherlands, this came at the cost of a decline in competitiveness in foreign markets.

Difficulties in obtaining voluntary wage restraint posed a dilemma. All governments after 1974 were caught between the brake of a hard currency policy and the engine of a reflationary surge for which there were insufficient resources. The immediate government response had been to rescue industries in difficulties with subsidies, job creation in the public sector and demand-stimulating measures. Another response had been the reduction of labour supply, through a recruitment ban on foreign workers (which was largely ignored), the early retirement of older workers and an additional year of education for young people. It did not matter much that in 1974 the Christian Democrats shifted coalition partner, from left to right, and in 1977 returned to the Social Democrats. All governments until 1982 were wedded to a Keynesian approach. Public employment expanded and the share of public in total employment rose between 1970 and 1982 from 23 to 32 per cent. It was not enough. Until 1975 heavy industry had absorbed redundant workers from labour-intensive industries such as textiles, clothing and leather, as well as coal mining, but this was now no longer the case. The employment ratio in manufacturing fell by more than four percentage points between 1973 and 1980. Total aid to business, combining subsidies, capital transfers, loans and government equity investment averaged 5.5 per cent of GDP per year in the second half of the 1970s and peaked at 8.9 per cent in 1982. This equalled 13 per cent of government expenditure at the time and was unsustainable. In later years it would fall to around seven per cent. The largest item in the budget was subsidies to traditional sectors and large firms, in compensation for the hard currency policy.

Before 1973, Belgium's main difficulties had been related to its outdated industrial structure, a problem which was compounded by the shifting economic balance between the two regions. As the first industrial country on the continent, it had inherited a large manufacturing base, concentrated in Wallonia. The decline in the demand for steel and coal began to hurt the region as early as 1960. Post-war industrialisation programmes and accommodating tax treaties had helped to attract foreign investment and solve the age-old problem of underemployment in rural Flanders. Unemployment had always been much higher in Flanders, but after 1970 the positions reversed and unemployment rates in Wallonia tend to be twice the national average.

With corporate profits under pressure, employers screamed for wage restraint and lower taxes. But they were internally divided and unable to attract the unions to a deal. In 1974 they signed what would turn out to be the last central agreement before long. In 1975, FBE pulled the brake and recommended a small wage increase, but this advice went unheeded. Similar attempts in later years failed and until 1982 wage increases outpaced productivity growth, with the implication that the competitive position of firms deteriorated and profits eroded. Failing to agree, each side maintained an interest in demanding social protection (unions) and subsidies (firms). Unavoidably, this development led to state involvement in wage bargaining and a shift from bipartism to tripartism. The government needed wage restraint, if only to limit the rising claims and costs of social security and the increasing deficit in public spending. Until 1981, attempts to encourage unions and employers to accept restraint failed. Each side had a sticking point: employers refused to discuss working time reduction, unions ruled out real wage restraint, and governments could not afford to give up the strong currency.[29] After 1981, the government took an authoritarian line, and from 1982 to 1986 free wage-setting through negotiations between unions and employers was suspended.

The central organisations lacked control over their members and disagreed over policies. As in many other European countries, Belgium witnessed a period of worker militancy and radicalisation of union demands after 1968. Ideologically, Belgian employers felt under attack.[30] With the slow-down of economic growth, it became less easy to compromise. In 1976 Fabrimetal, the metal employers, demanded the abolition of the indexation system, which had since 1952 guaranteed the automatic adjustment of wages to increases in consumer prices. The attack failed and made indexation the 'holy cow' of Belgian industrial relations. Unlike their Dutch colleagues, Belgian union leaders remained steadfast in defence of indexation.

The 1980s: Devaluation and Recovery

At the European Summit of 1980, Belgium was 'advised in strong terms' to modify its 'prejudicial system of wage indexation if it wants to stay in the EMS'.[31] Impressed, Prime Minister Wilfried Martens proposed a temporary suspension, apparently without consulting his Socialist coalition partners, whose ministers resigned. The next government, again with the Socialists, asked for special powers of parliament and, only 48 hours before a wage stop would have taken effect, unions and employers agreed on a package of voluntary restraint and working-time reduction for 1981. Soon thereafter the government fell (over the federalisation issue), provoking the fourth crisis in two years. In an unusual speech King Baudouin reminded politicians that time had come 'to put our differences aside' and 'give priority to survival', as one 'would do if we were at war'.[32] But the next government did no more than solve another piece in the federalisation puzzle and postpone what Belgian employers called 'the evident decision', by which they meant the suspension of wage indexation.

The general elections of 1981 resulted in large losses for the Christian Democrats in Flanders and gains for the Liberals. Forming his fifth Cabinet, CVP leader Martens chose to govern with the Liberals. Despite its narrow parliamentary majority, this coalition stayed four years in office and was continued after the elections of 1985. Martens V ruled by decree, obtaining special enabling powers in an annual vote of confidence. This silenced the Socialist opposition and the internal critics from the Christian union wing. Martens defended his 'less democracy for a better economy' approach as 'an unavoidable step in the recovery of our country'.[33]

1982 began with an 8.5 per cent devaluation of the franc, the largest since the start of the EMS. This was combined with a standstill in wages and a suspension of indexation for the entire year. Martens and his aides had secretly negotiated this manoeuvre with the veteran leader of the Christian Workers' association, who used his influence to assure co-operation from the Christian unions. They went along on condition that suspension of indexation would be temporary and special income protection applied to low-paid workers and large families. The Socialist unions were left in the dark, but their strikes were unsuccessful. Wage indexation remained, in part, suspended until the end of 1986. Real wages fell between 1982 and 1986, and productivity gains were captured by firms, leading to a sharp decline in labour's share in enterprise income. However, since the government raised the employers' social security contributions in order to meet rising costs, non-wage labour costs decreased less and the gap between labour costs and take home pay rose sharply. Since the government had agreed to exempt minimum wages and heads of (large) families from its measures, or offer compensation, the distance between minimum and average wages narrowed and the overall wage structure compressed.

There are similarities between the Belgium recovery plan of 1982 and the 'no nonsense' approach in the Netherlands. Both were responses to a severe crisis and were implemented by centre-right governments with a strong electorate mandate for the Liberals. In both countries, the Social Democrats had exhausted themselves as coalition partners by their failure to tame or convince the unions (as well as by their antagonism towards permitting a new generation of nuclear weapons on Dutch or Belgian soil). In both countries, the recovery plans aimed at the restoration of private sector competitiveness and profitability; fiscal consolidation; and a halt in the upward trend in unemployment through job sharing. The overall package was deflationary and at first increased unemployment. It implied a shift of incomes from households to enterprises, showing in a sharp fall in labour's share in net national income. The main difference, however, was that in the Netherlands recovery was consolidated by the Wassenaar agreement. This allowed the Lubbers government to concentrate on fiscal consolidation and uncouple public sector pay from private sector wage negotiations. In Belgium the lack of agreement placed the government in a more vulnerable position, with many risks of implementation failure and political horse-trading.

The choices of the Belgian government were constrained by the fact that it started the 1980s with a huge public debt. There was no money for lowering taxes or to boost consumer demand. While the cost crisis in social security was severe, the austerity measures tended to be rather piecemeal and drawn out over a longer period than in the Netherlands, possibly because the opposition of the more powerful Belgian unions and within the Christian Democratic Party was stronger. Belgian social security for workers is contributions-based, but in 1983 premiums covered only 62 per cent of total expenditure, against 84 per cent in 1970.[34] The deficit in social security, combining all programmes, had increased nearly tenfold, from 26 billion Belgian francs in 1970 to 254 billion in 1980, with the rise in unemployment benefits as the largest contributing factor. Expenditure on unemployment rose from 0.7 per cent of GDP in 1970 to five per cent in 1985. As part of the first austerity package, unemployment insurance entitlements had been differentiated between principle breadwinners with dependent families, single households and people earning a second household income in 1980. For the latter two categories, benefits were lowered and phased out earlier. In later reforms, an extended 'waiting time' of 150 days applied to school-leavers and from 1982 benefits no longer followed wage increases (a principle only introduced in 1975).

Early retirement also contributed to the cost explosion. Faced with the explosive growth in youth unemployment, affecting one in four under the age of 25, and the structural crisis in mining, steel, ceramics, textile and shipbuilding, Belgian governments believed that they had no choice but to encourage the early retirement of workers. It was the only policy response on which unions and employers agreed.[35] Its appeal showed in the sharp fall in the employment ratio of older males, now the lowest in Europe. Older workers received an early retirement payment until legal retirement age in case of unemployment, and public subsidies were available for early retirement in case of replacement by a young worker.

Work sharing was the third plank of the 1982 recovery plan. Under the so-called 5+3+3 operation, unions and employers were encouraged to negotiate a five per cent reduction in working hours in exchange for a three per cent wage sacrifice and a three per cent increase in employment. Attempts to negotiate a central agreement failed. Employers, assured of statutory wage restraint, needed to make no further concessions. Unions complained that they had been robbed of an instrument – wage pressure – to wrest concessions. Yet, in sectors and firms with over-capacity problems, agreements were reached for 1.3 million employees, with a net employment effect of 52,100 jobs, which was about half the government's target. Flexibility in working hours was encouraged through experiments allowing the suspension of mandatory norms on maximum daily or weekly hours, if firms could show positive employment effects and entered into agreement with the unions and the Ministry. Fifty-five plant agreements were signed between 1983 and 1986, affecting 26,000 employees in total, nearly all in large manufacturing firms like Siemens, Phillips, Samsonite, and General Motors, all of which were interested in increased flexibility and located in Flanders. The Socialist unions in Wallonia would have none of it.

The 1990s: Sluggish Growth but EMU Participation Ensured

In the 1990s Belgium exemplified Europe's principal economic malady: high structural unemployment and slow productivity and employment growth in private services. The international slow-down in economic growth and the restrictive policies in the run-up to EMU magnified the problems. On the supply side the problems were related to a compressed wage structure, allowing little variation across sectors, regions and skill levels, despite very large differences in unemployment, labour demand or productivity. Together with the strong bias towards passive labour market policies and the earnings-compensating role of social security, this helps explain why long-term unemployment is so persistent.[36] Unemployment traps appear to be related to the length rather than the level of unemployment benefits. Older workers can stay unemployed until retirement age and the small unemployment benefit for married women often serves as a small second income in the family. They have no monetary incentive to accept a job if it is not full time

In 1990, the monetary authorities, anxious to quell the occasional speculative frenzies against the franc, promised to preserve parity with the DM in the event of a realignment, and the Belgian central bank, the BNB, gained the same degree of independence as its Dutch counterpart, the DNB.[37] Following the EMU decision at Maastricht in December 1991, Belgium set itself the objective of belonging to the first group of participants. With the entrance of the Socialists into Martens' seventh cabinet (1988–91), fiscal control had been relaxed, however, and the link between price indexation, wages and benefits was re-established. Free wage bargaining had resumed, albeit under the 'shadow of hierarchy' defined by the 1989 Law on Safeguarding Competitiveness of Enterprises, which authorised the government to intervene, *ex post*, if wages in Belgium rose faster than the average trend among its five major trading partners. The Conseil Central Economique (CCE), with bipartite representation of unions and employers, as well as co-opted economic experts, was assigned the task of issuing a report on the state of the economy and, if need be, recommending corrective measures.

The balance sheet of this period of limited free wage bargaining (1987–93) is mixed. The central organisations were able to conclude (biennial) central agreements, but, according to some observers, these agreements were 'devoid of content and largely dictated by government'.[38] Wage increases, set centrally and based on productivity gains in manufacturing, outpaced the four times lower productivity increases in services. Hence, investment and employment in domestic services stagnated. The debt and competitiveness problems resurfaced. The new round of federalisation in 1988 had not encouraged 'the kind of fiscal behaviour associated with restricted monetarism'.[39] Following the EMS crisis of 1993, BNB had to accept a wider margin between the franc and D-Mark. The CCE report for 1994 stated that Belgium had again developed a handicap of six per cent against its trading partners. This figure was disputed by the unions, who blamed the deflationary policies of the Bundesbank and the restrictive EMU membership criteria agreed at Maastricht.[40] Formalised in its so-called EMU convergence plan of 1992, the government had in 1992 ushered in a fiscal consolidation package, aiming at reducing the deficit from seven to three per cent of GDP by 1997. Later a special three per cent EMU tax surcharge was implemented. Consumer spending was sluggish, while the savings rate surged to unprecedented heights, suggesting a lack of confidence in the economy.

Alarmed by sharply rising unemployment, in early 1993 Prime Minister Jean-Luc Dehaene (1992–95) proposed a 'Global Pact'. Infuriated by proposals to trim the cost-of-living index, the Socialist Union Federation FGTB, under pressure of its affiliates, ended the talks later in the year. The government, including its Socialist ministers, went ahead and excluded tobacco, alcohol and energy from the cost-of-living index. With the Global Plan becoming law in 1994, the eight-year interlude of limited freedom in wage setting was at an end.[41] Wage increases, beyond the watered down price indexation, remained banned until the end of 1996. Dehaene II

(1995–99), again a Christian–Socialist coalition, started with proposing a 'Pact for the Future of Employment', in pursuit of three objectives: to halve unemployment by 2002, improve the sluggish rate of GDP growth and secure the budget deficit target required for EMU membership. Consultations continued until April 1996, when the main employers' federation reached a draft agreement with the unions. Its content was, once again, wage moderation; a legal maximum working week of 39 hours in 1998; improved rights for leave of absence without pay, part-time retirement at age 58 and full-time retirement at age 60; an annualisation of working time; and a lowering of employers' social security contributions. The agreement failed, however, when the FGTB was unable to gain approval from its affiliates. The leadership of the Christian ACV slipped through with a slight majority.[42]

The government went ahead and enacted a new Law on Safeguarding the Competitiveness of Enterprises, proscribing that wage increases must remain below the *average* wage increases in Germany, France and the Netherlands. This was a clear tightening of the old law of 1989, as it introduced a wage norm *ex ante* instead of an *ex post* rationale for intervention. The 1996 Act stipulates that multi-industrial bargaining must take place every second year, on the basis of the CCE report, and lead to an agreement on the precise margin for sectoral bargaining. If no agreement is reached, as was the case in 1996, the government sets the margin – 6.1 per cent for 1997 and 1998, including a predicted 3.6 per cent rise in consumer prices.[43] The next round, for 1999–2000, did produce an agreement. This was eased by the government's decision to reduce social security contributions with 108 billion francs or 2.5 billion Euro over five years. The deal itself was complex and linked the future reduction in social contributions to compliance with the wage norm. Companies and sectors paying above the norm would not be penalised if they proved that it did not destroy jobs. Not only was this extremely difficult to monitor, it also required sectoral and regional data that is as yet unavailable.

Wage cost subsidies have been used since the early 1980s, but until recently they were targeted at industry only. Following the EMS crisis, there was a rapid expansion, from 15 billion francs in 1993 to 60 billion in 1996. As in the original Maribel scheme of 1981, subsidies were intended to compensate exporting firms for the hard currency policy and to slow down the decline of manual work. Because of its selective character, the European Commission has repeatedly criticised Maribel as a distortion of competition. In response, subsidies have been offered to all firms proportionate to 'labour intensity'. The revised scheme applies to about

770,000 workers, against 431,000 in the old programme. Unions criticise the subsidy as a hand-out to employers. But the proposal of Socialist ministers to make the subsidies contingent on explicit job targets was rejected. Since 1995, the federal government has also phased in an additional 'low earnings' subsidy scheme, applying to 782,000 workers at or around the minimum wage, whose social security charges are lowered by between two and 12 per cent of total wage costs. In 1996, one-third of total expenditure on tax- and charge-reducing subsidies went to Maribel, one-quarter to the low earnings scheme and one-fifth to special job creation plans for the long-term unemployed.[44]

Part-time employment has remained unpopular with the unions. Unlike the Netherlands, it never was or became the dominant choice for working mothers. The full-time employment/population ratio of Belgian women is double that of the Netherlands, whereas the part-time ratio is three times lower.[45] Historically, a much larger number of Belgian married women continued to work full time, and childcare facilities have been available on a much wider scale. The policies of Belgian governments concerning part-time work have been inconsistent. Around 1980, part-time work was encouraged, but in later years a scheme under which part-time employment could be combined with part-time benefits was stopped because of its costs. In recent years, especially for older workers, the government has reinstated the possibility of combining part-time work with part-time benefits. Part-time work is treated with ambivalence in labour law and social security, as well as in statistics. In Belgium, employment protection and minimum wage and vacation rights apply only to part-time jobs that exceed one-third of full-time jobs, with a minimum of three hours per day.

CONCLUSIONS

In negotiated political systems like Belgium and the Netherlands, constrained by the rules of consociationalism and corporatism, policy change is critically dependent upon the agreement of ruling coalition parties and support from the social partners. These systems suffer from what Fritz Scharpf calls a 'negotiator's dilemma'. Negotiators must simultaneously search for effective policy responses, in terms of policy content, while resolving distributive conflict, that is, find a 'fair' distribution of the social costs of adjustment between and among ruling coalition parties and the social partners.[46]

Both countries suffered from lack of consensus and co-ordination in the 1970s and went through a deep crisis in the early 1980s. With a fragile political consensus of Keynesian reflation, Dutch and Belgian unions, in part as a result of radicalising tendencies, were unprepared to forsake income redistribution for employment. As a result, central bankers and increasingly governments endorsed a hard currency stance. The resultant decline in competitiveness led to soaring unemployment, which in turn exacerbated the cost explosion in social security. In addition, Belgium experienced a depletion of its national reserves, a crisis of international confidence and a humiliating devaluation of its currency.

In the face of the acute unemployment and fiscal crisis, a severe challenge to their power and pent up frustrations over recurrent intervention, the Dutch unions resigned themselves to the new realities of the world economy and returned to a strategy of wage moderation. Rather than continuing the prisoners' dilemma game, in which third-party intervention had become unavoidable, they redefined their position in terms of 'battle of the sexes', preferring a co-ordinated policy over distributive privilege. From 1982 on, Dutch unions have consistently placed jobs before income. This learning process on the part of the trade unions led to a revitalisation of the social partnership in 1980s and 1990s. Employment growth, subsequently, created the economic and political precondition for the path-breaking transformation social security and labour market policies, despite initial disagreement.

Next to wage restraint, labour time reduction and labour time flexibility played a key role in job growth. Policy preferences shifted from across-the-board reductions in the working week towards the enhancement of part-time work and annualisation of working time. Two-thirds of the jobs created since 1982 have been part time. The surge in part-time employment coincided with the rapid increase in labour force participation by women, from 29 to 60 per cent between 1971 and 1996, the largest rise in any OECD country. While the labour force increased by one-fifth between 1970 and 1997, the female labour force more than doubled.[47] The positive interaction effects between wage moderation, part-time work, the shift to services and increasing participation have since the early 1990s been supported by social security reform. From 1983 to 1998, transfers to households in GDP came down from 31 per cent to 26 per cent and the share of government expenditure in GDP declined from 62 to 52 per cent. In relative terms, related to the size of the labour force, there are fewer people on disability and sickness benefits.

This painful learning experience of shifting preferences did not occur in Belgium, where the social partners remained stuck in a 'prisoner's dilemma' and, moreover, suffered from internal fragmentation. Belgian trade unions did not accept that wage restraint and a recovery of profits were necessary conditions for economic recovery and job growth. In part, this reflects the continued strength of the Belgian unions, compared with the Dutch. The result was that Belgian governments had to impose on trade unions and firms what in the Netherlands was negotiated between them. Whereas the Dutch social partners were successful in combining moderate wage increases with increased flexibility at the micro level, the Belgium strategy of imposed wage restraint sacrificed micro-flexibility in the labour market for the purposes of macro-adjustment. This restricted decentralisation and flexibility of wage bargaining in the Belgian case, made linkage with other policies, in particular work-sharing, more difficult and implementation failures more likely. Moreover, its continued need to beg for support for highly contested policies compromised the attempt at fiscal consolidation and welfare reform. Of course, the options of Belgian governments were also limited by the fact that more money had to be spent on interests and repayment of debts. Under conditions of permanent austerity, the slightest of setbacks in economic growth had extremely damaging consequences for the country's public finances.

Like the Netherlands, Belgium entered the 1970s with one of the lowest employment/population ratios in Europe. Thirty years later, unlike the Netherlands, this has hardly changed. Until recently, reducing labour supply was accepted as an alternative to overt unemployment and governments went along with subsidising early retirement for lack of alternatives. Unemployment has remained high, hiding a large regional variation, with Flanders approaching full employment, and includes a large structural component, with the highest share of long-term and youth unemployment in Europe outside Italy and Spain. Yet there was no second country where governments designed so many pacts, proposals and plans to coax unions into accepting wage restraint and employers into creating jobs, with so little success. Unions argue that these schemes fail to re-qualify workers and trap them in dead-end jobs. Economists argue that subsidies to firms exposed to international competition have lowered employer resistance to union wage demands and slowed down the rate of innovation.

It is tempting to distribute some blame to the linguistic conflict and the cumbersome federalisation process. It overshadowed other pressing problems, like industrial decline, unemployment, public administration, justice or environmental decline.[48] Michel Albert observed that the Belgians 'were amusing themselves with their linguistic squabbles' while the 'ship was sinking'.[49] The weakening of public policy was compounded by the partisan use of the state, with recruitment practices based on party membership, language and region. It is an open question whether the new political situation will create a new political and economic dynamic. The new Lib–Lab–Green coalition which gained power in 1999 has a mandate for change, after the string of scandals in recent years and the disastrous electoral results for the Christian and Social Democrats. Helped by the 1998 central agreement, this may be the time for a new start.

NOTES

This paper is based on a larger three-country comparison, including Austria, that we undertook together with Brigitte Unger (Economic University of Vienna), for the conference project, directed by Fritz W. Scharpf (Max Planck Institute for the Study of Societies, MPIfG, Cologne) and Vivien A. Schmidt (Boston University), on 'The Adjustment of National Social Policy Systems to Economic Internationalisation' in twelve advanced welfare states. This joint paper has greatly benefited from the collaboration with Brigitte Unger and comments and suggestions made by Fritz Scharpf and Vivien Schmidt. Martin Schludi (MPIfG) and Friso Janssen (University of Amsterdam) helped us with preparing the graphs, Myriam van Parijs with the Belgian Sources.

1. A. Hemerijck, 'The Historical Contingencies of Dutch Corporatism' (D. Phil. Thesis, Oxford University, 1993).
2. F.W. Scharpf, 'The Joint-Decision Trap: Lessons from German Federalism and European Integration', *Public Administration* 66 (1988), pp.239–78.
3. G. Esping-Andersen, *The Three Worlds of Welfare Capitalism* (Princeton: Princeton University Press 1990); and K. van Kersbergen, *Social Capitalism: A Study of Christian Democracy and the Welfare State* (London and New York: Routledge 1995).
4. P.J. Katzenstein, *Small States in World Markets. Industrial Policy in Europe* (Ithaca, NY: Cornell University Press 1985).
5. G. Lehmbruch, 'Introduction: Neo-Corporatism in Comparative Perspective', in G. Lehmbruch and P.C. Schmitter (eds.), *Patterns of Corporatist Policy-Making* (Beverly Hills, CA and London: Sage 1982), pp.1–27.
6. P.C. Schmitter, 'Interest Intermediation and Regime Governability in Contemporary Western Europe and North America', in S. Berger (ed.), *Organizing Interests in Western Europe* (Cambridge: Cambridge University Press 1981).
7. G. Dancet, 'Wage Regulation and Complexity. The Belgian Experience', in R. Boyer (ed.), *The Search for Labour Market Flexibility* (Oxford: Clarendon Press, 1988), pp.212–37.
8. J. Vilrokx and J. Van Leemput, 'Belgium: The Great Transformation', in A. Ferner and R. Hyman (eds.), *Changing Industrial Relations in Europe* (Oxford: Basil Blackwell 1997), pp.315–47.
9. J.P. Windmuller, *Labor Relations in the Netherlands* (Ithaca, NY: Cornell University Press 1969).
10. H. Slomp, 'België: naar "Nederlandse toestanden"?' in T. Akkermans and P.W.M. Nobelen (eds.), *Corporatisme en verzorgingsstaat* (Deventer: Stenfert Kroese 1983), pp.143–69.
11. J. Van Ruysseveldt and J. Visser, 'Weak Corporatisms going Different Ways? Industrial Relations in the Netherlands and Belgium', in J. Van Ruysseveldt and J. Visser (eds.), *Industrial Relations in Europe. Traditions and Transitions* (London: Sage 1996), pp.205–64.
12. B. Ebbinghaus and J. Visser, 'When Institutions Matter: Union Growth and Decline in Western Europe, 1950–1995', *European Sociological Review* 15/2 (1999), pp.135–58.
13. See H. Daalder, 'The Netherlands: Opposition in a Segmented Society', in R.A. Dahl (ed.), *Political Opposition in Western Societies* (New Haven, CT: Yale University Press 1966), pp.188–236; L. Huyse, *Passiviteit, Pacificatie en verzuiling in de Belgische politiek* (Antwerp and Utrecht: Standaard 1970); V.R Lorwin, 'Belgium: Religion, Class and Language in National Politics', in R. Dahl (ed.), *Political Opposition in Western*

Democracies; V.R. Lorwin, 'Segmented Pluralism: Ideological Cleavages and Political Cohesion in the Smaller European Democracies', *Comparative Politics* 3/2 (1971), pp.141–75; and A. Lijphart, *The Politics of Accommodation. Pluralism and Democracy in the Netherlands* (Berkeley, CA: University of California Press 1968).

14. A. Hemerijck, 'Corporatist Immobility in the Netherlands', in C.J. Crouch and F. Traxler (eds.), *Organized Industrial Relations in Europe: What Future?* (Aldershot: Avebury 1995), pp.183–226.

15. A. Romanis Braun, 'Indexation of Wages and Salaries in Developed Economies', *IMF Staff Papers* 23/1 (1976), pp.226–71.

16. J. Visser, 'Continuity and Change in Dutch Industrial Relations', in G. Baglioni and C.J. Crouch (eds.), *European Industrial Relations: The Challenge of Flexibility* (London: Sage 1990), pp.199–240.

17. OECD, *Economic Surveys 1979: The Netherlands* (Paris: OECD, 1980).

18. A. Hemerijck, 'Corporatist Immobility in the Netherlands', in Crouch and Traxler (eds.), *Organized Industrial Relations in Europe*, pp.183–226.

19. J. Visser and A. Hemerijck, *A Dutch Miracle: Job Growth, Welfare Reform and Corporatism in the Netherlands* (Amsterdam: Amsterdam University Press 1997).

20. Visser, 'Continuity and Change in Dutch Industrial Relations', pp.199–240.

21. J. Visser, 'The First Part-Time Economy in the World. Does it Work?' (Paper presented at Euro-Japan Symposium on the Development of Atypical Employment and Transformation of Labour Markets', Japan Productivity Center for Socio-Economic Development, Tokyo, 24–25 March 1999).

22. J.-P. van den Toren, *Achter gesloten deuren? CAO-overleg in de jaren negentig* (Amsterdam: Welboom 1996).

23. L. Aarts and P. de Jong, *Curing the Dutch Disease* (Aldershot: Avebury 1996).

24. J. Visser, 'Two Cheers for Corporatism, One for the Market: Industrial Relations, Unions, Wages, and Labour Markets in the Netherlands', *British Journal of Industrial Relations* 36/2 (1998), pp.269–82.

25. F. de Kam, 'Tax Policies in the 1980s and the 1990s: The Case of the Netherlands', in A. Knoester (ed.), *Taxation in the United States and Europe* (London: Macmillan 1996), pp.259–301.

26. R.A. Koole, *Politieke partijen in Nederland: Ontstaan en ontwikkeling van partijen en partijstelsel* (Utrecht: Het Spectrum 1995).

27. Visser, 'The First Part-Time Economy in the World. Does it Work?'

28. H.R. Sneessens and J.H. Drèze, 'A Discussion of Belgian Unemployment Combining Traditional Concepts and Disequilibrium Economics', in C. Bean, R. Layard and S. Nickell (eds.), *The Rise in Unemployment* (Oxford: Blackwell 1986), pp.89–120.

29. G. De Swert, 'Samen apart', in BVVA (ed.), *Vijftig jaar Arbeidsverhoudingen* (Bruges: De Keure and Belgische Vereniging voor Arbeidsverhoudingen, 3–16 1989).

30. J. Moden and J. Sloover, *Le patronat belge. Dscours et idéologie 1973–1980* (Brussels: CRISP, 1980).

31. Dancet, 'Wage Regulation and Complexity', p. 211.

32. M. Deweerdt and J. Smits, 'Belgian Politics in 1981: Continuity and Change in the Crisis', *Res Publica* 24/2 (1982), pp.261–72; W. Dewachter, 'La Belgique d'aujourd'hui comme société politique', in A. Dieckhoff (ed.), *La Belgique: La force de la désunion* (Brussels: Complexe 1982), p.262.

33. J. Smits, 'Belgian Politics in 1982: Less Democracy for a Better Economy', *Res Publica* 25/2–3 (1983), pp.181–217.

34. J. Peeters, 'De sociale zekerheid tien jaar later: naar een crisismanagement', in BVA (ed.), *Vijftig jaar Arbeidsverhoudingen* (Bruges: De Keure and Belgische Vereniging voor Arbeidsverhoudingen 1989), pp.197–228.

35. J. Bastian, *A Matter of Time. From Worksharing to Temporal Flexibility in Belgium, France and Britain* (Aldershot: Avebury 1994).

36. L. Goubert and F. Heylen, 'Loonvorming en de werking van de arbeidsmarkt in België', in J.J. van Hoof and J. Mevissen (eds.), *Loonvorming en werking van de arbeidsmarkt in België* (Amsterdam: Elsevier 1999), pp.87–110.

37. P. Kurzer, *Business and Banking: Political Change and European Integration in Western Europe* (Ithaca NY: Cornell University Press 1993).
38. Vilrokx and Van Leemput, 'Belgium: The Great Transformation', p.341.
39. P. Kurzer, 'Placed in Europe: The Low Countries and Germany in the European Union', in P.J. Katzenstein (ed.), *Tamed Power: Germany in Europe* (Ithaca, NY: Cornell University Press 1998), p.120.
40. C. Serroyen and J.P. Delcroix, 'Belgium', in G. Fajertag (ed.), *Collective Bargaining in Western Europe, 1995–96* (Brussels: ETUI, 1996), pp.31–56.
41. P. Blaise and T. Beaupain, 'La concertation sociale 1993–95', *Courier hebdomaire du CRISP* 1497/98 (1996).
42. Van Ruysseveldt and Visser, 'Weak Corporatisms Going Different Ways?', p.217.
43. Vilrokx and Van Leemput, 'Belgium: The Great Transformation', p.340.
44. L. De Lathouwer, 'Het Belgisch werkloosheidsstelsel: een evaluatie vanuit sociaal zekerheids- en arbeidsmarktperspectief', in J.J. van Hoof and J. Mevissen (eds.), *Loonvorming en werking van de arbeidsmarkt in België* (Amsterdam: Elsevier 1999), p.199.
45. Visser, 'The First Part-Time Economy in the World'.
46. F.W. Scharpf, *Games Real Actors Play* (Boulder, CO: Westview Press 1997).
47. SCP, *Social Cultural Plan 1998* (Ryswÿk: Social Cultural Planbureau, 1998).
48. M. Swyngedouw and M. Martiniello (eds.), Belgische Toestanden. De lotgevallen van een kleine bi-culturele demoncratie (Antwerp: Standaard 1998).
49. In M. Hansenne, *Emploi: Les scénarios du possible* (Paris: Duculot, 1985).

Building a Sustainable Welfare State

MAURIZIO FERRERA AND
MARTIN RHODES

ESCAPING THE EQUALITY–EFFICIENCY TRADE-OFF

The conciliation of economic growth – with its demanding 'efficiency' imperatives – and social justice – with its equally demanding call for 'equality' – was one of the most significant aspirations of the twentieth century. The creation of the welfare state (and, more specifically, social insurance) has turned this aspiration into a largely successful institutional reality. Yet, today, the welfare state is the object of heated controversy in all of the advanced economies. The 'conciliatory' capacity of social policy has been put in serious question, especially in the light of the so-called 'globalisation' process. More and more frequently, efficiency and equality, growth and redistribution, competitiveness and solidarity are referred to as polar opposites that can only thrive at each other's expense. There is, therefore, a risk that the new millennium may have opened under the shadow of a resurrected 'big trade-off',[1] offering only two possible coherent value-combinations and thus virtually only one viable institutional scenario, if functional priorities ('the pie first') are to be respected.

Plausible as it may sound, this trade-off logic is not inescapable. But finding a way out of it is certainly not simple. For the task entails the identification of new value combinations and institutional arrangements that are both *mixed* (in respect of their normative aspirations) and *virtuous*, that is, capable of producing simultaneous advances on all fronts. The search for these combinations and arrangements must start from an accurate diagnosis of the problems and challenges that are currently afflicting the Western welfare state and are disturbing its delicate relationship with the spheres of economic production and exchange. In the analysis which follows we seek answers to three broad questions. What exactly lies at the basis of the current welfare predicament? What reforms are needed in order to (re)create virtuous circles between social protection and its changed socio-economic context? And, finally, how can the reform agenda be realised, so that 'old vices' are turned into 'new virtues'?

GLOBALISATION VERSUS 'INTERNAL' CHALLENGES

Let us start with the thorny issue of 'globalisation', frequently assumed to be at the root of the predicament. As shown by recent research, there may good reasons for believing that the overall impact of globalisation has been exaggerated, as have its potentially adverse consequences for employment and social standards.[2] It is important to acknowledge that national economies have neither been wholly absorbed into a new global order nor their governments totally incapacitated. Non-traded sectors remain important in most European economies and national comparative advantage and specialisation remain critical for international competition. Good arguments for the compatibility of large welfare states with internationalisation are regularly rehearsed. Welfare states emerged in line with the growing openness of economies and facilitated the consequent process of socio-economic adjustment. Government consumption still appears to play a functional, insulating role in economies subject to external shocks.

Moreover, unemployment problems and the need for the modernisation of social protection systems should, on the whole, be attributed mainly to other developments (such as the 'post-industrialisation' of advanced economies) to which globalisation (greater trade competition, the internationalisation of finance) may make some contribution but cannot on its own explain. We discuss a number of hypotheses concerning the interaction of internationalisation with European labour market problems below. Serious attention should be paid, however, to arguments that financial market globalisation limits government policy-making autonomy, and that market integration and tax competition constrain the capacity of states to engage in redistributive tax policies. While the 'propensity to deficit-spend' has not been constrained by increasing trade and capital mobility (in the EU it has rather been checked by the construction of economic and monetary union), financial market integration and capital mobility have potentially a detrimental effect on the policy-making autonomy of governments. They certainly demand that policies prioritise credibility with the capital markets foremost amongst their other objectives.

Yet whatever the extent of the 'globalisation', which remains debatable, the potential incompatibility between national welfare states and increasingly integrated European markets may be much more important than the subjection of the welfare state to punitive global markets. At a time when EMU has forced a reduction in deficits and debts, and rendered competitive devaluation impossible for its member countries, and single market legislation is levering open product and financial markets to ever greater degrees of competition, the constraining nature of these developments must be acknowledged. All European welfare states must become 'competitive' to the extent that simultaneously meeting their fiscal, solidarity and employment-creation objectives requires a creative new mix of policies. That said, various types of institutional setting and forms of social, social security and labour market policy may be equally compatible with competitiveness. There is no need for (nor is there much evidence of) convergence on a 'neo-liberal' value combination and institutional model.

It should also be stressed that welfare states have generated many of their own problems and these would have created severe adjustment difficulties in the late twentieth century, even in the absence of greater exposure to flows of capital and goods. By helping to improve living standards and life spans, welfare states have created new needs that social services were not originally designed to meet. Rising health care costs and pension provision have contributed massively to welfare budgets and fiscal strains.[3] Other problems – for example, the decline in demand for low or unskilled manufacturing workers – stem from the increasingly post-industrial nature of advanced societies. Post-industrial change has created a 'service sector trilemma' in which the goals of employment growth, wage equality and budgetary constraint come increasingly into conflict.[4] Creating private service sector employment on a large scale entails lower wage and non-wage costs, while generating such employment in the public sector is constrained by budgetary limits. Given the limits on running high public deficits in the long run, once again there appears to be an inescapable trade-off: we either accept high unemployment or countenance greater inequality.

Even if compounded by external pressures, the roots of the current welfare predicament are therefore primarily internal – as, of necessity, must be the solutions. The social and economic transformations occurring within affluent democracies are generating mounting pressures on institutional arrangements which not only were designed under very different circumstances, but which in certain respects have also become increasingly rigid over time. This syndrome is aptly captured by the metaphor of *growth to limits*.[5] In the last couple of decades most of the ambitious social programmes introduced during the *trentes glorieuses* (especially as regards pensions and health care) have come to full maturation: they work 'in high gear' and apply to the vast majority of the population. As observed by Paul Pierson,[6] these extended government commitments produce persistent budgetary pressures and a marked loss of policy flexibility, making even marginal change inherently difficult.

The crux of the problem can be construed, as Pierson puts it, in terms of 'irresistible forces' (for example, post-industrial pressures) meeting 'immovable objects' (strong public support and veto points). Thus, the relative growth of the service sector implies lower productivity growth and entails either greater public spending or increased wage inequality if new jobs are to be created. The maturation of governmental commitments and population ageing demand reforms to health care provision and old age pensions (in 1996 these accounted for 75 per cent of all social protection outlays in the European Union) if costs are not to escalate and employment creation stymied by higher direct taxation and/or payroll taxes. Yet such policies are constrained by the popularity of generous welfare programmes and the commitment of a range of political and vested interests and beneficiaries to defending them. The path forward must of necessity combine creative new policy mixes with new social bargains, woven together with a high degree of political imagination.

BUILDING A SUSTAINABLE WELFARE STATE: THE AGENDA FOR REFORM

If our diagnosis is correct, then the current, persisting problems of the welfare state must be interpreted essentially in terms of an 'institutional maladjustment' between a set of old policy solutions, which are gradually losing both their effectiveness and their flexibility, and a set of new societal problems mainly stemming from internal transformations, but under tighter exogenous constraint. Of course, the challenges to the *status quo* and the capacities for adjustment differ widely across countries. Whichever the institutional configuration, the scope for policy innovation seems to lie between the twin constraints of (1) preserving social justice objectives and (2) solving those fiscal and policy failure problems that undermine economic imperatives – at both the macro- and the micro-level. At the risk of some simplification, we would like to indicate and discuss some possible broad guidelines for reform in the crucial fields of labour market policy, social insurance and health care.

The Labour Market: From Unemployment Insurance to Employability

Continental European countries have performed poorly in terms of job creation in recent years. Fluctuations in the European economic cycle have left larger numbers unemployed whenever there has been an upturn in the cycle ('hysteresis'). This suggests that employment creation lags behind growth and that the fruits of new growth are not evenly shared between insiders and outsiders[7] – a situation much more acute in some countries than others, created by over-protective regulations for those in full-time, standard employment.[8] In this respect, unemployment shows how different national systems have to face the sometimes adverse consequences of existing social contracts and swallow the bitter pill of reform. Thus, in the Scandinavian countries, the distributional costs of generous social contracts have been met by those in employment who have paid high taxes for an over-developed public sector to soak up the potentially unemployed. In continental Europe, governments, employers and labour unions have tacitly accepted that the price of adjustment should be shouldered by the unemployed, comprised largely of younger, female and older workers. In southern Europe, an acute 'inside–outsider' problem has developed as a result of the fragmentation and disparities in the income support system for those without work, with large differences in the level of protection given to core and marginal workers.

There has been intense disagreement about the causes of growing unemployment in Europe and the decline in the incomes of the low-skilled and unskilled, but not about the fact that it is occurring. One way or another, there appears to be a relationship between international competition (which for the European countries is primarily with their immediate neighbours in most sectors), technological change and the declining demand for certain types of workers. Christopher Freeman and Luc Soete[9] argue that the advanced economies are experiencing a shift from an older Fordist 'techno-economic paradigm' – based *on energy-intensive* production systems and services – to a new techno-economic paradigm based on *information-intensive* production systems and services. The rapid growth of e-commerce is just its latest manifestation, but one with potentially enormous implications for employment, the organisation of work and skills. The consequence is far-reaching managerial, organisational and distributive changes, including unemployment among particular categories of workers but new opportunities for others. Denis Snower[10] identifies four critical associated developments responsible for the greater dispersion of incomes – and a shift in labour demand – between versatile and well-educated workers on the one hand and non-versatile workers and poorly educated workers on the other: (1) the reorganisation of firms into flatter hierarchies with a large number of specialised teams reporting directly to central management; (2) radical changes in the organisation of both manufacturing and services linked to the introduction of flexible machine tools and programmable equipment, allowing a decentralisation of production and the adoption of 'lean' and 'just-in-time' methods; (3) dramatic changes in the nature of products and in seller-customer relations; and (4) and the breakdown of traditional occupational distinctions and of what is meant by 'skilled' versus 'unskilled' workers when employees are given multiple responsibilities, often spanning production, development, finance, accounting, administration, training and customer relations.

By making some jobs less secure, while rendering certain skills and workers redundant, these developments are creating greater reliance on unemployment insurance, public support for education and training and a wide variety of welfare state services. The risk is that this generates what Snower calls 'the quicksand effect' – the phenomenon whereby welfare structures designed for a different era become weighed down and generate negative effects, destroying incentives and making redistributive policies inefficient, while the productivity of welfare services declines and their cost increases.

However, the policy conclusions are not all pessimistic. In the labour market, Europe can adapt to the challenges of the information and communications technology revolution, and this revolution can be employment-enhancing in the long term, if it invests in a new form of flexibility for the workforce (in which occupational patterns and skills profiles are more important than inequality-increasing wage flexibility) and engages in extensive institutional innovation. Greater attention has to be paid to the spread of information and communications skills through the education and training systems, as well as substantial investment in telecommunications infrastructure (such as 'information highways'). There also needs to be a co-ordination of supply-side policies across all European countries, focusing on the rapid diffusion of the new techno-economic paradigm throughout the wider socio-economic system.[11]

The implications for the welfare state are wide-ranging, and we address some these broader issues – in pensions, social security and health care – below. To avoid the 'quicksand effect' of traditional welfare policies, a number of options need to be considered. These include incentives to choose between the public or private provision of welfare services; the introduction of elements of voluntary or compulsory savings and insurance into the current tax-and-transfer system and government subsidies for low-income groups to help meet equity objectives and the 'activation' of traditional benefits. At the same time, there needs to be an expansion of a non-traditional personal, social and environmental services sector to counteract the loss of jobs occurring due to the fact that many traditional services are now exposed to international competition. The creation of a new 'sheltered sector' could be encouraged by tax changes bringing activities that are now frequently in the black economy (for example, cleaning and repair work) back into the regular economy, while new jobs could be encouraged in education, caring personal services and repair and maintenance. The welfare state's financing and its benefit structure should allow for an expansion of employment at the lower end of the earnings scale – thereby tackling one angle of the 'service sector trilemma' – without creating a class of 'working poor'.[12] High levels of payroll taxes and social security contributions can be an impediment to the expansion of low-paid/low-skill private-sector service jobs. Social security systems which are financed out of payroll taxes tend to increase labour costs for low-paid employment above the corresponding productivity levels, if wages are sticky downwards.[13] A substantial reduction of social contributions for low-paid workers, as undertaken for instance in the Netherlands and in the United Kingdom, will be part of the strategy to resolve this dilemma.

Certain combinations of reform in labour market rules (including labour laws) and social security systems, plus policies to encourage a redistribution of work (some forms of work sharing) can counter hysteresis and help mobilise sections of the unemployed work force left behind by returns to higher levels of growth. Flexible employment patterns, buttressed by reform of the tax and social security systems, will play an important role in this respect. Otherwise, activation policies, designed to help welfare recipients to enter the labour market, while also strengthening obligations to accept suitable work and/or take part in training courses, will fail to tackle the unemployment problem.

To facilitate such change, there may have to be some selective deregulation of the labour market to enhance flexible (part-time or temporary) service-sector employment, and this will form an important part of many continental countries' labour market strategies.[14] But, as Peter Hall[15] argues, there is no reason why such adaptation will necessarily push Europe's organised, co-operative economies down the slippery slope to Anglo-American style deregulation and inequality. As demonstrated by Stephen Nickell,[16] a number of protective measures that are generally assumed to impede employment creation may in reality may have little effect. These include employment protection measures and general labour market standards, generous unemployment benefits (as long as they are accompanied by strict benefit durations and measures to help the jobless back into work) and high levels of unionisation and union coverage (as long as they are offset by high levels of co-ordination in wage bargaining). Rather than hampering economic performance because of alleged price distortion, many forms of labour market protection can enhance productivity and are beneficial for economic development. Thus, minimum wages pressurise firms into finding ways to raise productivity, whether through technological innovation or through training. As long as they are designed so as not to create or accentuate an insider/outsider dualism in the labour market, employment security regulations will improve the worker's commitment to the enterprise, creating trust and enhancing forms of work flexibility.

Moreover, there is no need to shift away from concertation towards a unilateral imposition of policy to secure the necessary changes. Indeed, periods of high unemployment and painful restructuring in the trough of the cycle seem to have bolstered the search for consensual solutions in which flexibility is matched by innovations in social security. Of particular importance is the way in which optimal forms of labour market regulation require collaborative industrial relations as well as corporatist bargains to cement them.[17] Selective deregulation, leading to an expansion of part-time employment, has been achieved in the Netherlands, for example, within the context of a broad social pact sustaining co-ordinated wage bargaining, while also minimising the impact on real income disparities.[18] As we argue in greater detail below, when discussing how best to bring about reform, the optimal way of tackling the employment problem institutionally is via negotiation, not the unilateral imposition, *à la* Thatcher, of looser regulation.

Employment and the labour market thus provide a good example of reform in a sensitive policy area where new techniques and new modes of negotiation have already been and will continue to be critical for policy innovation and policy success. There is now a whole menu of policy measures to choose from: modifying the funding of welfare by shifting the burden of costs, for example, away from pay-roll taxes to general taxation; by removing tax wedges and eliminating poverty traps; by introducing wage subsidies in various forms to employers and 'in-work' benefits (again in all forms including tax credits) as one way of easing the move from benefits and into employment; and, more specifically, via the 'activation of so-called 'passive' benefits. Examples of radical proposals made in this area are conditional negative income taxes (negative income tax conditional on, for example, evidence of serious job search by an unemployed person); and benefit transfer programmes (for example, providing individuals with vouchers that could be offered by the unemployed to firms that would hire them, and reducing correspondingly the amount of public money spent on traditional forms of unemployment benefit).[19] Denmark and the Netherlands have perhaps gone furthest in experimentation in these areas, and in both cases reforms have been introduced within a general context of policy concertation. Both hold lessons for other countries, now also experimenting with such policies on an ever wider scale, both in terms of the mix of policies and the consensual process through which such policies are designed and delivered.

Redesigning Social Insurance

As is well known, the institutional core of the welfare state in many European countries is constituted by the principle of social insurance. This comprises a rights-based guarantee of public support in cash and/or in kind against a pre-defined catalogue of standard risks, including old age, invalidity, the death of a supporting spouse, sickness and unemployment.[20] This rights-based guarantee rests in its turn on the compulsory inclusion of large sectors of the population (in some cases the whole population) in public schemes. These are mainly financed from contributions levied on the gainfully employed (with the partial exception of health care and family allowances in some countries). To a large extent, the crisis of the welfare state is the crisis of social insurance (especially pension insurance). Are there 'virtuous' ways of redesigning this core institution? And, even more fundamentally, should the institution as such be preserved?

A full answer to this latter question would obviously require an extended discussion of the advantages of public/compulsory over private/voluntary insurance in terms of risk pooling, adverse selection, moral hazard, interdependent risks, interpersonal redistribution, and so on. From the point of view of *positive theory*, the justification of public involvement and compulsory membership lies basically in the technical inability of markets to overcome the information problems inherently connected with insuring 'social' risks.[21] From the point of view of *normative theory*, the justification lies in the greater capacity of public social insurance to satisfy the fundamental principles of distributive justice (at least in their Rawlsian version), by safeguarding the position of the worst off in society.[22] 'Public and compulsory social insurance' is, however, only a general regulatory principle, which allows in practice a wide range of institutional solutions. Thus, the Italian pension insurance, overwhelmingly centred on state-run, pay–go schemes, with very generous formulae, and the UK pension system, centred on modest 'national insurance' pensions, supplemented by occupational or even personally funded benefits, illustrate the full range of forms which the principle of compulsory insurance can take in practice.

Defending the desirability of this principle – even in its minimal definition – is no trivial matter. The idea of 'dismantling' large-scale compulsory insurance crops up frequently in political debates around the OECD, opening up the risky scenario of universal systems degenerating into purely voluntaristic and/or localised (and therefore fragmented) systems of social solidarity. But finding 'virtuous' ways of redesigning this core institution – what kind of compulsory social insurance can be sustained? – raises two sets of issues. The first concerns the basket of risks to be included within the scope of insurance, while the second concerns benefit and funding formulae. We discuss each of these in turn.

What Risks?

As far as the basket of risks is concerned, the standard catalogue drawn up almost a century ago and which has survived largely due to institutional inertia now fits poorly with the prevailing socio-economic context. A revision of this catalogue is thus urgent, as regards both the range and the definition of covered risks. Is it still appropriate, for example, to keep in the basket the general risk of 'surviving'? Survivor's benefits represented almost two per cent of GDP in the EU on average in the mid-1990s. To the extent that this risk still generates real needs, are there not more effective ways of responding to them? Such needs could be dealt with via an adequate supply of services (health care, education, training and housing) and/or of targeted transfers (for example, scholarships or work grants, or benefits for single parents), and more generally through a policy of incentives for the formation of two-earner households. Why not leave to the private insurance market the task of satisfying the greater demand for security desired by some people in this field? Similar questions could be raised regarding other risks as well. Is it still appropriate to maintain in operation large-scale public schemes for work injury and invalidity (as distinct from basic disability insurance)? Why not transfer the responsibility for compensation directly to the employers (as recently experimented with in the Netherlands, for example)?

But the biggest challenge in the area of risk-redefinition is old age. At the beginning of the twentieth century, surviving beyond the age of 65 was indeed a risk for the bulk of the population. In Germany, France, Italy or

England an average male at the age of 20 could only expect to reach the age of 62; if he lived beyond his fortieth birthday, he could still only hope to reach the age of 68. Thus, remaining alive beyond the official age of retirement was indeed a 'risk' in the strict sense of the concept and the risk definition (old age equals life beyond 65) 'matched' the existing state of affairs. Once formalised into pension rules, however, this notion of old age became a social norm *per se*, a taken-for-granted principle for the organisation of the life cycle, regardless of socio-demographic change. Given longer life-spans, this norm became the subject – rather than the object – of contextual redefinition, offering a fertile ground for the social construction of 'retirement' as a distinct phase in people's existence and as a novel collective practice.[23]

The notion of old age is thus in need of institutional redefinition. To some extent, this process is already under way. In recent years, many countries have indeed raised the legal age of retirement – especially for women and civil servants, who could traditionally retire earlier. In a few cases, the principle of flexible retirement has also been formally introduced, establishing a range of possible ages for exiting from work (for example, in Belgium, Italy and Sweden). But so far this shift in policy has not proved very effective in actually re-orienting the choices of both workers and employers regarding labour market exit. As recently shown by the European Commission and the OECD, little improvement has taken place in the activity rates of older workers, and early retirement is still being used as a mistaken solution to the unemployment problem. The retirement issue must be integrated with the employment question and the introduction of the 'employability' policies discussed above. It is an objective that must be forcibly put on the reform agenda in all mature welfare states. In some countries, there are already signs of a reversal of labour-shedding strategies using early retirement, prolonged unemployment, sickness and disability as easy exit options. As labour-shedding substantially increased the financial burden imposed on the systems of social security, policy actors, most notably in the Netherlands, have come to recognise that a robust welfare state requires a high level of employment rather than a low level of open unemployment. Such a diagnosis has not yet taken firm root, however, in countries such as Italy and Germany, which have resorted massively to labour-shedding in the last couple of decades.

'Dependency', that is, the loss of physical self-sufficiency, typically connected with the chronic-degenerative pathologies of (very) old age, is a separate issue. There is in fact a range of options available to deal with this most important and growing risk.[24] The issue is debated in many countries, and in 1995 Germany updated this aspect of its social insurance system (*Pflegeversicherung*). But innovation is slow to come about in other countries. Besides long term care, the updating of social insurance should definitely also address the issues of gender equality and gender equity, neutralising the indirect penalties suffered by women and all 'carers' in general under traditional insurance regulations. The promotion of more equality and equity across genders is a very important and broad objective which cuts across all sectors of social policy. Social insurance schemes are in urgent need of being 'mainstreamed' in this respect in all countries.[25]

What Benefits?

The issue of benefit and funding formulae raises two main questions: a qualitative question (how to compute benefits and how to finance them) and a quantitative question (how much protection?). As for the first question, the emerging trends in most social insurance systems (especially in the EU) are for a rationalisation of the inter-personal redistribution implicitly incorporated in benefit and financing formulas and a strengthening of the 'contributory principle'. The elimination of transfers that can be identified as *inequitable* (because they are grossly disproportional to contributions), *outdated* (because they are out of step with the structure and distribution of needs) or *perverse* (because they generate significant work disincentives) appears desirable both for normative and practical reasons. Such a policy also has the advantage of being potentially self-legitimating in political terms, providing an effective solution to the blame-avoidance problems facing 'modernising' elites.[26]

In general terms, a closer link between contributions and benefits can be regarded with favour as well – but only up to a point. If nested within the wider logic of compulsory universal coverage, the contributory principle serves two important purposes. The first one is that it safeguards against the possible degeneration of social insurance via the 'inequitable' and 'outdated' transfers mentioned above. Those who think that this is only a minor risk should look at Italian developments in recent decades for evidence to the contrary (to some extent France is a parallel case).[27] The second purpose served by the contributory principle is that it strengthens the overall legitimacy of the welfare state, giving to each contributor the feeling that they have a real stake in the system.[28] Even if people are aware that contributory social insurance does not follow strict proportionality rules, they are willing to support a system that 'roughly' balances out burdens and rewards, in compliance with deep seated norms of 'strong reciprocity'.[29]

However, the contributory principle also has its drawbacks. An objection which is often raised is that in an increasingly flexible and heterogeneous labour market a close link between contributions and benefits will prevent many workers from accumulating adequate benefits – and especially adequate pensions – because of frequent spells out of work. A second drawback has to do with employment incentives. As discussed above, to the extent that contributions tend to be levied essentially on work earnings, they tend to create problems of employment-creation – especially at the lower end of the earnings spectrum. It is true that these two drawbacks can be partly neutralised by selective reforms of institutional regulations. Incorporating 'equitable' and 'updated' norms in the crediting of contributions for involuntary or socially valued interruptions of work (for example, training or caring periods) or relieving employers from paying social insurance contributions for low-wage workers are both feasible and desirable. But there are limits of a political and financial nature to such a strategy, not to mention institutional inertia. The optimal strategy could be one of combining the 'contributory' with the 'fiscal' logic and establishing two layers of benefits. A first layer of pay–go universal benefits could be tax-financed, ensuring an interpersonal redistribution based on criteria of 'equity of opportunity';[30] and a second layer of benefits could be linked to income-related contributions. As argued by Fritz Scharpf,[31] such a strategy would also maximise the immunity of the welfare state against the challenges of international tax competition.

The actual role that can be played by funding as opposed to pay–go – a thorny issue, hotly debated in many countries and internationally – is highly contingent on the institutional legacy of a particular country. In principle, a combination of the two mechanisms seems a desirable objective as they are subject to different risks and returns.[32] Pay–go systems are good at protecting against inflation and investment risks and in allowing vertical redistribution, but they are also vulnerable to population ageing and rising unemployment. Funding generates fewer distortions in the labour market and may contribute to developing financial markets, in situations in which real interest rates are higher that the rate of growth of employment and real wages. Funded systems can also provide workers with higher returns on contributions. On the other hand, they are vulnerable to inflation and investment risks and are also costly to administer. Regardless of their respective merits and disadvantages, the real problem is that for a given country at a given point in time the options between these two systems are heavily constrained by past choices.[33] Only a few countries have been able to overcome the 'double payment' problem involved in the transition from mature pay–go systems to funded or mixed ones. However crucial for the overall architecture of the welfare state, pension financing is one area in which desirable policy objectives must inexorably yield to the very limited possibilities offered by the institutional *status quo*.

But what of the 'how much' question? At the abstract level, there is little that can be said on this issue. Two general considerations can, however, be advanced. The first is that in an age of permanent austerity all 'how much' questions will have to be answered with an 'unpleasant arithmetic'. Thus, 'pluses' (a new benefit, service, or investment) must be balanced against 'minuses' within a highly constrained budgetary context, and the opportunity costs of the *status quo* must be constantly made explicit and carefully assessed.[34] A few fortunate countries may be able to escape this logic and enjoy the politics of surplus once again, but most will not. If this is true (and this is the second general consideration) then the one sector of social protection in which financial resources can be redeployed is pension insurance – especially the generous pension benefits offered by many 'Bismarckian' systems. In high-income societies where the elderly tend *on average* to wield considerable economic resources (both mobile and immobile) there is no compelling justification for concentrating public protection on this social group. In the wake of the social and economic transformations illustrated above, income insecurity is increasingly spreading across the earlier phases of the life cycle. This is especially true for women, as a consequence of their continued vertical and horizontal segregation in the labour market. The vulnerability to poverty has visibly shifted from the elderly to other social groups (the young, lone parents, workless households, ethnic minorities and so on), and within some of these groups there are also worrying symptoms of social dislocation (crime, teenage pregnancies, homelessness, substance abuse, educational exclusion and suchlike).

In this new context, a re-calibration of social insurance from 'old age protection' to 'societal integration' seems in order. As is well known, pension schemes are very 'sticky' institutions: they create long chains of psychological expectations and material interests and thus tend to 'lock' their members into the *status quo*. But even sticky institutions are not impervious to change. Most European countries have already taken many important steps in the field of pensions in the 1990s. Efforts on this front must definitely continue: pension reform remains the key for solving the allocative and distributive dilemmas of the welfare state, especially in continental Europe.

Universal, but not Unlimited Health Care

Considering demographic projections, the efficiency and cost problems inherent in the production of medical services and the 'unpleasant arithmetic' of permanent austerity, the reform agenda for public health systems of advanced welfare states is replete with dilemmas. As in the case of pensions, policy change is politically very difficult in this area, owing not just to the potential opposition of professionals, but also because the principle of public universal coverage remains extremely popular in OECD countries. Are there virtuous ways for reconciling universalism and sustainability in public health care? This is a complex question that needs to be addressed dispassionately.

Both at the macro and at the micro level, the allocative and distributive priorities of the health care sector have historically been the result of an implicit bargain between the medical profession and the big purchasers, typically large insurance companies, health funds and governments. In all countries, the total amount of resources destined to health care – as opposed to other sectors relevant to people's health status, such as environmental protection or job safety measures – has been defined essentially via 'automatic' criteria (such as past expenditures) or, more recently, based on macro-economic compatibilities. These methods appear to be less and less effective. A rich empirical literature has shown that: (1) there are remarkable variations in the utilisation rate of various medical treatments and technologies, not only across countries, but also across areas of a single country and even across providers of a single area; (2) the correlation between these variations and variations in the main indicators of health status is not strong; and (3) health status correlates positively with other indicators, such as the quality of the environment, income, employment or unemployment, nutrition and life-style, the safety of transport and so on.[35]

The literature also shows that a large degree of the variation in utilisation rates basically stems from clinical uncertainty: from the absence, that is, of reliable information on the actual effect of various forms of medical intervention. An open debate is therefore in order on the appropriateness of existing care methods and on public strategies of health promotion. Is it possible to identify practices that are really effective? And how can we define the overall amount of public resources that must be mobilised to finance such practices? This latter question has allocative implications that are both inter-sectoral (for example, how much should go to health care and how much to the environment?) and intra-sectoral (how much to this or that cure or pathology?). It also has clear distributive implications: that is, how much should go to whom?

The situation of budgetary 'emergency' during the last decade has not allowed a serious and coherent debate on the dilemmas of inter-sectoral allocation: the prime imperative has been that of cost-containment, wherever and whenever possible. On this front there will be much to discuss in the future. But the most urgent debate concerns the intra-sectoral allocations and distributions: and this is the most interesting aspect for a project of 'sustainable universalism' in health care.

Selecting Users or Selecting Treatments?

The classical doctrine of social security assumed that all full members of a society should have an unconditional right to receive all the forms of care made available by medical progress, with no formalised or fixed restrictions. Since the early 1980s, the first part of this assumption (all citizens unconditionally) has undergone a gradual redefinition. In many countries, the dimension of access (which has remained universal and unconditional – at least in countries with national health systems) has been increasingly separated from the dimension of financial participation: user charges have been introduced in many countries, but differentiated according to need. This 'neo-univeralism' has not, however, significantly altered the second part of the assumption (all forms of care, with no restrictions). It is true that all countries have always had to cope with rationing, especially as regards costly technologies. But the most widespread method of rationing has been *de facto* that of waiting lists, mainly based on the 'first come, first served' principle. It is also true that some countries have started to introduce restrictions to certain *forms* of care – usually at the margins of the system: plastic surgery, spa treatments and the like. But rationing has so far remained primarily implicit and marginal. The assumption of 'full comprehensiveness' (the third dimension of classical universalism) has not been squarely addressed. Yet some limitation of the principle of universalism seems desirable in this respect as well. Considerations of cost-effectiveness are also important not only to safeguard economic sustainability, but also to encourage a more responsible use of medicine and a reallocation of resources from the traditional fight against disease towards the promotion of health.

Yet how should universalism be limited in this respect? Is it possible to identify a package of 'essential' and effective forms of care to be maintained under public insurance (even if provided through 'internal markets' or contractual relationships between purchasers and providers)?

The main obstacle is of a methodological nature, that is, what are the relevant criteria for making a selection? The choice has profound implications in terms of both social justice and public finances. Is it appropriate, for instance, to adopt some sort of demographic criterion (limits to the treatment of incurable pathologies among the very old), following the suggestions of the so-called 'ageist' approach?[36] Or should resources be concentrated on the cure of all 'avoidable deaths' – those caused by pathologies that, based on existing clinical knowledge, should not lead to death if a patient is appropriately treated?[37] Or should we be more selective and invest only in treatments that promise a reasonable number of 'quality adjusted life years' (QALYs)?[38]

However intractable they may sound, these questions are no longer just the subject of purely academic discussions, and are now at the core of the policy-making debate. No country has been able so far to adopt formal and explicit rationing criteria in their health systems. But the use of positive and negative lists (for example, in the supply of pharmaceuticals), of medical protocols, of indicative guidelines, and suchlike, is becoming more and more widespread.[39] It is obvious that all attempts at introducing greater discipline on this front are bound to meet enormous resistance of an ethical, political and organisational nature. But the issue must be looked at in a dynamic perspective. If it is true that picking among treatments and technologies which are *currently* utilised is extremely difficult – organisationally and politically speaking – stricter rules can be established for *future* treatments and technologies. This is where the most difficult rationing dilemmas will occur, because of the huge costs of new medical technology, especially in its early phases, 'natural scarcities' (such as organ transplants) or the interval between the experimentation with new treatments and their wider availability. In other words, the definition of priorities *now* would be useful even if only with regard to *future* choices, based on cost-effectiveness considerations and forms of procedural equity.

Besides the establishment of some explicit criterion for limiting the content of public entitlements, two other strategies seem promising for making health care universalism more sustainable. One is the introduction of specific incentives at the micro-level for practising evidence-based medicine. This is slippery ground, as it interferes with professional 'freedom'; but there are compelling normative arguments and possible institutional solutions for making steps along this road.[40] The other strategy is that of encouraging patients themselves to become more responsible, allowing them a greater margin of choice on the quantity and type of care that they would like to receive – if appropriately informed. This is the direction followed by the US with the Patient Self-Determination Act of 1991 and which some European countries are following as well.

There can be little doubt that the opening of a public debate on the criteria and choices that affect life and death will generate acute moral tensions and political controversies. For the wider public, such a debate may even seem inadmissible. But in a world of scarce resources and characterised by the ultimate unavoidability of death, the health care systems are obliged to confront the issue of allocative and distributive rationing. Ultimately, what will differ among them will the mix between the explicit or implicit, rational or non-rational, deliberate or casual nature of the criteria they employ.

A New Public/Private Mix

One consequence of permanent austerity is that expanding health care and social services through the public budget will remain limited. Restricting universalism through user charges and priority setting will serve to filter demand based on equity and effectiveness considerations. But it will still leave a sizeable (and certainly growing) share of unmet demand. In many countries private expenditure for health care and social services has been rapidly increasing in recent years. Especially in the field of social personal services, the 'third sector' is also becoming increasingly active. But the potential for a further expansion of both the private and the third sector for services has not been fully exploited, despite its positive occupational implications for economies struggling with high unemployment. To some extent (especially in continental Europe) this is linked to the 'inactivity trap' caused by high wage floors, which constrains the development of a labour-intensive social services sector.[41] But there are other obstacles as well. The development of non-public forms of provision has traditionally been regarded with suspicion as possible sources of social differentiation and the erosion of welfare state legitimacy. Is this suspicion still well grounded? Can virtuous mixes between the public and non-public spheres be designed to help solve the 'resource' problem without also diminishing both the quality and coverage of care and the legitimacy of public provision?

In contemporary affluent societies, care services are highly valued goods, and the demand for them is not only constantly growing, but is also becoming more diversified, especially among higher income and educated consumers, who are interested in quality, freedom of choice and more personalised provision.[42] It is unrealistic to expect the state to maintain control of such developments. The emergence of an increasingly specialised private market for health and social services is thus unavoidable. The crucial question is whether there are ways to cater for a significant part of this new demand within the public arena? The advantages for the welfare state of doing so are that public institutions would remain the central locus of care provision and consumption, with no (or little) additional costs and no loss of social cohesion or legitimacy. The success of this strategy depends on two main conditions: the ability of public care services to satisfy 'new' consumer demand (a question primarily of innovation); and the willingness of these consumers to pay fees for services on top of their ordinary taxes and contributions.

In western Europe, the first condition is essentially a matter of regulation, organisation and management. Here public health institutions have traditionally been and still largely are *the* centres of medical excellence. In this respect, the European situation is very different from the US, where the long historical delay in the introduction of public health insurance opened an early opportunity for the expansion of private markets, creating a twin-track system of socially differentiated provision. The European middle classes trust public hospitals and think rather highly of their clinical quality. It should not be impossible for these institutions to adjust and upgrade their supply of services with a view to attracting fee-paying consumers. The second condition could be met by linking fees to new opportunities. It is certainly true that users of public services dislike and even resent the imposition of charges for what used to be provided free of charge. But their willingness to pay could increase if they are convinced that they have access to a wider array of (new) services and have more options regarding the timing, location and overall context of care. Paying for such high-grade care could be institutionally organised and encouraged, through collective forms of voluntary health insurance, for example. This would be greatly facilitated if it were possible to differentiate between 'essential' and 'non-essential' treatments, along the lines discussed above. The latter could in fact form the object of a second 'pillar' in health insurance.

FROM THE AGENDA TO POLICY: HOW TO BRING ABOUT THE REFORMS?

The third general question raised at the beginning of this discussion concerns the more practical problems of how to bring about the reforms. It is important to stress that timely and effective reforms do not simply follow from the pressures of functional problems. They depend most crucially on the ability of relevant policy actors (national executives, sub-national agencies and supranational bodies) to diagnose the problem correctly, elaborate viable and coherent policy solutions, adopt them through authoritative and legitimate decisions, and then implement these decisions in accordance with local conditions. Successful reforms depend also – more generally – on the ability of social policy systems to learn from experience, to develop new insights and make good use of relevant information stemming from other policy areas and from foreign experience. Even in the presence of intense functional pressures, welfare states may be unable to respond (or to respond adequately) owing to major institutional deficits with respect to policy diagnosis, communication between policy experts and politicians, political conflict and implementation failures.

At the same time, as the experiences of the 1990s have shown, there are powerful vested interests devoted to defending transfer-heavy welfare states and their traditional redistributive outcomes. Thus, reforms to health care systems, pensions and labour markets all require a careful process of adjustment if social cohesion as a governing principle is not to be sacrificed and if core constituencies and their representatives (welfare professions, social partners, citizens) are not to become hostile opponents of change. As shown by recent experiences, potential blockages in the process of reform are being avoided in some countries by the creation of new coalitions behind the reform agenda, most notably through new types of concertation and negotiation. On the other hand, some social and political 'challenging' of the *status quo* is required in order for reforms to become effective: changes that are purely marginal and incremental will not be enough to neutralise the old vicious circles.

Thus a successful policy adjustment strategy across the range of issue areas dealt with above requires an identification of the salient policy problems, a sequential strategy of policy reform (in other words a planned and incremental approach rather than a policy 'big bang') and a preservation of social consensus. In some countries (the 'Westminster models' of democracy, such as the UK and New Zealand), radical reform strategies of a neo-liberal kind have been implemented in the absence of strong constitutional constraints or coalition partners and have ruthlessly bypassed the involvement of social partners. But these two polities are really the exceptions to the rule amongst the advanced economies (and even New Zealand, with new electoral rules, has become a country of coalitions). Most continental European economies are 'negotiating systems' with coalition governments, federal arrangements or strong regional actors, and active social partnerships whose involvement in the policy process is a cornerstone of social stability and continued prosperity.

Policy reform in such negotiating systems is more likely to be constrained by 'veto power', and as a consequence more likely to follow an incremental pattern of policy change. In these countries an incremental and concerted process of reform is not only necessary but can also be more productive than radical and unilateral breaks with the welfare *status quo*. In the complex and 'organised' economies of continental Europe, the policy areas mentioned above are closely linked and reform in one area will quickly have impacts in others. Often policy-making competencies are shared between state officials and the social partners, which again constrains the political degrees of freedom for the government. Much more so than in the liberal Anglo-Saxon economies, with their predominantly tax-financed welfare systems, it is therefore essential to focus the attention of policy makers and social partners on particular problem constellations (such as illustrating the connections between pension reform, social charges and employability) in order to introduce an effective reform sequence. If institutional trust and co-operation are not to be the first casualties of the adjustment process, a social dialogue must be preserved or reinforced. Commonly accepted information, successive rounds of negotiation and the provision of widely acknowledged and coherent sources of expertise all assist in a process of policy 'puzzling' and learning in the search for acceptable and workable solutions.[43]

The implementation of agreed policies also requires the political power to avoid policy blockages and deliver side payments to potential losers. Implementation and legitimising reforms so as to avoid blockage will also require that broader social coalitions are accommodated and aligned with the reform process. Thus, not only does the interlocking nature of European social security and employment systems require simultaneous action on multiple fronts, but broadening and deepening the bargain may also compensate for the absence of conventional organisational prerequisites in those countries where the social partners are neither strong nor cohesive. The best way to generalise the process of exchange is to synchronise industrial and structural with social and employment policy and/or extend concertation levels upwards or downwards by making associational strength itself a part of the bargain.[44] This requires a complex and gradual process of coalition building, but one that is essential if countries are to succeed in putting the requisite institutions for a co-ordinated adjustment strategy in place.

In Europe, the supranational authorities clearly have an important role to play in this respect. National adjustment strategies and bargains can be reinforced and encouraged in their efforts to tackle existing inequities in welfare cover and introduce new forms of flexible work and social security and tax reform. One specific area where an EU role is required is in helping ensure that both labour and capital remained linked in national social bargains, for example, given the low exit-costs for these organisations in those countries without a corporatist tradition. This could be achieved by scheduling productivity-linked wage increases and employment creation in line with programmed non-inflationary expansion and growth at both national and European levels. The conclusion of the European employment pact in June 1999 and the launching of the so-called 'Cologne process' to co-ordinate wage developments with monetary, budget and fiscal policy and stressing the importance of education and training, could make an important contribution given adequate support by the member states. The Commission could also play a role in diffusing notions of 'best-practice' policy sequencing and linkages. Also of central importance will be the development of new 'soft' instruments for European intervention in the member state economies and labour markets. These are essential if the policy blockage encountered in recent years by more traditional European instruments (such as social and employment policy directives) is to be avoided.

In fact, almost by stealth, during the 1990s the dynamics of European integration have been playing an increasingly important role in shaping social policy developments within the member states. The European Union, acting as a 'semi-sovereign' policy system, seems slowly but surely to be carving out a distinct 'policy space' regarding social policy – a space which may gradually work to rebalance 'softly' and 'from below' the current structural asymmetry between negative and positive integration. This trend is clearly visible in the areas of gender policy and, since 1997, employment policy. In the area of social protection proper, the relevance and involvement of the EU is less marked and the logic of asymmetry still predominates: but here, too, the situation is in reality less depressing and certainly less static than it sometimes appears.

In the field of employment, the turning point has coincided with the launching of the 'Luxembourg process' in 1997 and the new employment chapter introduced in the Amsterdam Treaty. This chapter provides for the co-ordination of national employment policies using a 'management by objectives' approach, whereby EU institutions draw up guidelines and monitor their implementation through an institutionalised procedure. This neither 'binds' the member states in a hard, legal sense, nor foresees possible sanctions as in the case of budgetary policy. Despite its 'softness', this process of co-ordination is acquiring increasing salience for the shaping of public policy at the supra-national, national and sub-national levels. Though specifically focused on employment issues, the process has crucial implications for other social policies as well. This is so not only because boosting employment performance is, *per se*, a way of securing the viability of established welfare programmes, but also because of the close link between most recipes for employment promotion and the 'modernisation' of social protection systems, as discussed above. Not surprisingly, many of the employment guidelines drawn up so far in the new institutional framework call for an adjustment of various institutional features of existing welfare arrangements. A novel, promising 'concerted strategy for modernising social protection' is expected to take off in the course of 2000.[45]

CONCLUSION

In sum, the process of welfare state 'recasting' involves a number of dimensions of change in response to a largely domestically generated set of pressures. To the extent that external constraints are important, they do not render impossible diverse institutional and normative designs for the welfare state. And, in the European context, reconciling growth with social cohesion remains a feasible objective, even if achieving that goal will require resetting old instruments, introducing substantial innovation and changing in some respects the ambitions and objectives of welfare states.

As we have argued, neither outright welfare state retrenchment nor a radical process of labour market deregulation is necessary to meet the challenges posed to the welfare and employment *status quo*. Nor, it should be added, is there any *a priori* justification for an all-out assault on the public sector as such, even if, as we argue above, there is clear scope for a new equilibrium between the private and public sectors in welfare provision. Efficient public services are an important institutional condition for competitiveness, especially in innovative, high-skilled and high value-added forms of production and in promoting the transition to information-based services and production systems. To achieve this goal, social and welfare policies should be part of an institutional ensemble that fosters long-term relations of *trust*: close links between the state and the social partners; the construction of social and electoral coalitions around programmes of welfare reform; a system of social and labour market regulation that stimulates a longer term product development strategy, ensures a better educated and more co-operative workforce and makes managers more technically competent and willing to invest in generic and company-specific skills.[46]

Finally, although sequential and incremental reforms move at a slower pace than radical change, they are also less likely to endanger the overall stability of the economic and political system. 'Big bang' reforms tend to create massive uncertainty in the period of transition and generate social conflict, thereby easily undermining economic performance and reducing, at least in the short run, the propensity to take economic risks. An erosion of social cohesion, furthermore, is likely to undermine the degree of trust in the economic and political system, fostering an unstable environment for long-term economic investment, consumer behaviour and policy development.

NOTES

This article was initially prepared in an earlier form for the conference on 'Progressive Governance in the 21st Century', Palazzo Vecchio, Florence, 20–21 November 1999.

1. A.M. Okun, *Equality and Efficiency: The Big Trade Off* (Oxford: Blackwell 1975).
2. See, e.g., G. Garrett, *Partisan Politics in the Global Economy* (Cambridge: Cambridge University Press 1998)
3. P. Pierson, 'Skeptical Reflections on "Globalization" and the Welfare State', article presented at the International Conference on Socio-Economics, Montreal, July 1997.
4. T. Iversen and A. Wren, 'Equality, Employment and Budgetary Restraint: The Trilemma of the Service Economy', *World Politics* 50/4 (1998), pp.507–46.
5. First used in P. Flora (ed.), *Growth to Limits. The Western Welfare States Since World War II*, 4 vols. (Berlin: De Gruyter 1986/87).
6. P. Pierson, 'Coping with Permanent Austerity: Welfare State Restructuring in Affluent Democracies', article presented at the European Forum on 'Recasting the European Welfare States' (Florence: EUI 1999).
7. See P. Ormerod, 'Unemployment and Social Exclusion: an Economic View', in M. Rhodes and Y. Meny (eds.), *The Future of European Welfare: A New Social Contract?* (London: Macmillan 1998), pp.21–40.
8. See H. Siebert, 'Labor Market Rigidities: At the Root of Unemployment in Europe', *Journal of Economic Perspectives* 11/3 (1997), pp.37–45.
9. C. Freeman and L. Soete, *Technical Change and Full Employment* (Oxford: Blackwell 1987); and C. Freeman and L. Soete, *Work for All or Mass Unemployment? Computerised Technical Change into the 21st Century* (London and New York: Pinter Publishers 1994).
10. D.J. Snower, 'Challenges to Social Cohesion and Approaches to Policy Reform', in OECD, *Societal Cohesion and the Globalising Economy: What Does the Future Hold?* (Paris: OECD 1997), pp.39–60.
11. See Freeman and Soete, *Work for All or Mass Unemployment?*, and on the social implications of the new economy, see the recent report of the High Level Group on the Economic and Social Implications of Industrial Change, *Managing Change* (Brussels: European Commission 1998)
12. See Snower, 'Challenges to Social Cohesion and Approaches to Policy Reform'; and G. Esping-Andersen, 'Equality and Work in the Post-Industrial Life Cycle', in D. Miliband (ed.), *Reinventing the Left* (Cambridge: Polity Press 1994).
13. See the analyses of Palier, Manow and Seils and Hemerijk and Visser, this volume.
14. For interesting proposals on how to reform European systems of labour law, see A. Supiot

(ed.), *The Transformation of Labour and the Future of Labour Law in Europe* (Brussels: European Commission 1998).

15. P. Hall, 'Organized Market Economies and Unemployment in Europe: Is it Finally Time to Accept Liberal Orthodoxy?', article prepared for the 11th International Conference of Europeanists (Baltimore, 26/28 Feb. 1998).

16. S. Nickell, 'Unemployment and Labor Market Rigidities: Europe versus North America', *Journal of Economic Perspectives* 11/3 (1997), pp.55–74.

17. See M. Rhodes, 'The Political Economy of Social Pacts: "Competitive Corporatism" and European Welfare Reform', in P. Pierson (ed.), *The New Politics of the Welfare State* (Oxford: Oxford University Press 2000).

18. J. Visser and A. Hemerijck, *'A Dutch Miracle': Job Growth, Welfare Reform and Corporatism in the Netherlands* (Amsterdam: Amsterdam University Press 1997); see also their contribution to this volume.

19. See, e.g., Snower, 'Challenges to Social Cohesion and Approaches to Policy Reform'.

20. For a comprehensive historical survey, see P. Flora and A.J. Heidenheimer (eds.), *The Development of Welfare States in Europe and North America* (New Brunswick: Transaction 1981).

21. N. Barr, *The Economics of the Welfare State* (Oxford: Oxford University Press 1992).

22. See, e.g., the arguments offered by N. Daniels, *Just Health Care* (Cambridge: Cambridge University Press 1985), and by P. Van Parijs, *Refonder la solidarité* (Paris: Cerf 1996).

23. M. Kohli, 'The World We Forgot: A Historical Review of the Life-Course', in V.W. Marshall (ed.), *Later Life: The Social Psychology of Ageing* (Beverly Hills: Sage 1986), pp.45–72.

24. For a discussion, see A. Oesterle, *Equity and Long Term Care Policies* (Florence: EUI Working Articles EUF no. 99/14).

25. A. Orloff, 'The Significance of Changing Gender Relations and Family Forms for Systems of Social Protection', article presented at the European Forum on 'Recasting the European Welfare States' (Florence: EUI 1999).

26. J. Levy, 'Vice into Virtue? Progressive Politics and Welfare Reform in Continental Europe', and P. Pierson, 'The Comparative Political Economy of Pension Reform', articles presented at the European Forum on 'Recasting the European Welfare States'.

27. For illustrations, see M. Ferrera, *Le trappole del welfare* (Bologna: Il Mulino, 1998).

28. B. Rothstein, *The Universal Welfare State as a Social Dilemma* (New York: Russell Sage Foundation, Working Article no. 141 1999).

29. S. Bowles and H.Gintis, *Recasting Egalitarianism: New Rules for Markets, States and Communities* (London: Verso 1998).

30. As proposed by P. Rosanvallon, *La nouvelle question sociale* (Paris: Seuil 1995).

31. F.W. Scharpf, 'The Viability of Advanced Welfare States in the International Economy', in F.W.Sharpf and V.Schmidt (eds.), *Work and Welfare in Open Economies* (Oxford: Oxford University Press 2000, forthcoming).

32. For a discussion of these issues, see M. Buti, D. Franco and L. Pench, 'Reconciling the Welfare State with Sound Public Finances and High Employment', *European Economy* 4 (1997), pp.7–42.

33. Pierson, *The New Politics of the Welfare State*.

34. M. Salvati, 'I democratici di sinistra: un identikit riformista' (Rome: unpublished article 1999).

35. For a review, see A. Smith *et al.*, *Choices in Health Policy* (Darmouth: Aldershot 1995).

36. D. Callahan, *Setting Limits: Medical Goals in an Aging Society* (New York: Simon & Schuster 1987).

37. For a definition of 'avoidable deaths', see W. Holland, *European Community Atlas of 'Avoidable Deaths'* (Oxford: Oxford University Press 1991).

38. A. William, 'Economics, Society and Health Care Ethics' in R. Gillon (ed.), *Principles of Health Care Ethics* (London: Wiley 1994).

39. A survey is offered by J. Lenaghan, *Hard Choices in Health Care: Rights and Rationing in Europe* (Bristol: BMJ Publishing Group 1997).

40. Cf. the arguments advanced by Daniels, *Just Health Care*.

41. F. W. Scharpf, *Combating Unemployment in Continental Europe* (Florence: EUI Robert Schumann Center working article 1997).

42. M. Alestalo and S. Kuhnle, 'Introduction: Growth, Adjustments and Survival of European Welfare States', in S. Kuhnle (ed.), *Survival of the European Welfare State* (London: Routledge forthcoming).

43. We are indebted to the recent work and personal suggestions of Anton Hemerijck for this interpretation of the continental systems.

44. Rhodes, 'The Political Economy of Social Pacts'.

45. See the text of the communication on *A Concerted Strategy for Modernising Social Protection*, COM(99)347 final, adopted on 14 July 1999

46. For a fuller discussion of this issue, see M. Rhodes, 'Globalization, Welfare States and Employment: Is There a European "Third Way"?', in N. Bermeo (ed.), *Unemployment in the New Europe* (Cambridge University Press, 2000).

Abstracts

Interests and Choice in the 'Not Quite so New' Politics of Welfare

FIONA ROSS

A growing body of literature, broadly referred to as the 'new politics of the welfare state', seeks to explain the constellation of pressures that condition how affluent societies are restructuring their broadly popular and deeply entrenched welfare states. Yet, while greatly increasing our awareness of the processes of retrenchment and, to a lesser extent, reformulation, the new politics remains overly de-politicised. With the imperatives of post-industrial adjustment and globalisation impelling leaders to restructure their costly social programmes and watchful electorates, entrenched interests and sticky institutions obliging them to practise modesty, welfare state restructuring has been reduced to a collision between structural necessities and institutional and political constraints. This 'sandwiching' of political leadership circumvents the critical role political agency can play in crafting welfare reform.

Reforming Health Care in Europe

RICHARD FREEMAN AND MICHAEL MORAN

The wave of health care reform which has come over the systems of Western Europe in recent years is partly prompted by fiscal imperatives. But both the intensity and the direction of reform are shaped by other factors - both by the internal characteristics of health care systems as well as by the character of surrounding economic and political systems. As a result, reforms usually described in the language of market liberalism actually involve a complex mixture of market reforms and state intervention.

Timing and the Development of Social Care Services in Europe

VALERIA FARGION

In this study, *timing* is identified as the most crucial factor in explaining why local governments in Continental Europe were unable to adopt the Scandinavian model of social service provision. In these countries, greater local-level fiscal autonomy and service provision responsibilities occurred within a context of increasing social needs and strong economic constraints. Moreover, local governments lacked well-institutionalised social service systems at the time of these growing demands. Given these competing pressures, local governments were incapable of developing adequate policy responses. Trends towards greater fiscal austerity coupled with an expected increase in social needs render more expansive provision unlikely.

Motives, Means and Opportunities: Reforming Unemployment Compensation in the 1990s

JOCHEN CLASEN

This discussion of developments in unemployment compensation in three European welfare states in the 1990s argues that the introduction of obligatory activation policies particularly for young unemployed people in the UK and Denmark indicates an important type of welfare reform which is difficult to classify as either retrenchment or expansion. While Germany has also moved some way in the same direction, a similar restructuring has not occurred. Reasons for these differences are explored and it is argued that their understanding needs to take account of three interrelated aspects: motives of policy makers, the means which enable and constrain policy making (largely institutional contexts within which social security systems operate) and opportunities. A somewhat messy concept, the latter is influenced by a range of contingent factors conferring legitimacy on welfare reform.

'Defrosting' the French Welfare State

BRUNO PALIER

France is often said to have one of the most 'frozen' welfare states in Europe. When analysing the institutional reason for this, one realises that three different types of change have been introduced in France in the face of the 'welfare state crisis'. After increasing resources (1) the government then introduced limited retrenchment in social expenditure (2). However, French governments have also acted indirectly in reforming the institutional causes of welfare problems (3) and have initiated structural reforms (changing the types of benefits, financing mechanisms and management arrangements) which are making the French system more manageable and flexible.

The Employment Crisis of the German Welfare State

PHILIP MANOW AND ERIC SEILS

The mainstream of the academic debate on the German political economy attributes the problems of the welfare state and the labour market to unification rather than the traits of the German model. By contrast, we find a pathological response pattern to recessions which results from the interplay of the Bundesbank, the government and the social partners – the employers' and union organisations. While, on the one hand, the central bank forces the government to observe fiscal discipline, with the government then shifting costs on to the social insurance funds, on the other, employers and unions use early retirement as a key instrument of adjustment in the labour market. This process of dual cost externalisation leads to increasing non-wage labour costs which, in turn, contribute to the problem of unemployment.

Desperately Seeking a Solution: Social Democracy, Thatcherism and the 'Third Way' in British Welfare

MARTIN RHODES

New Labour's 'Third Way' and its innovations in employment and social policy can only be understood against the background of welfare state construction in Britain, the problems faced by all post-war governments in welfare policy and the nature of the institutional solution to those problems implemented by the Thatcher and Major governments. Several common assumptions concerning the past of British welfare need to be dispelled, including the concept of 'welfare consensus', the stability and invulnerability of the welfare state in the so-called 'Golden Age' and the idea that 'globalisation' is a recent phenomenon. The welfare state was the victim of Britain's relative economic decline from early on, constantly buffeted by currency and balance-of-payments crises, while the failure of British social democracy to institutionalise a consensus on the social wage contributed to the turbulence of the 'stop–go' cycle and economic mismanagement. The legacy of Thatcherism was an institutional 'fix' to these problems which heavily constrains New Labour. The 'Third Way' is, in reality, an imaginative amalgam of modest and incremental innovations which seeks to build and improve on that legacy in the absence of any obvious available alternatives.

Reforms Guided by Consensus: The Welfare State in the Italian Transition

MAURIZIO FERRERA AND ELISABETTA GUALMINI

A wave of reforms was introduced in Italy during the 1990s in the field of pensions and in the labour market. In many respects, these reforms have substantially redesigned the overall profile of the Italian welfare state as it had developed under the so-called First Republic (1948–92). Pension expenditure has been brought under control and the pension formula has been substantially rationalised. A clear shift from passive to active policies is visible in the labour market, which is also beginning to become more flexible. The reforms of the 1990s have been introduced via an increasingly well-articulated system of 'concertation' between the government and the social partners. The negotiated character of the reforms is largely responsible for their success. The politico-institutional transition of the domestic political system and the dynamics of European integration both explain in turn the emergence of this new style of policy making.

The Scandinavian Welfare State in the 1990s

STEIN KUHNLE

This study offers a broad outline of what has happened in the fields of social security and welfare in Denmark, Finland, Norway and Sweden during the 1990s. Reforms and reform efforts are analysed and an assessment is made of the status and prospects of the so-called 'Scandinavian type of welfare state'. Although the Nordic countries have not been immune to the international ideological winds of welfare state criticism, it is argued that economic rather than ideological factors have triggered reform activities. Social policy developments have varied across the Scandinavian countries during the 1990s, but all four nations seem to have overcome the economic challenges, which were particularly dramatic in Finland and Sweden at the beginning of the decade, with reasonable economic success and with welfare state institutions and programmes largely intact.

Change and Immobility: Three Decades of Policy Adjustment in the Netherlands and Belgium

ANTON HEMERIJCK AND JELLE VISSER

Although the 'negotiating economies' of the Netherlands and Belgium are similar in their consociational and corporatist structures, they have followed different paths of policy adjustment. While the Netherlands seems to have been cured from the 'Dutch disease', Belgium has not recovered (yet). What is the possible explanation? It cannot simply be economic since both countries were initially very similar in the sectoral profiles of their open economies. It also cannot be purely institutional, since Dutch institutions did not change fundamentally from the 1970s to the 1990s. What they have in common is a policy-making structure with plural veto positions which produce perverse policy outcomes if their occupants pursue narrowly defined interests. We show how after dismal failures Dutch governments and social partners relearned the importance of a more 'encompassing' approach which their Belgian counterparts could not embrace, in part because of the increasing salience of ethnic-linguistic conflict.

Building a Sustainable Welfare State

MAURIZIO FERRERA AND MARTIN RHODES

The conciliation of economic growth and social justice has been one of the most significant achievements of twentieth-century welfare states. Yet today it is the object of heated controversy. The 'conciliatory' capacity of the welfare state has been put in serious question, especially in the light of 'globalisation'. In this conclusion we consider first the relative influence of external versus domestic developments in generating welfare policy dilemmas and apparently unavoidable trade-offs between efficiency and equality, growth and redistribution, competitiveness and solidarity. Via an examination of employment, social security and health policy we then seek to identify the scope for new value combinations and institutional arrangements that are both mixed (in respect of their normative aims) and virtuous (able to produce advances on all fronts). We conclude by considering how this agenda can be advanced in political and institutional terms.

Notes about the Contributors

Jochen Clasen is Professor of Comparative Social Research in the Department of Applied Social Science at the University of Stirling. He is co-author of *Voices Within and Without. Responses to Long-Term Unemployment in Germany, Sweden and Britain* (with A. Gould and J. Vincent, 1998), and editor of *Social Insurance in Europe* (1997) and *Comparative Social Policy: Concepts, Theories and Methods* (1999).

Valeria Fargion is Senior Lecturer in the Political Science and Sociology Department at the University of Florence. In 1998–99 she was European Forum Fellow at the EUI in Florence and is currently engaged in two international projects jointly sponsored by ISSA and the School of Social Welfare, University of California, Berkeley. She is author of *Geografia della cittadinanza sociale in Italia* (1997) and of numerous articles on the Italian welfare state.

Maurizio Ferrera is Professor of Public Policy and Administration at the University of Pavia and directs the Center for Comparative Political Research at the Bocconi University in Milan. He has written extensively on Italian and comparative social policy. Recently he has authored *Le Trappole del Welfare* (1998) and co-authored *Salvati dall'Europa?* (1999).

Richard Freeman is Lecturer in European Policy and Politics at the University of Edinburgh. He is author of *The Politics of Health in Europe* (2000) and co-editor of *Welfare and Culture in Europe* (1999). He is currently working on policy transfer in the health sector.

Elisabetta Gualmini is Assistant Professor of Political Science at the University of Bologna. She teaches Comparative Public Administration.

She has recently authored *Le rendite del neo-corporativismo* (1997), *La politica del lavoro* (1998) and co-authored *Salvati dall'Europa?* (1999).

Anton Hemerijck is a Senior Lecturer in the Department of Public Administration, Leiden university, the Netherlands and visiting researcher at the Max Planck Institute for the Study of Societies in Cologne. He has published widely on issues of comparative social and economic policy and welfare reform. Together with Jelle Visser, he is author of *A Dutch Miracle: Job Growth, Welfare Reform and Corporatism in the Netherlands* (1997).

Stein Kuhnle is Professor of Comparative Politics at the University of Bergen. He is the author of *Velferdsstatens utvikling. Norge i et komparativt perspektiv* (The Development of the Welfare State: Norway in a Comparative Perspective) (1983), co-editor of *Government and Voluntary Organizations: A Relational Perspective* (1992), and editor of *The Survival of the European Welfare State* (2000).

Philip Manow is a researcher at the Max Planck Institute for the Study of Societies, Cologne. He is the author of numerous articles on the German welfare state and has written two books on German health policy. Recent articles include 'The Comparative Institutional Advantages of Welfare State Regimes and New Coalitions in Welfare State Reforms', forthcoming in Paul Pierson (ed.), *The New Politics of the Welfare State*.

Michael Moran is Professor of Government at the University of Manchester and author, most recently, of *Governing the Health Care State* (1999). He takes up a Leverhulme Major Research Fellowship in September 2000 to write a book on *The British Regulatory State*.

Bruno Palier is *chargé de recherches* in the *Centre d'études de la vie politique française* (CEVIPOF), Paris. He has recently published (with Giuliano Bonoli) 'From Work to Citizenship? Current Transformations in the French Welfare State', in J. Bussemaker (ed.), *Citizenship and Welfare* (1999), and 'Changing the Politics of Social Programmes: Innovative Change in British and French Welfare Reforms', *Journal of European Social Policy* 8/4 (1998).

Martin Rhodes is Professor of European Public Policy at the European University Institute in Florence. His recent publications on employment and welfare issues include 'Globalization, Welfare States and Employment: Is There a European "Third Way"?', in N. Bermeo (ed.), *Unemployment in the New Europe* (2000), and 'The Political Economy of Social Pacts', in Paul Pierson (ed.), *The New Politics of Welfare* (2000).

Fiona Ross is a Lecturer in Politics at the University of Bristol. She is currently completing a book on the changing politics of welfare state restructuring in affluent societies. She has written articles on the politics of the welfare state and institutions. This paper was written during a year she spent with the European Forum 1998–99 at the University Institute in Florence.

Eric Seils is a researcher at the Max Planck Institute for the Study of Societies in Cologne and is currently writing a Ph.D. on the political economy of the low-wage sector in Germany and the Netherlands.

Jelle Visser is Professor in the Sociology of Labour and Organisation at the University of Amsterdam and Fellow at the Max Planck Institute for the Study of Societies in Cologne. He is an expert on trade unions and comparative industrial relations and the author, with Anton Hemerijck, of *A Dutch Miracle' : Job Growth, Welfare Reform and Corporatism in the Netherlands* (1997).

Index